RETROSPECTA 33

THE YALE SCHOOL OF ARCHITECTURE

TABLE OF CONTENTS

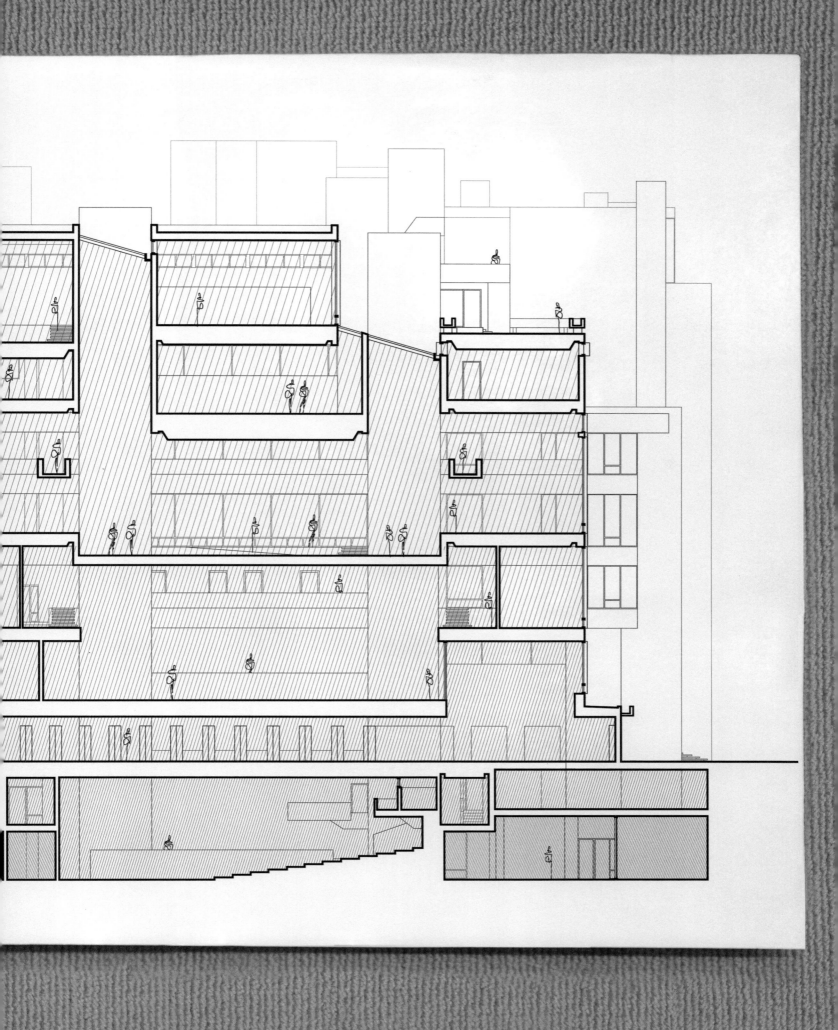

LETTER
FROM THE DEAN

At the Yale School of Architecture students are encouraged to trace a path for themselves across a wide range of courses in which theory and practice, too often considered in isolation, are intertwined. The diverse branches of the discipline--from landscape to building to planning, from the study of the past to projections of the future--are understood to comprise a continuum rather than discrete fields. Fundamentals of drawing, construction, historical analysis, and urban studies remain at the core of the curriculum, continuously informing and being informed by emerging theories and technologies.

As the discipline reevaluates its position and potential to effect change, we aim to embrace the future in a comprehensive and grounded manner. There is no fixed set of aesthetic or ideological qualifications that produces an architect. All we ask of our students is meaningful engagement with the history and possibilities of architecture and its ramifications in the world at large. That engagement is the thread that binds our diverse faculty; and it is that which will bind our students as they move the discipline forward.

Retrospecta, documenting a year in the life of the school, displays the fruits of this commitment to thoughtful and empathetic practice, as well as of the enormous efforts put forth by our students and faculty. It is the summation of two semesters' labor, but it can hardly do justice to the volume and diversity of excellent work produced over the course of eight short months. It is a glimpse of architecture to come, of the skills and ideas with which our students will define their own place in the world.

ROBERT A.M. STERN
Dean & J.M. Hoppin Professor
of Architecture

LETTER
FROM THE EDITORS

This year we reoccupied Paul Rudolph's Art and Architecture Building--rededicated as Rudolph Hall--and ever since it has preoccupied us. The building is an integral part of the architectural education at Yale, providing the students and faculty who work within it lessons in mass, volume, texture, and affect. To attend the Yale School of Architecture is to gradually discover the building's myriad spaces and surfaces. From its stairwells to its orange carpets to its collection of reliefs and sculptures, it is a vivid argument against the banal.

The diversity of work presented in this book is a testament to that argument. We have tried to imbue this year's Retrospecta with the material richness of our environment and have organized the book in the way that Rudolph Hall organizes our time at Yale. From the undergraduates on the seventh floor to the advanced graduates on the fourth, and through the electives, lectures, and exhibitions that enhance our education, we have attempted to reveal the spatial relations that exist between the occupants of the building. The building at once enforces a hierarchy of students and undermines it. Space flows within and between studios, fostering the dissemination of diverse ideas and agendas. It is this exchange that constitutes the legacy of the school and places it at the forefront of the discipline.

We must express our appreciation and admiration for Caspar Lam and Ke Cao, our graphic designers from the School of Art. We could not have asked for better partners in this complex process. Dean Robert A.M. Stern offered his keen eye and honest criticism from the start. Associate Dean John Jacobson, Richard DeFlumeri, Robie-Lyn Harnois, Monica Robinson, and Jean Sielaff answered innumerable questions. Michael Beirut of Pentagram provided support, advice, and the perfect typeface. Richard Kaplan and John LaRusso at Finlay Printing patiently transformed our wild ideas into the beautiful object in your hands today. Finally, this book would not be possible without the donors who generously support its publication and the faculty and students who produce the outstanding work that fills its pages.

ANNE MASON KEMPER
ANDREW SMITH-RASMUSSEN
KYLE STOVER
EMMETT ZEIFMAN

ENROLLED STUDENTS

Master of Architecture I, First Year

CHRISTOPHER PATRICK
 AUBIN
 BS Northeastern
 Univ. '08
MELISSA KATHLEEN
 BAULD
 BA Clemson Univ. '05
HILARY JANE BINGNEAR
 BS Univ. of
 Virginia '06
EMMA JANE BLOOMFIELD
 BA Harvard Univ. '08
KEVIN RICHARD
 BLUSEWICZ
 BS Univ. of
 Maryland '08
MARIJA BRDARSKI
 BS Ohio State
 Univ. '06
BRIAN OLIVER
 BUTTERFIELD
 BA Washington
 Univ. '04
AMY ELIZABETH CHANG
 BA Univ. of
 California,
 Berkeley '06
CHRISTY LAUREN
 CHAPMAN
 BA Univ.
 of Memphis '07
THOMAS ROBERT CHASE*
 MA Wesleyan
 Univ. '07
CHRISTOPHER STUART
 CONNOCK
 BS Univ. of
 Virginia '03
JACOB LAWRENCE
 DUGOPOLSKI
 BS Univ. of
 Michigan '06
FRANCES SARAH EDELMAN
 BA Yale Univ. '06
KIPP COLBY EDICK
 BS Columbia
 Univ. '06
KATHRYN JOAN EVERETT
 BS Univ. of
 Virginia '06
MARK ALLEN GETTYS
 BA Clemson
 Univ. '08
WILLIAM GRANDISON
 GRIDLEY
 BS Bucknell
 Univ. '08
ELIZABETH ROSE HABER
 BS Univ. of
 Virginia '05
JUSTIN CHARLES HEDDE
 BA Univ. of
 Florida '07
LINDSAY NICOLE
 HOCHMAN
 BS Univ. of
 Virginia '07
SHIRLEY NANSHING
 HSU
 AB Dartmouth
 College '02
VIVIAN SHING-WEI HSU
 BA Univ. of
 California,
 Berkeley '04
KYUYOUNG HUH
 BS Seoul National
 Univ. '08
KEITH MARTIN JOHNS
 BS Ohio State
 Univ. '06
JOHN JOSEPH JOURDEN
 BS Univ. of
 Michigan '99
HOMIN JUNG
 BE Myongji Univ. '07
DOUGLAS JOSEPH KANE
 BS Univ. of
 Maryland '04
ANNE MASON KEMPER
 BA Rice Univ. '07
JAEYOON KIM
 BA Swarthmore
 College '07
ALFRED KIM KOETTER
 BS Cornell Univ. '07
KEE HYUN LEW
 BA Univ. of
 Michigan '06
RONALD CHYI-TUNG LIM
 BA Wesleyan
 Univ. '06
LIAM PATRICK LOWRY
 BS Univ.of
 Wisconsin '07
DANIEL GREGORY
 MARKIEWICZ
 MEng. Princeton
 Univ. '06
RAFAEL NG
 BA Brown Univ. '07
JONAH ASHER ROWEN
 BA Carnegie Mellon
 Univ. '08
SEO YOUNG SHIN
 BArch. Hongik
 Univ. '08
ANDREW BENJAMIN
 SMITH-RASMUSSEN
 BA Calvin
 College '03
BRIAN DOUGLAS SPRING
 BS Ohio State
 Univ. '06
KYLE RICHARD STOVER
 BS Univ. of
 Cincinnati '08
TYLER G. SURVANT
 BA Washington
 Univ., Missouri '06
ALEXANDRA FOX TAILER
 BS Univ.
 of Michigan '07
MARK TALBOT
 BA Ohio State
 Univ. '08
LAURA CLARK WAGNER
 BA Brown Univ. '05
LETICIA WOUK ALMINO
 DE SOUZA
 BA Barnard
 College '08.
JIA-JUN YEO
 BA National Univ.
 of Singapore '07
JI-YOUNG YOON
 BS Ohio State
 Univ. '05
EMMETT ZEIFMAN
 BA McGill Univ. '06
DARIA ZOLOTAREVA
 BFA Univ. of
 Pennsylvania '07
MATTHEW AARON ZYCH
 BS State Univ.
 of New York
 at Buffalo '08

Master of Architecture I, Second Year

CATHERINE ANDERSON⁂
 BDSN Univ. of
 Florida '05
BRETT PATRICK APPEL
 BS Univ. of
 Michigan '04
ANNE-MARIE PAULA
 ARMSTRONG
 BA Univ. of
 Waterloo '06
ANDREW LEON ASHEY
 BS Northeastern
 Univ. '03
JULIANNE REBECCA
 AUGUST-SCHMIDT
 BA Univ. of
 Washington '05
AMINA BLACKSHER
 BA Connecticut
 College '99
JASON M. BOND
 BED Texas A&M
 Univ. '07
CARMEL GREER
 BONFIGLI
 BS Univ. of
 Virginia '01
THOMAS BRADY
 BA Columbia
 Univ. '05
HELEN PEARSON BROWN
 BA Stanford
 Univ. '04
JOEL R. BURKE
 BS Ohio State
 Univ. '07
A. TALLEY BURNS
 BA Yale Univ. '05
STEPHANIE CAIUS
 CARLISLE*
 BA Wesleyan
 Univ. '05
CHRISTINE CHANG
 BA Univ. of
 California,
 Berkeley '04
CRAIG WILLIAM CHAPPLE
 BS Arizona State
 Univ. '06
HARVEY HO WANG CHUNG
 BS Univ. of
 Michigan '05
ANDREEA COJOCARU
 BA Wellesley
 College '06
CORY COLLMAN
 BS Univ. of
 Illinois,
 Champaign-
 Urbana '06
PATRICK ROBERT CONNER
 BA Univ. of
 California,
 Berkeley '04
COURTNEY ERIN CROSSON
 BA Duke Univ. '04
YIJIE DANG
 BA Univ. of
 Hong Kong '07
GINA MARIA DI TOLLA
 BA Barnard
 College '05
AIDAN JOSEPH DOYLE
 BS Clemson Univ. '06
KURT EVANS
 BS Univ. of
 Michigan '04
AURORA VIRGINIA
 FAREWELL
 BA Yale Univ. '05
ALEJANDRO FERNANDEZ
 DE MESA
 BS Univ. of
 Virginia '06
DONGFANG GAO
 BFA Tokyo National
 Univ. '07
REBECCA GARNETT
 BS Univ. of
 Virginia '03
PALMYRA STEFANIA
 GERAKI
 BA Yale Univ. '06
TALA GHARAGOZLOU
 BA Yale Univ. '06
JEROME W HAFERD
 BS Ohio State
 Univ. '07
JANICE YUMI HAHN
 BA Univ. of
 Pennsylvania '07
JACQUELYN PAGE
 WITTKAMP HAWKINS
 BA Princeton
 Univ. '04
ZACHARY RUSSELL
 HEINEMAN⁂
 BA Harvard Univ. '03
RACHEL CHING-MEI HSU*
 BS Stanford
 Univ. '06
AUDE HELENE JOMINI
 BFA Rhode Island
 School of
 Design '01
JIN HYU KIM
 BS Seoul
 National Univ. '07
K. BRANDT KNAPP
 BA Arizona
 State Univ. '06
GARY TEIN-LI KU
 BA Univ. of
 California,
 Berkeley '06
JANG HYUNG LEE
 BA Hongik Univ. '07
TAE KYOUNG LEE
 BS Univ.
 of Toronto '06
CALEB COKER LINVILLE
 BA Haverford
 College '04
MEREDITH MCDANIEL
 BA Pomona
 College '99
GREGORY KAHN
 MELITONOV
 BS Skidmore
 College '04
JOSEPH DART MESSICK
 BFA Rhode Island
 School of
 Design '01
IAN WESTBROOK MILLS
 BA Yale Univ. '03
ANDREW BOODY O'BRIEN
 BA Colby College
EMILY SULLIVAN
 OTTINGER
 BA Wellesley
 College '06
MATTHEW DAVID
 PERSINGER
 BS Ohio State
 Univ. '06
ELIJAH PORTER
 BA Swarthmore
 College '00
ZACHARIAH JAMES
 PURSLEY
 BED Univ. of
 Colorado '06
JAMES DUGGAN SCHRADER
 AB Princeton
 Univ. '06
TOMASZ SMIERZCHALSKI
 BS Ryerson
 Polytechnical
 Univ. '04

SUSAN HIDEKO SURFACE
  BFA Parsons School
  of Design '04
KATE THATCHER
  BS Univ.
  of Virginia '04
ADAM JOESPH
  TOMSKI
  BS Ohio State
  Univ. '05
CHAT TRAVIESO
  BFA Maryland
  Institute College
  of Art '07
ANJA TUROWSKI
  BS Georgia
  Institute of
  Technology '04
TYLER BALDWIN VELTEN
  BA Pomona
  College '04
YU WANG
  BS Univ. of
  Michigan '04
RYAN WELCH
  BA Amherst
  College '03
PHILIP LEGARE WINN
  BA Columbia
  Univ. '99
CRAIG A. WOEHRLE
  BS Washington
  State Univ. '01
JUENAN WU
  BA Wellesley
  College '07
STEVE ANTHONY YBARRA
  BA Yale Univ. '05.
HOEY YIP
  BA Univ. of
  California,
  Berkeley '03
HILARY ZAIC
  BA Princeton
  Univ. '05
CARLOS ZEDILLO
  BA Yale Univ. '06

Master
of Architecture I,
Third Year

ANGEL ARTURO BEALE
  BFA Rhode Island
  School of
  Design '05
JAMIE ANNE BERG
  BA Univ. of
  Pennsylvania '04
BRYAN WILLIAM BERKAS
  BA Univ. of
  Washington '05
REBECCA ELIZABETH
  BEYER
  BA Univ. of
  Pennsylvania '05
JOHN CAPEN BROUGH,
  III
  AB Princeton
  Univ. '04
TERRENCE LIN CHEW
  BA Univ.
  of California,
  Berkeley '05
CHENG HUI CHUA
  BA National Univ.
  of Singapore '05
GERARDO DEXTER
  CIPRIAN
  BS State Univ.
  of New York
  at Buffalo '06
ROBERT ALEXANDER COLE
  BA Wesleyan
  Univ. '04

DANIEL DAVID COLVARD
  BA Dartmouth
  College '04
CODY WILSON DAVIS
  BS Ohio State
  Univ. '06
PHILIP GARFIELD DREW
  BA Wesleyan
  Univ. '89
TRAVIS ROBERT EBY
  BS Univ. of
  Cincinnati '05
SEHER ERDOGAN
  BA Yale Univ. '04
ISIDRO GARCÍA TORRES⁕
  BS Massachusetts
  Institute
  of Technology '05
LESLIE E. GOEDKEN
  BFA Parsons School
  of Design '05
NICHOLAS HANNA
  BS McGill Univ. '04
REUBEN AZRIEL HERZL
  AB Univ. of
  California,
  San Diego '06
PARSA KHALILI
  BS Univ. of
  Illinois,
  Champaign-
  Urbana '06
JASON JOON KIM
  BA Univ. of
  California,
  Los Angeles '99
ISAIAH J. KING
  BS Univ. of
  Michigan '04
ERIC BRYANT KRANCEVIC
  BA/BS Kent State
  Univ. '06
JANGWON LEE
  BS Seoul National
  Univ. '06
LOUISE CHRISTGAU LEVI
  BA Yale Univ. '05
JOSHUA WADE
  LEWANDOWSKI
  BA Univ. of
  Minnesota '05
NINA YEN-LING LIU
  BA Yale Univ. '00
PATRICK ROBIN LUN
  BS Univ. of
  Michigan '06
ROBERT ARAM MARKS⁕
  AB Harvard Univ. '04
FELICIA GABRIELLE
  MARTIN
  BFA Otis College of
  Art & Design '02
ALEXANDER MAYMIND
  BS Ohio State
  Univ. '06
PATRICK J. MCGOWAN
  BA Univ. of
  California,
  Berkeley '04
MARIANNA FERREIRA
  DE MELLO
  BDSN Univ. of
  Florida '04
LAUREN J. MISHKIND
  BA Scripps
  College '03
KRISTIN ELIZABETH
  MUELLER
  BS Texas Technical
  Univ. '06
SHANE B. NEUFELD
  BA Amherst
  College '04

MIEKO OKAMOTO
  BA Columbia
  Univ. '96
CHEON-KANG PARK
  BE Handong
  Univ. '05
MIRIAM LYNN PETERSON
  AB Cornell
  Univ. '04
RACHEL ALEXANDRA
  REESE
  BS Univ. of
  Idaho '93
KAREN GRACE RIZVI
  BFA Art Institute
  of Chicago '93
MATTHEW A. ROMAN
  BA Princeton
  Univ. '03
ROBERTO ATTILIO ROSSI
  BA Princeton
  Univ. '84
MEREDITH JAYE SATTLER⁕
  AB Vassar Coll. '95
TAL SCHORI
  AB Brown Univ. '03
ZAKERY M. SNIDER
  BS Ohio State
  Univ. '06
TRISHA SNYDER
  BS Princeton
  Univ. '05
MEGHAN ELIZABETH
  SPIGLE
  BS Univ. of
  Virginia '06
SOHYUN SUNG
  BE Korea
  Univ. '05
TOM Y. TANG
  BS Univ. of
  Illinois,
  Champaign-
  Urbana '04
JULIANNA VON ZUMBUSCH
  BA Columbia
  Univ. '04
LEAH ROSA WEINBERG
  BS London School
  of Economics &
  Political
  Science '03
EMILY ARDEN WELLS
  BA Univ. of
  Pennsylvania '04

Master
of Architecture II,
First Year

NICHOLAS ANDREW
  GILLILAND
  BArch. Univ. of
  Kansas '01
KATHARINE M. GILLIS
  BArch. Univ. of
  Notre Dame '05
ELIZA WEYLAND HIGGINS
  BArch. Roger
  Williams
  College '06
PAUL BENJAMIN
  HOWARD
  BArch. Auburn
  Univ. '05
CHING-WEN HSIAO
  MArch. National
  Taipei Univ. '06
QIWEI LIANG
  BArch. Tsinghua
  Univ. '08
SCOTT BRANDON O'DANIEL
  BArch. Univ. of
  Kentucky '04

CYRUS DINYAR PATELL
  BArch.
  Visveswaraiah
  Technical
  Univ. '06
CARLOS FELIX RASPALL-
  GALLI
  BArch. Univ. of
  Buenos Aires '04
FRANCESCA GIULIA
  SINGER
  BArch. Politecnico
  di Milano '05
ANDREA VITTADINI
  BArch. Politecnico
  di Milano '08

Master
of Architecture II,
Second Year

NICHOLAS JAMES CARUSO
  BArch. Rensselaer
  Polytechnic
  Institute '03
SHU H. CHANG
  BArch. Cornell
  Univ. '03
CHRISTINE MEI LING
  CHOW
  BArch. Univ.
  of Southern
  California '04
MARC ALLEN CUCCO
  BArch. Univ. of
  Texas at Austin '06
MWANGI GATHINJI
  BArch. Univ. of
  Notre Dame '04
MARK ROBERT GAUSEPOHL
  BArch. Univ. of
  Cincinnati '97
LEYLA KORI
  BArch. Istanbul
  Technical Univ. '06
TERRI W. LEE
  BArch. Cornell
  Univ. '04
DAVID CHRISTIAN
  PETERSEN
  BArch. Cooper
  Union '07
YIJUN QIAN
  BArch. South
  China Univ. of
  Technology '07
SAIFULLAH SAMI
  BArch. Indus
  Valley School
  of Art &
  Architecture '04
CHRISTOPHER NEAL
  STARKEY⁕
  BA Rice Univ. '01
ZACHARY PAUL STEVENS
  BArch. Rhode
  Island School of
  Design '05
DANIEL ROBERT YODER
  BArch. Kent State
  Univ. '07

Master of
Environmental Design,
First Year

NATHAN BRIGHT
  BArch. Univ. of
  Texas at Austin '99
OZLEM CAGLAR TOMBUS
  BArch. Middle East
  Technical Univ. '98
DAVID BIJAN SADIGHIAN
  BA Yale Univ. '07

Master of
Environmental Design,
Second Year

LUCAS TURNER COHEN
  BA Bard College '02
IBEN ANDREA FALCONER
  BA Brown Univ. '06
OLGA PANTELIDOU
  MArch. National
  Technical Univ.
  of Athens '07
ZACHARY MORGAN WHITE
  AB Univ. of
  Chicago '01

Major in Architecture,
Yale College
Class of '09

MICHAEL C. BARRY
MEGAN ENYEART
KEIR EVANS
MAIRAN FOLEY
MARCUS HOOKS
MICHAEL HUANG
ANDREA KWOK-YAN LEUNG
MARILYNN LY
VANESSA MENDOZA
NANCY NICHOLS
CHRISTIAN ONCESCU
CHRISTOPHER PALENCIA
MICHAEL PEARCE
ADLER PRIOLY
NATHALIE RAZO
BENJAMIN SACHS
WILLIAM SANKEY, JR.
TROY SUTTLE
YASMIN TARHAN
GARRET WONG
WILLIAM WONG

Major in Architecture,
Yale College
Class of '10

ELIZA ANGILA
EMILY APPLEBAUM
KYLE BRISCOE
LAURA BRITTON
VIRGINIA CALKINS
JOSHUA BREMNER
  FELDMAN
IAN JANER
ELIZABETH KUWADA
ADRIAN LATORTUE
RUSSELL LESTOURGEON
LULU LI
CHRISTOPHER MACKEY
NATHAN MEJIAS
JOSE MEZA
ERENE MORCOS
THOMAS MURDOCH DUNCAN
ELIZABETH NADAI
KRISTIN NORTHWEHR
MAHDI SABBAGH
JOSEPH TRAYNOR
DANA WU
JIE ZHANG

7

FACULTY

D. MICHELLE ADDINGTON
VICTOR AGRAN
JOHN APICELLA
CHARLES ATWOOD
  Edward P. Bass
  Distinguished
  Visiting
  Architecture Fellow
  Fall 2008
THOMAS AUER
JAMES W. AXLEY
SUNIL BALD
DIANA BALMORI
  William
  Henry Bishop
  Visiting Professor
  Fall 2008
DANIEL BARBER
STEVEN BAUMGARTNER
THOMAS H. BEEBY
ANDREW BENNER
DEBORAH BERKE
PHILLIP G. BERNSTEIN
LJILJANA BLAGOJEVIĆ
JOHN P. BLOOD
KENT C. BLOOMER
KARLA BRITTON
TURNER BROOKS
PAUL B. BROUARD
BRENNAN BUCK
LUKE BULMAN
MARTA CALDEIRA
ARAN CHADWICK
HO-YAN CHEUNG
CRISTINA CHU
KATHERINE CLARKE
  Louis I. Kahn
  Visiting
  Assistant Professor
  Spring 2009
DARIN COOK
MARTIN P. COX
NIKOLAS DANDO-
  HAENISCH
B. TAYLOR DANSBY
ELIZABETH DANZE
NAOMI DARLING
PEGGY DEAMER
PETER DE BRETTEVILLE
BROOK DENISON
KYLE DUGDALE
KELLER EASTERLING
JOHN C. EBERHART

PETER EISENMAN
  Louis I. Kahn
  Visiting Professor
MAKRAM EL KADI
SUSAN FARRICIELLI
MARTIN J. FINIO
LIZA FIOR
  Louis I. Kahn
  Visiting
  Assistant Professor
  Spring 2009
KURT W. FORSTER
  Vincent Scully
  Visiting Professor
  Fall 2008
BRYAN FUERMANN
MARK FOSTER GAGE
ALEXANDER D. GARVIN
MARTIN D. GEHNER
  Emeritus
KENNETH GIBBLE
ANNE GILBERT
MARIO GOODEN
KEVIN GRAY
J. KIMO GRIGGS
SOPHIA GRUZDYS
RACHEL GRUZEN
STEPHEN HARBY
KARSTEN HARRIES
STEVEN HARRIS
ARIANE LOURIE
  HARRISON
ANDREI HARWELL
ERLEEN HATFIELD
ROBERT HAUGHNEY
KRISTIN HAWKINS
DOLORES HAYDEN
MIMI HOANG
ADAM HOPFNER
JOYCE HSIANG
SANDY ISENSTADT
JOHN D. JACOBSON
KATHLEEN JOHN-ALDER
ANDREA KAHN
SARRAH KHAN
SANGMOK KIM
GEORGE KNIGHT
FRED H. KOETTER
KEITH A. KRUMWIEDE
AMY LELYVELD
JENNIFER LEUNG
M.J. LONG
TIM LOVE

GREG LYNN
  William B.
  & Charlotte
  Shepherd Davenport
  Visiting Professor
  Spring 2009
FRANCISCO MANGADO
  Eero Saarinen
  Visiting Professor
  Fall 2008
DINO MARCANTONIO
ANDREW MARCHESIN
BIMAL MENDIS
EDWARD MITCHELL
KYOUNG SUN MOON
JOEB MOORE
DIETRICH NEUMANN
  Vincent Scully
  Visiting Professor
  Spring 2009
HERBERT S. NEWMAN
TIMOTHY NEWTON
ALAN W. ORGANSCHI
HIDEAKI OTA
PALOMA PAJARES
S. EDWARD PARKER
JOHN PATKAU
  William B.
  & Charlotte
  Shepherd Davenport
  Visiting Professor
  Spring 2009
EEVA-LIISA PELKONEN
BEN PELL
EMMANUEL PETIT
ALAN J. PLATTUS
DEMETRI PORPHYRIOS
  William
  Henry Bishop
  Visiting Professor
  Spring 2009
ALEXANDER PURVES
  Emeritus
CRAIG RAZZA
KEVIN ROTHEROE
JOSHUA ROWLEY
ELIHU RUBIN
  Daniel Rose '51
  Visiting Assistant
  Professor
DEAN SAKAMOTO
HILARY SAMPLE
JOEL SANDERS

DAVID M. SCHWARZ
  William B.
  & Charlotte
  Shepherd Davenport
  Visiting Professor
  Fall 2008
MASSIMO SCOLARI
  William B.
  & Charlotte
  Shepherd Davenport
  Visiting Professor
  Fall 2008
VINCENT J. SCULLY, JR.
  Sterling Professor
  Emeritus of
  the History of Art
WILLIAM W. SHARPLES
  Louis I. Kahn
  Visiting Assistant
  Professor
  Spring 2009
BENJAMIN SHEPERD
DANIEL SHERER
EDWARD M. STANLEY
ROBERT A.M. STERN
  Dean &
  J.M. Hoppin
  Professor
LINDSAY S. SUTER
BARRY SVIGALS
NEIL THOMAS
SHANTA TUCKER
LAURA TURLINGTON
MICHAEL WANG
CARTER WISEMAN
THOMAS ZOOK

AWARDS

Faculty Awards

Professor King-lui
Wu Teaching Award
ALEXANDER PURVES

Student Fellowships

William Wirt
Winchester Traveling
Fellowship
PARSA KHALILI

Gertraud A. Wood
Traveling Fellowship
    Awarded 2008
MATTHEW A. ROMAN

George Nelson
Scholarship
    Awarded 2008
JOHN CAPEN BROUGH III
PARSA KHALILI

David M. Schwarz/
Architectural Services
Good Times Award
ISAIAH J KING

Student Medals & Prizes

American Institute
of Architects Henry
Adams Medal
JOHN CAPEN BROUGH III

American Institute
of Architects Henry
Adams Certificate
ZAKERY M. SNIDER

Alpha Rho Chi Medal
MWANGI GATHINJI

William Edward
Parsons Memorial
Medal
MIRIAM LYNN PETERSON

The H.I. Feldman Prize
EMILY ARDEN WELLS

    Nominees
BRYAN WILLIAM BERKAS
    Spring 2009
SHU H. CHANG
    Fall 2008
TRAVIS ROBERT EBY
    Fall 2008
SEHER ERDOGAN
    Fall 2008
    Spring 2009
ELIZA HIGGINS
    Spring 2009
PARSA KHALILI
    Fall 2008
JASON JOON KIM
    Spring 2009
ISAIAH J. KING
    Fall 2008
    Spring 2009
PATRICK ROBIN LUN
    Fall 2008
FELICIA GABRIELLE
    MARTIN
    Fall 2008
PATRICK J. MCGOWAN
    Fall 2008
LAUREN J. MISHKIND
    Spring 2009
KRISTIN ELIZABETH
    MUELLER
    Fall 2008

YIJUN QIAN
    Fall 2008
CARLOS FELIX RASPALL
    GALLI
    Fall 2008
MATTHEW A. ROMAN
    Fall 2008
ZAKERY M. SNIDER
    Spring 2009
TOM Y. TANG
    Fall 2008
EMILY ARDEN WELLS
    Spring 2009

Wendy Elizabeth
Blanning Prize
    Awarded 2008
CODY WILSON DAVIS

Sonia Albert
Schimberg Prize
OLGA PANTELIDOU

Janet Cain Sielaff
Alumni Award
IBEN ANDREA FALCONER

Moulton Andrus Award
SEHER ERDOGAN

The Drawing Prize
SHANE B. NEUFELD

Gene Lewis Book Prize
FELICIA GABRIELLE
    MARTIN

David Taylor
Memorial Prize
ALEXANDER MAYMIND

Student Internships

Takenaka Corporation
Summer Internship
    Awarded 2008
ISAIAH J. KING

David M. Schwarz/
Architectural Services
Summer Internship and
Traveling Fellowship
    Awarded 2008
SHU H. CHANG

Student Scholarships

Franklin U. Gregory
Memorial Scholarship
LOUISE CHRISTGAU LEVI

Charles O. Matcham
Scholarship
FELICIA GABRIELLE
    MARTIN

Everett Victor Meeks
Graduate Fellowship
CODY WILSON DAVIS

Eero Saarinen Memo-
rial Scholarship
BRYAN WILLIAM BERKAS

Carroll L.V. Meeks
Memorial Scholarship
ALEXANDER MAYMIND

Samuel J. Fogelson
Memorial Award
PATRICK ROBIN LUN

Christopher Tunnard
Memorial Fellowship
KAREN GRACE RIZVI

Anne C.K.
Garland Award
SEHER ERDOGAN

Robert Allen
Ward Scholarship
JASON JOON KIM

Kenneth A. House-
holder Scholarship
    Awarded 2007
JOHN CAPEN BROUGH III

Henry A. Pfisterer
Scholarship
JASON JOON KIM

James Gamble Rogers
Memorial Fellowship
    Awarded 2008
BRYAN WILLIAM BERKAS
TRAVIS ROBERT EBY
SEHER ERDOGAN
REUBEN AZRIEL HERZL
LOUISE CHRISTGAU LEVI
FELICIA GABRIELLE
    MARTIN
ALEXANDER MAYMIND
ZAKERY M. SNIDER

Enid Storm
Dwyer Scholarship
MATTHEW A. ROMAN

Herman D.J.
Spiegel Scholarship
PARSA KHALILI

Ulli Scharnberg
Scholarship in Memory
of Carroll L.V. Meeks
MARC ALLEN CUCCO

John W. Storrs
Scholarship
PATRICK J. MCGOWAN

Harvey R. Russell
Scholarship
JULIANNA VON ZUMBUSCH

Yen and Dolly Liang
Scholarship
TRAVIS ROBERT EBY

Robert Leon Coombs
Scholarship
GERARDO DEXTER
CIPRIAN

Federick T. Ahlson
Scholarship
ROBERT ALEXANDER COLE

David C. Morton II
Scholarship
JOHN CAPEN BROUGH III

Stanley Tigerman
Scholarship
ZAKERY M. SNIDER

Cesar Pelli
Scholarship
PARSA KHALILI

Federick Bland
Scholarship
ERIC BRYANT KRANCEVIC

Clarke Family
Scholarship
TOM Y. TANG
MARIANNA FERREIRA
    DE MELLO

Pickard Chilton
Fellowship
REUBEN AZRIEL HERZL

Dean's Scholarship
MARC ALLEN CUCCO

Charles Gwathmey
Scholarship
KRISTIN ELIZABETH
    MUELLER

Kenneth A. House-
holder Memorial
Scholarship
ANGEL ARTURO BEALE

Ruesch Family
Scholarship
MEGHAN ELIZABETH
    SPIGLE

Dilworth Family
Scholarship
LOUISE CHRISTGAU LEVI

Richard D. Cohen
Scholarship
FELICIA GABRIELLE
    MARTIN

Frank D. Israel
Scholarship
SEHER ERDOGAN

Norman R. Foster
Scholarship
MATTHEW A. ROMAN

DONORS

Friends
42/40 Architecture INC
Louis M. Aledort
Ruth Aledort
Nancy Alexander
  '79 BA, '84 MBA
Stephanie Allen
The American Institute
  of Architects
Ernest A. Anderson, Jr.
Mary Ellen Anderson
Suzanne L. Anderson
Philip F. Anschutz
Architecture Class
  Of 1983
Drew C. Arena
ASSA ABLOY
Charles L. Atwood
Autodesk, INC
Mr. & Mrs. Charles
  Balbach
Meta Barton
J. Peter Baumgartner
BCER Engineering
Deborah L. Berke
Charles Berry
Maria Berry
Carmen L. Bieker
Charlene D. Bieker
Jack Bistricer
Roberto Bonetti
  '64 BE
Rhonda Boswell
Robert Boswell
Howard M. Brenner
  '54 BA
Leigh Luter Brewer
Carolyn Brody
Donna L. Brown
Margaret F. Brown
Trevor S. Brown
Coleman P. Burke
Bryan Vision
  Associates Doctors
  of Optometry
Edward F. Buckley
George R. Bunn, Jr.
  '68 LLB
Mark M. Carhart
  '88 BA
James F. Carpenter
Mr. & Mrs. Richard M.
  Chanzit
Mrs. William G.
  Chester‡
Mr. & Mrs. James C.
  Childress
Rebecca S. Chopp
  '01 MAH
Carla Cicero
Fred W. Clarke, III
Laura Weir Clarke
Sheila M. Cleworth
CNI Contractors, INC
Ann Coggeshall
Communication Arts,
  INC
Sheila Levrant
  de Bretteville
  '63 BFA, '64 MFA
David Dechman
James M. DeFrancia
Gary Desmond
Rosemary Desmond
Gayer G. Dominick
Peter H. Dominick, Jr. ‡
  '63 BA
Philae Carver
  Dominick
Robert Donner, Jr.
  '53 Ugrd
Lewis W. Douglas, Jr.
  '45 BA
Mr. & Mrs. Bruce Ducker

Enid Storm Dwyer
Stefan T. Edlis
Elkus Manfredi
  Architects, LTD
Barbara Fey
Kari U. Foster
John E. Freyer
Virginia M. Freyer
Kathryn Scott Fuller
Gaines International
Sandy Gallun
Alan G. Gass
Sally R. Gass
Caleb F. Gates, Jr.
Gensler Denver
Scott Gerber
Tracey Gerber
Salma Gibara
Sam Gibara
Mary G. Golonka
Lauren M. Goodman
  Haddon, Morgan,
  Mueller, Jordan,
  Mackey & Foreman,
  PC
Jane M. Hamilton
Tracy Hart
Hart Howerton
  Partners, LTD
Mr. & Mrs. D. E. Harvey
Murray P. Hayutin
Phyllis Hayutin
Andrew Philip Heid
  '02 BA
Herschend Family
  Entertainment
Harley G. Higbie, Jr.
  '49 BS
David Hilder
Dale Hodges
Susan G. Hodges
George Hopfenbeck, Jr.
Jane Holzman
Mel Holzman
Betsy Hoover
George Hoover
Kip Hughes
Elise Jaffe &
  Jeffrey Brown
Jeffrey Beers
  International, LLC
Helayne Jones
Larry Jones
Teresa Jordan
  '77 BA
Coiman H. Kahn
George D. Kirkham
Ken Kuchin
Marianne Ladenburger
Robert W. Ladenburger
Alexandra Proctor
  Lange
  '94 BA
Leonard & Evelyn Lauder
Luisa Law
Sydney L.W. Lea, Jr.
Charles Leavell
Lindsey Leavell
Edward J. Lenkin
Linbeck Construction
  Company
Kent A. Logan
Victoria T. Logan
Catherine W. Lynn
  '78 MA, '81 PhD
Nancy P. Magoon
Robert Magoon
M. Grey Maher
J. Landis Martin
Sharon Martin
Joan S. Mathews
Ann Maurer
Gilbert Maurer
Jan Perry Mayer

Kathleen Doheny McCoy
Peter McCoy
Susan J. McFarlane
Gerald E. McNally, Jr.
Susan Mead
Michel Mercure
David J. Miller
Lisa Farber Miller
Nancy Lee Miller
Richard N. Miller
Montgomery Little
Soron & Murray, PC
Michiko Murao
  '03 BA
Paul Nakazawa
Gael Neeson
Jane P. Nichols
Bradley Nitkin‡
  '69 BA
Howard B. Noble
Susan T. Noble
Sheila K. O'Brien
Hilda Ochoa-
  Brillembourg
Roy O'Connor
Susan E. O'Connor
Deirdre Mary
  Ofarrelly
Thomas P. Owen
Owen Blicksilver
  Public Relations, INC
Judith E. Parker
Leonard Passano
  '52 MS
Neil Peck
  '62 LLB
Cesar Pelli
  '76 MAH, '08 DFAH
Miriam E. Perrin
Annzo E. Phelps
Pikes Peak Community
  Foundation
Jim Pinkard
Pinnacle Atlantic City
Geoffrey Platt
Katharine F. Plum
Sam Pluss
Zondra Rae Pluss
William Jethro Pott
  '05 MEM, '05 MBA
Mr. & Mrs. Reichborn-
  Kjennerud
William K. Reilly
  '62 BA, '94 MAH
Robert S. Rich
  '63 LLB
Debbie Richards
William P. Richards, Jr.
Riverview Park
  Associates, INC
The RMH Group, INC
Sam H. Roberson
Robert H. Malott Insur-
  ance Trust
John F. Roberts
Linda Z. Roberts
Marcia Robinson
Richard Robinson
Jane & E. Kevin Roche
  '95 DFAH
John M. Rocholl
Gideon G. Rose
  '85 BA
Joseph B. Rose
  '81 BA
Carolyn Greenspan &
  Marshall S. Ruben
  '82 BA
Jeanne W. Ruesch
Saiber Saiber, INC
Architecture
  S.A. Miro, INC
The San Isabel
  Foundation

William S. Saslow
Saunders Construction,
  INC
Paul H. Scarbrough
Mr. & Mrs. Thomas
  Schieffer
June Schorr
Paul C. Schorr, III
Vincent Scully
  '40 BA, '47 MA,
  '49 PhD
Norman C. Selby
  '74 BA
Brenda Shapiro
Carole Shaw
George Shaw
Barbara S. Sheldon
David B. Sheldon
John J. Sie
Robert E.W. Sinclair
Slifer Designs, INC
Mr. & Mrs. Albert H.
  Small
Gordon H. Smith
  '57 BE
Tania W. Stepanian
Allan M. Striker
Helena Striker
Sundance Square
  Management Company
Stephen Daily Susman
  '62 BA
Sutherland Foundation,
  INC
Svigals + Partners
Yuko Takenaka
  '97 BA
Elaine Tillinghast
Michael Touff
Trademark Property
  Company
Libby C. Trevor
Humberto Trueba, Jr.
Kimberly J. Trueba
University of
  Notre Dame
Urban Design Group, INC
Melissa G. Vail
  '74 BA
Alyce Van Gilder
Dell G. Van Gilder
Michael Vlock & Karen
  Pritzker
Harry R. Wadsworth
Betty L. Wagner
Charles L. Warren
Emily Webb
Anne C. Weisberg
Leslie M. Wileman
Margaret Wilfley
John Wittemyer
Nancy Wittemyer
Frank M. Woods
Pei-Tse Wu
  '89 BA
Xcel Energy Services,
  INC
Yale Club of New Haven
Zaidy's of Cherry
  Creek, INC
Morton Zeppelin
Zing LLC Zing
  Magazine

1935
David Norton Yerkes

1938
Gardiner Angell

1940
Russell P. Morse
Cope B. Walbridge‡

1941
Peter K. Ogden

1942
Edwin B. Crittenden
H. Dickson McKenna

1944
Leon A. Miller

1947
David N. Cybul
Henry Kibel
Bertram Lee Whinston‡

1948
Ekmel Moran
Joseph Richmond
  Tamsky

1949
Frank S. Alschuler
Theodore F. Babbitt
Jack Alan Bialosky, Sr.
Charles H. Brewer, Jr.
Russell C. Cecil
Elvia Fernandez
Abigail M. Hamilton
Bruce P. Helmes
George A. Hinds
William S.
  Kirkpatrick
Augustine J. Palmieri
Edward A. Sovik
George D. Waltz

1950
John A. Carter
R. Paige Donhauser
Elford A. King
Edward Humphrey
  Nelson
Herbert L. Seigle
Morris Simon
D. Jack West

1951
Stanley B. Brundage
Phelps H. Bultman
Earl P. Carlin
Frederick A. Craggs
Ross H. De Young
Martha Cantwell
  Meeker

1952
Thomas C. Babbitt
Donald Z. Bailey
Frank C. Boyer, Jr.
James A. Evans
George C. Holm
Morton Kass
Donald C. Mallow
William H. Metcalf, Jr.
Vincent M. Milone
James Elwell Palmer
Howard M. Y. Wong

1953
Duncan W. Buell
Andrew S. Cohen
Frank D. George
Stanley V. Greimann
Gordon Griswold

Milton Klein
Julian E. Kulski

1954
Charles G. Brickbauer
George R. Brunjes, Jr.
James H. Fitts, III
James D. Gibans
John F. Lee, Jr.
John V. Sheoris
Roger L. Strassman

1955
Vica S. Emery
John L. Field
Duncan M. Graham
Thomas F. Graves
Estelle T. Margolis
James Stewart Polshek
Edwards F. Rullman
Patricia V. Tetrault

1956
Richard W. Chapman
Thomas W. Connally
William B. Grindereng
Gerald E. Henniger
Walter D. Ramberg,
Stanley B. Wright, Jr.

1957
Ernest L. Ames
Edwin William
  de Cossy
Charles Augustus
  Ferrari
Edmund J. Glenny
James H. Handley, Jr.
Clovis B. Heimsath
Lee Mogel
Richard A. Nininger
William L. Porter
Howard W. Shoemaker
Richard Elliott
  Wagner

1958
Arthur H. Corwin
James S. Dudley
Harold D. Fredenburgh
Mark H. Hardenbergh
J. Arvid Klein
Herbert P. McLaughlin
Allen Moore, Jr.
Charles O. Perry
Jacques Richter
Malcolm Strachan, II
Michael W. Stuhldreher
Harold F. VanDine, Jr.
Donald W. Velsey

1959
George J. Alfano‡
Bernard M. Boyle
Frank C. Chapman
Peter B. Frantz
Thomas G. Green
Franklin D. Guidone‡
Louis P. Inserra
Robert Michael
  Kliment
Eugene J. Lorincz
Herbert S. Newman
Earl A. Quenneville
Frederick A. Russell
Ulli Scharnberg
Bruce W. Sielaff
Lee Anthony Syracuse
Terry G. Twitchell
Ralph J. Warburton
Carolyn H. Westerfield
Andrew C. Wheeler

1960
James B. Baker
Thomas L. Bosworth
Richard Spofford
  Chafee
John K. Copelin
Robert Melik Finkle
Alexander Grinnell
Michael Gruenbaum
David P. Jeffrey
Louis B. Joline
Julia H. Keydel
James D. McNeely
Oscar E. Menzer
Robert A. Mitchell
John J. Molloy
David L. Niland
Walter Rosenfeld
Gertrude O. Seibels
Stanley Tigerman

1961
Edward R. Baldwin, II
Paul B. Brouard
Robert W. Carington
Peter Cooke
Warren Jacob Cox
Francis W. Gencorelli
Charles T. Haddad
William J. Hawkins,
  III
Alvin H. Holm, Jr.
W. Eugene Sage
Wallace E. Sherriff

1962
James L. Alcorn
Brian D. Bagot
George E. Buchanan
Robert A. Cordingley‡
David W. Fix
Norman R. Foster
Charles Gwathmey
Richard A. Hansen
Tai Soo Kim
Keith R. Kroeger
James Morganstern
William S. Nichols
Renato Rossi-Loureiro
Meredith M. Seikel
Donald R. Watson
Myles Weintraub

1963
Austin Church III
A. Robert Faesy, Jr.
John Ming-Yee Lee
Ward Joseph Miles
F. Kempton Mooney
Louis H. Skidmore, Jr.
William A. Werner, Jr.
John V. Yanik

1964
Philip Allen
Lucinda L. Cisler
Theoharis L. David
Edward T. Groder
Peter Jeremy Hoppner
Charles D. Hosford
Augustus G. Kellogg
Judith A. Lawler
Charles L W. Leider
Robert J. Mittelstadt
Robert A. Nerrie, III
Ramesh Baldevbhai Patel
Joan F. Stogis

1965
Michael J. Altschuler
Thomas Hall Beeby
Richard C. Fogelson
Peter L. Gluck
Neil Goodwin

Sherman St. C.
  Hasbrouck
Norman E. Jackson, Jr.
Arthur A. Klipfel, III
Isidoro Korngold
Thai Ker Liu
Charles G. Meyer, Jr.
Gary L. Michael
John I. Pearce, Jr.
Alexander Purves
Elliot A. Segal
Robert A.M. Stern
Frederick C. Terzo
Leonard M. Todd, Jr.
Jeremy A. Walsh
Arnold N. Wile

1966
Andrew Andersons
Emily Nugent Carrier
Richard C. Carroll, Jr.
James Scott Cook
John J. Damico
Michael Hollander
William F. Moore
Peter H. Nuelsen
William L. Riddle
W. Mason Smith, III
Henry H. Smith-Miller
Lester R. Walker
Marja H. Watson

1967
William H. Albinson
Edward A. Arens
Robert A. Bell
R. Caswell Cooke, Jr.
Charles M. Engberg
Alexander D. Garvin
Glenn H. Gregg
Walter A. Hunt, Jr.
Eugene J. Lai
Chung Nung Lee
John W. Mullen III
A. Ramirez
  de Arellano
Charles S. Rotenberg
Theodore Paul
  Streibert
Darius Toraby
William H. Willis, Jr.
Robert M. Winick

1968
Frederick S. Andreae
Robert A. Busser
Gail H. Cooke
Peter de Bretteville
David M. Dickson
John Fulop, Jr.
Christopher C. Glass
Susanne Feld Hilberry
John Holbrook, Jr.
Gerard Ives
Erno Kolodny-Nagy
Peter Papademetriou
Franklin Satterthwaite
Donald R. Spivack
Salvatore F. Vasi
John J. Vosmek, Jr.
Thomas R. Welch, Jr.
James C. Whitney

1969
Jeffrey K. Abrams
John L. Allen
Jane K. Cahn
James E. Caldwell, Jr.
Samuel R. Callaway, Jr.
Robert J. Cassidy
David B. Decker
George B. Dudley
George T. Gardner
Harvey R. Geiger

Edward J. Gotgart
William H. Grover
Eric R. Hansen, Jr.
Peter Hentschel
Roderick C. Johnson
Raymond J. Kaskey, Jr.
James W. Peoples
William B. Richardson
John H. Shoaff
Bobby Votava

1970
Judith L. Aronson
Roland F. Bedford
Paul F. Bloom
F. Andrus Burr
Roc R. Caivano
Michael G. Curtis
Steven B. Edwins
Brin R. Ford
Morgan H. Grace, Jr.
George T. Hathorn
Peter Van W. Hoyt
David C. Jamison
James V. Righter
Steven G. Rockmore
Laurence A. Rosen
Daniel V. Scully
Walter C. Upton
Jan A. Van Loan
F. Anthony Zunino

1971
John R. Benson
William A. Brenner
Jay Warren Bright
An-Chi H. Burow
Rockwell J. Chin
Mark J. Ellis
Ronald L. Gonzalez
Anita Holland-Moritz
H. Rodriguez-
    Camilloni
Susan St. John
Peter J. Wood

1972
Marc F. Appleton
Paul B. Bailey
Edward P. Bass
Frederick Bland
Phillip M. Caldwell
Roberta Carlson
    Carnwath
Heather Willson Cass
William A. Davis, Jr.
John L. Delgado, Jr.
John H. T. Dow, Jr.
Joseph A. Ford, III
Richard N. Gould
William H. Maxfield
Keiichi Okamoto
David B. Peck, Jr.
Barton Phelps
Jefferson B. Riley
Robert L. Robinson
Paul W. Scovill, III
Mark Simon
James L. Strickland
Henry B. Teague
Brinkley S. Thorne
Carl H. Wies
Roger Hung Tuan Yee

1973
Arthur F. Duncan
J.P. Chadwick Floyd
Robert P. Hoffman
Stephen R. Holt
Everardo A. Jefferson
James O. Kruhly
William M. Mack
Nancy Brooks Monroe
Robert D. Orr, Jr.
Robert S. Page
Karen Rheinlander-
    Gray
Steven C. Robinson
William A. Sterling

J. Lawrence Thomas
Stephen C. Thomson
John W. Whipple
Robert J. Yudell

1974
Gordon M. Black
Sara E. Caples
Eric A. Chase
Andres M. Duany
Barbara L. Geddis
William E. Odell
Eleftherios Pavlides
Thomas C. Payne
Elizabeth M.
    Plater-Zyberk
Barbara J. Resnicow
David M. Schwarz
Richard A. Senechal
George E. Turnbull
Joy A. Wulke

1975
Tullio A. Bertoli
Martha A. Burns
S. Fiske Crowell, Jr.
Douglas J. Gardner
Karyn M. Gilvarg
Susan E. Godshall
Margaret R. Goglia
Keith B. Gross
Edwin R. Kimsey, Jr.
Francis C. Klein
Larry W. Richards
Hervin A.R. Romney
Mana Sarabhai
    Brearley
Andrew K. Stevenson
Hughes W. Thompson, Jr.
J. David Waggonner, III
Denis T. White

1976
Benjamin M. Baker, III
S. Shalom Baranes
Henry H. Benedict, III
Robert S. Charney
Anko Chen
Stefani Danes
Barbara R. Feibelman
Anna Marie Howell
Kunio Inoue
Daniel F. Kallenbach
James R. Kessler
Roy T. Lydon, Jr.
William A. McDonough
Eric Jay Oliner
Herschel L.D. Parnes
Richard H. Perlmutter
Stuart N. Silk
John K. Spear
Barbara Sundheimer-
    Extein
Philip B. Svigals

1977
C. Douglas Ballon
Calvert S. Bowie
Louise M. Braverman
Peter D. Clark
Bradley B. Cruickshank
W.J. Patrick Curley
Barry G. Donaldson
Eric W. Epstein
Barbara Flanagan
Carl M. Geupel
Jonathan S. Kammel
James Hirsch Liberman
Kevin P. Lichten
Randall T. Mudge
Davidson Norris
Paul J. Pugliese
Andrew K. Robinson
Raymond G. St. Francis
Charles B. Swanson
Stephen M. Tolkin
Alexander C. Twining

1978
Frederic M. Ball, Jr.
Paul W. Bierman-Lytle
Judith M. Capen
Kenneth H. Colburn
Kathleen Anne Dunne
Lisa J. Gelfand
Ralph A. Giammatteo
Robert W. Grzywacz
Cynthia N. Hamilton
William S. Mead
Kevin R. O'Connor
William Hall Paxson
Daniel Arthur
    Rosenfeld
Julia Ruch
David Spiker
Leonard Taylor, Jr.
Margaret T. Weidlein
Brigid C. Williams

1979
Steven W. Ansel
Jack Alan Bialosky, Jr.
James Leslie Bodnar
Richard H. Clarke
Jeffrey P. Feingold
Bradford W. Fiske
Patti Lee Glazer
John Charles Hall
Kevin E. Hart
Patrick C. Hickox
Michele Lewis
Michael B. Lipkin
Gavin A. Macrae-
    Gibson
George R. Mitchell
Thomas N. Patch
Jon K. Pickard
Miroslav P. Sykora

1980
Jacob D. Albert
Beryl E. Brown
David W. Carter
Turan Duda
Peter T. Ernst
J. Scott Finn
Stephen W. Harby
Mariko Masuoka
Ann K. McCallum
Julia H. Miner
William A. Paquette
Beverly Field Pierz
Stephen Lee Porten
Laura Herry Prozes
Michael I. Zenreich

1981
Mark T. Binsted
Donald W. Blair
Richard L. Brown
Douglass W. Cooper
Mark Denton
Eric W. Haesloop
Brian E. Healy
Mitchell A. Hirsch
T. Whitcomb Iglehart
Howard W. Kielley
Michael G. Kostow
Jonathan Levi
Jane Murphy
Frances H. Roosevelt
Daniela Holt Voith
Spencer Warncke
Diane L. Wilk

1982
John A. Boecker
Michael B. Burch
Domenic Carbone, Jr.
J. Peter Devereaux
Bruce H. Donnally
Raymond R. Glover
John E. Kaliski
Thomas A. Kligerman
Charles F. Lowrey, Jr.
Theodore John Mahl
Donald C. McBride

Jay D. Measley
Paul W. Reiss
William H. Sherman
Martin K. Shofner
Constance A. Spencer
R. Anthony Terry

1983
Maynard M. Ball
Anthony Stephen
    Barnes
Phillip G. Bernstein
Aaron A. Betsky
Carol J. Burns
Margaret D. Chapman
Stuart E. Christenson
Ignacio Dahl-Rocha
Charles D. Dilworth
Jane Backus Gelernter
William H. Gilliss
Anne Ridker Jaffe
Erica H. Ling
Frank M. Lupo
Elizabeth Ann Murrell
Jacques M. Richter
Gary Schilling
Brent Sherwood
Sonya R. Sofield
Robert J. Taylor
Michael R. Winstanley

1984
Kenneth A. Boroson
Paul F. Carr, Jr.
Michael J. Chren
Marti M. Cowan
Mark B. DuBois
Michael Coleman Duddy
Teresa Ann Dwan
Douglas S. Dworsky
Elysabeth B. Gamard
Frederick R. Groen
Blair D. Kamin
Elizabeth M. Mahon
Michael L. Marshall
David Chase Martin
Kenneth E. McKently
Jun Mitsui
Lawrence S. Ng
David L. Pearce
John R. Perkins
Ted Trussell Porter
Jill S. Riley
Jennifer C. Sage
Kevin M. Smith
Mary E. Stockton
Sherry L. Williamson
Sarah E. Willmer

1985
Barbara A. Ball
Rasa Joana Bauza
Bruce R. Becker
William N. Bernstein
William Robert
    Bingham
Robert L. Bostwick
M. Virginia Chapman
Frank R. Cheney
Bruce Coldham
Jonathan M. Fishman
Craig W. Fraulino
Kristin E. Hawkins
Lucile S. Irwin
Andrew M. Koglin
Charles H. Loomis
Peter B. MacKeith
Chariss McAfee
Richard G. Munday
Mark D. Rylander
Roger O. Schickedantz
R. David Thompson

1986
William Bartow
    Bialosky
Timothy Burnett
Margaret J. Chambers
David D. Harlan, Jr.

Richard W. Hayes
David J. Levitt
Aaron E. Rumple
J. Gilbert Strickler
John B. Tittmann

1987
William D. Egan
R. Andrew Garthwaite
E. Baker Goodwin
Elizabeth P. Gray
David B. Hotson
Andrew B. Knox
David G. Leary
Arnold C. Lee
Douglas S. Marshall
Craig D. Newick
Lilla J. Smith
Duncan Gregory Stroik
Andrea M. Swartz
Jennifer Tate
William L. Vandeventer
Lester Y. Yuen

1988
Atowarifagha I. Apiafi
Hans Baldauf
Andrew D. Berman
Cary Suzanne
    Bernstein
John David Butterworth
Aubrey Leon Carter, III
Allison Ewing
Stephen Clarke
    Fritzinger
Drew H. Kepley
Ann Lisa Krsul
Oscar E. Mertz, III
Ken Okamoto
Alan W. Organschi
Elaine M. Rene-
    Weissman
William Taggart Ruhl
Gil P. Schafer III
Matthew Viederman
Robert Duncan Young

1989
Larry G. Chang
Dale B. Cohen
William F. Conway
Darin C. Cook
John DaSilva
Steve Dumez
Thomas J. Frechette
Jennifer A. Huestis
Hidetoshi Kawaguchi
Kevin S. Killen
Scott A. Kirkham
Frank Koumantaris
Stephen D. Luoni
Juan Penabad
Rossana H. Santos-
    Wuest
Susan L. Seastone
Robert Ingram Tucker
Claire Weisz

1990
Thomas Randal Bader
Charles S. Bergen
Stephen Brockman
Matt Bucy
Elizabeth Ann Danze
Andre D. DeBar
Stancliff C. Elmore, Jr.
Roberto J. Espejo
Kristen L. Hodess
Jeffrey E. Karer
David M. Levine
Marc D. L'Italien
Catherine Mercer
Erik Bennett Oldham
Lori B. Arrasmith Quill
Deborah R. Robinson
Marie B. Wilkinson
Scott Wood
Mark A. Yoes

1991
David M. Becker
Carrie M. Burke
Sophie Harvey
Amy B. Janof
Dominic L.C. LaPierre
Joseph W. Moore
Linda Stabler-Talty
Alexander M. Stuart
Lindsay S. Suter
Claire E. Theobald
Michael W. Wetstone
Kevin Wilkes
Erika Belsey Worth

1992
Andrew James Abraham
Peter Kevin Blackburn
Kelly Jean
    Carlson-Reddig
Betty Y. Chen
Larry Greg Cohen
Frederick Adams
    Farrar, II
Bruce Marshall Horton
Deborah Aaronson
    Judelson
Douglas Neal Kozel
James Arthur Langley
Laura Auerbach
    Lapierre
Marc A. Turkel
Lynn Waskelis
Marion Converse
    Winkler

1993
Sari Chang
Richard G. Grisaru
Celia C. Imrey
Jordan J. Levin
Tara L. McCay
Craig Jeremy Moller
Gitta Robinson
Allen Douglas Ross
Evan Michael Supcoff

1994
Brendan Russell
    Coburn
Mark C. Dixon
Pamela J. Fischer
Anne G. Haynes
Benjamin J. Horten
Paul W. Jackson
Mark R. Johnson
Thomas Allen Kamm, Jr.
William J. Massey
Tania K. Min
Craig N. Schultz
Albert J. Tinson, Jr.
Mimi H. Tsai

1995
Matthew Karl Bremer
Ethan P. Cohen
Clemon A. Johnson
Allison Eden Karn
George C. Knight
Aaron Matthew Lamport
Rodney Leon
Michael Henry
    Levendusky
Jonathan Paul Siegel
Zon Sullenberger
John Christopher
    Woell

1996
Douglas C. Bothner
John L. Culman
Don M. Dimster-Denk
Russell S. Katz
Michael V. Knopoff
Chung Yin J. Lau
Thomas A. Lumikko
Nancy Nienberg
David A. Thurman
Mai-Tse Wu

1997
Victor E. Agran
Andrew Joseph Cleary
Leslie Ann Creane
Leah Simone Hall
S. Drew Lang
Peter Downing Mullan
Samuel Edward Parker, III
Raj Nalin Patel
Jeffery Ryan Povero
William James
    Voulgaris
Shawn Michael Watts
Aicha Schleicher Woods

1998
Carl F. Bergamini, Jr.
Paul John Boulifard
Melissa L. Delvecchio
Marjorie K. Dickstein
Glenn T. Fearon
Clifton R. Fordham
Arianne Marie Groth
Edward B. Gulick
Emily Sheya Kovner
Karl A. Krueger
Martina Y. Lind
Ceu Guilhermina
    Martinez
Marc A. Roehrle
Elizabeth P. Rutherfurd
Paul D. Stoller
Jennifer L. Taylor
Gretchen V. Wagner
Maureen R. Zell

1999
Elizabeth Marie Bester
Kimberly Ann Brown
Celia K. Civello
Martha Jane Foss
Taeik Kim
Bruce D. Kinlin
Elizabeth Rahlfs
    Manegold
Ajit Pai
Aaron W. Pine

2000
Urapong Amornvivat
Benjamin Jon Bischoff
Bing Bu
Frederick P.H. Cooke
John Christopher Ferri
Oliver Edmund
    Freundlich
Wen-Wei Huang
Donald Wayne Johnson
Thomas Matthew
    Morbitzer
Lesli Sarah Stinger
Michael James Tower
Cheng-Hsun Wu

2001
Ghiora Aharoni
Paul J. Arougheti
Siobhan A. Burke
Scott Garland
    Campbell
Yulee Carpenter
Natalie Sze-Wan Cheng
Mathew M. Combrink
Kay Frances Edge
Claude Daniel
    Eshaghian
Mark Foster Gage
Jeff Allan Goldstein
Jaehee Kim
Christopher M. Pizzi
Elizabeth Weeks
    Tilney
Juliana Chittick
    Tiryaki
Joan Y. Young
Jorge A. Zapata

2002
Dee Christy Briggs
Pengzhan Du
Joseph P. Ferrucci
Alexander Haskell
    Jermyn
Rashid Jamal Saxton
Jeffrey Paul Straesser
Victoria Partridge
    Walsh

2003
Edward Fox Baxter
Andrew William Benner
Marcos Diaz Gonzalez
Jian Hei
Li-Yu Hsu
Peter E. Kosinski
Olaf Lewis
    Recktenwald

2004
Abir Ahmad
Graham W. Banks
Valerie Anne Casey
Christopher H. Cayten
Stephen Yuen-Hoo
    Chien
Zhigang Han
Patrick James Hyland Jr.
Christopher A.
    Marcinkoski
James C. Nelson III
Benjamin Rosenblum
Adam Sokol
Stephen Kenneth Van Dyck
Na Wei

2005
Benjamin Thomas
    Albertson
Francesca R. Ammon
Emily Alice Atwood
Ralph Colt Bagley IV
Nora Ingrid Bergsten
Brent Allen Buck
Christopher A. Fein
Diala Salam Hanna
David Charles Hecht
Derek James Hoeferlin
Mang Tat Louis Lee
Brandon F. Pace
Jean Y. Pelle
Noah Riley
Brett Dalton Spearman
Nicholas Martin Stoutt

2006
Angel Paolo Campos
George B. de Brigard
Brent Wayne Fleming
Palmyra Stefania Geraki
Michael Joseph Grogan
Andrei Simon Harwell
Sean A. Khorsandi
Christopher John
    Rountos

2007
Joseph D. Alguire
Brook G. Denison
Heather Nicole Loeffler
Karl Rajiv Mascarenhas
Allen Slamic
Joseph M. Smith
Audrey Vuong

2008
Anton N. Bosschaert
Alexander S. Butler
Marc Charles Guberman
Kyung Sook G. Kim
Lorenzo Marasso
Maria C. Melniciuc
Marc C. Newman
Garrett T. Omoto
David J. Riedel
Leo Rowling Stevens, IV

7TH FLOOR

Faculty

JAMES AXLEY
TURNER BROOKS
BRENNAN BUCK
ANDREI HARWELL
DOLORES HAYDEN
ADAM HOPFNER
SOPHIA GRUZDYS
ARIANE LOURIE HARRISON
GREG LYNN
BEN PELL
ALAN PLATTUS

Guest Jurors

FORTH BAGLEY
KELLER EASTERLING
PETER EISENMAN
LIZA FIOR
MARK FOSTER GAGE
NICK JOHNSON
JOHN KALISKI
JAMIE VON KLEMPERER
GEORGE KNIGHT
IRVING LAVIN
RALPH LERNER
BARBARA LITTENBERG
LESLIE LU
ED MITCHELL
ADRIANNA MONK
BEN PELL
ALBERT POPE
HILARY SAMPLE
DAI SONGZHOU
BILLIE TSIEN
HUIJIN TU
BOWEI WANG
ADAM YARINKSY

Students

ARIANA BAIN*
ANGEL BEALE
MICHAEL BERRY
KEVIN BLUSEWICZ
JASON BOND
NICHOLAS CARUSO
CODY DAVIS
TRAVIS ROBERT EBY
SEHER ERDOGAN
KATEY EVERETT
JOSEPH FAMELY*
JOSH FELDMAN
REUBEN HERZL
MARCUS HOOKS
JASON KIM
JANG LEE
JOSH LEWANDOWSKI
LULU LI
MARIANNA MELLO
SHANE NEUFELD
ROBERTO ROSSI
JONAH ROWEN
BENJAMIN SACHS
TRISHA SNYDER
KYLE STOVER
GARRETT WONG
JUDE WU*
JUENAN WU

* STUDENT, YALE SCHOOL
  OF FORESTRY

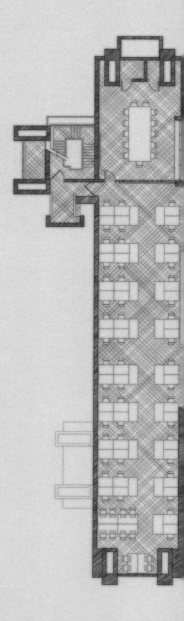

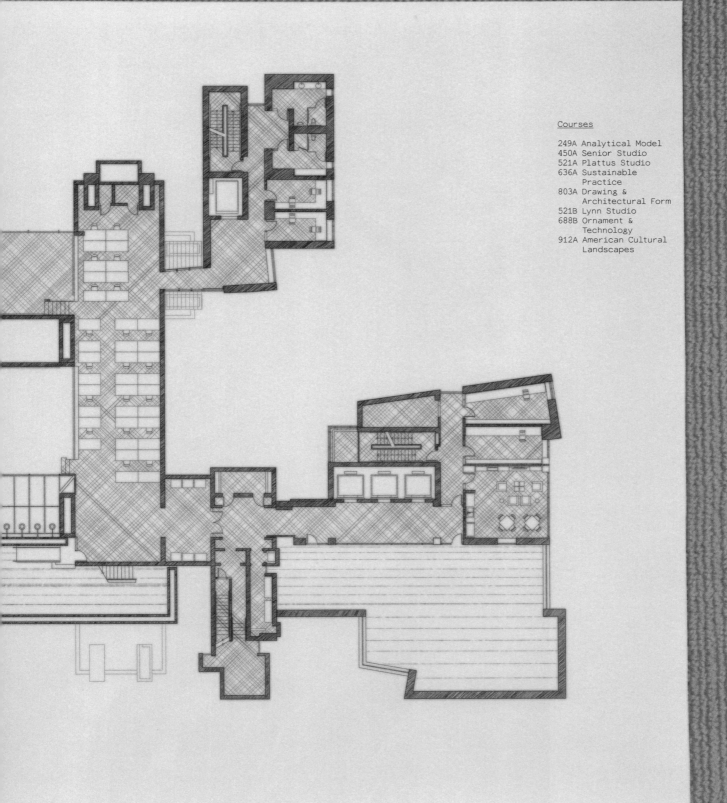

Courses

249A Analytical Model
450A Senior Studio
521A Plattus Studio
636A Sustainable
     Practice
803A Drawing &
     Architectural Form
521B Lynn Studio
688B Ornament &
     Technology
912A American Cultural
     Landscapes

ANALYTICAL MODEL*

An introduction for undergraduates to the history and practice of architectural analysis. Students produce drawings, models, and diagrams of significant architectural works in order to facilitate a comprehensive understanding of specific architects, buildings, and contexts. There is a description of a variety of approaches and the relationship between analysis and design.

249A

*
YALE COLLEGE COURSE

I
ARATA ISOZAKI'S PLAYING CARDS
JOSH FELDMAN
This is a study of the Oita Prefecture Library through a "mass and void analysis". Section cuts throughout the entire building depict the voided space. Exterior volumes are rendered in bass wood while the interior profile is carved out. Further study of the external and internal views visible throughout the building is depicted in teal. Nodes of rest within the library demarcate private observation points. An orange underside portrays the shared public space.

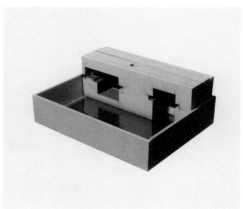

I

II
THE NELSON-ATKINS MUSEUM EXPANSION:
AN ANALYSIS THROUGH MODEL
LULU LI
Steven Holl's expansion of the Nelson-Atkins Museum in Kansas City is analyzed and reinterpreted through a series of models and diagrams focused around four themes: massing, tectonic, movement/contour, and program. The analysis also emphasizes the relationship between the expansion and the pre-existing museum as well as the formal geometries of this new "archipelago" building type.

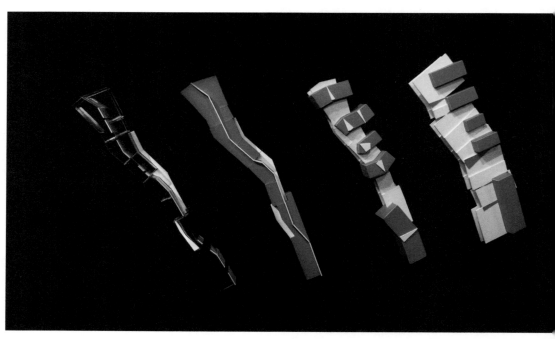

II

JOSH FELDMAN   LULU LI

SENIOR STUDIO*   450A

Advanced problems for undergraduates with emphasis on the architectural implications of contemporary cultural issues. Exploration of the complex relationship among space, materials, and program. Emphasis on the development of representations (drawings and models) that effectively communicate architectural ideas.

I
DOMINANT VOID
MARCUS HOOKS

I

II
THE CUSHING COLLECTION
BENJAMIN SACHS

II

III
INTIMATE IMMENSITY
GARRETT WONG

III

MARCUS HOOKS   BENJAMIN SACHS   GARRETT WONG

ANDREI HARWELL

ALAN PLATTUS

FORTH BAGLEY   JAMIE VON KLEMPERER   LESLIE LU   BILLIE TSIEN
KELLER EASTERLING   GEORGE KNIGHT   ALBERT POPE   HUIJUN TU
NICK JOHNSON   RALPH LERNER   HILARY SAMPLE   BOWEI WANG
JOHN KALISKI   BARBARA LITTENBERG   DAI SONGZHOU   ADAM YARINKSY

521A

PLATTUS STUDIO

This studio marked the tenth year of a three-way collaboration between architecture students and faculty at the University of Hong Kong and Tongji University in Shanghai. While past studios have focused on a variety of waterfront sites, especially along the Suzhou Creek and the Huangpu River, the site for this year's studio was, like the 2007 site, a block in the heart of the historic, but rapidly developing, French Concession. Once occupied mainly by the characteristic Lilong-style housing of the early twentieth century that covered so much of the city of Shanghai, the block is targeted for the sort of large-scale mixed-use redevelopment that has spread through the French Concession, especially along major corridors such as Nanjing and Weihai Roads. Although the only historic building actually remaining on the cleared site is one of Mao Tse-Tung's several Shanghai residences, the studio provided an opportunity to analyze and evaluate the character of both the historic and contemporary urban fabric in Shanghai, and their collision. At a more detailed level of design, the studio also considered the relationship between historic and contemporary architectural and landscape vocabularies, and the ideological questions these entail. Also, given the enormous size of a typical Shanghai block, the urban design issue of the superblock was studied in relation to this specific site.

I
PODIUM FRAGMENTED
TRAVIS ROBERT EBY & SEHER ERDOGAN,
H.I. FELDMAN NOMINEES

The site is located on a busy stretch of Nanjing Road--Shanghai's answer to Broadway. Initial observations of Nanjing Road's recent development have focused the project on a study of urban fabric and the existing commercial pressures.

The analysis identified the "podium tower," a typology consisting of two oversized parts, as the prevalent figure in the coarsening of the grain which has led to an undifferentiated streetscape and segregated urban flows.

This critique led the project through a process of fragmentation of the podium. These fragments are determined by a matrix of commercial and residential unit types, which allow for different modes of aggregation and thereby the production of a highly heterogeneous environment. The series of configurations integrate the site's various morphologies with existing urban context.

As a result, four quadrants with distinct urban characteristics arise, displaying the versatility of the fragmentation method on the ground plane. The development strategy scripted for the project fosters the involvement of multiple parties.

TRAVIS ROBERT EBY
SEHER ERDOGAN

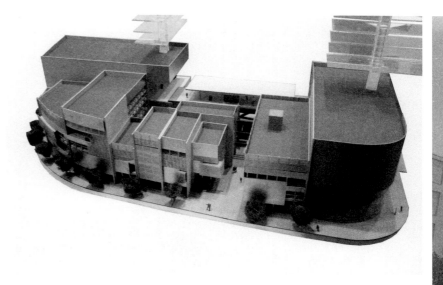

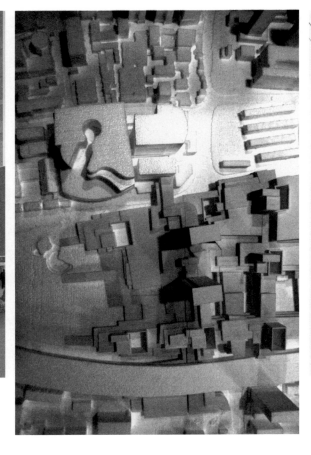

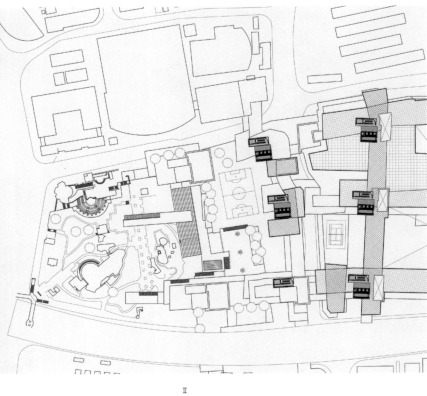

II

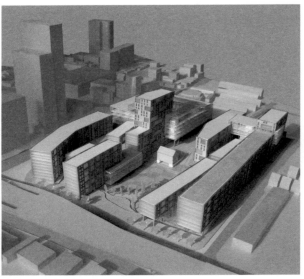

III

ANDREI HARWELL   ALAN PLATTUS

FORTH BAGLEY   JAMIE VON KLEMPERER   LESLIE LU   BILLIE TSIEN
KELLER EASTERLING   GEORGE KNIGHT   ALBERT POPE   HUIJUN TU
NICK JOHNSON   RALPH LERNER   HILARY SAMPLE   BOWEI WANG
JOHN KALISKI   BARBARA LITTENBERG   DAI SONGZHOU   ADAM YARINKSY

JOHN KALISKI „The one part of the idea I worry about from a critical perspective is the notion that you can make a convention center work vertically, in terms of circulation. I would challenge that because you're moving huge and heavy things of indeterminate weight around, so your entire convention center is based on the size of the freight elevator that you're capable of designing. I think the mechanics of it are fascinating.

NICK JOHNSON „I'm interested in your objectives but I'm not persuaded by your narrative as read because you described this thing as a kind of non-object, a neutral, and then you are trying to contextualize it according to what is around the site--and yet black boxes are the one thing that convention centers typically are. It's about making this a desirable experience of place, and that's where you haven't gone far enough.

JOHN KALISKI „Your initial motivator was this program that would activate everything else around it, and I think that is really smart. Then you made the second move to tie it into everything that was already there, and that is really smart. There are a couple of problems where you didn't take the program far enough. The forms you've generated seem to want to have a more programmatic aspect to them.

NICK JOHNSON „One quick point about money, because it's interesting. Money is an old concept, especially with the developer. I think what will quite rightly overtake our singular obsession of money in the forthcoming years will be environment.

BARBARA LITTENBERG „Can I just say, I'm fascinated with the design process. I love that site planning idea, and when I look at that my mind just wants to go there and find out what's going on. But I think you get into a conflict with your building type--when I see these big

conference halls and the nature of that space I say to myself, uh-oh. Somehow you killed the intrigue of that plan by trying to shoehorn these boxes inside it. I think it's an aspect of an investigation where you say, 'I want to make a piece of a city.' Programmatically, it could come and go, but then you want to take that organization and use it with something else. It should be an organism that is flexible enough to accommodate, and convention centers are the exact opposite.

BILLIE TSIEN „I totally appreciate what you're saying, but I also appreciate the nobility of taking the thing that everyone hates, a convention center, and trying to make it an anti-convention center. I do think you make an interesting point in talking about hybridizing it and making it more than one thing. I think it's very interesting and subversive.

JOHN KALISKI „But getting back to your point about the notion of money and environment and a nexus between these two--I think that's where the project fails. In my mind what was interesting was that you created this organizing principle in the landscape, which in essence is the environment. That environment was like a park you go to for no other reason than to simply go. It has parts of the program above it and parts below, but that open space, whatever it was, was something you could comprehend and move through. Then I think it would have worked. Part of the problem was that you had the organizing principle of this open space with the organizing principles of the vertical cores, and it just became too much where one was unable to become dominant.

BARBARA LITTENBERG „But was there an idea to create a piece of the city or to create a convention center?

JOSH LEWANDOWSKI „It was to create a piece of the city.

II
PLAID URBAN LANDSCAPES
ANGEL BEALE & JOSH LEWANDOWSKI

Our observations of the site reveal a Shanghai development boom in this urban fabric of podium buildings and the effects this has had on the city in terms of isolating its grid into individual street blocks. The podium blocks create nodes that facilitate transportation systems. Our response was to create a similar web of pedestrian sky walk ways and to jump start development through a convention center. Through time it would develop into the urban landscape. We hope to re-imagine the city typology as more interconnected and more integrated as program is deployed around the convention center. We have developed a plaid programmatic deployment in the urban fabric in an attempt to counteract our initial observations.

NICK JOHNSON „My response is driven from what I found out last year (at the Fall 2007 Studio Review) because of that year's existing site. We found that indigenous people were being displaced because the perceived conditions were inadequate for contemporary living.

ROBERTO ROSSI „Yes, and that's why we are leveraging one situation for another, a desirable real estate reality that people want to pay money for, so that the people who have been forced out may return again.

JOHN KALISKI „What I was saying gets back to a point of view of yesterday about displacement, whether housing displacement or social displacement. What's interesting about the project to me is the notion that the choice exists to value this land in terms of values other than strictly monetary ones. So what's interesting for me is that it creates social value as opposed to economic value, but in the process of doing that it might create values of another type in this area that might be monetized.

NICK JOHNSON „The reason for my comment is that you did state these are actually high end apartments, and that brings up this whole notion of palatable displacement with these kinds of facilities.

JOHN KALISKI „I was going to ask about that as well, because not only is there a financial dimension to it, but 'is it really necessary.' In looking at these, I keep thinking, what if they are high rise condominiums? What are the spatial devices that go into high rise condominiums, and are those built in to a certain degree? Because I think there is a bit of discontinuity between the typology of the housing blocks and the idea that they are actually luxury apartments. Then I wonder, do they even need to be luxury apartments given that the program might be thought of as economically contributing to this area in a completely different way?

ALBERT POPE „There is an extension to that argument because the program you've taken is ideologically loaded. On the left side you have this convention center, where you have made a powerful capitalistic icon. You might be telling us that monuments shouldn't be so big and they should pay for themselves with luxury amenities, and in some ways you're updating the notion of monumentality. An argument for this side is that the maximum value is not about displacement but about devoting the site to the public value. What you're really doing is updating the idea of monumentality.

ALAN PLATTUS „You know Albert, I hadn't thought of it before you said that, but in a way it is a formalization of what happened to a lot of cultural facilities ex post facto.

JOHN KALISKI „If you want to have a discussion on the financial mechanisms, one should simply recognize that if you expand your terms of financial mechanisms to include building and maintaining things, then there are other things besides paying for itself.

NICK JOHNSON „They aren't fundamentally different, are they? It's that cigarette paper between Communism and Capitalism. The way in which monumentality was created historically was to capture the wealth of the workers and redistribute that to monuments was just done on a larger scale--a national scale--where all this is doing is capturing that notion of value and contribution and localizing it.

JOHN KALISKI „I do like how the box of the Ping Pong Palace got wrapped though. I think that if it hadn't been wrapped there would have been a different challenge, which would have been the fact that those buildings tend to be giant walls.

FORTH BAGLEY „If this is an arena where you want people to come play, you have to be able to say, 'meet me at the front door.' It seems to me that your Ping Pong Palace is the least open of all the buildings.

III
THE PEOPLE'S PING PONG PALACE
MARIANNA MELLO & ROBERTO ROSSI

The malls and hotels of Nanjing Road, Shanghai's great commercial strip, grow on the rubble of the city's demolished residential districts. The local population is relocated to projects ever further away on the periphery as developers saturate the center with a monoculture of tourism, business, and shopping. Our proposal for this nodal site on Nanjing Road is for a complex of athletic and leisure facilities open to the public and intended to draw displaced Shanghainese back downtown. The anchor of for the project is the People's Ping-Pong Palace: an 8,000 person table tennis arena and training center that functions both as a world-class venue for international tournaments and as a recreational facility for public use. Mixed with the sports program (and subsidizing it) are two hotels and 750 high-end residential units, arranged around a green plaza at the heart of the development to create a dense community.

ANGEL BEALE   MARIANNA MELLO
JOSH LEWANDOWSKI   ROBERTO ROSSI

636A

SUSTAINABLE PROCTICE

YALE SCHOOL OF FORESTRY

This seminar looks broadly at sustainable architectural design--reviewing environmental issues, key documents, and larger-scale strategies--and then narrowly at the current and emerging detailed methods used to support design development of sustainable buildings, communities, and cities. Devised to complement 633a, Environmental Systems in Buildings, this seminar reviews the evolution of the notion and need for sustainability; considers case studies of innovative community, urban, and regional-scale strategies of sustainable design; surveys recent sustainable design assessment methods, design guidelines, and standards; considers case studies of innovative buildings shaped by these methods; and provides a broad overview of advanced simulation methods used in the design development of these innovative buildings and communities.

I
GINKGO CITY
ARIANA BAIN, NICHOLAS CARUSO, JOSEPH FAMELY, REUBEN HERZL & JUDE WU

The design of Ginkgo City was informed by the site. The expansive wetlands and mangrove swamps around the new city were left untouched and devoted to the ecosystems that provide critical services to sustain human life and overall ecological resilience in the region. A high-density corridor was generated along the high ground of the peninsula before fanning out across a collection of existing villages to the south, thus shaping the form of Ginkgo City as an extremely dense community surrounded by extensive nature preserves for rainwater catchment, wildlife retention, and general recreation.

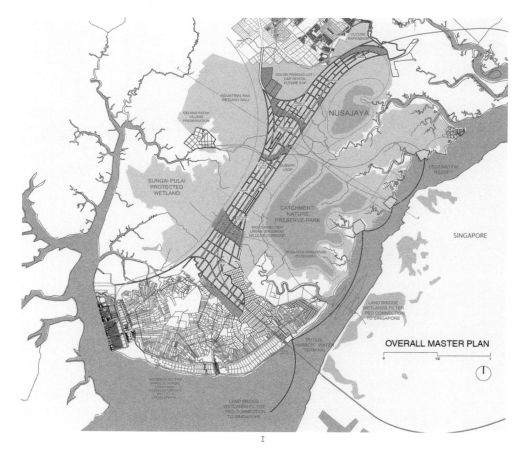

I

II
URBAN MANGROVES
JOSEPH FAMELY & REUBEN HERZL

Coastal tropical cities occupy a tenuous space, often having profound impacts on the surrounding ecosystems, while simultaneously being subject to forces of nature. For years, mangroves have been used as passive tools to bi-directionally buffer the stresses between sea and city, yielding a plethora of study on mangrove restoration and large conservation efforts. This paradigm misses the opportunities that emerge from framing mangroves as active tools in urban development. The proposed experiment intends to develop a base of investigation into how mangrove systems can inform urban design, serving simultaneously as green infrastructure and a framework for studies of urban ecology.

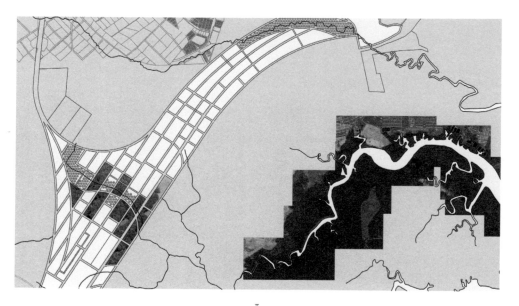

II

ARIANA BAIN*
NICHOLAS CARUSO
JOSEPH FAMELY*
REUBEN HERZL
JUDE WU*

JOSEPH FAMELY*
REUBEN HERZL

DRAWING &
ARCHITECTURAL FORM

803A

This course examines the highly rigorous constructed architectural drawing through the tools of descriptive geometry, cast perspective, and sciagraphy. These tools have evolved within an historical and theoretical context of architectural representation, and can inform strategies toward the conception of architectural form. The process of the constructed drawing reveals the building through the tactile materials of its own construction. Thus, media such as pencil, ink washes, and watercolor are an integral part of the articulation of these drawings. The appropriateness and meaning of drawn construction and its articulation are examined through a series of drawn investigations, which use the Yale campus as a point of departure.

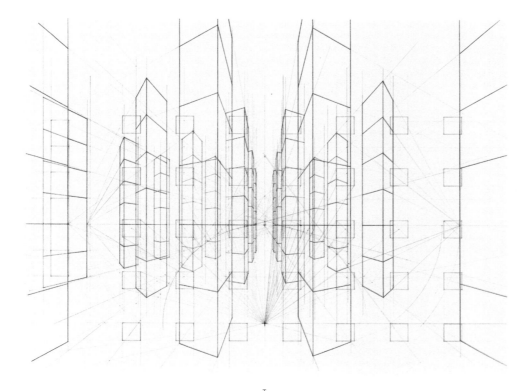

I

I
PANORAMIC PROJECTION
TRISHA SNYDER
Standing in a field of columns: an overlay of plan and panoramic projection

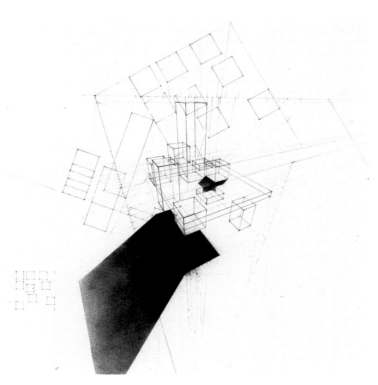

II

II
THREE POINT PERSPECTIVE
JUENAN WU
A field of nine squares projected in space with shadows using three-point-perspective.

521B

LYNN STUDIO

For the last decade, architects have used the digital medium of surface modeling tools primarily for the design of sloped, curved and topological floors. In this studio we will focus on the surface of building façades with some attention to the design of a large single volume and its walls and ceiling as it relates to the façade. The contemporary language of surface modeling from the fields of automobile, yacht, aerospace and industrial design will be given an equal value to the architectural context for the project.

The site and program for the studio will be a contemporary solution to the 1657 urban design proposal of Bernini for the Piazza San Pietro. Despite its scale, the duomo was not visible from the piazza due to the extensive depth of the building. Much like Alberti's Sant Andrea in Mantua, the ambition was to conceal the dome; yet unlike Alberti's design of a superimposed façade that precludes and represents the volume and mass beyond, Bernini masked the duomo's appearance on approach to the oval forecourt by projecting an opaque screen into the city as a "terzio braccio" or "third arm". Mussolini's axial development of Via della Conciliazone (for the design of which he consulted with gothic campus architect Ralph Adams Cram, who encouraged Mussolini to build horizontal towers instead of a vertical tower) compounded the un-built solution to the problem Bernini perceived with the visibility of the duomo from a distant frontal approach. The present situation with an allée of Mussolini era blocks leading to the church can be improved by returning to Bernini's original urban vision with a contemporary design sensibility.

I
TERZO BRACCIO
JASON KIM,
H.I. FELDMAN NOMINEE

The ambition of this project is to retain the unprogrammed public space created by the original two arms designed by Bernini, while incorporating the program of a library with very restricted access, and all without reducing the efficacy of either. As with the original urban gesture, it was crucial to maintain the porosity of the original colonnade in the third arm. I approached the problem by considering the façades facing the Vatican and Rome as a porous public space and considering the ceiling as the surface that would exist between the public and the private users of the library-- effectively creating a third façade.

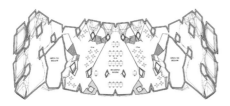

IRVING LAVIN „I have a question about the re-
„ lationship of the so-called diamond shape,
„ where all the radii are generated from the
„ same points. You know that's not true of the
„ piazza itself--that's not the way it works.
„ That is, the piazza is a fake ellipse in the
„ sense that there's a common one, but it's made
„ of two circles of larger diameter, so the col-
„ umns here, if there had been one, would not
„ have met in this corner, they would have met
„ here. The other thing is that, had you done it
„ the other way, had these been the same, you
„ would've ended up with lozenges of different
„ shapes. So my point is basically an infor-
„ mation question: to what degree is this lie
„ you're telling a deliberate one, and what is
„ its purpose rather than having done presumably
„ what Bernini would have done, namely have the
„ colonnade respond to this center.
PETER EISENMAN „But you wouldn't have had
„ lozenges, you're making a very good point.
IRVING LAVIN „Am I wrong?
PETER EISENMAN „No, you're right but you wouldn't
„ have had lozenges because you only have one
„ point of inflection rather than two.
IRVING LAVIN „They would've crossed, they
„ would've intersected, and there wouldn't be
„ these spaces in the center. Anyway, the ques-
„ tion is one of geometry, because the subtlety
„ results from the geometrical interpretation.
PETER EISENMAN „I would say the two sections are
„ the best part of the project in there, number
„ one; and they don't have to come down into
„ lozenges. They could…
LIZA FIOR „He's got the message, and he's not
„ wedded to his lozenges. What I liked about
„ your presentation was that you did start with
„ an ambition to capture these public spaces
„ of pause, which is so explicit in the sec-
„ tion--that the bulk of the place you can't
„ go, making the place you can go, terminating
„ the two arms, but then actually making a way
„ through into the piazza. And that was quite an
„ ambitious thing to do, where the buffer becomes

„ the means through.
IRVING LAVIN „I want to say, this last time,
„ this lozenge-mania up there is the prime char-
„ acteristic of Guarini at the Sindone. That's
„ what goes on up there. Now wait a minute,
„ there's another comment in there, that every-
„ body recognizes that that dome is profoundly
„ influenced by Islam…
PETER EISENMAN „But it doesn't come down in plan.
IRVING LAVIN „Absolutely not. That's why I want
„ you to look at it. But it does come to some-
„ thing else in this case that it doesn't inform;
„ namely, it's transparent. That's light. And
„ therefore you're looking up as though you were
„ looking up at a Late Gothic fan vault, as they are
„ called, which consists of intersecting lines,
„ except here, its glass up there, so you're
„ looking into diamonds which are transparent.
MARK FOSTER GAGE „That dome (in the Sindone
„ Chapel) is also made of components instead of
„ a surface, which makes it even more interest-
„ ing; it's stacked pediments. I think it's one of
„ the best examples of what a Baroque dome can
„ be, versus a Renaissance dome, which is often
„ the ribs with painting in between, which is a
„ surface; the Baroque dome in the Guarini sense
„ is a collection of components; in that sense
„ it's corbelled, like a mosque. That's what this
„ project needs, something that breaks up the
„ continuity of surface with a component.
IRVING LAVIN „Sorry, Jason has it. These are
„ not identical. It's the same as in the case
„ of the Guarini. It does that because the dome
„ is convex. Whatever the diagrammatic pattern
„ he has makes, they're not identical. They do
„ swell and diminish and they have little…
GREG LYNN „The only thing about Jason's is that
„ it's extruded in a topological way, but it's
„ extruded. So it's missing that thing of…
MARK FOSTER GAGE „And that's what Guarini isn't.
PETER EISENMAN „Is not. Guarini is not that. And
„ the question of extrusion…
GREG LYNN „So it has no façade, by definition,
„ because it's extruded.

+3M: RARE BOOK VAULT REFLECTED CEILING PLAN

+6M: READING ROOM

LONGITUDINAL SECTION - AA

II

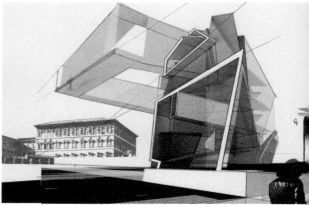

III

MARK FOSTER GAGE „He has the first project to take a component-based system, like what exists in the original colonnade, and over a course slowly translate it into a surface. And I think a lot of the other students had either components or surfaces, but this is the first one to blend the relationship between the two, and I think that's incredibly fascinating. I also think, as Greg was mentioning, the quality of the scrolls, which you see as far back as Alberti on Santa Maria Novella, trying to create a relationship between a surface like this and a surface like this, the use of a scroll—I mean, you're using it in a completely new way, not to create a relationship between a vertical and a horizontal surface, but to create a relationship between a surface and a component, and I think that's incredibly rich conceptual territory.

PETER EISENMAN „Mark, let me ask you a question. Because Robert (Stern) and I, when we start thinking alike, I start to get worried. What happens if you take the centerpiece away? You could do exactly the same…

GREG LYNN „Oh, no. No, take the other stuff away, leave the center.

PETER EISENMAN „Either way. You could do exactly what you said without the centerpiece.

GREG LYNN „No.

PETER EISENMAN „What Mark just said?

GREG LYNN „Can we go look at the drawings?

MARK FOSTER GAGE „But I think it's more interesting as a dome; I think you might want to re-address the gaping…

GREG LYNN „Let's go over here, because he's got an even bigger one. Here, he's got a giant one over here you should see.

MARK FOSTER GAGE „It looks really great here. It's actually really successful.

PETER EISENMAN „Boy, look at it next to the dome though. Look at this perspective. The dome turns into a phallic symbol.

ROBERT A.M. STERN „Was it your intention to make these anatomical references, or beyond that? Or is it a product of your fervent imagination?

MARK FOSTER GAGE „I think it is a rather lovely mass. You're taking an idea about rustication, which is incredibly important to Baroque architecture, and scaling up ideas of massing— I think there's a lot more to talk about than this, whether it's a relationship with the mass or the rocks. There's something else happening here which is much more interesting and more successful than just—I could give a fuck about the ramps, to be honest. It's much more interesting for me to look at this thing, than to stand in it and look out at the pope's balcony.

PETER EISENMAN „Rusticated?

MARK FOSTER GAGE „When you look at the Palazzo del Te do you wonder why the little pieces of rustication are shaped as such?

PETER EISENMAN „I know why.

MARK FOSTER GAGE „You do?

{Laughter}

PETER EISENMAN „But if you just take the interior—let's strip away the outside for a minute and take this ramp system, which is really a very radical interior gesture. And then you say, well we have the problem of decorum. It seems to me that he's caught between a radical gesture and the context that he's in. And my question is, are there other forms of the exterior? Because I would never expect, seeing the plans, that these are the façades. And my only question is, how come? Because the ramps have a much more wild, radical…

MARK FOSTER GAGE „Why do we think—why are the ramps radical? I mean, the Vatican is rife with ramps.

PETER EISENMAN „No, no, no, the way they're used is a bit extreme, let's say. They crisscross, they're like Piranesian Carceri, let's say.

IRVING LAVIN „Yeah.

PETER EISENMAN „Let's say they're Piranesian, rather than Wrightian.

IRVING LAVIN „I agree, you're right.

PETER EISENMAN „Let's say they're Piranesian, I would never expect that this decorum; since the outside doesn't relate, except in moments,

---

GREG LYNN „See, this is honestly where symmetry gets you in trouble.

{Laughter}

MARK FOSTER GAGE „See, that's what I was trying to say.

ROBERT A.M. STERN „I want to hear Cody's reply.

CODY DAVIS „Those are definitely interpretations, but I think the ambition was to produce a certain grotesque, distorted quality of the forms that are respectful of the proportions of the site, but it's very apparent that these things have misshapen, altered forms that are alluding to the things that are already there: a big, massive dome, that has a very, very strong presence in the city.

ROBERT A.M. STERN „You are not answering the question.

LIZA FIOR „Just say yes or no.

ROBERT A.M. STERN „Was sex on your mind?

CODY DAVIS „Sex is always on my mind.

{Laughter}

MARK FOSTER GAGE „Well I also think that one reason you get so many biomorphic readings from it is that the surface is unarticulated. I mean, you could scallop it, flute it, there's a whole range of surface articulations that it could use that would take it away from being read as skin.

GREG LYNN „I want to be critical; I think there's a problem with the scale. Right now it's too big to develop a logic of interior spaces, so you just throw these slabs in it. And on the site, it is like a decorative element blown up large. And it doesn't yet have an idea about how to make a space, other than at that urban scale.

MARK FOSTER GAGE „I agree with Greg's comment. Right now he does not have a logic of how to make a room in this space. If you had designed an interior and had it not be coincident with the exterior, it would allow you a little bit more design freedom. It's weird because you are making a dome, but there are no domes in the Renaissance where the dome's exterior is the same as the interior.

I wonder if there are other decorous forms that could do something more--my only objection to the project is not the Piranesian interiors, which I think would be stunning, and the elaborate section—I just say to myself, it seems that the façades are styled in some way, and I don't know where they come from.

MARK FOSTER GAGE „I was making a case for the exterior, and you keep blaming the exterior on the ramps of the interior, and that frustrates me because I think you're making moves here, either intuitively or you thought about it—but for me, these distances that you're using are incredibly similar to the distances of the colonnade. The pavilions at the ends of Bernini's colonnade, which no one has talked about all day, are about the same size as your pavilions. Like when you see the perspective here, these facets are about the same size as the dome. I mean, everything is somehow resonating contextually, and to say that the exterior is because of the ramp system—it's…

PETER EISENMAN „It's not because of the ramp system.

SHANE NEUFELD „I didn't say that though, I actually said…

MARK FOSTER GAGE „The language existed before the ramp, right?

SHANE NEUFELD „No, yeah, the idea…

MARK FOSTER GAGE „Quit arguing with me. I love your project.

{Laughter}

ADRIANNA MONK „One thing I like about your project is that it's the only one that takes advantage of the fact that you've got a building that can give a different perspective on the whole piazza. You're using it as an entrance to the whole piazza, and yours takes the opportunity of saying, 'Hey you know what? I could give you different levels, and different views that you don't want to miss. And by giving you a ramp so you can zigzag through the building, I'm going to show you what you should look at, because sometimes you're just overwhelmed.' You come to these places and you're in awe. But that's what I think is really good about it.

II

VATICAN READING ROOM IN THE CONTEXT OF GIOVANNI LORENZO BERNINI

CODY DAVIS

This project is a manipulation of the Baroque forms found in Bernini's sculptural compositions, replete in the two arms encircling Piazza San Pietro and in the baldacchino at the heart of the church. Respecting the principles of plasticity, proportion, and symmetry, the proposed "third arm" finds a state of transition between the horizontal continuity of the surrounding colonnades and the vertical rhythm of the columns themselves. Undulating surfaces culminate in a dome volume which is suspended by looping scrolls.

III

TERZO BRACCIO

SHANE NEUFELD

Historically, the "third arm" was intended to complete the Piazza San Pietro, sealing off the Oval Piazza from the rest of the city. However, Bernini's vision never came to fruition. This project for a new reading room extension for the Papal Library completes Bernini's intended design while bringing a new monument to Rome's dense urban fabric.

The project combines two ambitions. The first is to inject the commissioned building with a secular function by elevating the public's visual experience of the Piazza through the design of a ramp that would enable public circulation throughout the entirety of the building.

The second is to generate—through formal analysis of Borromini and an experimentation with various contemporary techniques—a façade that references the contrasting chiaroscuro of the Baroque while creating a new monument for Rome.

688B

ORNAMENT
& TECHNOLOGY

Through a close reading of twentieth century practices of the decorative, this course examines contemporary interests in digital fabrication relative to the historically complex relationship between technology and the production of ornament. The seminar surveys the history of ornament from 1851 to the present in order to identify various definitions of the term (from notions of the joys of handicraft, to associations with excess, deceit and sin) and to examine a series of diverse case studies (from architectural projects to wallcoverings, textiles, fashion, graphic and furniture design). The intention is to outline the potential for digital fabrication to contribute to renewed considerations of ornament today, exploring strategies of figuration, organization, technique, and application to which these technologies readily lend themselves. The course begins with a series of weekly readings presentations and case study analyses, gradually identifying the current discourse on ornament and possible new trajectories. Subsequent material investigations using in-house CNC fabrication resources serve to clarify student positions relative to this discourse, and to define new territory for the confluence of ornament and technology in contemporary architectural practice.

I
AMERICAN GRAFFITI
JASON BOND & JANG LEE

Using the roadside diner façade as our site for investigation, we sought to develop a concept for ornament that is simultaneously representational and affective. This was achieved through half-tone graphic abstraction and operable apertures. The stainless steel façade appears as a coherent graphic image from a distance, but when approached these graphics dissolve into their abstracted components. The operable panels similarly dissolve the surface, presenting their own formal evocations that fragment their representational effects.

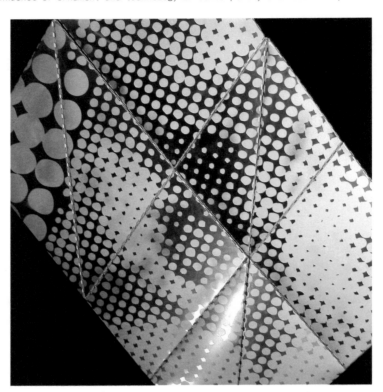

I

II
STAIR BANISTER
JONAH ROWEN & KYLE STOVER

Our project seeks to interrogate the traditional understanding and component relationship of a stair banister. Traditionally, banister design has employed forms of ornamentation that deal with material removal as a volumetric process, although in today's suburban homes banister design has been reduced to a thinness of surface in part due to construction technique. Our banister design seeks to blur the relationship of volume, mass, and structure through geometric patterning achieved by a technical means of graduated material removal.

II

JASON BOND
JANG LEE

JONAH ROWEN
KYLE STOVER

AMERICAN CULTURAL LANDSCAPES

The cultural landscape in the United States, a combination of natural and built environments, has evolved through decisions about the use of land and natural resources, the planning of towns, the development of transportation and infrastructure, and the promotion of various building types and architectural styles. After a brief review of Native American and colonial settlement patterns, the first portion of this lecture course surveys the growth of towns and cities between 1800 and 1920. The second portion examines 1920 to 2000, when residential and commercial activities shift away from city centers into diffuse, automobile-dependent metropolitan regions.

I

In the evolution of modern American cities, Washington, D.C., is a singular example of restrained and regulated urban planning. From its conception as a planned capital city in the late eighteenth century, Washington, D.C., has continued to strive towards the emblematic image of an impressive monumental and democratic center. Yet beyond the legible core of government complexes and landmarks, the development of the community of Washington, D.C., has reflected the same general patterns of growth and social trends evident in other major American cities. Unique to Washington, D.C., however, is the uniform scale of its downtown. With no modern high-rises and a skyline capped only by the Washington Monument and the dome of the Capitol, the city remains vertically regulated due to the role of one pivotal building in its history. The construction of the daring Cairo Hotel in 1894 prompted the city government of Washington, D.C., to establish a height limit, a regulation that persists today under much debate. Surrounded by a neighborhood of typical two and three story row houses in fashionable Dupont Circle, the massive twelve story Cairo, with its Moorish and Romanesque detailing, could not have been more out of place in its day. The height limit inspired by the audacity of the Cairo will continue to be controversial as different trends in the economy and attitudes towards urbanism emerge. Regardless of its controversies, however, the height limit legislation has been instrumental in choreographing the growth of the city and defining its contemporary character and cohesive image.

II

For over one hundred and fifty years, the American public library has assessed the needs of its public and responded accordingly. Each manifestation of the downtown, urban library seeks to reconcile the modified architectural tastes, shifting programmatic needs, and expanding technological prowess of American society. From 1854 to today, libraries have sought to balance their role in knowledge acquisition with their interest in community affairs. The first stage of library design, occurring between 1854 and 1889, reflected an isolated focus on public education through the loan of authorized books and periodicals. From 1889 to 1917, Andrew Carnegie initiated a second design typology that attached community annexes to the traditional public library. A third stage of library design occurred in the 1960s when programmatic flexibility was limited and libraries again shifted focus toward book-learned knowledge, seeking to increase load capacity and book accessibility.

Library design in the twenty-first century has launched a fourth phase of societal adaptation. For the first time in history, the focus of American libraries has shifted from information center to cultural center. In 2003, the Seattle Central Library, designed by the Office for Metropolitan Architecture, broke the decades-long trend in which community involvement in library design was limited to the presence of exhibition space and meeting rooms. In a more Carnegie-esque arrangement that bridges the idea of library as information center and community center, the Seattle Public Library includes programmatic elements like auditoria, music practice rooms, a gift shop, and a coffee cart. In the process of adapting to digital technologies and changing forms of communication, the library's role as community organizer has almost completely surpassed its role as knowledge provider. Reading, once the defining activity within the library, is now a relatively minor activity, supplemented by social spaces and public forums.

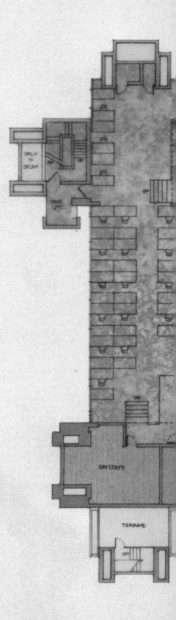

<u>Faculty</u>

SUNIL BALD
PHILLIP G. BERNSTEIN
LJILJANA BLAGOJEVIC
PETER DE BRETTEVILLE
PAUL BROUARD
BRENNAN BUCK
MARTIN COX
LIZA FIOR
KURT FORSTER
ADAM HOPFNER
JOYCE HSIANG
KATE JOHN-ALDER
JENNIFER LEUNG
AMY LELYVELD
BIMAL MENDIS
JOEB MOORE
HERBERT S. NEWMAN
ALAN ORGANSCHI
BEN PELL

<u>Guest Jurors</u>

MICHELLE ADDINGTON
KUTAN AYATA
ANDREW BENNER
MICHAEL BELL
STELLA BETTS
STEPHEN CASSELL
LILY CHI
PEGGY DEAMER
KELLER EASTERLING
KURT FORSTER
DOUGLAS GAUTHIER
MARIO GOODEN
CATHERINE INGRAHAM
MAKRAM EL KADI
PETRA KEMPF
JANETTE KIM
GORDON KIPPING
JONATHAN KNOWLES
KEITH KRUMWIEDE
AMY LELYVELD
PETER LYNCH
DAVID LEWIS
FRANCISCO MANGADO
CHRIS MARCINKOSKI
MICHAEL MEREDITH
PABLO CASTRO OBRA
ALAN ORGANSCHI
EEVA-LIISA PELKONEN
CHRIS PERRY
ENRIQUE RAMIREZ
SHAWN RICKENBACKER
NICOLE ROBERTSON
ROB ROGERS
RAYMUND RYAN
HILARY SAMPLE
JOEL SANDERS
ASHLEY SCHAFER
GALIA SOLOMONOFF
JOHN STUART
MARK TSURUMAKI
ENRIQUE WALKER
MARK WASIUTA
CLAIRE WEISZ
MABEL WILSON
MICHAEL YOUNG

<u>Students</u>

ANNE-MARIE ARMSTRONG
CHRIS AUBIN
HILARY BINGNEAR
KEVIN BLUSEWICZ
MARIJA BRDARSKI
AMY CHANG
TOM CHASE
ANDREEA COJOCARU
PATRICK CONNER
JACOB DUGOPOLSKI
TRAVIS EBY
KIPP C. EDICK
MARK GETTYS
JUSTIN HEDDE
LINDSAY HOCHMAN
SHIRLEY HSU
JASON KIM
ALFIE KOETTER
KEITH JOHNS
TERRI LEE
LOUISE LEVI
KEE LEW
RONALD LIM
MATT ROMAN
ROBERTO ROSSI
JONAH ROWEN
BRIAN SPRING
KYLE STOVER
TYLER SURVANT
ALEXANDRA TAILER
MARK TALBOT
CHAT TRAVIESO
ANJA TUROWSKI
JIA-JUN YEO
EMMETT ZEIFMAN

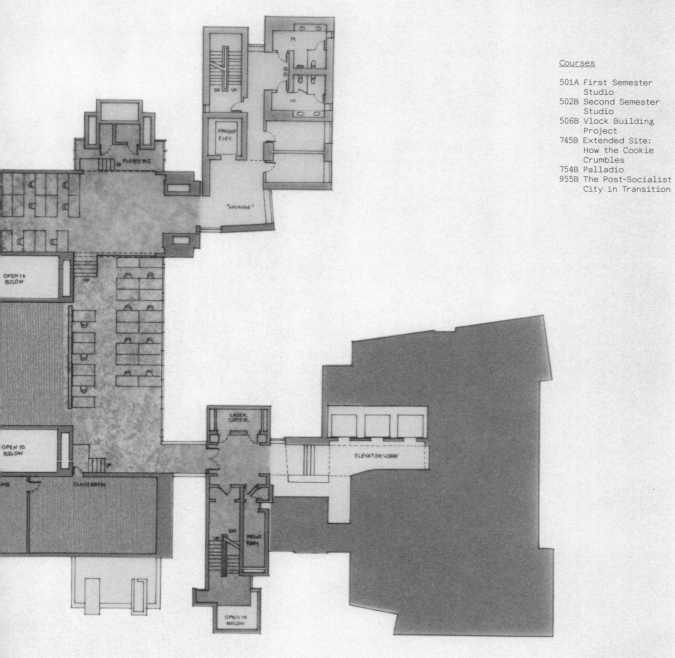

Courses

501A First Semester
     Studio
502B Second Semester
     Studio
506B Vlock Building
     Project
745B Extended Site:
     How the Cookie
     Crumbles
754B Palladio
955B The Post-Socialist
     City in Transition

FIRST SEMESTER STUDIO

501A

STUDIO COORDINATOR
BEN PELL

LANDSCAPE CONSULTANT
KATE JOHN-ALDER

This first semester of architectural design at Yale is intended to introduce students to problems, techniques, and terminology of contemporary practice. These include tangible issues of formal and programmatic organization and structural and material systems, and more abstract but no less integral questions of scale, inhabitation, perception, and affect. The ambition is to blend critical thinking and a fresh cultural awareness with an emerging technical expertise, and to rehearse the methods by which architects are today utilizing these faculties of inquiry and analysis to pursue a more culturally engaged practice.

Over the course of three projects the studio examines a sweep of critical approaches, with an emphasis on developing methodologies of research, analysis, and design and situating this work relative to contemporary discourse. To that end, the projects this semester reflect real-world opportunities and challenges. While the programs of each are specific and prescribed, they are intended to provide an operational context within which to explore various sets of architectural issues (e.g. form, program, site, enclosure, structure, surface, material) while addressing specific cultural and physical parameters. The first project, Skins and Sculls, asks students to propose a small building on the New York City waterfront. The project focuses on questions of the vertical surface, examining the nature of building enclosure as both membrane and threshold. The second project, MuseumPark, asks students to consider the relationship between building and site, interior and exterior, as a composite landscape; a field condition of varied textures and programs that operate simultaneously as discrete and networked entities. And finally, the third project, BAM_West asks students to develop an infrastructure for urban spectacle to support a new performance and arts center in the DUMBO neighborhood of Brooklyn.

I
OVERLAPPING AGENDAS
CHRIS AUBIN
This project seeks to reconcile the diverse needs of the Socrates Sculpture Park and the Long Island City Community Boathouse through a communal mechanism which adapts its function and scale to facilitate the project's disparate programmatic requirements. Angled paths weave between the enclosures and provide an integrated circulation network for boats, bikes and pedestrians, establishing a clear directional grain to moderate the park and the river.

II
WALK IT OUT
KEVIN BLUSEWICZ
Strutting, people-watching, and attitude characterize New York City spectacle. BAM as a piece of urban infrastructure is necessarily more of a stage for this public spectacle than a container for performance spaces. This project positions the pedestrian as the performer, and attempts to establish an attenuated promenade through the building that forces the individual to be on display. The procession is defined and activated by the carving of the ground plane and the pliability of a light, modulated roof plane. Theater spaces exist as folds in the roof plane, hanging above the more public program of the shifting ground.

III
RE-STITCHING THE FIELD
KEITH JOHNS
Sited at the intersection of a fairly diverse demographic, the museum park seeks to re-situate and engage the disparities of its cultural constituents through the medium of art. Formally, the museum tethers itself to specific constituent zones--inviting them in through didactic inlets that ultimately terminate within the body of the building. They are then re-configured or overlapped to produce a spatial 'knot' that blurs building and landscape as well as social allegiances.

MARION WEISS „We haven't really talked a lot
„ about technique today, but I think there
„ are certain things that you may think are
„ interesting to represent, but a uniform
„ grid where you just take little things out
„ says nothing about the rest of your project.
„ Had you just drawn the section and put a scale
„ figure without all of the rest of that you
„ would have realized you have this desire for
„ monumentality that you keep feeding in to by
„ all these others things.
ROBERT A.M. STERN „If you're going to do that
„ drawing I would suggest a one-point perspective
„ that allows you to see deep into the building,
„ which is the famous drawing of this building
„ as I'm sure you know. I don't know if you were
„ looking at Paul Rudolph when you created this
„ composition, and the more I look at it, it
„ is very Rudolphian, much like his courthouse
„ in New York. It is an interesting composition,
„ and it's not that there isn't an idea; it's that
„ you did your best to hide it.

SUNIL BALD „I think if you consider Rudolph
„ and those drawings, your project has not yet
„ transformed into something that uses those
„ planar elements to actually make real volumes.
„ I think you do yourself a bit of disservice in
„ shying away from those moments where you're
„ going to have to confront the types of volumes
„ this might create, programmatically, where
„ they might become solid. I think it becomes
„ more successful at the points where the ground
„ meets those areas, but once it begins to rise
„ up it's not really holding itself together by
„ making an architectural space.
BEN PELL „One thing I think you can do with that
„ drawing is that it reveals a certain sensibil-
„ ity of scale, and I feel like there is some-
„ thing appropriate about the scale in relation
„ to the site and the program. I think what would
„ help is if you provided context, in that we're
„ seeing this thing against the backdrop of the
„ bridge. We're seeing the overhang and we're
„ seeing the activity of the city.

JENNIFER LEUNG „Looking at the project, I pick up
„ on your language of first creating some kind of
„ complex circulatory system, the knot. Then what
„ you're doing, in terms of the device you've used
„ to re-orient, is programmatic and landscape and
„ I appreciate that as an intent. That intent is
„ very substantiated and important to the site.
SUNIL BALD „I think there is a kind of tension
„ in the understanding of the knot as a single
„ system that winds itself up. I do think it's
„ important to take a system like that and begin
„ to cross it with materiality to get some dif-
„ ference. The second thing is taking this other
„ system and bringing it over the site is another
„ major tectonic, and those types of moves, and
„ the intensity that is required to do them seem
„ to be something that you want to have cross
„ register with this iconic formalism.
JENNIFER LEUNG „I think the project would really
„ have gained by a jump in scale, that is keeping
„ this same system in terms of circulation and

„ knotting, and jumping scale. For the moment it
„ is only a result of the analysis and it doesn't
„ push back. I think it's having scale issues,
„ and maybe you can choose elements that allow
„ you to understand A to B rather than building
„ to site.
STELLA BETTS „For me this project is easier to
„ pull apart, no pun intended. Because I was
„ thinking about your knot, and whether it was
„ a loose knot or one of those knots that you
„ could never get undone and even if you do
„ you've altered the threads too far, and what I
„ mean by that is, what is that translation? In
„ one sense, you say, 'I'm thinking about a knot
„ and I'm thinking about program' and it's which
„ bits of program can be intertwined--or you go
„ into materiality or go into the experiential.
„ I think in taking that idea of 'knot' you have
„ to ask, what is it doing programmatically,
„ what is it doing materially, what is it doing
„ to the site?

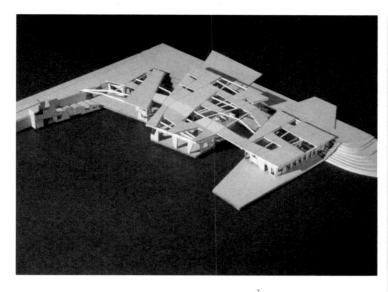

I

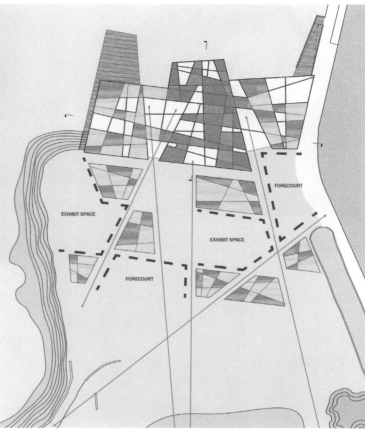

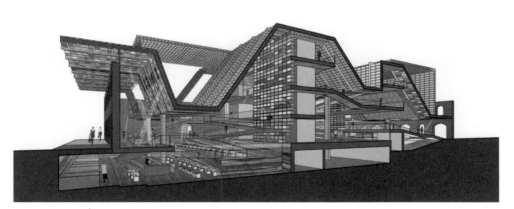

II

III

I

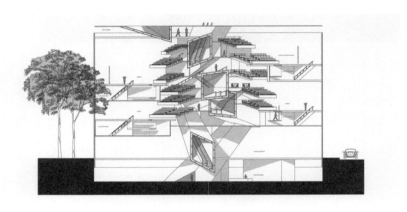

II

III

KUTAN AYATA   KATE JOHN-ALDER   ALAN ORGANSCHI   GALIA SOLOMONOFF
STELLA BETTS   PETRA KEMPF   EEVA-LIISA PELKONEN   CLAIRE WEISZ
JONATHAN KNOWLES   ENRIQUE RAMIREZ

CLAIRE WEISZ „It's funny because I think most of our questions are just orientation and organization questions. I think we were all just figuring out how to get in and how are things organized. I do think that museums are organizational projects because they essentially organize time. I think because you relied on a sectional idea to build your model, the sections are very clear in their spatial delineations.

KUTAN AYATA „It's all in relation to the program. You can have multiple routes through the project, one for a glance, another for linear engagement, and another for a more in depth cross section between art works. You could use the landscape strategies you are developing to orchestrate or curate the exhibitions on the inside.

SUNIL BALD „Your project is palimpsestual of your own process. I think the one thing that seperates it from a time-based palimpset is that they seem more a collection of stacking processes as opposed to overlay. I think as a process of stacking, each unit maintains it's own integrity to a certain degree, rather than overlay where different units have to compete for the same space. In competing for space, there is a possibility for these units to blur and become something else.

GALIA SOLOMONOFF „I think that what's really provocative is the way you define the generative grid. You took analytical tracings of the polemic conditions and drew them from the site, and that was the point of departure, which generates some pretty interesting patterns that you developed with other criteria to generate a project. I think it would help if you added a second system to deal with surfaces that does not deal with your original striations. That somehow these surfaces could intersect your striations and help define the section.

STELLA BETTS „One thing that is key in this project is that you are not making enough difference. In fact, I would expect that if you have these two tubes and these two pods, then that somehow those might have a difference between them--that if I was going to see one kind of a performance it might lend itself. It has really become about these two paths through the thing, and the spaces they create around them.

ENRIQUE RAMIREZ „In your project I think there is an interesting paradox--that if you're referring to Pompidou and Fun Palace, the two projects are primarily a structure where a number of things could happen. Basically, concert halls, cinemas, and theaters are very different kinds of theaters, and they begin to be separate. In your case the interesting thing would be to play in reversal. Instead of designing an oval structure that structures paths of movement that can then be populated with any program and therefore give the project a programmatic value, I would play it in reverse and design a number of very precise elements that then can be plugged up in a structure that you still don't know so the project would be an investigation of structure on the other end.

BEN PELL „I think that's a really good piece of criticism. But the point that you've reached here is where a project begins--you realize that thing you have is where you can strategize both the aberrations and the normative conditions and turn it into architecture. That's where I'm losing track of the project because I don't understand how that's becoming generative for you.

ALAN ORGANSCHI „The danger of it is that you end up with this sort of fissure between conceptualization and information about program, and whatever it is you choose to take on and what you actually end up producing. The fear that I have is that you have something that you do not fully understand. As a result, when you begin to interrogate it and begin to examine it, it's a found object in and of itself.

EEVA-LIISA PELKONEN „There's a kind of cellular interest, and the thing is floating in the air. There's the water of course, as a thing that effects your strategy, and the sun above. I think it's very provocative, this much, in section, when you have the sky and it's floating, and you're under, and you're sitting--can you see the water? I mean, why couldn't you see the water, trickling under your feet? Suddenly it's such a letdown to have this guy in a box, where you wish he could get his feet wet, you know?

JONATHAN KNOWLES „This thing is a stiff, thick membrane that's going to crack, it's going to break, it's going to tear itself apart if you put it out in the east river. So, I think the sensibility is, ok, this thing is floating. Well, then, how does the roof respond to that? How does the enclosure respond to these things moving not in tandem?

KATE JOHN-ALDER „But he's also, basically, torturing himself by saying that this roof has to extend up and be a cantilever, and here where it hangs down, you've captured something about what happens on a water's edge with growth and erosion, and allowing that water to actually sieve through--if that roof just kind of fell down into the water and the water could sieve through, you're actually capturing something that's very much about a water's edge and what happens over time with any built form that meets something that is so powerful and so strong.

PETRA KEMPF „I think if you just erase the name 'roof' from your project completely and find a new name for your project--I think that's what's hindering you to overcome, sort of, your desire. Because I think that project--the thickness that you show there is so much richer than here because here you, again, fell into the roof idea.

{Laughter}

I think it's surface, surface, surface; I think you have to just find another name.

I
GROUND-FIGURE
AMY CHANG

Taking cues from the idiosyncrasies of the Grove Street Cemetery, this project investigates the idea of dissonance between layers of horizontal strata. The project creates a site specific grid, and the program emerges out of this field as a series of gallery bands and courtyards. In complicating figure-ground and solid-void relationships, the project creates dramatic spatial conditions that disrupt the clear definition of the ground plane. The overlapped graining of museum circulation and site circulation (as the swelling of the adjacent greenway into a park landscape) provides a multiplicity of ways to experience museum and park.

II
THIS IS NOT GORDON MATTA-CLARK
KIPP C. EDICK

This project was the culmination of a tumultuous first semester, and in it I chose to explore how a platonic mass can be affected as a reaction to the conditions that surround it, and then reiterated to fit the unique functional quality requirements and overarching structural logic of the site. The context is DUMBO, Brooklyn, and the site experiences an observable disturbance induced by a highly complex transportation system that complicates traditional methods of mobility such as walking and biking. That is, the superfluous infrastructure in place confuses/disorients pedestrians upon arrival, dislocating areas such as this site. The building is therefore a platonic solid of generic height pierced by framed attractions, 'luring' its subjects from various vantage points from which spectator may arrive. The large perforations are then connected within the core, creating a winding helix organization that is both utilized structurally and reminiscent of the reverberating consequences that have shaped this portion of DUMBO.

III
ROOF AGGREGATION
RONALD LIM

The proposed floating structure is a landscape extension into the water that is also a roof housing the required functions underneath. This roof is an intricate aggregation of porous layers that weaves through variously programmed box pavilions, resulting in a complex roof plan that weaves two separate systems. The roof's complexity also results in intricate and varied cast shadows underneath. Because it floats on water, the structure can move with the tide, becoming a living organism in its own right.

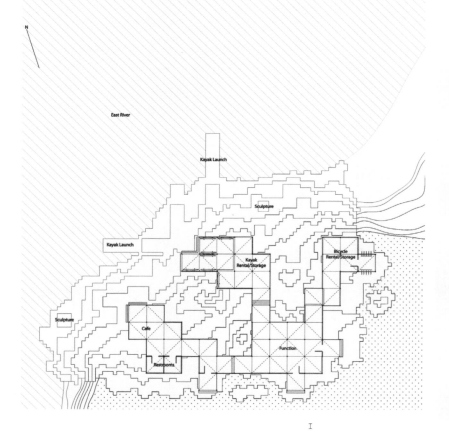

East River

Kayak Launch

Sculpture

Kayak Launch

Kayak
Rental/Storage

Bicycle
Rental/Storage

Sculpture

Cafe

Function

Restrooms

I

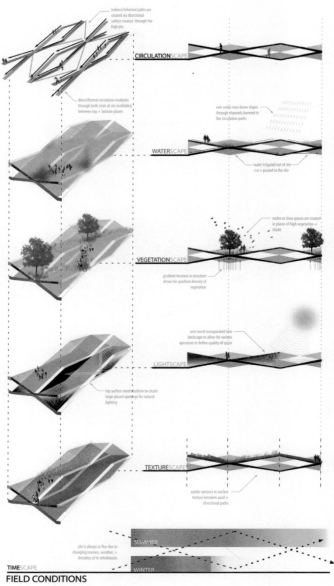

CIRCULATIONSCAPE

WATERSCAPE

VEGETATIONSCAPE

LIGHTSCAPE

TEXTURESCAPE

SUMMER

TIMESCAPE   WINTER

FIELD CONDITIONS

II

III

KELLER EASTERLING „When you present your „ project, I'm kind of on board because of the „ intelligence behind it. It's smart, and there „ is a kind of comedy in it that I like that it „ establishes this crazy little box in the land- „ scape. I keep on wondering if what constitutes „ these kinds of boxy enclosures is also going „ to be an aggregate like their plugs.
BEN PELL „Do these things move around?
TOM CHASE „Yes. They are ten-by-ten-foot, the „ idea is that they can be built simply out of „ steel posts and can be moved together to form „ all these aggregates.
BEN PELL „Then as much as I agree with Keller

„ about her reading of the site as a skin, I'm „ curious about the buildings as a skin. Maybe a „ better analogy for them is a kind of virus, and „ I don't mean that in a negative way, rather as „ something that has a kind of logic of self orga- „ nization to it. That would lend a kind of conti- „ nuity to it that you don't get because it isn't „ a skin, but it is still an organism. And be- „ cause of that, the way you would really want „ to pitch it wouldn't be with one plan, but „ with six plans, where we see that there are „ multiple ways in which we could configure these „ things and better understand the logic of „ their configuration.

I
EDGE FEEDBACK
TOM CHASE
A tidal marsh is a constantly variable environment: tidal pools fill and empty twice daily; plant and animal communities vary with the seasons; and the overall topography fluctuates from year to year. Socrates Sculpture Park hosts daily, monthly, and annual exhibitions, inhabiting the site's semi-exposed pier and landfill land- scape as well as the tidal river shoreline. Edge Feedback blurs the line between building and site, permitting natural ecologies to re- take and activate the site while the building adapts to ever-changing program requirements. The building responds to the smooth space of nat- ural conditions (via movable modular building units) while natural con- ditions are cultured in and around the striated space of built forms (fostered by site scale "eco-blocks"). Site occupies building and building occupies site.

BEN PELL „Your project is really fascinating in „ a lot of ways and I think it's really elegant, „ and one of the things I like about it very „ much is the kind of economy of means with „ which you achieved a great deal of complexity. „ As an intervention on the site I feel it's „ limited, meaning that it doesn't extend to the „ extents of the site; it's actually very precise „ about where it is and where it isn't. As a kind „ of figure that emerges from the site I think „ there is something very powerful about that.
BRENNAN BUCK „I think that the spaces are in- „ teresting down there, but part of the problem „ is that you're working with topologically „ continuous surfaces; a problem of an architec- „ ture of surfaces is how to deal with openings „ within that surface. It raises the question of „ what that surface is and can that surface be „ porous or work at different scales rather than „ as a sort of single continuity.
DOUGLAS GAUTHIER „I think it goes back to that „ red and blue diagram. I think you could be „ able to manipulate that in three dimensional

„ space: up, down, and sideways, and you would „ be able to get a lot more difference than what „ you're giving us.
BEN PELL „Combined with the circulation diagram, „ which I think is a powerful way to approach „ the project, it gives you a set of geometrical „ relationships which then set up this kind of „ figure--a bowtie. in fact it seems like that is „ the only device you need to accomplish what „ you are after. You don't have to excavate--it „ inherently has conditions of topology which „ can be translated into landscape, it inher- „ ently has conditions of convergence which can „ be translated into circulation, it inherently „ has conditions of interiority which can be „ translated into architecture or program.
MARK TSURUMAKI „What I would like to see played „ out more is the hard and fast logic of the „ bowtie; the most interesting part is actually „ the slow gradation of these planes as you move „ in the lateral direction and how that could „ begin to make connections between programs „ and landscapes and other programs.

II
W[E]AVE: INTERWOVEN FIELD CONDITIONS
MARK GETTYS
W[e]ave is a landscape that intertwines discrete programs such as galleries, book stacks, seating, and administra- tive programs and distributes them into a networked field relationship across the site. The undulating form mediates between an open ground layer and an enclosed underground layer. The upper layer serves as a landscape park with exterior galleries while the lower layer houses the closed galleries, café, and book stacks. The landscape's "bowtie" shape establishes a series of openings and enclosures that allow for a complex field of interwoven condi- tions of program, landsca.pe, light exposure, water irrigation, structure, entrances, and circulation at various densities and intensities over the site.

III
BAM_WEST GLIMPSE
JUSTIN HEDDE
The intention is to create a space where theater and dance can be experienced intimately or casually, traditionally or experimentally. This range is sought through the establishment of two grains within the site. The lower, running from street to park, uses long gestural moves to allow for free pedestrian movement around two screened box the- aters. The upper, running East-West and containing more enclosed program- matic spaces, breaks into seams allowing light to pierce down through to more public spaces below. It orients itself based on views looking towards Manhattan and the Brooklyn Bridge.

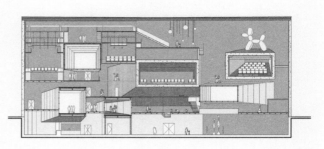

I

II

III

KURT FORSTER „ It's really like a visual megaphone „ for the city, where you're looking through, as „ opposed to, say, reflection. So ideally one „ should say that the parts of the building that „ aren't the visual cones should go away. So my „ question is, would that be an ideal state to „ achieve?

MARIJA BJDARSKI „ Yes, I think there are differ- „ ent ways to do it, but I want to make the cones „ dominate and highlight the view through that, „ which I think has to do with materiality.

PEGGY DEAMER „ What works with what you are „ saying is to feel the tension between the „ front and back of the building. To me that „ is complicit with your idea of being caught „ between Brooklyn and Manhattan. It's those „ two planes that are the recognition of that „ materiality--now what's problematic is that „ the project is either about those two walls or „ it's about those cones. You need to establish „ that hierarchy.

STEPHEN CASSELL „ Your project, interestingly „ enough, hinges on the inversion of typically „ understood spaces. You've taken the theater „ spaces, which are typically dark, and placed „ them in the most open spaces, and the typi- „ cally most open spaces have been moved to the „ darkest, most enclosed areas of your form. „ But it becomes problematic where those cones „ aren't one or the other.

GORDON KIPPING „ The thing about the object is „ that every time you move it, it's another idea, „ another proposition. That's the power of the „ object. You told us so clearly how this came „ to be, but I would pull it off its base and „ reposition it. I wonder about how BAM would „ want to brand itself and if is it necessary to „ have the picture postcard view.

I
OBJECT INVERSION
MARIJA BRDARSKI

Conceived as an object situated between the Brooklyn and Manhattan skylines, the Brooklyn Academy of Music investigates various object-void relationships as an idea of establishing several degrees of dialogue both within the context of the site and as organizational strat- egies of theater program.

Abstaining from the traditional model of a sequence of spaces leading up to the main performance, the pro- ject proposes the conical shape as a method of addressing program, light and entrance within the interior organizational system of the building, while using the absence of the cone to establish a dialogue with the urban condition.

BEN PELL „ It seems like you stumbled upon the „ blocks too late in the process to really go back „ and explore it far enough, so you felt like, „ 'I just know my plans need to be clear.' „ It does seem that as a system, that would yield „ a very different kind of architecture that would „ come out in the plans and section and that „ would force you to ask other questions of it-- „ and it might also, at least in my mind, „ justify some of the plan jogs here because „ they would just be a function of the aggregate „ condition produced by adding up a bunch of „ those guys.

KEITH KRUMWIEDE „ It's an intriguing proposal. „ I mean this return to traditional load bear- „ ing masonry walls and this reinvestigation of „ poche, whether it's additive or subtractive in „ your case, is really intriguing. Even taking „ it to its natural logical extreme, as Frank „ Zappa would say, right, with the courtyard „ spaces that you have throughout, there's quite „ a bit going on. Unfortunately the drawings, „ your section cuts, just don't mirror or match „ what your proposal is. Disjuncture.

JOYCE HSIANG „ It's just an interesting thing for „ your process to see that you have to acceler- „ ate and realize that you get to that so you can „ go back to this and reinterpret this and find „ what the crutches are that you need to elimi- „ nate to be able to have trusted yourself.

KELLER EASTERLING „ But I just have a feeling „ in the end that that you don't get as much „ pleasure from the sort of isomorphism of „ the system as you would get pleasure in that „ model. You like that model, and it works, and „ it was fun, and it's a discovery. I think it „ would also be fun to draw that. To draw it „ in--I never say this--to draw it in straight „ ahead orthographic projection. I think you „ would love that drawing. If you did it then you „ would have a little bit more confidence that „ you didn't have to just gigantic-size it.

II
THE ALFOS COMPLEX
ALFIE KOETTER

Inspired by coastal break-water barrier systems, this project uses a mono- modular system of interlocking compo- nents, termed Alfos Blocks, to create a dynamic skin that responds to circulatory and programmatic needs. Through a series of offsets, one is able to use the Alfos Blocks to create a variety of increasingly permeable walls that provide greater degrees of light and views to the more public spaces within the Complex. Conversely, by set- ting the Alfos Blocks flush with one another, one is able to create a solid wall to enclose the more private spaces within. Through offsets and intersec- tions, the building as a whole diffuses circulation from the land, through the building, and finally to the water.

CLAIRE WEISZ „ You're kind of playing in that „ larger arena where the sort of bipolar discus- „ sions of landscape and architecture are less „ meaningful but in fact you feel like you can „ play with many different aspects of both to „ create something. I think this project starts „ to do that because it starts out very clear. „ It has a kind of intentionality I find reason- „ ably convincing in the scale of the repeated „ element, the stacks, and the cases, and the „ kinds of things that might make up a collec- „ tion in the university start to get deployed in „ a larger area and it does comment, I think, on „ the particular landscape you happen to have „ across the street, which is the cemetery, and „ the kind of particularity of using a whole site „ without using a whole site. There's something „ interesting in this case that happens.

ROB ROGERS „ The qualities of the carriage of „ light and sky and landscape merge amazingly „ beautifully. For instance, it happens in this „ drawing, and it doesn't mean you have to „ have some kind architecture performing like „ landscape, landscape performing like archi- „ tecture; it is a really subtle marriage of the „ experience that's inside.

PEGGY DEAMER „ My sense is you're dexterous „ enough to come up with a programmatic rein- „ terpretation that is not necessarily what they „ asked for but kind of pushes this approach „ slightly more radically, because it operates „ formally; I think you're getting mileage from „ the formalism.

MICHAEL YOUNG „ To bring this back to the regis- „ tration from the diagram to the architecture, „ one of the things that I appreciate about what's „ going on over here is that the organizations „ are loose enough that we are asked to actually „ participate in them, not only as critics but „ now as potential users, potential subjects in „ the space. The organizations are not spelled „ out, and when you come to a moment like that „ slightly displaced theatre seating, where the „ section also moves down, and escapes just „ for a moment, that to me is the most charged „ element in this entire configuration. Because „ that's there it causes me to ask questions „ about all the other things that appear to be „ more clearly defined, but it's bringing in an „ ambiguity that sparks the composition.

III
CATALOGUE
EMMETT ZEIFMAN

The dominant programmatic elements of the project--vitrines, trees, and stacks-- are run through one another, estab- lish-ing a continuous catalogue to be browsed by the visitor. This initial gesture develops out of the analysis of adjacent and projected conditions, par- ticularly circulation routes and library and park typologies. As the constituent elements of the museum, park, and li- brary are combined, rigid organization- al structures dissipate. The resultant gradients of density, intermixture, and exposure provide opportunities to expe- rience these programs in both isolation and synthesis. A rectilinear envelope modulates light and provides necessary areas of enclosure in response to the organizations of objects. The catalogue and its envelope blur the distinction between figure and ground, suggesting the simultaneous presence of a discrete architecture and landscape.

I

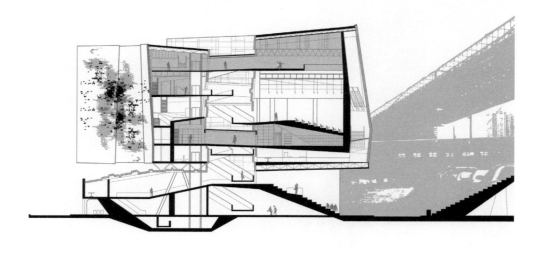

II

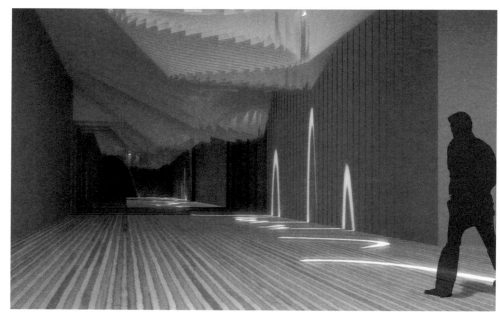

III

KUTAN AYATA   STELLA BETTS   CHRIS MARCINKOSKI   CLAIRE WEISZ
MICHAEL BELL   PEGGY DEAMER   ALAN ORGANSCHI

PEGGY DEAMER „I'm fascinated that you have
„ this programmatic approach and there is this
„ rigorous way in which you come up to the proj-
„ ect. With this very elegant scheme, you have
„ what I would call a marketplace typology, or
„ a hypostyle, which is not uninteresting but
„ you haven't identified it. So I have a much
„ more positive relationship to this project
„ but I also feel like something has happened
„ that is not what you said. And I also feel
„ like we've gotten to a project that is all the
„ things you said and but has yielded something
„ that is just different. I think we should talk
„ about that different thing and not just your
„ intentions.
MICHAEL BELL „I think it's when you decided to
„ locate walls, which is exactly what this sys-
„ tem is not about, with its amorphic quality.
„ When you're inside, outside, and inside again
„ you need to maintain that freedom when it's
„ time to draw it up and assign the program like
„ a marketplace in which it's ambiguous space--
„ it may be a different user tomorrow, and it
„ doesn't necessarily need that same hierarchal
„ assignment. You should allow yourself that
„ same level of freedom to the finish.

CLAIRE WEISZ „I think one of the tough parts
„ about where you ended up versus where you
„ were trying to explore is that ultimately you
„ ended up with something that is recognizable
„ as a site plan. And you look at that and you
„ say what kind of site plan is it? So I have a much
„ plan sort of gives up the ghost too early, and
„ I want to use the word exaggeration where I
„ think you should allow yourself to exagger-
„ ate your intentions and not resort to timid
„ drawings. If you exaggerate your intentions
„ sometimes the model you make from that or the
„ drawing you do tells you more. I feel like
„ you're holding back your intentions.
MICHAEL BELL „Instead of setting up a disjunc-
„ tion between architecture and landscape
„ that says landscape is smooth, horizontal,
„ undifferentiated and architecture is discrete,
„ enclosed--instead of positing that, through
„ these subtle deformations and the changing
„ in scale from aperture to opening, you are
„ starting to have the possibility of displacing
„ what is structure and what is enclosure. That
„ starts to speak to relational qualities and
„ radiant changes with hierarchal shifts. They
„ are no longer oppositional.

I
DISPLAY:COLLECT
LINDSAY HOCHMAN
This scheme highlights the relationship
between African Art and quotidian programmatic activities using the typology
of the urban market as an organizational
strategy. Semi-public spaces for the
display of African art, books and mer-
chandise provide a backdrop for the social activities of a reading room, café
and gallery all under a unifying roof.
The roof delineates a new urban passage
that links the expanded Yale library
and museum network with the Dixwell
community while also moderating light
conditions to respond to the programmatic differentiation between display
and collection spaces. The intervention
also serves as the at-grade terminus
for the Farmington Canal Bike Path.

ROBERT A.M. STERN „Is that it?
BEN PELL „No, he already presented.
ROBERT A.M. STERN „Oh. I thought it was one of
„ those projects where he says, 'There it is, it
„ speaks for itself.'
                {Laughter}
„ There is a problem in our world of too much
„ architecture. Sometimes you need to know when
„ to stop, and the computer does not help. Those
„ do not look like computer drawings, they are
„ nice, but the simple solution is what is right.
ALAN ORGANSCHI „This is a beautiful presenta-
„ tion. I am made aware of the size and the
„ gesture and the way it is resolved in the
„ skin, but it makes you do things in your plan
„ and section that do not actually support the
„ optimum experience of the programs. The thick
„ walls that you take great care in producing
„ around the theater spaces do not create any
„ traction in the building. It is a graphic-heavy
„ device. There are many beautiful passages and
„ you should be commended for that sophistica-

„ tion. But you could focus more on the spatial
„ experiences--qualities that relate to that
„ undercut theater and the flyspace. They feel
„ interrupted by the way the plans develop.
BEN PELL „What are these material studies?
BRIAN SPRING „My main emphasis was within that
„ slot. It is no longer tied to the preservation
„ of the original wall, but is a sampling of
„ it. The weathering and oxidation of that wall
„ becomes the impetus for a series of studies
„ of how those effects can be deployed as a
„ planar graphic surface against something that
„ is extremely volumetric. It begins to have
„ specular qualities of distorted views within
„ the slot. There is a constant interplay of
„ something that is being distorted, something
„ that is being revealed, something that is be-
„ ing concealed.
ROBERT A.M. STERN „The walls have been removed
„ from the warehouse? I can understand why you
„ would not want them there. You would just as
„ soon take half of New York down.

II
(RE)SURFACING PERFORMANCE
BRIAN SPRING
The design of a new Brooklyn Academy
of Music re-articulates the typically
hidden back of house support spaces and
casts them as "impromptu stage sets"
for a series of occupant instigated per-
formances. The traditional relationship
of performance theatre to support
functions is altered--the two are pulled
apart to create an interstitial slot
that becomes an extension of the urban
promenade that starts at the ground
level. The interior surfaces of the slot
are set into a gridded matrix of panels
derived from the weathered wall of an
existing historical building on site.
These panels oscillate between graphic
surface and volumetric wall with dif-
fering degrees of transparency, thus
phenomenally mediating the relationship
between occupant (actor) and perimeter
back of house space (temporary stage
sets). As occupants ascend vertically
through the slot, they are afforded sur-
face-altered glimpses of multiple back
of house functions--ultimately hybridizing the performance via jump cuts
through impromptu "stage sets."

STELLA BETTS „I would say that it's either not
„ site specific enough or it shouldn't be site
„ specific. See, when you take on a system,
„ and you're obsessed with it, which I think is
„ great--it's then that I don't understand the
„ parking. You've got to just run the system and
„ let it distort and what happens when it has to
„ take on parking.
KUTAN AYATA „You could place it somewhere else,
„ but the specificity, the floor pattern, the
„ column pattern, could not happen anywhere.
„ This specificity is interesting to me.
STELLA BETTS „But then he leaves the landscape
„ behind.
CHRIS MARCINKOSKI „It would be the organiza-
„ tional pattern manifesting in the formal pat-
„ tern. What's compelling about this is that
„ it's about use and relationships. And those
„ relationships are very dynamic--you could
„ imagine it becoming, deforming, and becoming
„ static and that relationship is on the floor
„ pattern. The idea I am compelled by is the

„ organizational pattern.
KUTAN AYATA „I think it's great that you've
„ placed an incredible investment in trying to
„ marry material specificity to the program-
„ matic requirements. The project immediately
„ takes on the question of the white box for
„ the exhibition and why we exhibit in the
„ same space. You look at the pattern, which is
„ distinctly different where you used different
„ approaches and for the ornamental and the
„ programmatic. Look, I think it's great, I
„ love it, it's a bit too specific--it's very
„ seductive, but then you show this, and it's
„ yet another system and maybe there are just
„ too many.
STELLA BETTS „In this project there is a really
„ interesting initial diagram that I am fixated
„ upon--that drawing that you began with where
„ you began with the center pushing out to the
„ perimeter and this idea of light. I'm kind of
„ wishing that that strategy got deformed and
„ placed upon the site.

III
AFFECT MUSEUM
KYLE STOVER
This project seeks to establish new
organizational criteria to expand the
museum's capacity to collect, organize,
and display art and books to staff,
museum-goers, and other visitors. By
providing programmatic organization
both around a linear narrative of
collect/display and around spatial affect, the collection can be experienced
both traditionally and phenomenally.
In allowing for an expanded experience
of the museum, possibilities for both
curatorial and user are designed into
a cross grain, thereby enriching
the museum's programmatic possibilities.

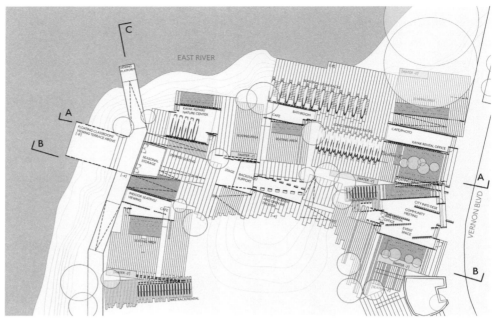

I

II

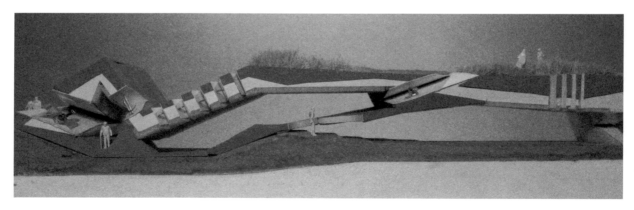

III

KEITH KRUMWIEDE „It's really an incredibly thor-
„ ough presentation, very detailed, the large
„ scale model--everything is developed to the
„ same level, so it's really clear, it's easy to
„ understand what you've done, and it's some-
„ times to your detriment that you can really
„ see what you've done.
                    {Laughter}
„ But it tells me you need to recognize putting
„ other elements into play, so the fact that
„ it's the bands and the movement of the bands
„ from the horizontal condition to the vertical
„ plane--that sets up an idea about the atmo-
„ sphere and the organization of the site; it
„ doesn't necessarily need to be all you allow
„ yourself in a tectonic strategy. Looking at the
„ types of rooms you're creating, there could
„ be structurally necessary secondary elements,
„ or maybe they're actually primary structural
„ elements, that become secondary elements.

„ That's okay within the framework of the idea;
„ it doesn't diminish the idea. I think it would
„ enrich it because at the very least it might
„ allow you to understand that no, there can be
„ two surfaces riding at the same time: one is
„ beneath the other, and if one goes away I still
„ have another ground. Or it might be the recog-
„ nition that you construct the ground first, and
„ then you layer the sticks in over it.
JENNIFER LEUNG „It may not be extreme enough,
„ in a sense. The other thing is that the best
„ moments in the plan are suggestions of a cir-
„ culation that crosses the grain.
KEITH KRUMWIEDE „I find the actual rotation of
„ the pieces problematic. It introduces a noise,
„ an unnecessary noise complication into it, and
„ the site plan is where it's most evident. That
„ rotation is what you're saying is where two
„ geometries come together? To me that rotation
„ is not helping you.

PERCOLATE/PROLIFERATE
JACOB DUGOPOLSKI
Making use of the visual and experiential effects of the moiré pattern, this
project uses shifted programmatic grids
to filter and connect Socrates Sculpture
Park, the Long Island City Boathouse,
and the greater Long Island City community. Maintaining the outer path that
follows the edge of the East River and
creating an urban street edge along
Vernon Boulevard, the intervention connects both edges through a network of
paths around the overlaps of three mis-
aligned striations. These overlaps are
composed according to external influences and become pavilions or enclosed
spaces which at the speed of movement
across the site create moirés intensi-
fied according to a catalog of speeds.

II
SKINS AND SKULLS
ALEXANDRA TAILER
This project is a sculptural extension
of programmable landscape from the
existing sculpture park to the south.
The landscape of the sculpture park
changes biannually--similarly, bicycle
and kayak storage as well as intimate
and public meeting spaces have the
freedom to relocate to any unit in which
those programs can be dimensionally
accommodated within these programmable delaminations. The horizontal
datum surfaces have been lifted to
create the expression of floor and roof
systems and to exaggerate their physical detachment from the ground plane.
The overall movement of this project is
determined by paths of least resistance
within the varying program placement.

BRENNAN BUCK „The thick series of sectional
„ layers are pretty successful, but they're most
„ successful when they disassociate from the
„ plan or at least the programmatic layout,
„ particularly in places like this where the
„ red layer forms the ceiling of one space,
„ the ground of the next, and then goes up and
„ creates a ground condition.
JOEL SANDERS „And what I love about this sec-
„ tion is that it's like a baroque architectural
„ section revisited, where there doesn't have
„ to be a literal correspondence between what's
„ happening on the top and what's happening on
„ the bottom--each can have its own logic.
MARK TSURUMAKI „I think all the strange condi-
„ tions that occur are fantastic--I like the
„ weird window slippage where you can see this
„ thing where the ground becomes a gallery and
„ the gallery becomes a ground. I keep thinking
„ that there's a fantastic promise here in how
„ this thing is a kind of inhabited thickness,

„ and there's this sense that it's really growing
„ from both sides; there's this pressure of this
„ kind of planting, these crops or whatever the
„ landscape is above pushing down, and then
„ programs and other sorts of inhabitation re-
„ quirements pushing up from below. And somehow
„ the form of this thing is not something you've
„ just applied and made up--it is somehow a
„ byproduct of understanding these two forces
„ relative to one another. But it almost seems
„ that to play that out you would have to know
„ the logic of the planting to begin with to
„ generate the logic of the section.
DOUGLAS GAUTHIER „It seems to me if you'd actu-
„ ally followed your research you would have had
„ some kind of hydroponic system, some kind of
„ landscape system and it would've played out
„ your Sir John Soane kind of language of the
„ museum in a way that actually educated and was
„ a heuristic language, that wasn't a graphic
„ language.

III
LANDSCAPE TATTOO
MARK TALBOT
Landscape is not two dimensional,
it is a series of highly specific layers
that form a three dimensional mat.
This project exploits this layered condition of landscape, providing pockets
of occupiable space within its thickness. Each pocket contains specific
program corresponding to the material
condition of the layer in which it
resides. For instance, libraries and
auditoria are located within pockets
of sound absorbent foam and children's
play areas are located upon bouncy
rubber material. Each material layer
is further divided by thickening and
thinning. Thickening the soil layer
increases the potential root depth
for plants and allows the plant layer
to chicken, as well. The production
of these pockets and thicknesses is
reminiscent of the art of tattooing.

502B

SECOND SEMESTER STUDIO

The studio examines the conceptual implications of the architectural program as both a subject of research and a catalyst for design innovation. Through the design and construction of the house, the studio explores the physical and psychological dimensions of a home and the aggregation of homes that creates an urban community. A series of analysis and design problem traverse scales that range from the intimate spaces in which a single body resides to the increasingly complex, urbanized, and socially interactive systems of multiple-unit housing. These problems, assigned both as individual and collaborative projects, challenge student to reconsider the familiar and intuitive program of dwelling space and the architecture it generates.

STUDIO COORDINATOR
ALAN ORGANSCHI

I
ADAPTIVE PREFABRICATION
JACOB DUGOPOLSKI

Reacting to the constantly changing family size of the immigrants entering the neighborhood and church, this assemblage of units addresses flexibility and community integration. Through stacking and shifting the main living spaces along the south façade and interlocking the utility functions and public circulation on the north, the units form an adaptable network. Each room can be easily divided in half or connected by a half stair to the adjacent unit, allowing for hundreds of combinations. At the urban scale, the distribution of public spaces is staggered at key locations while site paths are cut through to link the interior of the block to the sponsoring church and community outlets.

II
COHABITATION
JIA-JUN YEO

By conceiving two dwellings as volume within volume, vertical separation is achieved between two very different occupants. The discrete volumes of a young trader's habitat act as mediators of light for the singular space below, home to a retired archivist requiring comfortable levels of ambient light. Here, the archivist's bookshelf walls double as structure, supporting the trader's rooms above while creating a horizontal datum which plays against the vertical displacement of any one room depending on the task at hand. This results in sectional variation in the ceiling heights below that offer spatial articulation to the archivist's dwelling.

III
TRANSMOGRIFICATION
DE BRETTEVILLE STUDIO

Through an analysis of the typical pre-war New Haven duplex and Rudolph Schindler's Pueblo Ribera Court Houses, the project seeks to synthesize the open-ended and combinatorial logic of Schindler's project with the density and environmental requirements particular to the New Haven duplex typology. The resulting model is, in fact, one instance of a new and adaptable hybrid, the formal and massing properties of which are dependent on the local site conditions. However, each instance is derived from the same analytical mechanism.

+36

+32

+28

+24

+20

+16

+12

+8

+4

+0

II

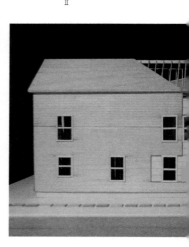

III

I

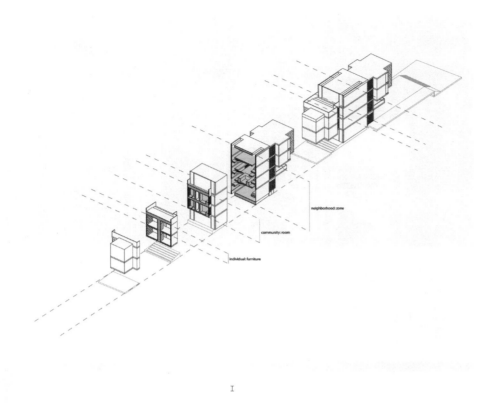

I

I
A HOUSE IS NOT A HOME
HILARY BINGNEAR
How do you make public housing domestic? This project makes use of thresholds at multiple scales to address this issue. The largest of these is that of the building's community space which is an exchange between the residential community and the Hill neighborhood. The utility cores are buffers between the public community areas and the semi-private study areas. The integrated cabinetry of the individual SRO units become thickened thresholds between these semi-private spaces and the private bedrooms.

II
CHIASMUS
JONAH ROWEN
This project was formulated based on the wall as the singular site of division between two spaces, whose shapes are rotationally symmetrical with one another; they are formal inversions of each other. However in spite of their apparent equivalency, the spaces are imbued with drastically different ambient characteristics based on the form of the space itself. That is, the two units' topological symmetry is belied by their competing differences which are continually made apparent by absolute directions. This makes the architecture as much an inhabitant of the space as the two people who live in it.

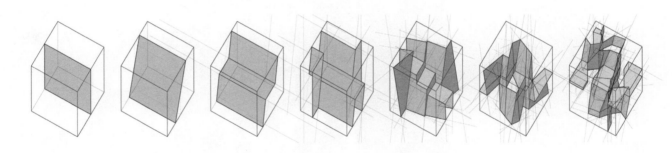

II

III
TRANSMOGRIFICATION
LELYVELD STUDIO
A precedent analysis of the Forbidden City provided our studio a conceptual groundwork centered on programmatic coupling, axial shifting in order to establish ceremonial order, and a tension between the perception of spatial as opposed to actual user access. When applied to a theoretical two tenant New Haven house, this analysis creates a unique solution that couples the occupants together while articulating their symbolic and actual disjuncture. The dynamic tension that comes into play allows us to unpack the loaded assumptions of habitation, thus, engaging the question beyond the object of the house itself and establishing an order that can extend beyond basic necessities.

III

I
BLOGGER & BIBLIOPHILE
KEE LEW

The blogger's space is considered a contusion generated by his movement. The bibliophile occupies the peripheral space which serves as a programmatic armature for the excess of storage surface he requires. The progression of the bibliophile along this armature becomes a scroll in which activities and spatial experience are inscribed relative to the sectional disposition of the nested blogger. The unfolding and folding of the constructed site reveals the hidden narrative quality of the project.

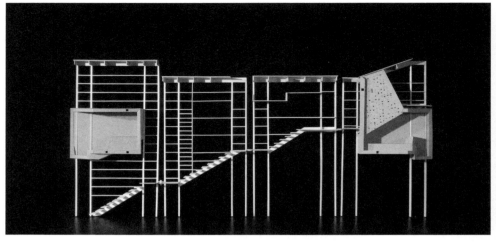

I

II
MUTABLE DOMAINS
TYLER SURVANT

This SRO is sited within the economic context of New Haven's fluctuating population. Through a simple mechanism of the operable wall, the internal organization of the building allows for a dynamic and reciprocal response to the cycles of the urban decay and growth. Four floors provide a varied character of habitation: each a different ratio of public to private space; of vacancy to occupation; and of figure to ground. Standard bedroom/bath units along a double-loaded corridor provide a plan typology for the lower, more communal floors, but the introduction of a larger unit type in the upper floors consumes the corridor, ensuring a denser, private habitation and further questioning boundaries of ownership.

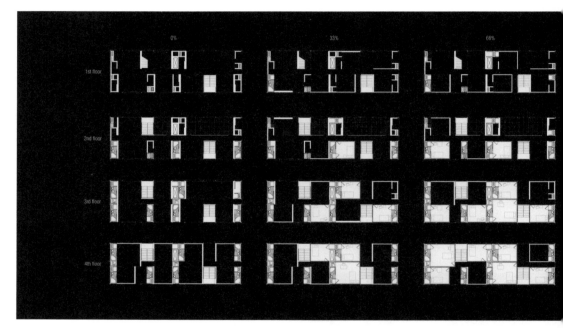

II

III
TRANSMOGRIFICATION
MENDIS STUDIO

The Mendis Studio studied the Hasan Rashid House (1986), designed by Hassan Fathy and located in Tanta, Egypt. In this transmogrification the formal diagram, spatial sequencing, and tectonic logic of Fathy's house displaces that of the traditional two-unit New Haven house. An exchange of walls and a shift from an inward to outward orientation introduces open corner courtyards into the New Haven house and initiates a syncopated spatial rhythm of portals and walls that both references and reimagines the order of the Fathy house.

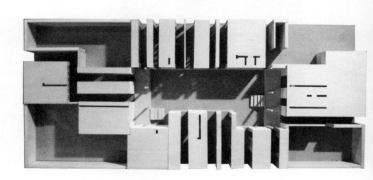

III

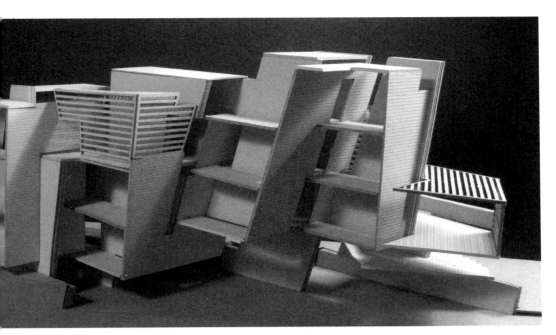

I

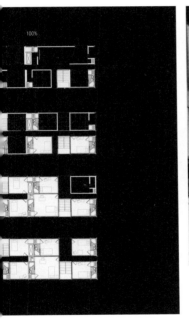

II

III

III

I
REPLICATION
SHIRLEY HSU

Tilted slabs interlock with one another other in series to form a system that articulates and organizes the program and circulation of a 10-unit SRO, creating contrasting spatial experiences of light and dark, expansion and compression. The heavy walls fit loosely, letting the building breathe by allowing light, air and people to circulate. Facing south to take advantage of thermal mass, the walls tilt to respond to programmatic needs, allowing light to flood down into the living spaces while sheltering and keeping cool the more protected spaces.

II
MANIFOLD STORAGE
BRIAN SPRING

The project negotiates the storage desires of two distinct personality types: the blogger and the bibliophile. Mediating between the two living units is a storage manifold that modulates the exposure of each inhabitant depending upon the amount of storage used. The tectonic systems deployed respond to the various storage types (analog vs. digital), thus the majority of the wood lattice system resides within the unit of the obsessive compulsive bibliophile. The two systems are knotted together in such a way that at different moments one is supporting the other and vice-versa. Independent of the tectonic assemblies is a graphic wallpaper that wraps the perimeter and temporally reveals itself in modulated expanses depending upon the amount of storage used on the perimeter.

III
TRANSMOGRIFICATION
MOORE STUDIO

The interbreeding of the Schindler House and a typical New Haven duplex produces a wood-framed compound exploded across a generic urban lot. The courts and gardens of Schindler's Los Angeles project are defined over two stories by unfolded and tilted-up fragments of East Coast vernacular architecture. The threshold between interior and exterior is extended through the delamination of the wood-framed walls, siding becoming louvers, studs mullions, and wallboard sliding partitions. The shifting ground of the model reveals analytic studies and superimpositions, while further blurring the distinction between lot and building.

I
LINK
ALAN ORGANSCHI
AMY CHANG

Taking advantage of the SRO's programmatic flexibility for shared kitchens and baths, this project uses an alternating coupling mechanism, whereby a single resident shares a bath with a neighbor of the same sex and a kitchen with a neighbor of opposite sex. The resulting string of individual, but linked, dwelling units is organized around a series of void spaces, which provide shared circulation, light and air. There are no party walls between units, but there is a sense of linked space which extends the dwelling unit beyond the narrow bounds of efficiency dimensions. Marrying a rowhouse and mat condition, the SRO provides the privacy and autonomy of separate apartments, with the community and efficiencies of shared program.

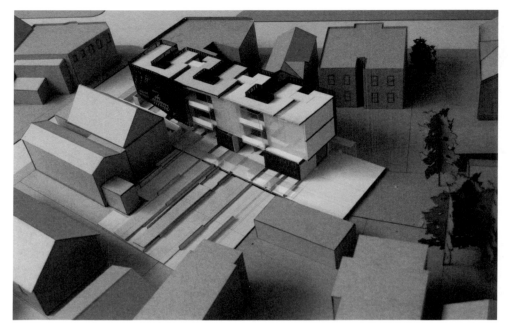

I

II
CO-HABITATION
ALFIE KOETTER

This co-habitation exercise focuses on the symbiotic relationship of two individuals living within a fourteen-by-sixteen-by-sixteen foot volume. Though formally distinct, each unit is informed by the spatial and programmatic characteristics of the other.

The program within the bibliophile's unit is organized by privacy. Three levels within the unit organize program with the most public space, the living room on top, the bedroom in the middle, and the bathroom on the bottom. The resulting form of this organization is a wrapper extending to the ground where access is provided to both units.

Within the wrapper of the bibliophile, the blogger takes form, filling the cavity spaces left underneath the wrapper and rupturing the wrapper itself for access to light. This invasion of the bibliophile's wrapper also benefits him. Instances of rupturing also result in the formation of beds and tabletops within the bibliophile's unit.

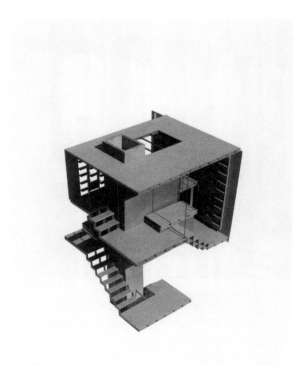

III

III
TRANSMOGRIFICATION
ORGANSCHI STUDIO

With the stimulus of Charles Correa's 1983–1986 Incremental Housing project in Belapur, India, this transformation of New Haven's urban fabric more than doubles the city's density through a low-rise, component-based system of free-standing housing units that could be constructed incrementally. While the resulting scheme maintains the integrity of certain structural and infrastructural elements relevant to New Haven's own climate, culture, and architectural vocabulary, the figure-ground relationship and gradient hierarchies of private/public and open/closed space in Correa's project inform the dissection of the typical New Haven house and the subsequent multiplication and reorganization of its parts at the scale of the lot, the block, and the city.

II

AMY CHANG   ALFIE KOETTER   ORGANSCHI STUDIO

CHARLES W. MOORE
BUILDING PROJECT INTERNS
MELISSA BAULD, EMMA BLOOMFIELD,
MARIJA BRDARSKI, TOM CHASE,
JACOB DUGOPOLSKI, FRANCES EDELMAN,
KIPP EDICK, ELIZABETH HABER,
JUSTIN HEDDE, LINDSAY HOCHMAN,
VIVIAN HSU, MARK GETTYS, WILLIAM
GRIDLEY & DANIEL MARKIEWICZ

49

PHILLIP G. BERNSTEIN   PAUL BROUARD   ADAM HOPFNER   HERBERT S. NEWMAN

506B

VLOCK BUILDING PROJECT

I
TEAM A

Our proposal considers the atypical family structure and its unforeseen future needs. It designs for the unknown. Adaptability is the key.

Programmatically, the tenant apartment stacks neatly above the secondary bedroom and bathroom spaces of the owner unit. This collection of rooms is expressed as a core (a house-within-a-house) with a gable roof. The owner's master suite and communal spaces (kitchen, dining, living) wrap the core as a flexible porch-like space visually open to the garden backyard.

The design is adaptable at three scales: neighborhood, house, furniture. By altering the dimensions of the L-shaped flex space the house can adapt to different sites; thus the house is deployable across a neighborhood. Through the mechanism of two hinged walls, ownership of the owner's secondary bedrooms and bathroom can toggle to the tenant, enabling proprietary adaptability within the house itself. Within the owner's flexible band of space, two cabinet-walls containing closet space and a desk subdivide the space. Their mobility (on wheels and tracks) allows them to reconfigure according to fluctuating spatial needs--adaptability at the scale of a large piece of furniture.

With this house, Team A proposes dynamic habitation, an adaptable domain where form, ownership, and space can accommodate fluctuating site conditions, economic motives, and lifestyles.

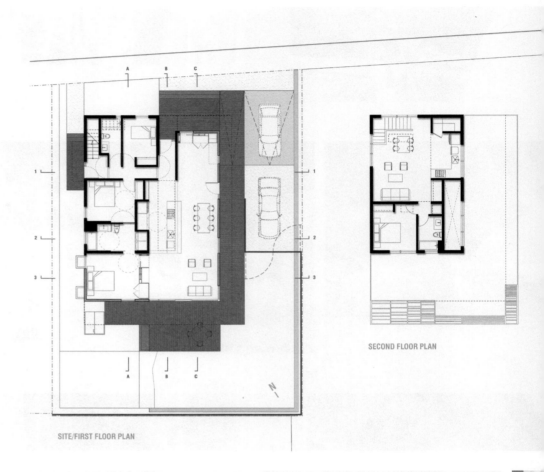

SECOND FLOOR PLAN

SITE/FIRST FLOOR PLAN

NORTH

I

CHRIS AUBIN   BRIAN BUTTERFIELD   THOMAS CHASE   LAURA WAGNER
HILARY BINGNEAR   AMY CHANG   JAEYOON KIM   JI-YOUNG YOON

II
TEAM B
SELECTED SCHEME

Fundamental to the design of our team's house are two methods of construction that facilitate a relationship between an internal system and a neutral shell. Our design proposes an outer envelope of Structural Insulated Panels (SIPs) and an internal armature of stud-framed partitions that swell to encompass all utility functions. We define utility functions as service-related program that assists the owner. These programs encompassed in the stud-framed partitions include entry, kitchen, bathrooms, laundry, facilities, and storage. It also includes the entire tenant program, as the income earned from this rental unit can be used to supplement the owner.

NORTH ELEVATION

WEST ELEVATION

FIRST FLOOR PLAN

EAST ELEVATION

SOUTH ELEVATION

ROOF (9 1/4" core)
22 panels, approx 415 lf

WALL (5 1/2" core)
42 panels, approx 555 lf

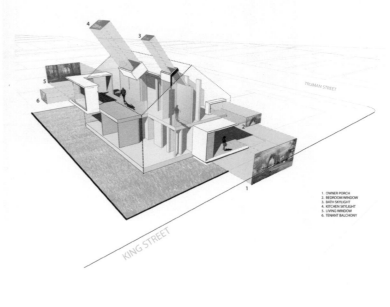

1. OWNER PORCH
2. BEDROOM WINDOW
3. BATH SKYLIGHT
4. KITCHEN SKYLIGHT
5. LIVING WINDOW
6. TENANT BALCHONY

TRUMAN STREET

KING STREET

II

III
TEAM C

We approached the building project as an exploration of the house's inherent asymmetries. Between the tenant and owner units, there is an asymmetry of footprint, of program, and of movement. We see asymmetry as a liberating and productive condition, wherein difference has benefit for both units in the dwelling. Each unit is designed as a coherent volume that responds to its unique program and the conditions of the site. When brought together, a reciprocal relationship develops between the two units, the owner unit providing services and structure that support the tenant above, and the tenant shaping the owner's experience through its position and effect on the section below.

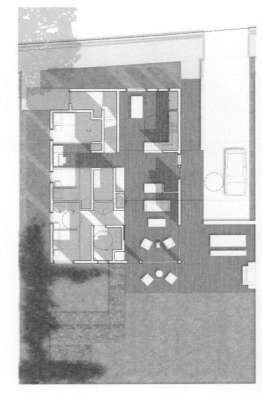
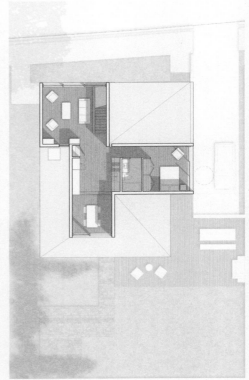

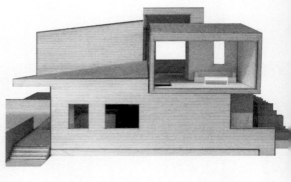

III

MELISSA BAULD
CHRISTOPHER CONNOCK

LINDSAY HOCHMAN
KYUYOUNG HUH
VIVIAN HSU

HOMIN JUNG
KEE LEW
JONAH ROWAN

JIA-JUN YEO
EMMETT ZEIFMAN

IV
TEAM D

Directional views and paths of circulation running from deep in our site's backyard and extending across King Place encouraged the differentiation between the glazed and open front and back elevations and the more opaque and insulating side elevations. In opposition to the strong directionality of this view corridor, program of the owner and tenant units organizes along opposing diagonals, connected by a central hinge which allows each to experience all four elevations. The more introverted program of the owner's bedrooms and bathrooms fits into the lower, intimate space beneath the second floor tenant unit, while the roof, also aligned with the diagonal of the tenant unit, depresses slightly to cover the owner's open, light-filled kitchen and living room in the other two corners of the house.

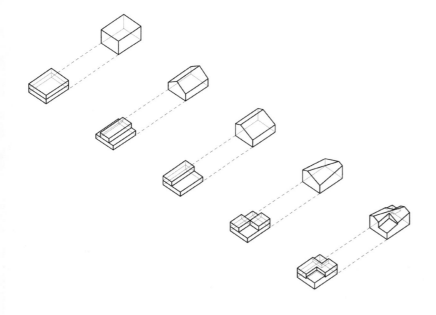

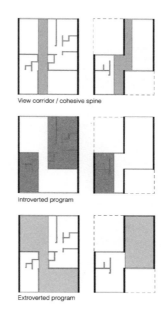

View corridor / cohesive spine

Introverted program

Extroverted program

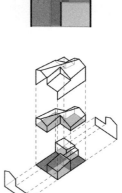

IV

V
TEAM E

Our approach is grounded in the idea
that the design of each space has a
positive impact on the other resident.
  The plan for the owner's unit
developed out of a critical analysis
of BP08 where we determined which
strengths could be applied to our own
site. The organization of the house
is split between zones of public and
private, which are distributed between
three bars of programmed space defined
by distinct spatial experiences.
  The interior space of the tenant unit
is organized around a central kitchen
delineated by a concentrated boundary
of built-in furniture and utilities.
The thickened built-ins define areas of
activity by dividing the plan and by
serving each of the spaces individually.
The overall form of the tenant unit
was manipulated to produce desired spatial effects for the owner below. The
result is a house containing two
units that equals more than the sum
of its parts.

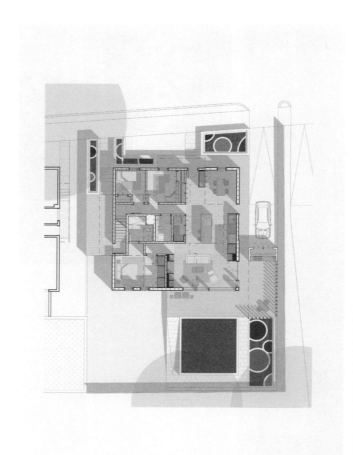

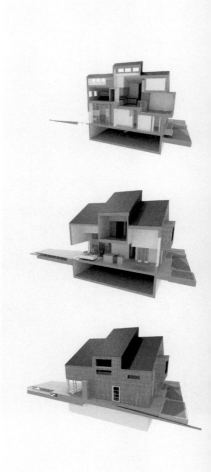

V

LETICIA WOUK ALMINO   ELIZABETH HABER   JOHN JOURDEN   ALEXANDRA TAILER
WILLIAM GRIDLEY   JUSTIN HEDDE   LIAM LOWRY   MARK TALBOT
KEITH JOHNS   DANIEL MARKIEWICZ

EXTENDED SITE: HOW THE COOKIE CRUMBLES

The architectural project does not begin or end with its building line--its influences and repercussions are elastic. This seminar asks a simple question: how does a building have an impact beyond its building line? Theoretical issues are explored in their own right but also in respect of the way in which they can inform practice.

There are some familiar references, for example the post-industrial landscape that remains long after the factory responsible is no longer visible and the much-explored effects of the Robert Moses expressways. Some cases have an immediate and localised impact that can be tracked within 5 years of the first move: for example the University of Syracuse's temporary relocation of the architecture department downtown and the investment and activity which followed.

The seminar also takes on the converse (outside in) question. It examines how forces external to the architect's usual way of doing things inscribe themselves on the city, from the strictures of apartheid on Johannesburg, to the very different (and benign) codes of datum, signage modules and value that make up the 42nd Street rulebook and the way these have determined the current properties of the street.

Through the analysis of examples the seminar explores the value of a methodology that is awake to the potential spatial and social impact of a proposition. The course not only takes examples and unpacks their influences and repercussions but also analyzes different methodologies and means of reflexive representation. Reference is made beyond architecture to include philosophical examples and art practice.

I

Since 1967 the Yale Building Project has engaged first year graduate students in the design and construction of built projects, moving architectural education out of the studio and into the "hands-in-the-dirt experience of pouring foundations and putting up siding" (Progressive Architecture, 1967). Representing a dramatic break in the curriculum of the school, the Building Project began during a period of important social upheaval, which would serve not only as impetus for the program itself, but would influence the nature of its work until today. From a radical past to what seems now a more passive endeavor (in terms of social idealism, at least), the Building Project has seen a host of clients and programs--from community centers to park pavilions to affordable one and two family homes. Likewise, the ambitions of students and the pedagogical imperatives of the project have changed over the last 40 years. Economic conditions, paradigms of construction, client ideology, and architectural culture (the politics of aesthetics) all play their part.

The task of this research was to unpack these influences, towards a new understanding of the pedagogical and social objectives of the project, and the ways in which they might intersect. As such, the Institution--Ivy League, ivory tower (or rather, the concrete tower of Rudolph Hall)--and the New Haven neighborhoods in which the Building Project operates--economically depressed and affected by a legacy of white flight and urban renewal--become subjects for study. Each and every summer, Yale meets New Haven through an extension of the classroom into the city. But these moments are brief and the relationships, thin. Might there be ways to intensify, prolong, or build upon these exchanges?

I
EXTENDED CLASSROOM
AMY CHANG
The Yale Building Project

PALLADIO

754B

I

This paper argues that theatre is an important aspect of Andrea Palladio's architecture; most visible in the urban palaces, civic and religious buildings and rural villas that are dispersed throughout Vicenza or sited beyond its city walls in the countryside.

Due to the somewhat sparing and efficient writing style found in Palladio's Four Books on Architecture, the relationship between theatre and architecture might at first glance appear vague and coincidental, such that the task remains to trace close parallels between theatricality and architectural theory and practice. The springboard for this investigation must fall to his lucid description of the dramatic qualities of the Villa Rotunda and its panoramic setting in Book II:

The site is as pleasant and as delightful as can be found; because it is upon a small hill, of very easy access, and is watered on one side by the Bacchiglione, a navigable river; and on the other it is encompassed with most pleasant risings, which look like a very great theatre, and are all cultivated, and abound with most excellent fruits, and most exquisite vines: and therefore, as it enjoys from every part most beautiful views, some of which are limited, some more extended, and others that terminate with the horizon; there are loggia's made in all the four fronts…

Palladio consciously employs the simile of theatre to describe the scenography of the villa and landscape. The villa acts to articulate the dramatic qualities of the topography and as if in tandem, the verdant, sweeping landscape is able to heighten the meaning of the activities taking place within the villa. While explicit only in this particular text within the Four Books, one could argue that a strong current of theatricality runs throughout Palladio's other projects, such as the Piazza dei Signori and Villa Barbaro at Maser.

In order to test this assumption within the wider spectrum of his work, this paper discusses external influences ranging from painting, to patronage and the architectural theory of his time. Additionally, it analyzes key works of Palladio's through the conceptual lens of three theatrical genres; the comic, tragic and satiric scenes as illustrated and described by Sebastiano Serlio in his Four Books on Architecture.

Vitruvius, and Serlio thereafter, defined the hierarchy of theatrical genres and related them to the social and spatial order of the city. For each of these classical genres a specific stage set was deemed appropriate. In Serlio's etchings of the three scenes, a square unit of pavement underpins the single point perspective of each composition. A terminated backdrop of a crumbling church façade defines the comedy, a triumphal arch with a platonic, funereal landscape beyond is deemed appropriate for the noble tragedy, and the depths of a clear cut forest trail are applied to the satiric scene. These three represent the theatrical types of public and private urban space and convey an implied hierarchical relationship between them.

II

The Palazzo Chiericati and the Villa Chiericati stand as two counterpoints to a generalized thesis of Palladio's work that would suggest a tendency toward synthetic and rational resolution. While the projects are typologically different, they share a formal and diagrammatic energy that is at its most volatile in the limits of their façades. One compresses and one expands. One is an introvert, one an extrovert. One makes ambiguity explicit, one makes expression ambiguous.

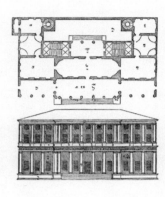

While the Palazzo is oriented to a public piazza, the Villa is surrounded by private grounds. Yet both projects are front-loaded. And both projects follow an apparent A-B-A organization from front to back. The critical moment in both buildings occurs at the corner of the façade: how does the façade relate to the volumes beyond it? The façade is charged with a dual role, as both backdrop and proscenium. Schinkel's Altes Museum provokes the same problem: how to resolve the classical order of the façade as it turns the corner and either expresses or suppresses the legibility of the interior volumes beyond. Schinkel's loggia-- the A-space of Palladio's palazzo--makes even more apparent this challenge. Le Corbusier's Villa Savoye, in a rather strange way, negotiates the problem of the façade in both the palazzo and the villa type. The co-planarity of the first and the ground floor on the "rear" façade suggests a dominant elevation in a project apparently intended to be seen from its four sides.

Through a series of analytic drawings and diagrams this project establishes a particular lineage from Palladio to Schinkel to Le Corbusier based not only on typology but on diagrammatic proposition. The investigation attempts to locate the formal energy of Palladio in the small yet highly charged (and very real) dimension of the façade as a way to interrogate a contemporary obsession in architecture practice with the surface and its politics. The paper does not propose a definitive genealogy from Palladio to Schinkel to Le Corbusier, but rather uses the latter to reconsider the former.

THE POST-SOCIALIST CITY IN TRANSITION

955B

This research seminar delves into the profound changes in architecture and urbanism of the post-socialist cities of Central and Eastern Europe and the former Soviet Union. The course explores how the structure of the modern socialist city yields to the processes of socio-political and economic transition. What are the outcomes and effects of the contemporary global transformation of these cities, initially invested with the vision of communist inter-nationalism? Case studies include shrinking cities, energy cities, the modern city in the free market landscape, and imported starchitecture. Students actively participate in seminar debates, perform research on a mutually agreed-upon topics and present it in class, and develop their own research portfolios on the selected topic. The ultimate goal is to famil-iarize students with key processes and to enable them to engage critically with transnational contemporary practice in this part of the world.

I
SEMINAR RESEARCH PORTFOLIO
POST-SOCIALIST CITY IN TRANSITION
CLASS RESEARCH

I

MARIJA BRDARSKI
ANDREEA COJOCARU

PATRICK CONNER
TRAVIS EBY
JASON KIM

TERRI LEE
LOUISE LEVI
ROBERTO ROSSI

CHAT TRAVIESO
ANJA TUROWSKI

5TH FLOOR

Faculty

ANDREW BENNER
LJILJANA BLAGOJEVIC
PETER DE BRETTEVILLE
PEGGY DEAMER
MARTIN FINIO
MARIO GOODEN
MAKRAM EL KADI
ANDREA KAHN
KEITH KRUMWIEDE
MIMI HOANG
TIM LOVE
BEN PELL
ALAN PLATTUS
ALEX FELSON

Guest Jurors

TOBIAS ARMBORST
THOMAS AUER
SUNIL BALD
STELLA BETTS
TOM BURESH
MARK CHABIN
RICK COOK
CLAUDE CORMIER
MARTIN COX
KATHRYN DEAN
KEVIN DALY
JULIE DORSEY
LIZA FIOR
MICHELLE FORNABAI
LESLIE GILL
PE'ERA GOLDMAN
KEN GREENBERG
STEVEN HARRIS
ARIANE LOURIE HARRISON
LAURIE HAWKINSON
PHU HOANG
DENISE HOFFMAN-BRANDT
MARK HUSSAR
MARIANA IBANEZ
MARK KROECKEL
DAVID LEVIN
GIUSEPPE LIGNANO
BARBARA LITTENBERG
MJ LONG
TIM LOVE
MARGARITA MCGRATH
ANA MILJACKI
ED MITCHELL
JOEB MOORE
DIETRICH NEUMANN
DAVID NILAND
ALAN ORGANSCHI
LUIS ORTEGA
ALBERT POPE
LYN RICE
ELIHU RUBIN
THOMAS SCHROEPFER
JOHN SZOT
GEORGEEN THEODORE
STANLEY TIGERMAN
TOD WILLIAMS
MABEL WILSON

Students

BRETT APPEL
ANNE-MARIE ARMSTRONG
ANDREW ASHEY
JULIANNE
    AUGUST-SCHMIDT
JASON BOND
HELEN BROWN
JOEL BURKE
TALLEY BURNS
CHRISTINE CHANG
HARVEY CHUNG
ANDREEA COJOCARU
CORY COLLMAN
PATRICK CONNOR
YIJIE DANG
AIDAN DOYLE
KURT EVANS
AURORA FAREWELL
REBECCA GARNETT
PALMYRA GERACKI
TALA GHARAGOZLOU
JEROME HAFERD
RACHEL HSU
AUDE HELENE JOMINI
JIN HYU KIM
JANG HYUNG LEE
TAE KYOUNG LEE
CALEB LINVILLE
ALEJANDRO DE MESA
IAN MILLS
ELIJAH PORTER
KATE THATCHER
ADAM TOMSKI
ANJA TUROWSKI
TYLER VELTEN
YU WANG
CRAIG WOEHRLE
HOEY YIP
HILARY ZAIC

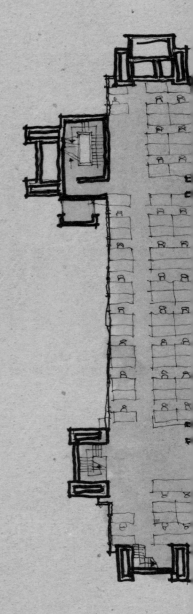

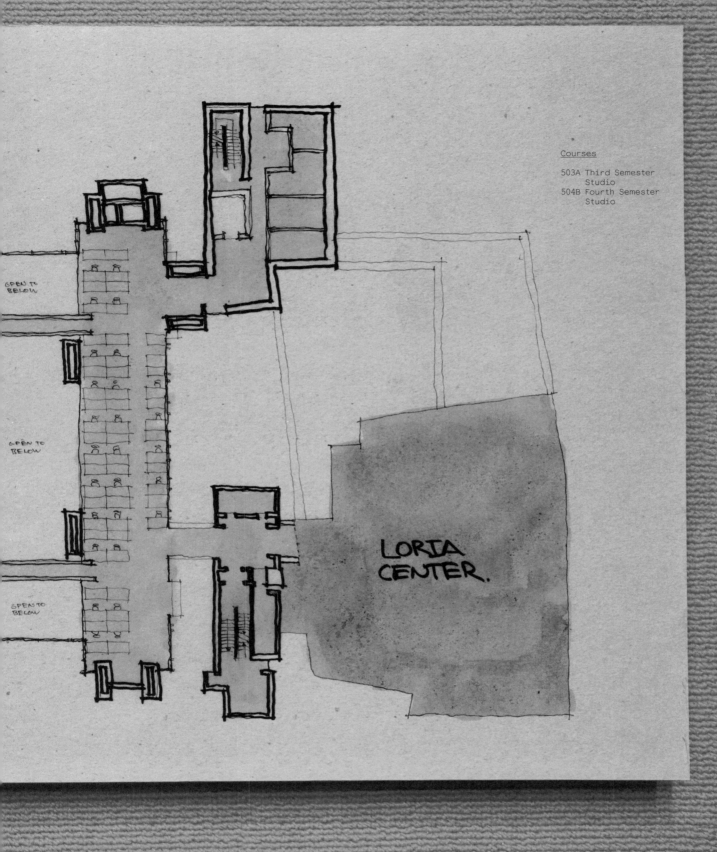

GPEN TO BELOW

GPEN TO BELOW

GPEN TO BELOW

LORIA CENTER.

Courses

503A Third Semester
    Studio
504B Fourth Semester
    Studio

503A

THIRD SEMESTER STUDIO

This comprehensive building design studio explores the theme of public architecture through the design of a medium-scale public building on Prospect Street at Yale University. It focuses on the development of a detailed building proposal with particular attention given to the intelligent integration of programmatic, spatial, environmental, structural and material factors. Each year a different building type--museum, library, courthouse, school--is selected in order to rigorously examine the operational and representational dimensions of architecture.

 The project for this year's studio is the Yale Center for Computing and the Arts, home of the newly constituted Computing and the Arts initiative at the university. This initiative will focus on "the interdisciplinary study of artistically-motivated problems involving mathematics, computer science, and information technology in an attempt to better understand traditional art through rigorous, formal methods, and to use modern technology as a means of artistic expression." Simply stated the goal is to publicly leverage the power of computing for the development of new modes of analysis and creative expression.

STUDIO COORDINATOR
KEITH KRUMWIEDE

I
ACADEMIC PLAYGROUND, MEDIA PARK
JULIANNE AUGUST-SCHMIDT
This project invites you to come play. Claim space, improvise, and create. You don't need a classroom to learn or a theater to share work. All is fair game when you are playing. By positing open program as verbs and moments, this project encourages an organization that opens itself to the curious. Horizontal meandering and vertical continuity encourage exploration and the collision of various activities and occupants. Visitor, Student, and Instructor circulate through, access, and occupy the same spaces. There are spaces that have explicit program out of necessity and those that absorb program based on adjacencies to other fixed program. As the activities maneuver and fluctuate so do the edges that bound them.

TOM BURESH „ I think you are lost in your building,
„ and I consider that to be a very positive at-
„ tribute. You say you wanted it to be free, which
„ I translate to being lost. In some ways you can
„ try and fix it and make it clearer, but it seems
„ to be a working analogy for you. This is what
„ I want to argue about: your project becomes
„ something I am completely lost in and that
„ becomes an attribute.
MARTIN FINIO „ I think that the architecture is
„ at half the scale it should be, that all the
„ spaces feel very small based on the proposal.
„ I love the ambitions and your engagement with
„ the project feels very infectious. It's a spec-
„ tacular failure as a building but it is a total
„ success as an interior investigation into how
„ someone makes a building. I hope you see that

„ as a real compliment. The idea of the core and
„ the sense of obligation to organize the build-
„ ing has basically gone out of its way to thwart
„ the organization of the building because there
„ are just so many ideas and scales within the
„ building itself that I cannot see how they can
„ do anything but make me lost. They thwart that
„ sense of coming to the building and leaving
„ and having that sense of how I moved through
„ yesterday and how I get to somewhere I was
„ the day before. I feel like all of that is
„ okay based on the way you talked about your
„ building. I feel like this is the first project
„ that I've seen where you maybe think about
„ the building in a different way than when you
„ started. There was a real ambition behind
„ what you were after. I think it is great.

II
FRACTURE
AURORA FAREWELL
My project seeks to accomplish two goals. The first is to create an open public commons at the ground floor as a continuation of the streetscape that draws the public into the entire ground floor of the building. The second is to create a visual connection between that public realm and the lab spaces above and below. These goals are accomplished by fracturing the building at the ground plane--between the lab spaces above and below--and along the axes of circulation. These fissures are drawn up through the building to define a series of boxes that float above the public ground. The boxes are then fractured at a smaller scale, the fractures again following the lines of circulation, and are registering on the roof plan and façade as glazing.

MARK HUSSAR „ I have to say that in principle it is
„ a great relief not to see another atrium, and I
„ think it is about gaps in between in such a way
„ that things come close enough that there is a
„ real tension between them. I think that princi-
„ ple, that way of using tight quivering space to
„ kind of stitch things together is a really good
„ strategy for this building, because it does
„ link things in ways that bigger open spaces
„ do not do. The use of the screens to bring
„ you back up against the slots is very clever.
KEITH KRUMWIEDE „ Is it no atrium? Or, is it one
„ of the first atriums we've seen where there
„ is control? There is discipline and it is
„ working at different scales and it is not solely
„ a shaft.
MARK HUSSAR „But the slots in the façades over
„ here--this is one of the first ones where there
„ is a relationship between the skin and what is

„ on the inside. To me it becomes the imagery
„ of what is being smartly done on the inside. I
„ wonder if the façade could be more homogenous
„ around the entire thing, if it was a little
„ dumber in that way? Because what the pathways
„ do on the inside is a lot more work three-
„ dimensionally, programmatically, and all of
„ that. But when they get rendered on the façade
„ as a window or slit it is very flat looking.
KEITH KRUMWIEDE „To me it should not have any-
„ thing that registers as a window, but also
„ not a slit that is indexing a thing behind.
„ The only thing that should be indexed at the
„ limits of the building are these two slots,
„ and you want to put a whole other level of work
„ on the envelope. These gaps maybe allow you to
„ control light and ventilation and you really
„ put it through the paces of what it needs to
„ do as a boundary.

III
SINUOUS CONNECTION
KATE THATCHER
The primary move is a crack, or split, running through the building in the north-south direction, allowing the east and west sides of the buildings to be separated by a half-level. The connective tissue, the circulation, is a spiral of stairs and ramps that jog diagonally through the building, connecting a variety of spatial and programmatic conditions, and choreographing internal as well as external views. Intermediary landings along the spiral provide another opportunity for flexible meeting, working, or display spaces within the public realm. The sequence of compressed and open spaces on the circulation path provides for views into the adjacent lab spaces, between floors vertically, through and across spaces horizontally, and to the outside. By maintaining a clear and relatively simple programmatic organization throughout, the complexity and richness of the project is expressed in the sinuous connection between the landings, floor plates, and programs.

MARK KROECKEL „Your stair is still acting too
„ much like a stair. I am wondering if it does
„ not actually become circulation and commons
„ much more mixed together--so that it is always
„ mediating the two sides of the building as it
„ is bouncing up in there, rather than having
„ stair, and then, distinctly, the commons off of
„ it. Ramps are cheap. They look good to draw
„ but they are a bitch to actually get to work
„ out, and then when you work them out they have
„ lost all their charm. I think you can do it
„ with a stair, there is nothing wrong with that,
„ but is the stair too constant? Does it always
„ have the same rhythm, does it always work the
„ same way, does it change or adjust as it moves
„ up through depending on which things it is
„ relating to?
MARIO GOODEN „Maybe it is a 'stramp'--a combina-
„ tion of stair and ramp--but I am also wonder-
„ ing, does it have the potential to push back
„ against the program here? Just thinking about
„ your issue of head heights, the length of run
„ that is required. And then maybe there could
„ be some blurring of this program.
MABEL WILSON „Give yourself some more breath-
„ ing room. This feels like the most compressed
„ scheme I have seen so far--not necessarily

„ a bad thing--but you end up with things like
„ the auditorium just kind of crammed into the
„ bottom. Given the amount of space that you
„ do have, you could give it more of a pres-
„ ence. There are some really key spaces that
„ could also be brought closer in relationship
„ to the common space and the circulation areas
„ and if you gave a bit more breathing room to
„ the building in general you might be able
„ to resolve some of the problems that you
„ are having.
MJ LONG „It is a smart scheme, it works very
„ well. My only comment about the stairs: the
„ answer is to be careful. It is nice that it
„ is fairly densely organized, this climbing
„ space, but it ought to more clearly link what
„ it is linking. You can get it working that way
„ instead of crumpling it up into a corner and
„ then having a corridor that flops down into
„ one of the common rooms. The other thing that
„ you have got to be careful about is how those
„ walls work. The idea is very good, and it is
„ nice to see something like that coming out
„ of the environmental workshop and into the
„ building, but you have got to be sure that the
„ anatomy of it strengthens the most important
„ facts of the stair and vice versa.

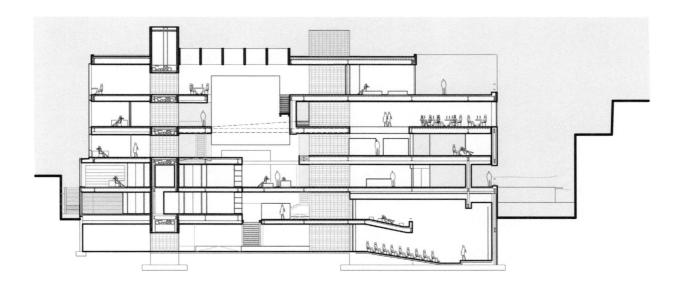

I

II

III

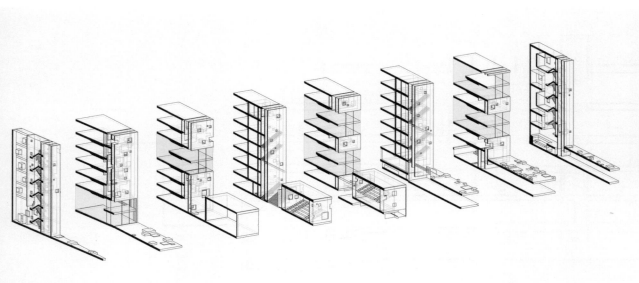

I

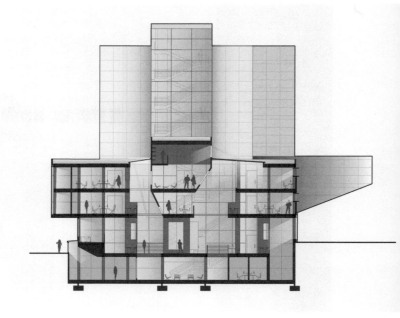

II

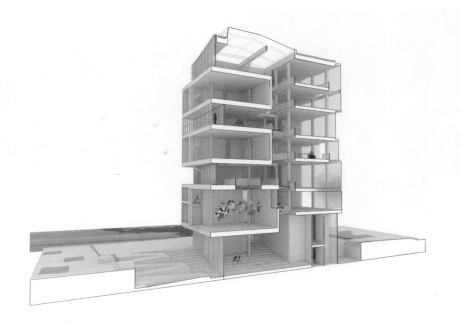

III

MJ LONG   ALAN ORGANSCHI   GEORGEEN THEODORE   TOD WILLIAMS
DAVID NILAND   ALBERT POPE   STANLEY TIGERMAN

ALAN ORGANSCHI „Can the building on the ground floor be different than on the upper floors with very different kinds of programs that also connect directly out to a garden space? I wonder if you could look at some of those programs given and bury them. Could you go down and out, and take some of the bulk out of the building? We do not assume that this is sloping; we know you are going to study it. It might become a really varied landscape. You own this--it could be anything--and it seems like you want to make something that relates to the internal workings of the site, and the wall that Fred (Koetter) and Suzie (Kim) have created, and the garden and all these things that are so suggestive, the street. There is a lot to work with there. I accept the formulation. I want you to test all of it.

PETER DE BRETTEVILLE „The green in front wants to engage the garden in the back. I would very much like to see you draw some sense of other perimeters. Start anticipating what those are beyond your rectangle as a means of engaging the landscape.
GEORGEEN THEODORE „One thing you could also consider is investing yourself more in the design of the landscape itself, and thinking about this kind of strategy--pulling that out into the site itself. So, for example, what would happen if you were to begin to think of a pathway system, or a system of linear benches, or whatever it may be, that would follow the diagram that you have been developing, but would then be applied to the landscape and would allow you to take ownership over that terrain?

I
LAYERED INTERACTION
TALLEY BURNS
Understanding the YCCA's desire to be a catalyst for collaboration that spans currently disparate disciplines, my design emphasizes common and circulation spaces in order to encourage student gatherings. These common exhibition spaces will facilitate the assimilation of a new computer-arts discipline. The building programs are enclosed by thickened stair walls on the south, east and west, which serve as environmental controls. The main stair, which provides direct linkage between the double height common-exhibition spaces, runs within the southern wall. A layered programmatic condition--from public to private-- is set up behind this stair wall, as the more private programs are organized behind the thickened southern wall and the most public along the glazed northern wall.

STANLEY TIGERMAN „Are you going to have someone in the entryway to help people decipher your code? My contention is that you have not yet achieved command of the language that you wish to use to convey to the public the obvious and more subtle aspects of your design. I am not trying to placate you. I think it is marvelous to be this optimistic, but to convey at this subliminal level and not be too subtle and devious with the clues that you use.
MJ LONG „I really appreciate that you began your project with an ambition to critique public space and create a new kind of public space, but somewhere between then and now, I got lost. How is this different from any other public space I know? How is this better?
PATRICK CONNOR „I wanted to create a series of overlooks so that when you are in the public space you can understand what is happening

in the rest of the building. There would be people working around the public space, so when you come in you are made aware of what is happening throughout the building.
TOD WILLIAMS „I appreciate the objective and the ambition outside the program. You said, 'I am going to take on something that I am interested in this semester: what is the status of public space?' and then you bracketed it and set up the conditions for the critique. And maybe that was not ambitious enough--maybe the critique should have included more of the context or an expanded idea of what is public. I guess maybe the critique is limited, but if you expanded it, maybe you could have achieved much more radical results. You have a very calibrated relationship between public and private, and maybe that could have been more radicalized.

II
THE DIFFERENCE LINK
PATRICK CONNOR
This project employs an elevated, linear, and formally distinct system of performance spaces, public media labs, and lecture halls to draw the casual visitor into the very heart of the building. This device acts as the key link between a seven story administrative tower that maximizes northern exposure and a low-slung student research center. At the north and south extremes, public program explodes out of the confines of the exterior envelope to indicate this inner logic.

DAVID NILAND „You don't consider those to be pejorative terms, do you? Offset, misalignment?
PETER DE BRETTEVILLE „The point is not gratuitous misalignment, but rather that by misaligning you call attention to a change in position, a change in use, a change in function, different constituents or different activities, so that the shifts that are a little hard to see are all about snapping your fingers--you are going somewhere else, and so you shift vertically, diagonally.
MAKRAM EL KADI „But the emphasis on disconnection is too much given to one façade. The location of the core is problematic. If you look at this amazing gap that you have created in the building, it is pointing to an elevator, half of an elevator, and that is a misalignment in the pejorative sense. And on the other side it is pointing to a bathroom. I love bathrooms, and I spend a lot of time in them, but it could be a locus of an amazing space.

ALBERT POPE „I think it is a very powerful scheme. It is an interesting scheme in relationship to a lot of the projects we have seen today because it has a very clear diagrammatic organization to it, but then there is also this overlay of idiosyncratic shifts. In some ways, offset and misalignment are useful tools because they become devices that allow you to evolve out of the diagram and set up more nuanced relationships between the different programs. There is a kind of density to it that is quite powerful. You seem to be very intentional about that dimension of the atrium space. You could say it is too tight, it should be more open, there should be more light, but you have been very careful about calibrating that dimension.
DAVID NILAND „This is a very interesting project not just because of the intentions, but because you tried to develop a language with which you can deliver what you hoped to achieve.

III
OFFSET YCCA
AUDE HELENE JOMINI
The Yale Center for Computing and the Arts aspires to connect different disciplines, suggesting an informal gallery-like space as an ideal home. However, nearly half of the program requires controlled light, sound or security. By articulating the controlled programs as distinct volumes within a fluid space of public circulation and group interaction, both needs are met. Art spaces and specialized labs are offset from the main floor plates to delineate a continuous, shifting, compressed vertical void that provides visual connections between floors-- light bouncing off the textured surfaces of the staggered volumes. The entry-level media steps carve downward into the site, accentuating the existing topographical change while bleeding from outdoors through the interior to create a dynamic public space that serves as a computing lounge, informal theater, and a place to gather.

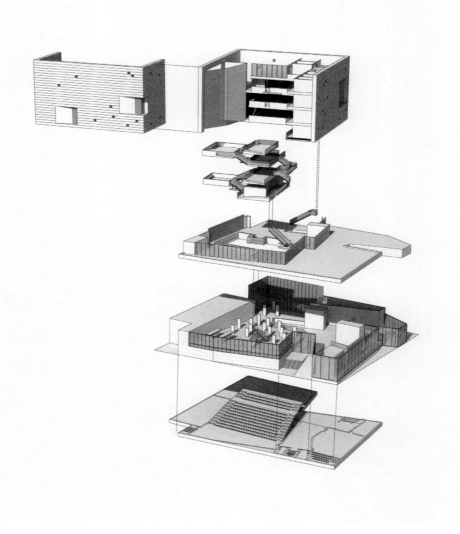

I

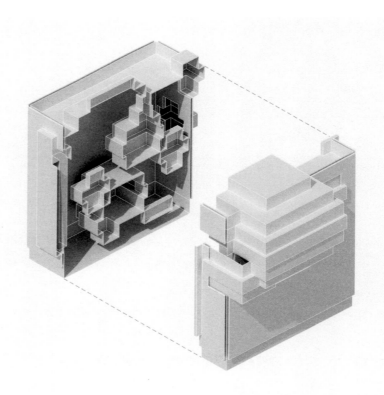

II

TIM LOVE „It is as if the Kieren Timberlake building that you were in last year has had a baby. It is so deeply embedded in where you have been the past two years, it is kind of fascinating. You have done a very creative sampling of spatial experiences that you have had on campus. That is a superficial crit, I am sorry, but we have been whispering over here and I wanted to know you to know what we have been whispering about.

TOD WILLIAMS „I am attracted to entering in that first floor plan. What I find peculiar is that it seems there is no space between this new public datum, the plinth, and the box above. So I wonder whether you could not do exactly the same thing by descending slightly so that you can ultimately find a greater separation. Your void between your plinth and your zinc building above seems way too squashed and there does not seem to be enough life in it.

LYN RICE „There is a real care taken on that first floor that I love. It is like you pushed the site into the building and allowed the building at times to finger out into the site and I think there is a really nice play of interior-exterior. And you have created space by modulating the section. I think part of the problem is that it completely disappears at the roof of the plinth. When I look at that it ends up looking like a Gap storefront, when actually there is much more sectional complexity going on in the floor.

STELLA BETTS „The lower level has a sort of care taken to the relationship to the site, but that movement through and the possibility of actually occupying the solid that you have above mostly just occurs in that middle zone, in a very regularly dimensioned stair.

TIM LOVE „It is a great set-up. You have all of the moving parts here. It is suggestive of so many secondary avenues the project could have taken and I think taking the risk of defining it was the right thing to do.

MARTIN FINIO „All I can say is that you guys have described every avenue that this guy has been down, which is a compliment to you. Brett has been to every one of those places, and he has been there through model making, through drawing. He has really tested this thing, and maybe in the end it succumbs to a sense of control, as opposed to being less controlled and more what you are all asking for.

I
WEAK TIES
BRETT APPEL

The proposal utilizes formal techniques to strategically separate and connect the programmatic elements and mediate the influences of the surrounding site. The laboratories are located in a volume hovering over a site-sensitive ramped plinth that mediates the topographical variation. The arrangement of the programmatic elements organizes the disparate computing laboratories to establish a series of visual and physical connections with mid-level common spaces and overlapping double-height review areas. The architecture attempts to provide a framework to promote a collaborative environment.

TIM LOVE „I agree with Christina that there is a conceptual thoughtfulness to your programmatic decisions, but I am not sure you found the right diagram and got all of the things in the right places. What I mean by that is simple things like where the public stair is—where the private stair, the fire stair, and the bathrooms are in relationship to the large spaces. The earlier models seem clearer and maybe because you were too careful about getting the square footages right you started to upend the diagram slowly and incrementally, but you did not say that maybe my diagram is not quite right. So it is a nice project, but there is a methodological question about when you nail the diagram in the process and when you are allowed to monkey with it again. This project in particular is such a Swiss watch that it really requires diagram management. You need to use a different part of your brain to figure out that maybe that diagram is not the right diagram.

STELLA BETTS „When you first described the diagram I was curious to see where the intersection of the X, Y, Z was going to occur, programmatically, physically, and in your model. What I really like is the sort of core of the Carpenter Center effect—that there is this passage that is happening in the site through the lower part of the building. I agree that if you revisit the diagram that I would want to see that circulation experience as the thing that connects those three points. I feel like that kind of movement is actually tying these in, and if you rethought your project in those terms it would begin to critique some of these locations and some of the other proximities.

TOD WILLIAMS „I am not sure about the diagram. One part I am sure about is that the movement from a historical smaller scale to the futuristic public pathway seems to be pretty resolved. The section is quite an interesting section; you can feel a desire to change. I do not understand the other one, the postproduction—what is the acquisition? I do not know how that factors into the building in a meaningful way. I would have said this axis really has to do with—well, what does it do relative to the street? Is there something that tells me about the street? I wish those things were more physical and less intellectual, because I think it is really hard to intersect X,Y,Z axes. I have a feeling that your elevator vestibule is not great or your stair into the vestibule is not great. My feeling is that it is not a joyful building to move through yet.

II
DEGREES IN POSTPRODUCTION
KURT EVANS

The new Yale Postproduction Center is a hybrid building that marries the Computer Science, Music, Art and Architecture departments. The design interrogates the provided departmental White Paper and re-conceptualizes the program along a series of three axes: (x) acquisition-postproduction; (y) historical-futuristic; and (z) extractivity-intractivity. What the project borrows directly from Koolhaas' Zentrumfür Kunst und Medientechnologie (ZKM)—principally the sliding relationship between old and new media—is further informed by Bourriaud's Postproduction. He presents the contemporary artist as a mixer of data, rather than the autocrat of a particular media. While the x,y,z axes in the Cartesian grid predicate a point zero, here the objective is to undermine such certainty. The ability of the YPC to avoid a conscious origin and instead suggest one's editable relationship to the meeting of axes is its greatest success.

I

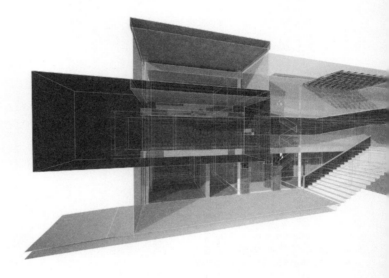

II

III

TOM BURESH   LAURIE HAWKINSON   GIUSEPPE LIGNANO   MABEL WILSON
KATHRYN DEAN   MARIANA IBANEZ   THOMAS SCHROEPFER

MARIANA IBANEZ „Your original strategy about „ finding the weave--and the fact that of course „ the weave produces an intersection--could „ have been pushed a lot further by this weav-„ ing and what you are calling the generic, „ which does not necessarily have to be generic. „ It could be the moments of inspiration that „ are fighting about this brief and trying to „ architecturalize those spaces. At this point „ your building looks like it is well-calibrated „ in the sense that your plans are solid and the „ program is distributed with a certain logic, „ but I think you did not take the opportunity of „ speculating about how the program introduces „ a new type of space. Thomas's comment about „ how the façade is the same for a lab as it „ is for a studio--the recognition that there „ has to be an introduction of difference, and „ that the introduction of intersection would „ produce different architectural responses. I „ think the elements are there, but they are „ very discretely resolved. You have a system „ for your façade, a system for organizing your „ plans, but there is nothing that is producing a „ tension between these parts of the program and „ then producing different spaces. Try to rep-

licate more than just one grey box. There are „ moments where you could have parts at different „ scales. Try to embrace the idea of difference, „ rather than this discrete sameness.
THOMAS SCHROEFER „There is a really good level „ of sophistication, but there is a very funda-„ mental question from where you started, which „ is with this idea of producing the weave. How „ do you go through the project so that all of „ a sudden it is not the same, it is all about „ difference and emerging from this into that?
ANDREW ASHEY „There was obviously an intent to „ keep the boxes the same, and then the activity „ and surface inside would be the difference. „ There was an intent to keep the generic box.
MARIANA IBANEZ „It is an interesting starting „ point. But with this argument about sameness „ and the articulated surface there is the point „ where you want feedback, so it is not just a „ one-way, staid, relationship.
LAURIE HAWKINSON „Why would you want to produce „ something generic? You would not. How do you „ find difference in the sameness that you set „ up, so that you are always looking for the „ difference to try to articulate in spatial ways „ and programmatic ways?

I
YALE CENTER
FOR COMPUTING AND THE ARTS
ANDREW ASHEY

This project re-conceives the YCCA and its pedagogical methods as expressed in the White Paper, changing it from a "problem-process-solution" framework to that of "recycled" investigation, wherein solution becomes content. This notion of recycled investigation between the arts and computer science is manifest in the logic of the building. Here the programmatic "bars" are used as studios and labs, representing the arts and computer engineering, respectively. At their juncture lies the grey box, an unprogrammed zone left for unforeseen uses produced by their overlap. This versatility is carried over to the perim-eter, through an interior skin that can respond to a diversity of furniture needs at the studios and a panel system that can serve as projection screens, white boards, pinup spaces, and light-blocking curtains at the labs.

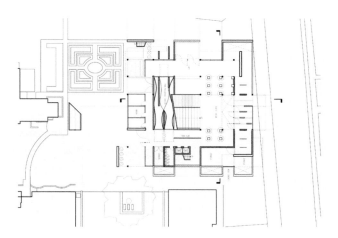

II
WEAVING BANDS
JANG HYUNG LEE

Computing and arts programs are encouraged to support each other and to stimulate and affect both the public and the school. Through the weaving of various programmed bands, the building consists of overlapped spaces. These spaces can merge or separate-through temporal shifts in use. Several bands extend into other programs and the furniture and the featured walls are repeated from the public realm into the school, blurring the program by making ambiguous adjacency.

MABEL WILSON „The way you make something is „ intelligent, you are thinking, and often times „ you need to abandon that and get into the inte-„ rior and figure out the logistics of how program „ works--the spatial sequence of the interior. „ But then there is some kind of intelligence in „ your previous moves that can always get pulled „ back into the process. I feel like you just „ said, 'This is what it should be.' Go back.
GIUSEPPE LIGNANO „We cannot do this. We cannot „ do all of these investigations and experimen-„ tations when it is just about a form, and then „ when it becomes architecture and do everything „ to put the windows and the glass in instead „ of making it work. That model is architecture. „ That must be architecture and do everything „ that architecture does. Cover you, give you „ light, a place to walk on, everything. And you „ definitely had it. That does everything.
KATHRYN DEAN „I am wondering if there is some-„ thing in between the two where you can take the „ places--like right here, this is an incredibly „ beautiful landscape--and start to understand „ how to fuse it with a normative construction. „ Because I just see the hundred and eighty foot

long truss, and the members are huge, and it „ is not even doing anything.
GIUSEPPE LIGNANO „But that is not the way to look „ at it. That is an intuition and that intuition „ becomes architecture not by cutting it and „ putting something else there, but by working „ on it until it becomes architecture, until it „ does everything it needs to do.
TOM BURESH „There is a whole other half of your „ project we are not even seeing. There are two „ floors underground. It seems like it would be „ harder and harder to carry through its logic as „ it gets up in the air. I love how you presented „ your project. You were really clear and you „ are making pretty amazing jumps from, 'I wrote „ this, I found this equation,' and all that. It „ shows a really agile mind, so I am hopeful „ for your future. However, this is really an „ extravagant figure, the one everyone is in love „ with here, and I do not know how successful „ it is at four floors. It looks like a really „ beautiful figure floating on the ground. There „ is another idea in how you are dealing with „ the foundation that this figure sits on top of „ and I feel you have to reconcile them.

III
AFFECT/FORM_SPACE OF FRICTION
TAE KYOUNG LEE

I envision YCCA as a place where the collision of human imagination and lim-itless technology happens. It is where the friction between artists and com-puter scientists creates something new. Here, an artist becomes a scientist, a computer engineer becomes a musician--deterritorializing their own trajec-tories to establish a new area of study.

   Architecturally, I understand the project as an exploration of the tension between sensation and representation. The project aspires to articulate a close relationship between the built form and its affect on the users by juxta-posing heterogeneous programs next to each other and mediating different users through permeable or split surfaces. As Deleuze describes sensation as an event that happens prior to cognition, which acts immediately upon the nervous system, the project highlights spaces of friction between its form and affect.

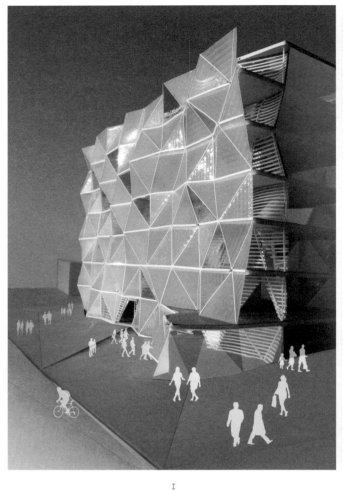

I

II

III

PHU HOANG „You are so constrained in giving yourself really no bar in this bar building that you cannot do much in here. Maybe a lower flatter building, or some other massing, would allow you to explore the implications of this leak space and what happens when it expands into the space.

MARTIN FINIO „The site work is successful, the building itself is successful on many levels, but the building as it is sited is not successful. The surface, the way you have treated it and related it to the building itself, is successful, but the building inside is probably the least successful thing about it. And it is a matter of both how it operates on the urban scale, at the street, and in its interior organization. But it is a wonderful way to the end the day--the craft and an absolutely clear idea.

MIMI HOANG „I think you've gone through a very long arc through the semester, from being absolutely tied to a really geometric logic to being a little more loose with that geometric system. I feel like the comments now are asking you to make that system be even more performative. I find really interesting the idea of tying a structure to it. I think that you have done an excellent job linking the environmental to how this façade performs and it is great to see that you have entered into the building. Those images are really interesting. It is not just an outside-in exploration, but you have been able to show how it performs on the inside. The difficulty of a strategy like this is obviously that it is really hard to figure out how it touches the ground. Wondering When to let go of the system and when to use it to do even more is a good place to be.

I
LEAKED SPACE
CHRISTINE CHANG
At the Yale Center for Computing and the Arts, academic disciplines have no distinct boundaries.The building is a flexible laboratory in which computer science cross-pollinates with the arts. As one moves through the thickened exterior envelope into the open interior core, one encounters an array of spaces varying in scale, privacy, and specificity. The thresholds between these spaces are part of the enclosed system, thus blurring the distinction between contained and public space. The activated envelope creates an architecture of leaked space. Both visitors and daily users weave through spatial sequences that exist between solidity, permeability, reflection, transparency, and occlusion. In suggesting an abstraction of physical space, the YCCA begins to embody the very discipline it aims to explore.

PHU HOANG „I think as a diagram it is an interesting idea about these two envelopes, but what is making it very difficult for us is that the drawings just rely on tone to differentiate the spaces, so you have this invention, this device you have created, that we have to believe would create different spatial qualities on one side of it versus the other.

PALMYRA GERAKI „I do not want different spatial qualities.

PHU HOANG „Then what is it for?

PALMYRA GERAKI „This is for the equipment and it is fully enclosed. This is for the more private program such as offices and workstations.

PHU HOANG „That is what I am saying. When you say more private, that is a different spatial quality than the public. This wrapper separates what you just said is more private versus public. In a way this is a presentation comment, but if you want us to understand what this thing does then the drawings should support it. You should see not just two tonal differences but the spatial differences.

MARTIN FINIO „I think the project is actually

much clearer and much more successful and much more interesting than you have been able to show us in your drawings. These drawings are like a disservice to the whole thing. But I think it is actually a very elegant solution, and through relatively simple and few deeds you have established difference, you have established a real argument about the program.

LAURIE HAWKINSON „The model is super clear. You can actually see the complexity, the subtle shifting that is occurring.

PALMYRA GERAKI „There is actually no shifting. The core is continuous all the way down.

LAURIE HAWKINSON „It looks like shifting from here. That was a compliment. But I think these drawings are really interesting--the idea of trying to demonstrate this promenade is very interesting and when I go up close to those drawings they are not as muddy. There is a lot of information in that unfolded elevation and the lower drawing of the LED that wraps up as this larger scale device that is swerving through the building. I see how it lends itself to a form inside the building.

II
ON CENTER
PALMYRA GERACKI
In an obstinate response to the variability of the programmatic requirements for Yale's new Center for Computing and the Arts, this design proposes a centrally organized building that continually reinforces and disrupts the power of its center. The public promenade, consisting of exhibition and performance spaces, spirals into the building as an extrusion of the landscape in a rotating motion countered by the motion of the other main circulatory route through the building. Disparate programmatic elements are brought together by the presence of a solid core consisting of highly conditioned spaces that gets voided selectively and treated in different materials to throw off the static and overpowering hierarchy of the alleged center.

PHU HOANG „First I want to say that I commend you for getting it to this point in terms of the plan. Looking at it, I know that was not easy, both in plan and section and structure, and this conversation that we are having I think is partially because you could get it to here. But for me, whether it is the Guggenheim model, where the atrium allows for a range of interactive relationships or interior relationships, or the trifoil of Ben van Berkel, you get difference within the interior. Right now it is kind of an object, and I can accept that you want to make a showcase and show people doing their activities at night, but still there is a pretty conventional sense of interior core and dark space and then everything spiraling around on the outside without much thought about the experience--what is at stake for those who are working here.

MARTIN FINIO „I'm fixated on the fact that it is always glass. My sense is the last thing you want to do is have an object building; that is

the last thing you want for this semester, and in fact you are far more interested in this idea of landscape. This is something we were talking about earlier--you were much more interested in that horizontal surface and this was a way to kind of play that out but as soon as you have to clad that in something opaque, it becomes this impossible object for you.

LAURIE HAWKINSON „So that was the glass.

MARTIN FINIO „Yeah. You are understanding this as a landscape that ends up coiling itself in this case.

MIMI HOANG „Martin, you are saying for you the more important idea is that he has invented this landscape that departs from the ground and reconnects to other parts of the program- it does not necessarily mean that it has to be clad in glass.

MARTIN FINIO „Right, it should definitely not be. But I can see your resistance to anything other than glass because this is the only way that it becomes phenomenal.

III
GRADUAL
JIN HYU KIM
This building has two kinds of gradient.First is the gradient of program. Rather than occupying separate rooms, each program appears within a continuous flow of space. Depending on relationships between dedicated labs and specified facilities, the programs inhabit the flow in the double helix structure (sound lab to editing rooms, editing rooms to visual lab, visual lab to fabrication lab, fabrication lab to device lab). Second is the gradient of light. Through the circular shape, the building resists directionality. The light level in spaces varies, so that people can choose their seats according to their own preferences.

I

II

III

STELLA BETTS   STEVEN HARRIS   MARK KROECKEL   JOHN SZOT
                MARK HUSSAR   ANA MILJACKI

MARK KROECKEL „I will just stick with the form for a little bit, and this is probably your last shot before the wolves eat you--but you beat it through everything, at every different scale, and it never differentiates. So when you say diagram, you do not have a diagram here because a diagram is able to operate in a scalar way, and it does not actually have to look like the thing that it is. It is the intelligence of how you are going to employ this thing.

KEITH KRUMWIEDE „Let's look at this in another way. I love the form. I love the circulation. I just want to get past that. The problem is, you were more or less at this point at the midterm. It is better now in terms of the circulation. The program is working better, it really was a disaster at the midterm as a working research lab. What you have not done is take advantage of your skills to learn something this semes-ter about developing this as a building, as a proposition about building. So I look at this, and I do not know where that section of steel comes from or why it is sitting in the ground right there. It is not an idea about build-ing. And I am going to pick on you because I think you can do it and have not done it. Your struggle is not a formal struggle. You can do it. These renderings, they are a little more polished than they were at midterm, but they are really not anymore informed. They are not telling you more about any kind of detailed resolution or another sort of scale of interrogation of the work. These plans, yes, they are at eighth-inch, but they might as well be at thirty-second. They have no detail that demands they be this size, except for the sheet that you got that says, 'Give me a plan at eighth-inch.'

I
INTERLOOP
HARVEY CHUNG
The Yale Center for Computing and the Arts functions as a mediator between Yale's main campus and Science Hill. Conceptually, the building is an inver-sion of the enclave typology of the Yale quad. It connects the surroundings and performs as a short cut to move people across the site. The building is formed by two interlocking sectional loops containing private programs such as studio and lab space. Students ac-cess the building at the four corners and the public enters through the inter-secting space embraced by the loops. It creates a transient public space that delivers the atmosphere of the comput-ing and the arts.

STEVEN HARRIS „Do you know how they catch mon-keys? They build a cage. And in that cage the bars are slightly closer together than a monkey's hand holding something. They hang bananas in the cage. The monkey puts his hand in there, grabs the bananas, and will not let go to get his hand back out. You have about eighteen ideas, many of which are good. But in combination each one is subverting the next. It seems to me that you started with something that as a diagram has a really clear ordering principle, the nine square grid. Then your idea about transparency is extraordinary, but the combination of doing this rotational second section and then throwing stairs to the perimeter and then doing this with inverted pyramids and then covering the outside in a perforated skin is making a stew out of the whole thing. If you took two of those ideas you could make it really precise and exquisite.

ANA MILJACKI „I would have gone with the mat as the main space-making idea, not the nine-square. The great thing about mats is that you can have a system that will recur. Certain things are held steady, but these are mostly to do with the openings and not so much what occurs around the openings. Your unit, your piece, your DNA, could be more intelligently programmed. That is what you could clarify.

PETER DE BRETTEVILLE „The mat is repetitive but responsive. It is not local and idiosyncratic in its overall notion, but it becomes idiosyn-cratic as you occupy it.

ANA MILJACKI „At what volume do you have differ-ent ideas playing? Right now they are all at the same volume, so we have mat in plan and in section it is something else. If you treated each of these units as a sectional piece of the mat, so that each floor plate does not just add up easily, then once you get here each of these units is understood on its own. I would have made them first strong on their own so that your section is not a series of strata that come from somewhere else.

KEITH KRUMWIEDE „Mark said, 'I like the roof,' and your immediate response was, 'I like it too.' You need to turn up the volume on one thing and actually see what the consequences are. And then maybe you turn it down and you turn up something else. The question of 'is it a mat, or is it nine squares?' has not really been tested because you found a point of comfort.

ANA MILJACKI „When you get really good as a designer you can identify that you have locked yourself in a place of comfort because you like something. This is the place where you want to actually induce distance from your project. Somehow simulate distance, try out several ideas in the extreme.

II
NINE SQUARE MAT
IAN MILLS
The final form of the building is a result of the specific spatial require-ments of it user groups--undergraduate students, graduate students, PhD stu-dents and the public--and the nature of their interactions. All public facilities such as theatres, the café, and exhibition spaces are on the ground floor. Some of these spaces have a visual connection to the student floors above in the form of open atria. The student groups are organized by floor with undergraduate on the fourth floor, graduate on the third, and PhD on the second. This organization reflects both the nature of work conducted by each group as well as their relationship to each other. The undergraduate floor is an open plan that encourages explo-ration while the PhD floor consists of more compartmentalized and special-ized spaces.

PETER DE BRETTEVILLE „I am intrigued by what you are saying--you are letting the analog and digital disciplines collide in plan. The model is the most convincing to me. If I do not look at the ground floor, those upper floors really look like they are colliding and overlapping, and there is some sense that you have backed that up by programmatic juxtapositions and collisions and maybe--there is enormous skill in this three-dimensional assembly here--you are just stumbling over the words a bit.

STELLA BETTS „Some of the ideas of the diagrams are super intriguing. I like how simple they are. I get it really fast and I agree that there is something really interesting looking at the plans and the transformation of the organization of the form. This stitching could be almost like a snowball that starts to col-lect different bits of both programs and by the time you get up to the top it is a mix of both. I could imagine a transformation in each floor-plate and perhaps even in section because the different bits of program that it is collecting along the way have different dimensions that demand different criteria. What are the speci-fications for different bits of program--what do you need for a lab? I think you need to clarify that to understand where cross-pollenization occurs. It does not just occur in this literal stitching bridge. You actually start to mix the programs; it is very exciting.

JOHN SZOT „I am not convinced. Admittedly, it generates a bias within me. I would recom-mend a different approach: 'here are my initial diagrams, and here is the abstracted version floor by floor.' Start to make decisions about where walls land as a result of these arbi-trary divisions that came from this idea of blending.

MARK HUSSAR „I think there is a lot of poten-tial there in your very first diagram, but I think you have to go back and really think about the idea. Do these two walls--they are such dominant aspects of your scheme--what do they actually represent? Do they represent the digital and analog, and if so what is the stuff in the middle? Or do they represent the two component parts of the program, visual and acoustic manipulation, and what happens in the middle is all about generating that stuff?

III
BLENDED TRANSITIONS
HOEY YIP
The conceptual approach for this project is blending: the blending of space; the blending of program; the blending of discipline; the blending of users. The goal of this project is to create a building where different activities in-teract and cross breed into hybrid mixed media. The formal and spatial approach to the building refers to Kazuo Shinohara's theory on "savage machine" and transparency ideology. The planning for the building provides a porous setting for multiple layers of inter-action among users. The Prospect Street and courtyard façades serve as the main supporting structure, with program spanning as bridges between these two external structural frames, allowing the spaces in the building to be as free flowing as possible.

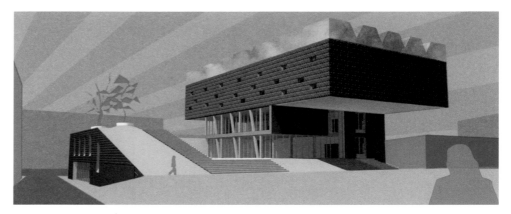

I

II

III

MICHELLE FORNABI   ALBERT POPE
MARK HUSSAR

MARK HUSSAR „The very top floor has a kind of „ stasis about it because it has resolved all „ the idiosyncrasies of context. Everything else „ seems like it is obligated to something else. „ And for that reason--and this is a nice qual- „ ity of the project--on one hand you can look „ at certain spaces and read a subtractive argu- „ ment, that it is the larger solid that has been „ eroded, and on the other hand it really seems „ like it is trying to suture something else „ together and therefore it has had to become a „ contortionist to do so. And those are two very „ different readings that are not conceptually, „ but formally and organizationally, at home „ with one another, which is a strength.
ALBERT POPE „You have got these buildings, the „ British Art Center--these really rich ingredi- „ ents--and you put it together and made a Twinkie. „ You are making something that resonates on a „ very different level than the ingredients.
MARK HUSSAR „I think there is an acknowledge- „ ment that after a while something adds up

MARK HUSSAR „This speaks to your image of what „ the public's experience of this would be and „ to the degree to which it would be spectacular „ in the sense of being pre-programmed as op- „ posed to being more spontaneous. Is that fair? „ I like this diagram on the left, the yellow „ one; it has the clearest urban relationship I „ have seen so far. It is very traditional with „ regards to the street and its life, but I like „ the idea, and I like the idea of being drawn „ underneath this volume and into something that „ spills out into this green space, which is „ sequestered, but not completely controlled. „ Certain aspects suggest to me that things „ could be more relaxed, but others suggest to „ me that you are imagining these uses as very „ structured and formal.
ALBERT POPE „The façade is also an interpreta- „ tion of the program, because it is scaffold- „ ing; it has a bit of the Fun Palace in it--

that allows you to say that the project is „ this and not that. In other words, it is not „ easy to extract a piece of this and substitute „ another one. I think this project says I can „ continue the idea of sourcing but I also want „ to synthesize.
ALBERT POPE „This building that we are sitting „ in owes its debt to other buildings. To chop „ the top two floors of the British Art Center „ and to change out the pewter with chrome is a „ slightly different level of quotation. It may be „ more straightforward. Rudolph would probably „ bristle at the suggestion that the building „ is unoriginal, but your attitude is different. „ It is not disrespectful, but it is certainly a „ very different model of trickle down.
KEITH KRUMWIEDE „So here we are: the thirty, „ thirty-five year anniversary of post-modernism. „ You could say there is a kind of retread going „ on, but there is another set of ambitions and „ operations here needs to be claimed.
ALBERT POPE „It is interesting but inconclusive.

all in support of 'anything' without trying to „ pinpoint what it is. However, it is interesting „ that you would have seats for something you „ cannot anticipate. I kind of wish that the im- „ provisational aspects of the scaffolding would „ have influenced more of the program.
MARK HUSSAR „The thing about the Thinkbelt „ and the Fun Palace idea is that you do not „ necessarily need to abide by the traditional „ program once you have identified that as your „ idea. There can be these unrelated moments „ where you choose to stack cubes, whereas on „ the other side there is another tectonic idea. „ Whether that all gets wrapped together with a „ uni-skin, which we've seen several times to- „ day, is less important because of the concept „ of the Fun Palace. It liberates you to treat „ the different programmatic areas in different „ ways, and maybe even represent some as being „ as fluid as the performance space itself.

I
CRYSTAL CRENELLATIONS
JASON BOND
Take the Yale courtyard and blow out one side. Grab Kahn's British Art Center and place it on top. Melting these two campus mainstays into one satisfies the unique demands of the polyvalent program while confronting Yale's rich architectural legacy. The courtyard type addresses issues of site: cap- turing and defining space. The British Art Center employs a field of cells, lit from above and penetrated by voids; here re-appropriated to provide a flex- ible space to house production facili- ties and studios. The fusing of these two types results in formal ambiguity employed alongside a caricatured use of material and detail to reflect on campus architectural tropes.

II
HALL FOR UNSETTLED ENCOUNTERS
ADAM TOMSKI
The agenda of the YCCA is to provide an environment of innovation for computer scientists and programmers who are dealing with technological issues in the arts. This includes the disciplines of architecture, fine arts, music, drama and any activity that can be categorized across those core groups. The program required space for public exhibition and performance as well as for private studio activity and production.
    My proposal creates a large public realm that is continuous with the street and is constituted by a one-hundred-by- sixty foot public room. This room is defined by a steel framework which sup- ports gantries, moveable partitions, and other mechanisms that make the space ultimately flexible. A unique aspect of the YCCA is the availability of Yale's impressive art collection to the sci- entists. My project seeks to foster an environment of freedom and security for them to interact with these artifacts.

KEITH KRUMWIEDE „Are you strongly committed to „ the opacity and solidity of this front piece „ versus the total transparency at the back? I „ think it is really important. The project has „ begun to exceed the graphic of the diagram „ that gave birth to it, and the strong distinc- „ tion between this thick bar at the front and „ this transparent--it is actually quite nice the „ way you have rendered it, but the continuity „ through there is too stark right now.
MARIO GOODEN „That contrast should be height- „ ened, because there are some very intelligent „ things that you are doing, things that you are „ doing very nicely, but they seem very timid at „ the moment. There is this heavy to light, dark „ to light--this stark, or what should be this „ stark difference between the two.
KEITH KRUMWIEDE „It is not about the going from „ the solid in the front to the transparent in the „ back across the middle, but actually looking „ for ways to intelligently let mass percolate „ through and maybe transparency percolate.

MICHELLE FORNABAI „I really love the way you have „ used the landscape and mirrored that in the „ theatre and lecture hall. In general, it has a „ very clear agenda. It has some very beautiful „ moves in section. It makes me vertiginous to „ think of the amount of activity, noise, lack „ of privacy that would be in this space--the „ lack of controlled environment. I am not sure „ to what extent this fosters real openness and „ productivity or just intense competition for „ these small private spaces. I think it is a „ very interesting problem that you have posed „ to yourself, because you are forced to use „ perhaps emergent materials and technologies „ to have this degree of openness with a real „ degree of potential for privacy and work to be „ accomplished here. It is really beautiful.
KEITH KRUMWIEDE „This is the architect's dream „ since 1858. Rudolph did it pretty well here „ because you are all the same kind of people „ working in this building and you are willing „ to accept a certain lack of privacy.

III
EXPERIENTIAL GRADATION
HILARY ZAIC
The project was conceived as a series of spatial gradients addressing site, program, and sequence. The strong urban edge fronting on Prospect Street dis- solves into the landscape towards the rear and Hillhouse Avenue. The program moves from public to private as one moves up into the building. Closed pro- gram for individual work, requiring a degree of privacy, is densely packed along Prospect Street, while the open and collaborative program flows out towards Hillhouse. The circulation is continually programmed, formally and informally, to allow for constant collaboration, planned or accidental. The skin structures and serves the building with systems, while screening between the exterior and the interior and its various bays.

LJILJANA BLAGOJEVIC

TOBIAS AMBROST   DAVID LEVEN   ANA MILJACKI   DIETRICH NEUMANN
CLAUDE CORMIER

504B

FOURTH SEMESTER STUDIO

STUDIO COORDINATOR
TIM LOVE

Lower Allston Landing, the 77-acre site for the core studio, is currently a freight rail yard and adjacent industrial properties recently acquired by Harvard University in the Allston neighborhood of Boston. The studio focused on an emerging trend in redevelopment: the creation of new transit-oriented mixed-use neighborhoods on post-industrial sites.

Harvard's original impetus for acquiring the parcels was to create a market-driven "research park" that would generate productive intellectual and economic synergies between Harvard's new science campus and spin-off life science and emerging technology companies.

Students were encouraged to begin their design speculation by understanding the regulatory, social, economic, and technical logic of the market-driven building types called for in the brief. Students were provided an illustrated handbook that qualified specific dimensional rules, circulation strategies, and conventional structural solutions for each of the types. Innovative new types were encouraged, but their "success" was measured against the multiple rationales of the types introduced at the beginning of the studio.

A second goal of the studio was to envision a multi-dimensional ground plane that made explicit the programmatic and physical relationship between buildings and the urban landscape. Moving away from the tendency to view post-industrial sites as a blank slate for development, students were challenged to address the spatial constraints, historical layers, evident and hidden ecological abuses, and the legal and political frameworks that characterized the site.

I

HAH! HARVARD-ALLSTON HUB
JULIANNE AUGUST-SCHMIDT
& JANG HYUNG LEE

For the first time in Allston's history, this site--a prominent location along the Charles River, will be open to the public, begging the question: If greater Boston has never claimed this site, what can it offer back now? This project asks Harvard University to reconsider its role not just as a private institution, but as a social instigator as well. Already a traffic hub for wider Boston, this project operates as an urban hub, networking commuter rail, highway, bicycle, pedestrian and vehicular transportation around outdoor venues, recreational parks, local market, retail, student housing and offices, and producing a relationship to the city through choreographed views and adjacent businesses along an elevated landscape that challenges the typical urban model of public on the ground and privatized above. Taking cues from urban street culture, this scheme proposes that the identification with place is claimed through scenographic discoveries and the impetus to explore.

II

URBAN GEOLOGY
HARVEY CHUNG & CRAIG WOEHRLE

This project grew out of a desire to invert the auto centric nature of the extant site by making use of proximity to the riverfront and mimicking geologic conditions with residential and commercial development. The irregularity of the site's southern lobe inherently rejected orthogonal organization in favor of a tessellated block grid. Each block consists of live/work units, offices, and retail and leisure facilities. The form of these developed from careful calibration of solar and water treatment goals. Vibrant commercial archipelagos are created by extruding skylight shafts at freeway interstices to feed zones beneath roadways.

III

URBAN SPACE OF PRODUCTION
AIDAN DOYLE & ADAM TOMSKI

Instead of simply ignoring the existing rail yard, we used it to enhance the site's value by reimagining CSX's flow of bulk and cargo freight as an asset to stimulate an industrial presence. We used the technology of the automated stacking crane and unmanned conveyer systems to turn the southern site into a twenty-four hour intermodal hub. The bottom layer is essentially an urban space designed around circulating and organizing objects. The upper layers contain R&D space while the eastern site is a gateway for international travellers, with a hotel, convention hall, commercial space, parking space, and student apartments. A skirt of playing fields connects the student living with the present recreational edge along the Charles river.

ANDREA KHAN „There is an interesting conversa-
„ tion that can happen here about different ways
„ of engaging people in urban space. My sense
„ of the project is that you are trying to estab-
„ lish a dispersed network of opportunities for
„ urban life and activity that are predicated
„ on a fundamental set of spec buildings that
„ have a set of rules for where they engage this
„ critical level, the linear civic center as you
„ call it. You are redefining the relationship
„ of the place as not having a center itself,
„ but forming a centralized location for the
„ larger arena and site as a whole. I think it
„ is a project about establishing a new way of
„ deploying an animated urban ground, which I
„ think may not be coming through as strongly as
„ you would like.
DIETRICH NEUMANN „I think, as you know from the
„ midterm, you have a convincing design for a
„ well functioning urban center, and the con-
„ nections are actually quite well thought out,
„ well proportioned, and have a certain density,
„ visual excitement and such. The ways you have
„ designed the passages under the buildings and
„ highways is quite thoughtful. Every project

„ has had to deal with this problem, but you have
„ really addressed it, which is a hard thing
„ to do. There was a lot of thought put into
„ not only function, but the urban questions
„ as well.
DAVID LEVEN „You are on to something that is
„ obviously provocative in your project. I think
„ there are certain fascinating features; the
„ plan is almost amazing in the way you use
„ the typology and give little clues that show
„ that you read the Think book. But the thing
„ that I think is really missing are some very
„ clear diagrams, more architectural than the
„ ones you have, that really show some reading
„ of the collaged site plan, what you are plug-
„ ging in to, and what you are connecting. The
„ project is about the critique of ground--you
„ don't care about the buildings above it--and
„ connection. You actually have all the connec-
„ tions to the neighborhood; they are all there.
„ You use ground in several distinct ways, but
„ I think by not leveraging the power of the
„ diagram, you have lost some of the power. I
„ think it requires a diagramming process that
„ really shows what it is all about.

ANA MILJACKI „Did you say why you decided to
„ break up the big moves? You do these unprec-
„ edented topographical manipulations and then
„ you differentiate it into these small suburban
„ scale units. I can't not see BIG in it; now
„ it is contemporary architecture. Why not just
„ keep the strong formal proposition?
DIETRICH NEUMAN „I think after the midreview,
„ we had similar comments. I had no idea if you
„ could carry it off and continue it and I think
„ this is an attempt at bringing scale into the
„ project by giving it a formal skin, which I
„ think is quite exciting. It is not so much a
„ collection of small pieces anymore. I think
„ it speaks to the scale, and there are so many
„ exciting things going on, I'm really happy
„ with the way it looks, too. The iceberg thing
„ is really promising. I'm really impressed by
„ how far you've taken this from the midterm.
TIM LOVE „The granulated scheme is an exten-

„ sion of how one sees the city. It becomes
„ a habitat or artificial village typology. It is a
„ question of scale and intent as much as au-
„ thorship, too.
CLAUDE CORMIER „You have a diagram in which
„ you describe how you want the energy from the
„ ground level to continue up through the other
„ units, but you don't see that in the project.
„ There is no differentiation between the ground
„ floor and the top floor units. It is not ex-
„ pressed, but it seems like it should be.
TOBIAS AMBROST „I think it is quite interesting
„ to blur architecture, infrastructure, land-
„ scape, street, et cetera. As a strategy, it is
„ very challenging and we haven't seen much of
„ it in other projects. That is the difference
„ between this project and the others. Here, you
„ have challenged these typologies and invented
„ a new one. You are getting excited by all the
„ possibilities! That is quite successful.

ANA MILJACKI „I agree that this was a great pre-
„ sentation and the kind of stuff that is on the
„ wall--the way you took us through it and even
„ the humor--was really fresh. I'm with you; I
„ want to be awake enough to talk about it. I
„ know that, of course, the distinction between
„ the site and the rail becomes problematic.
„ You are interested in the railroad because it
„ gives you all the stuff, but by the time you are
„ done working through it, woops, you haven't
„ looked at the site with the same rigor. The
„ rest of the site requires us to supply a lot of
„ the story.
DIETRICH NEUMANN „I have a few concerns. Obvi-
„ ously this whole Cedric Price machine you've
„ made here for the transport and exchange of
„ goods is fantastic and a great urban piece,
„ but as someone else mentioned, the fact that
„ you've invented your own program--I don't know
„ where that comes from, it is very unusual, it

„ will never happen. In creating your own prob-
„ lems, you are the architect and the client; you
„ run into this strange form of cancer where you
„ keep inventing to fill space. It takes away the
„ restrictions that lead to really good design
„ in the end.
ANA MILJACKI „I agree that you don't have enough
„ restrictions, but I actually think you don't
„ have enough program. When the market was at
„ its peak, architects could produce unsolicited
„ projects and show people what could be imag-
„ ined on a site. I think that is legitimate and
„ within our realm as architects.
TIM LOVE „It happens all the time. If a city
„ comes to an architect they have some ideas
„ about what they want or that they need a
„ certain amount of residential space. That is
„ relatively fixed, but when it comes down to the
„ detail level a lot of the program is really up
„ to the architects.

JULIANNE AUGUST-SCHMIDT   HARVEY CHUNG   AIDAN DOYLE
JANG HYUNG LEE   CRAIG WOEHRLE   ADAM TOMSKI

I

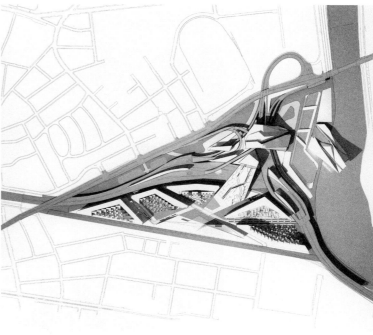

II

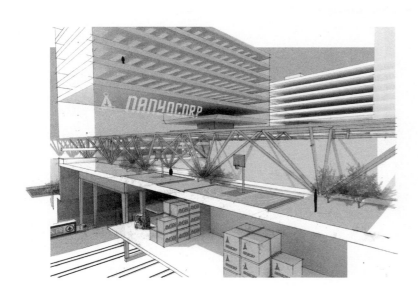

III

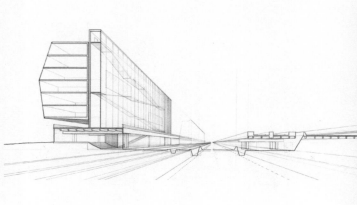

I

II

TOBIAS AMBROST   CLAUDE CORMIER   ANA MILJACKI   ED MITCHELL

CLAUDE CORMIER „What I like about this is that „ it achieves a beautiful balance between the „ public and the private. You are able to go „ from completely open and public, to very, very „ private. It makes sense. And I think the north „ side can certainly work with the same level of „ rationality as the south side; maybe it could „ be a bit more open or exploded. Sort of like „ Habitat '67 cut open and turned on its side.
ANA MILJACKI „I think its intuition, not rational „ or systematic. I cannot account for the moves „ by looking at a system. I think it is a work of „ intuition. But that is okay too!
TIM LOVE „There is a level of specificity to „ each building that makes it seems more like a „ single object though.
ANA MILJACKI „I'm interested in the change „ between the two models; what's up with the „ gradient? Is it contextual?
TIM LOVE „Yeah, it is contextual. I have a rule „ in my section, which is: never bring old „ models to reviews!
{Laughter}
CLAUDE CORMIER „You are trying to shape space by „ using oddly shaped buildings, which is actu-„ ally kind of successful. It makes me think of „ James Sterling. And I think you might really „ be onto something. I also think the creation „ of little hotspots of activity, almost like „ a High Street in English planning, is really „ interesting. I'd love to see a ground plan so „ we could see the landscape.
TIM LOVE „I want to come back to the robust „ boxes versus the figure thing. If the project „ had become that because of the choice of hand „ drawings, then the choice of hand drawing „ doesn't make sense. You only found these forms „ by hand drawing. The choice of representa-„ tional technique and where you ended up in the „ project are the same things.

ALAN PLATTUS „Are you averse to building „ anything on top of the mall complex? It is „ right on the water but it really doesn't take „ advantage of it.
ANDREEA COJOCARU „Well, we have the pier that „ elongates and becomes activated, but yes, we „ could have built a tower on top of the mall, „ but we wanted to move away from that; we didn't „ want to fetishize the mall by making it too „ much of an object.
ALAN PLATTUS „Ok, you've told us about your „ ground investigation, the storm water in-„ vestigation and such, but the piece of this „ discourse that hasn't made it through yet is: „ what is this as an urban place? Who is here? „ What are they doing? There are people here, „ not just water. We know how a mall works, „ we might like it or not, but we know how it „ works. But this other realm, which I find very „ tantalizing--I just don't know what it is.
ED MITCHELL „I like a lot of things about this „ project. I really like the diagrams. But it „ is too bad you guys could not go further with „ your water analysis--how the water works on „ the façades of the buildings, or how the pipes „ are articulated. The mall aside, this scheme „ is really interesting. There is a really clear „ idea of how the composition comes about from „ a detailed systems analysis. I just wish you „ could have taken it even farther.
ALAN PLATTUS „I agree, I think you guys should „ focus on the things that you invented and not „ get distracted by things like malls, because „ the project is really interesting.
ED MITCHELL „There is a real compositional thing „ here, but you are very clear about how that „ comes about through your analysis of the water „ systems, how they move together and relate. „ I think you just need to push it to the next „ level of detail and speculation. Otherwise „ what you get after all that work isn't all „ that appealing.

I
INFRASTRUCTURAL LAMINATION
JOEL BURKE & KATE THATCHER
Faced with the strong formal and functional limitations of a highway interchange the project created a lamination that organized the various speeds of traffic on the site, facilitating vehicular, mass-transit and pedestrian circulation. A continuous elevated commercial plinth provided for pedestrian access to the architecture as well as addressing both the infrastructural lamination and the public open space. The architecture took full advantage of the open space created by the lamination and began to define more localized conditions within the open public park. We organized a light rail system to and from Harvard and by utilizing a train station made the site a new destination for commuters.

II
COMMERCIAL LANDSCAPE
ANDREEA COJOCARU & ANJA TUROWSKI
In attacking the problems posed by site and program requirements, we attempted to synthesize three distinct issues--neighborhood context, water management, and phasing--into one coherent strategy that could be employed throughout the entire site while addressing internal and context specific conditions. While small scale residential lots and the train station connect to the existing urban fabric, the water front is transformed into a commercial landscape including a mall and pier, and the main part of the project is divided into a series of artificial watersheds that are organized around Research & Development nodes. In later phases the individual watershed nodes are integrated with each other as they are constructed and thereby connected to the central wetlands. Formally, these nodes seek to reinterpret and relate to the larger institutional context of Harvard/Allston by providing local specificity and connecting the larger context and the landscape with elevated walkways.

JOEL BURKE
KATE THATCHER

ANDREEA COJOCARU
ANJA TUROWSKI

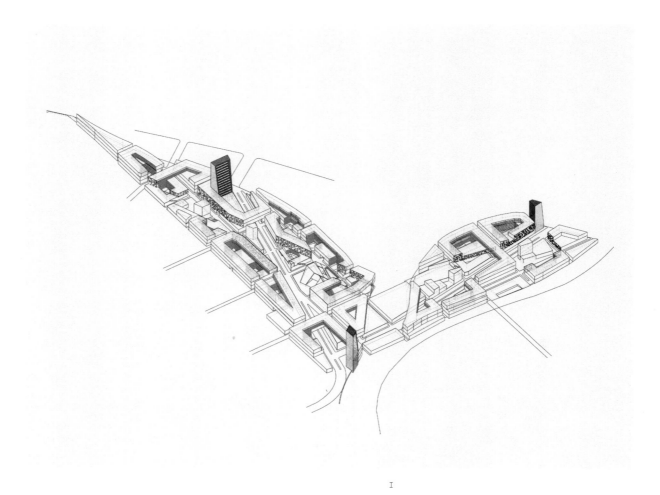

I

I
GRAFTING ALLSTON
ANNE-MARIE ARMSTRONG & ANDREW ASHEY
The proposal 'grafts' prevalent urban typologies representative of the context surrounding the site. It takes as its primary cues the courtyard 'microblock' of Harvard University to the north, the urban strip 'block' expansion of Boston University to the south, and most notably Interstate 90 which dominates the site and connects it to the greater Boston area and extended suburban 'superblock' landscape. At the building scale, this layered sectional diagram is pierced by landscaped 'pits' which allows for light, air and internal circulation. An open space network intensifies connections across the site through the dialectical and cross-axial insertion of the car-oriented 'miracle mile' on the street level and an elevated 'culture mile'--an undulating pedestrian landscape that spans the site and unifies key public projects.

TIM LOVE „ I think this is a very sensible and sen-
„ sitive urban proposition. One thing, just as a
„ very pedagogical thing: you've almost over done
„ it, you've almost done too much. For example,
„ you have this big tower, which is fine, this
„ tower can be like this or it doesn't have to be,
„ but then you make almost a little child of it.
„ This needed to be much more abstract, this un-
„ dulating cultural mile. It is a very fine scheme.
BARBARA LITTENBERG „ There are very brilliant
„ urban moves here. I think you're a little too
„ clever by half, that's all. And there are maybe
„ one too many layers, which I think is getting
„ to the point you're making, which is that these
„ bridging elements that pertain to the larger
„ infrastructure actually inhibit the develop-
„ ment of the street. I see a series of blocks
„ surrounding--essentially this is like the in-
„ frastructure of Broadway, you have this bowtie
„ space in here, which I think is potentially
„ great. The simple move of pulling back, in
„ this linear park, that goes into an on-grade
„ piece of ground, allowing those little houses
„ essentially to stand up to this diagonal ge-

„ ometry is great. And whether or not this ought
„ to be up in the air, you should be able to see
„ that--I would almost make it a little dumber,
„ you know.
TIM LOVE „ That's the issue. Finally, what's
„ emerged and what we do with that pedagogically
„ in this studio and other urbanism studios? I
„ suppose if you had written a script for this,
„ this would be an illustration of one possible
„ outcome, this would be one way to do it, right?
„ And then you would have gotten to this point
„ by your own rules. It's a question of whether a
„ single author for that with all of the twitches
„ and things is actually okay after all. So you
„ can get away with a single authorship because
„ the composition is so complex.
ANA MILJACKI „ I love it, I just cannot see it
„ as many other things. Maybe that's what you
„ needed to do, actually see it as a series of
„ variations on a theme, and see to what extent
„ you can actually take this being a different
„ façade even if you are the author of those
„ differences. I actually think--it's hard for
„ you, you want to design this.

ANNE-MARIE ARMSTRONG
ANDREW ASHEY

I

II

PE'ERA GOLDMAN „I don't mind that you haven't „ shown us the relationship between your ty- „ pologies and Boston because I what is really „ strong is the way in which you focused on „ how open and green space can be used as a „ foil against large buildings. That's really „ different from a lot of the projects we've seen „ today. It is a really strong conceptual agenda „ to focus on three scales of green and use them „ to create or deform these typologies you were „ given at the beginning.

DAVID LEVEN „This civic infrastructural space „ that you set up in the very beginning of your „ presentation with this huge move--you embed „ the train station there, that little block of „ wood, and you reference the Kendall Square „ idea of creating a neighborhood around the „ civic space, but this is unclaimed to the hilt; „ even the large scale spaces are unclaimed. And „ although you claim to have cracked the block, „ you may have just put a hole in the street, at „ the expense of this potentially amazing space „ where you bundled the infrastructures--a huge

„ move that ends up in a courtyard. I commend „ you for everything you've done, but that piece „ needs to be looked at in more depth.

RICK COOK „I agree. I don't know where the idea „ that this is Boston fabric came from; it is „ European fabric. Back Bay, Beacon Hill, and „ Southend--it is not this typology; the typology „ is an open square with a surrounding street. „ This project isn't about Boston typology.

ANDREA KAHN „It is important to note that you „ could have more closely integrated the larger „ urban moves with your commitment to really „ study the experience of the place on the „ ground. These aren't mutually exclusive. A „ collection of urban spaces does not necessar- „ ily make a network of open space. This project „ has an ambition to think about the network „ of open urban space at different scales, and „ so you got a little lost by focusing on one „ scale. That said, the project is impressively „ complete and does represent how much atten- „ tion you did pay to the details and is a lovely „ thing to see.

I
URBAN NETWORKS
TALLEY BURNS & REBECCA GARNETT
Our proposal for Lower Allston seeks to reconnect the isolated site to Boston by creating a series of open space networks that operate at three scales: the city, the community, and the block. We adjusted and deployed the currently underutilized Boston block courtyard typology along with additional residential, live/work and R&D courtyard typologies to create three reciprocal systems. The larger, composed of civic and educational programs, serves to link Allston to the Emerald Necklace and the active waterfront. Interior block spaces and strategic pass-throughs form networks of recreational and community based program that specifically benefit the Allston community and foster a new sense of place in a currently underserved neighborhood.

PE'ERA GOLDMAN „The location of the train sta- „ tion adjacent to the river is interesting. The „ redevelopment of the river could mean that „ in a successful station you could come as a „ business person and leave as a person going to „ the beach! It's a fantastic transformation.

ALAN PLATTUS „Yeah, into the phone booth…
{Laughter}

KEN GREENBERG „I love the fact you called it the „ 'Multi-Modal Transportation Hub.' That is how „ you plan for the future. And celebrating the „ highway as-is is really interesting as well-- „ the highway gets sucked up within the project. „ It's interesting how you linked the T, railroad „ station, water connection, and turnpike, a „ huge barrier, which you made into a bridge „ building and celebrated. The connection to „ the water might override as a conceptual study „ at this scale. It's really the fact that you „ view the water as a major transportation link, „ and I think it's great to use the waterfront as „ a way to connect neighborhoods.

ALAN PLATTUS „My concern is that this is a kind „ of miniature urbanism, and I don't mean this „ as a 'gotcha,' but you have a kind of mini- „ downtown and a train station, and the little „ research alley, et cetera. At a certain level „ it is very persuasive because I think it is „ built around a really smart set of connec- „ tions. But I think it breaks down downtown, „ where there is the illusion of these mini „ buildings, whereas each of these blocks is „ about the size of eight Boston row houses. The „ juxtaposition could be beautiful if you get it „ just right, but there isn't enough information „ at this point.

KEN GREENBERG „What I like about this is the „ loose and simple block typologies, each of „ which seems suited to its position in the plan. „ I think the big moves, especially on the wa- „ terfront, are very persuasive. There are a lot „ of funny little things and you're sort of sug- „ gesting that there is a lot of different archi- „ tecture by a lot of different people over time.

II
PRODUCTIVE TENSIONS
AND POLITICS OF SPACE
KURT EVANS & ALEJANDRO DE MESA
In asking the nature of the interchange, one provokes its dual role. As a connector, the interchange is a cog in the federal highway system, reaching as far as the western United States. As a divider, it physically severs Commonwealth Avenue from the proposed Harvard-Allston Plan to the north. This proposal, as a broader urban strategy, utilizes the operands of connection and division to produce a cohesive open space network at a myriad of scales. By amplifying existing fault lines between certain site constituencies, the expanded space is minimally programmed, providing for the distinct politics of place. The termini of these axes become the libraries, transit hubs, and riverside plateaus of the new Allston--zones of cosmopolitanism amid the landscape of interchange.

I

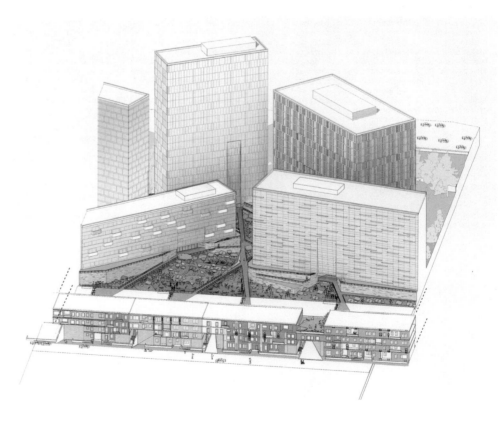

II

ANA MILJACKI „The only place where I am really uncomfortable is where there is that first moment of Voronoi for no particular reason. Generally we use it to find equidistant situations, so there needs to be some kind of motivation. That is not what you want from it; you just want to criss-cross the site without using a grid. Adjust it to the streets so it actually starts working for you, but that initial move is completely random.

BARBARA LITTENBERG „I love it. My only question is how you have determined the relative street layout. This is a real urban idea that shakes things up. But the layout of streets is not insignificant; some blocks might be bigger than others, certain places might need to be highlighted. You should agonize quite a lot about why they are the way they are.

ANA MILJACKI „The first move is the weakest move. I'm going after it because if you think it makes perfect sense I want to problematize it. If you had to give this to someone as a strategy that one point will not translate. It is either the thing you made or it is not. Or, you distill it to something that is more strategic; it is about distance, grid dissolution, et cetera. For me, it is helpful to think of this in terms of the agencies that would actually pull this kind of thing off; how could you hire someone to build this?

PEGGY DEAMER „Did you do the street layout because you wanted the blocks like that, or did you design blocks like that to get the street layout you wanted? I ask because the Voronoi doesn't tell us any judgment about it. Then the issue of local character could be brought in, not just mapping something that has a size of an office building, yielding a more complex relationship between the architectural conditions. How is it that you build up something that is more articulate that this?

ANA MILJACKI „I think where you are stuck--and there are many great things about this scheme--it is fun to look at and I want to go on the ride with you, but the thing you need to look at when you take on this rhetoric of discovery--it becomes very problematic. It works when you are talking to a developer who doesn't participate in the academic project or expect intelligent explanations. This linearity of that narrative isn't something you should embrace so quickly, as I think you did. You were trying to give it to us linearly, as if first you did this, then this, and so on. The project is smarter than that.

PEGGY DEAMER „It would be unfair for me not to say that I actually hate the spaces that this project yields. So everyone is trying to come up with reasons why they love it, but I don't like it. So I'm having a hard time finding all the rationales for why we should justify nonlinear thinking that looks like linear thinking because we all want to get here; I don't want to get here.

I
DEVELOPER MADE IN AMERICA
BRETT APPEL, JASON BOND
& YIJIE DANG
Is it possible to make great urban space today out of the large scale buildings preferred by developers? What is the minimum amount of control necessary to allow the market to produce vital places? In addressing these questions we created an urbanism of networked open space that choreographs the market-driven build out of the urban plan into an aggregate of community-forming blocks. Each community is inflected by a set of design guidelines that address issues of storm water, identity and place-making. A hybrid garage and student housing tower punctuates these communities and activates the remaining build out.

ED MITCHELL „There is a lot of merit in this project. However, like many projects, each logic is its own logic and the synthetic moments aren't all that convincingly articulated. So even building to building--you guys know this--they seem to react to each other, but if you test the logic it isn't the optimal logic of how things relate to each other. The next step in the process is to figure out how one system effects, in a positive way, the other systems. Your pathways are only pathways, all I can do is to move from point A to B.

ALAN PLATTUS „There is a logic of autonomy here, though. The world of the twentieth century super block allowed the freeing of the ground plane according to strict criteria. The buildings were then arranged according to views, sun, wind, et cetera. There was a functional and climatological logic to it. And yes, they were autonomous, but they were made autonomous precisely so they could obey that rational logic. You guys, on the other hand, had an agenda to ensure the autonomy of your blocks for fundamentally compositional reasons, and that what worries me. When I see a parking garage, for example, treated compositionally in exactly the same way as a residential building which is the same as a R&D building, all sort of dispersed on the ground plane, getting close to the perimeter but not touching, getting close to each other and not touching--and then to emphasize the autonomy, the path is precisely the rhetorical device you use like a moat, as you said, in case we missed the point. There is a foreground, a middle ground and a background. It is compositional.

ED MITCHELL „It is all about view. Developers think this way too. The use of the space is always autonomous, as if view is an idea of autonomy.

STELLA BETTS „What has happened is that the idea of autonomy has overridden everything else; all other space just becomes interstitial and fragmented.

II
LOWER ALLSTON LANDING
JEROME HAFERD, RACHEL HSU
& AUDE HELENE JOMINI
This project proposes the creation of a non-affiliated campus on the Lower Allston Landing site as a means of generating collaboration and mediation between Harvard and Boston universities. The street-front logic of the Boston University campus is explored through the development of a linear prototype complete with phasing, programmatic, and façade logics. This 'front' is juxtaposed with an inner campus that contains larger office and residential buildings. These "big buildings" are tied together programmatically to create an interconnected whole through the manipulation of the ground plane. Each of the large interior buildings has a unique street address, as well as a lobby that is embedded into the street liner. Thus, a campus is formed by these two components and their spatial and programmatic dialogue.

BRETT APPEL
JASON BOND
YIJIE DANG

JEROME HAFERD
RACHEL HSU
AUDE HELENE JOMINI

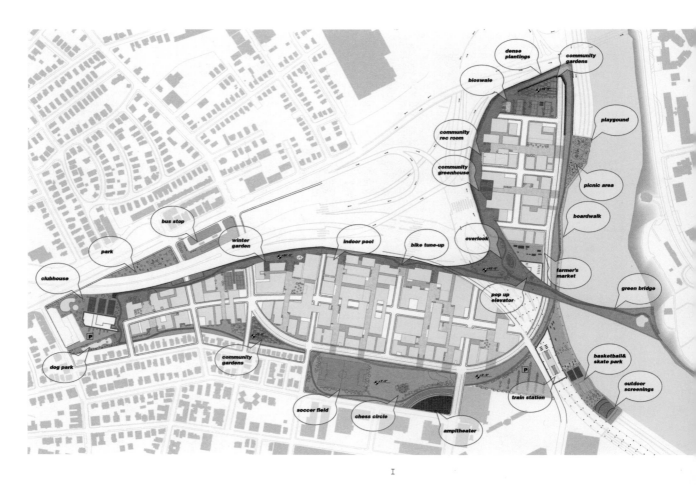

dense plantings

community gardens

bioswale

playgound

community rec room

picnic area

community greenhouse

boardwalk

bus stop

park

winter garden

indoor pool

bike tune-up

overlook

clubhouse

farmer's market

green bridge

pop up elevator

dog park

community gardens

basketball& skate park

soccer field

chess circle

train station

outdoor screenings

ampitheater

I

II

BEN PELL

ED MITCHELL

ED MITCHELL „How do you characterize the initial „ response to the green belt? I mean I think the „ green belt is interesting but it is not clear „ once that's established what the secondary ar- „ chitectural intentions are. What's the design „ datum? Why is gradient one, and why is that „ continuous green space a thematic strategy „ in your project? To be quite blunt, I would „ expect more of the relationship to that green „ space. It is a question of the gradient; how „ does a gradient produce values? I think the „ green scheme is really smart, how it blocks „ certain things and creates a new development „ opportunity at a bigger, bolder scale. It is „ a big urban proposition--these buildings down „ here are huge, and the rest of the stuff is so „ fragmented.

ROBERT A.M. STERN „The only times they come „ close to coming to grips with giving a char- „ acter to their diagrammatic intentions are in „ the perspectives with the surface shacks. The „ buildings look like they are two stories tall. „ The computer doesn't tell you how to scale „ things or how to make things, you have to draw „ it using your hands and eyes. Draw it up!

ALAN PLATTUS „I think it needs more contrast. „ Ed mentioned the gradient; I think it is the „ evenness of things. Yes, things are bigger by „ the time they reach the highway, but you al- „ most don't appreciate that. Given the strength „ of your armature, I'd like to see episodes of „ radically different typology and density that „ speak to the difference between various parts. „ The apparent similarity between the world by „ the river and the world by the highway, which „ everyone has struggled with, is the problem. At „ some level they are un-connectable. It seems „ that this difference is what is lacking. The „ block structure is very sensible, but you've „ overridden the strength of the grid.

I
GREENBELT
HELEN BROWN & YU WANG

The proposal approaches the project primarily through a "greenbelt" open-space strategy, which operates in four primary ways: as a means of introversion, mediation, extroversion, and infrastructure. The greenbelt unifies the three disparate parcels of the site, connects the site to its adjacent neighborhoods, and mitigates the presence of the highway. As the loop changes in elevation and works its way around the site, it provides numerous opportunities for outdoor programming that in turn inspire adjacent development.

Solidifying basic infrastructure and open space on the site sets the stage for development within. Vehicular traffic remains on the ground plane while pedestrian traffic moves above. As the ramped pedestrian passages move through the site, the entry level of adjacent buildings increases in elevation. Larger buildings occupy the center; smaller buildings populate the edge to better negotiate the varied condition of the belt. The ramps therefore provide a datum for 'light' and 'dark' programs that traverse the site.

II
URBAN INTERSTICES
CALEB LINVILLE & ELIJAH PORTER

In the proposed scheme, three "campuses" occupy the site. The first, a series of bio-tech R&D super-blocks contain large volumes of perpetually flexible, easily serviced lab space. The second, a large, dense blocks of student housing, consolidates Boston University's student housing, relieving housing pressure on the surrounding low rise neighborhood of Brookline. Another housing group at the river's edge provides apartments for both Harvard and B.U. graduate students. Wide corridors of urban connective tissue bound these blocks, linking residential neighborhoods to the river and tying the new corporate and university campuses into the existing urban fabric of Brookline. The connective tissue consists of streets, sidewalks and planted areas. Packed along its length are programmatic insertions at multiple scales ranging from market stands to outdoor movie theaters to playing fields. The open space of the corridors relieve pressure from the density of the campuses while the set program pieces foster interaction between the two populations creating moments of public theater. Furthering this emphasis on interaction, University amenities demolished in the redevelopment of the site--lecture halls and athletic facilities--reappear as insertions into the R&D blocks, becoming negotiated space for use by both the university and the corporate tenants.

HELEN BROWN
YU WANG

CALEB LINVILLE
ELIJAH PORTER

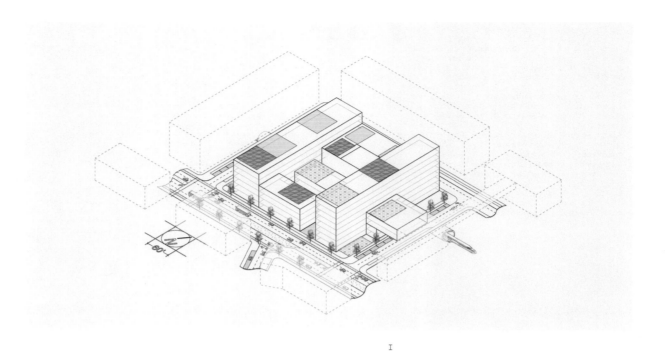

I

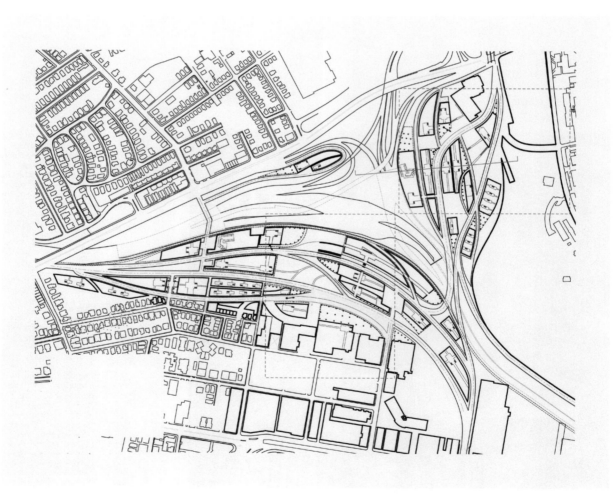

II

ED MITCHELL „I like a lot of the stuff that I see; „ it's really smart, from the midterm. But the „ urban gesture was good and then the pixeliza-„ tion destroyed it. When I look at it carefully, „ at first glance it seems like it works, and „ then a lot of the streets that seem connected „ have pretty major barriers in them, which is „ indicative of not very great urbanity if it's „ a city of blocked streets. There are a lot of „ little pieces and enclaves. I suspect--this „ thing, which is rendered like it's a boulevard „ dead ends over here and this street that is „ a highway traps these streets up here, which „ isolates this piece, isolates this piece, and „ then makes this part its own thing. So given „ that, what I would like to see is what you've „ done to establish what the long connections in „ the city are that this thing is a part of, and „ look at that again, because I think that would „ reestablish whether these actually do operate „ as streets, or they operate as nodal points. „ Therefore, the plexiglas stuff comes from the „ kind of analysis I don't like, which creates „ certain positions, and so on. But I don't think „ you'd call those centers of any kind, I think „ they'd just be buildings.

TIM LOVE „One place where you recover territory „ that was lost before is the part that faces „ the Charles River, because working at that „ interchange…

ED MITCHELL „That's very convincing.

TIM LOVE „Which is fairly realistic.

ALAN PLATTUS „I'm a little disappointed that „ you didn't get a chance to render some version „ of the plan, because I think it would have „ supplemented and maybe helped this issue of „ having to call out the hinges by differentiat-„ ing the building mass--rather, by saying that „ what they create is space. The other spaces „ you create are largely courtyards, these are „ the spaces where they externalize to the „ community. And so what I'd prefer to focus „ on rather than some differentiated building „ material would be the role that those spaces „ play. You're starting to get at it in the little „ partial plans, but you see it in the overall „ context better.

TIM LOVE „Those pieces drop down with their own „ morphological characteristics. But I do agree „ with Ed that they became too differentiated as „ monuments in the fabric, and it wasn't logical „ in the overall plan in a way. It's more about „ relocation of logic, less in terms of prospect, „ view, or an important space. That's a differ-„ ent qualification. The only one that does both „ are the towers that frame the Harvard view.

RICK COOK „I want to commend you on your „ way of working through issues logically. I „ appreciate that one of the first images that „ you show is trying to understand the scale „ of Back Bay, Beacon Hill, North End--in many „ ways it addresses the comments that we just „ had about how long it takes for real cit-„ ies to develop and the scale at which they „ develop. When I first saw your project I jumped „ to a conclusion that it was about form-making „ inspired by highways and I questioned that as „ a starting point, even though it has a fluidity „ and it is kind of sexy and interesting. But „ I appreciated that you talked about streets „ having scales and speeds--a fast street and „ a boulevard and the way this works. Because „ it is true, all great cities have streets that „ you pass through at a certain speed or that „ you walk very slowly. And I appreciated that „ you thought about textures of wall types and „ how deep walls are. This is a really inter-„ esting example, right here where we are, of „ how walls work, the depth of walls, and how „ people feel next to them--what Louis Kahn did „ versus what Paul Rudolph did versus what the „ historical colleges are. But I found that to „ be lacking. This idea of skin became pasted „ on. And I wanted to hear you guys talk about „ green roofs. If you have not seen this month's „ National Geographic there is a whole piece on „ green roofs. We happen to be in it. It is not „ just, 'Hey, this is cool.' It is a place where „ nature is so much richer.

ALAN PLATTUS „I can't resist--architects making „ National Geographic along with the other „ threatened species.

{Laughter}

RICK COOK „And one other thing. You should redo „ these graphics on your sections. Your project „ is much richer and more interesting than the „ graphics of these horizontal floor plates.

ALAN PLATTUS „You did the section to try to „ get spaces, and you wished--wished--that the „ buildings would be neutral. But of course as „ soon as you poché all the cross-floors they „ are anything but. You guys really went for it „ in your presentation. There is nothing that „ is hidden in this scheme. And I think laying „ it all out like that--if you were making this „ presentation to a client, you would take down „ about fifty percent of the drawings because „ they are not ready to see them.

4TH FLOOR

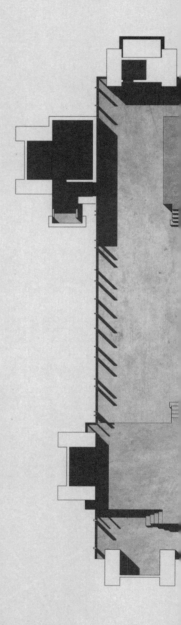

Faculty	Guest Jurors	Students
CHARLES ATWOOD	CONSTANCE ADAMS	ANGEL BEALE
THOMAS AUER	LUCIA ALLAIS	BRYAN BERKAS
DIANA BALMORI	AMALE ANDRAOS	REBECCA BEYER
THOMAS BEEBY	SUNIL BALD	NATHAN BRIGHT
CHRISTINA CHU	DIANA BALMORI	NICHOLAS CARUSO
KATHERINE CLARKE	ED BASS	DEXTER CIPRIAN
DARIN COOK	THOMAS BEEBY	TERRENCE CHEW
BROOK DENISON	BERRY BERGDOLL	CHENG HUI CHUA
PETER EISENMAN	LJILJANA BLAGOJEVIC	ROBERT A. COLE
JOSH EMIG	KENT BLOOMER	LUCAS TURNER COHEN
LIZA FIOR	MICHAEL BLUM	CODY DAVIS
KONRAD GRASER	DAVID BONDERMAN	SEHER ERDOGAN
RACHEL GRUZEN	LARRY BOOTH	IBEN ANDREA FALCONER
ANDREI HARWELL	DEBORAH BURKE	MARK GAUSEPOHL
KATE JOHN-ALDER	ROBERT CAMBELL	NICHOLAS GILLILAND
SANGMOK KIM	VISHAAN CHAKRABARTI	MWANGI GATHINJI
GEORGE KNIGHT	HENRYY COBB	REUBEN HERZL
FRED KOETTER	MARTIN COX	ELIZA HIGGINS
KEITH KRUMWIEDE	KEVIN DALY	ISAIAH KING
FRANCISCO MANGADO	CYNTHIA DAVIDSON	ERIC KRANCEVIC
ED MITCHELL	PEGGY DEAMER	PARSA KHALILI
TIMOTHY NEWTON	BROOK DENISON	JASON KIM
JOHN PATKAU	ANNA DYSON	LOUISE LEVI
EEVA-LIISA PELKONEN	KELLER EASTERLING	PATRICK LUN
DEMETRI PORPHYRIOS	PETER EISENMAN	ALEX MAYMIND
JOEL SANDERS	MERRILL ELAM	FELICIA MARTIN
DAVID SCHWARZ	KAREN FAIRBANKS	PATRICK MCGOWAN
MASSIMO SCOLARI	LUIS FERNÁNDEZ-GALIANO	MARIANNA MELLO
WILLIAM SHARPLES	KENNETH FRAMPTON	LAUREN MISHKIND
MICHAEL WANG	RICHARD FIELDS	KRISTIN MUELLER
	KURT FORSTER	MIEKO OKAMOTO
	ROBERT FREY	OLGA PANTELIDOU
	DOUGLAS GAUTHIER	CYRUS PATTELL
	KARSTEN HARRIES	MIRIAM PETERSON
	STEVEN HARRIS	YIJUAN QIAN
	DOLORES HAYDEN	CARLOS FELIX
	DAVID HAYS	RASPALL-GALLI
	BRIAN HEALY	MATT ROMAN
	PATRICK HICKOX	DAVID SADIGHIAN
	DENISE HOFFMAN-BRANDT	SAIFULLAH SAMI
	CARLOS JIMÉNEZ	ZAK SNIDER
	SERGIO KIERNAN	TRISHA SNYDER
	JEFFREY KIPNIS	CHRIS STARKEY
	DIANA KLEINER	TOM TANG
	GEORGE KNIGHT	OZLEM CAGLAR TOMBUS
	LEON KRIER	ANDREA VITTADINI
	KEITH KRUMWIEDE	EMILY ARDEN WELLS
	ARIANE LOURIE HARRISON	DANIEL YODER
	TIM LOVE	JULIANNA VON ZUMBUSCH
	BARBARA LITTENBERG	
	GREG LYNN	
	IAN LOMAS	
	FRANK LUPO	
	FRANCISCO MANGADO	
	SELINA MASON	
	ANURADHA MATHUR	
	GREG MILLER	
	ED MITCHELL	
	ROWAN MOORE	
	FERNANDO MUT OLTRA	
	DAVID NILAND	
	DIETRICH NEUMANN	
	JUAN MIGUEL OCHOTORRENATO	
	ALAN ORGANSCHI	
	KEVIN OWINS	
	JOHN PATKAU	
	GREGG PASQUARELLI	
	CESAR PELLI	
	STEVEN PETERSON	
	ALAN PLATTUS	
	ALBERT POPE	
	ALEXANDER PURVES	
	JAQUELIN ROBERTSON	
	INGEBORG ROCKER	
	MARK ROWEN	
	JOSHUA ROWLEY	
	ELIHU RUBIN	
	CAROL RUIZ	
	JOEL SANDERS	
	MASSIMO SCOLARI	
	CHRIS SHARPLES	
	WILLIAM SHARPLES	
	MARTY STEIN	
	SARA STEVENS	
	STANLEY TIGERMAN	
	ANTHONY VIDLER	
	CHARLES WALDHEIM	
	MARK WAMBLE	
	MARION WEISS	
	SARAH WHITING	
	DAN WOOD	
	FIKRET YEGUL	

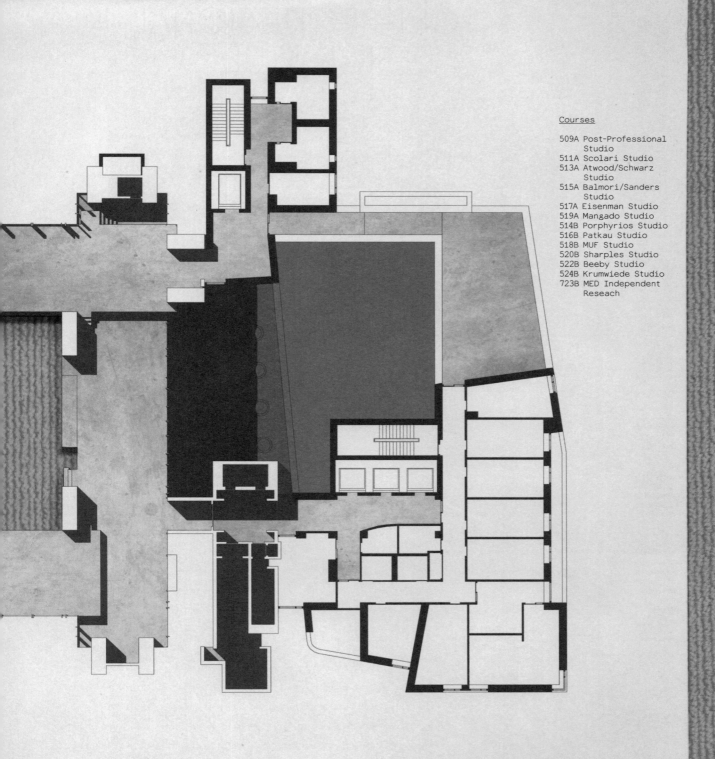

Courses

509A Post-Professional
     Studio
511A Scolari Studio
513A Atwood/Schwarz
     Studio
515A Balmori/Sanders
     Studio
517A Eisenman Studio
519A Mangado Studio
514B Porphyrios Studio
516B Patkau Studio
518B MUF Studio
520B Sharples Studio
522B Beeby Studio
524B Krumwiede Studio
723B MED Independent
     Reseach

FRED KOETTER   ED MITCHELL

ROBERT CAMBELL   DOUGLAS GAUTHIER   PATRICK HICKOX   DAVID NILAND
KAREN FAIRBANKS   BRIAN HEALY   FRANK LUPO   MARK WAMBLE

509A

POST-PROFESSIONAL
DESIGN STUDIO

Over the past several years the post professional studio has explored the problem of 'Temporal Urbanism.' The term, "Temporal Urbanism," seems to imply a neutral architecture sufficiently open to any given situation to provide a suitable container for content. While the standardized solution may seem to be the most flexible, much of the banality of our contemporary built environment is a product of this concept. The infinitely flexible is not necessarily a desirable agenda for architecture; neutrality is the undesirable outcome of modernism's universal aspirations.

Recently the State Treasurer of Massachusetts called for cities to cut costs for their school building programs. Taking the example of Florida and the southwest, the Treasurer requested that prototypes be developed in order to better track costs and speed up construction time. Local communities have questioned whether the difficult sites of New England are conducive to this kind of investigation. One can also assume that pre-fabrication and prototyping a community building would meet with resistance in neighborhoods that value the identity and unique programmatic aspirations of their public schools.

We also realize that a school's pedagogic program changes over the lifespan of any building. We examine and analyze examples of school projects within the historic canon that physically embody the ideologic values of various educational paradigms and evaluate the potentials and limitations of program driving the architectural solution. The sites for the project are in downtown Boston and we test preliminary prototypes against three sites and two programs to explore the potential for this methodology and to test the efficacy and ideology of prefabrication in architectural and urban form making. A flexible or mutable prototype that addresses the specificity of site but also the development and variability of program challenges the precept that form necessarily follows function.

The studio course is partially coordinated with the course in digital representation and fabrication required for incoming post-professionals. Exercises in that course help to inform the projects. Students work individually but research and analysis in the beginning of the semester is done in teams.

I
FRACTURES--SCHOOL FOR
THE PERFORMING ARTS IN BOSTON
CARLOS FELIX RASPALL-GALLI,
H.I. FELDMAN NOMINEE

As an alternative to the traditional school organization of linear corridors between anonymous classrooms, this project expands the notion of public spaces of school buildings. A dynamic interior landscape inspires the students to exchange their ideas outside the formal environment of the classroom. As in urban systems, this interaction and circulation space is the negative space, the cracks in-between the private functions of the school.

Two different material systems organize these private programs: facing the exterior, a set of massive blocks encloses the classrooms; in the heart of the building, an arrangement of folded planes contains the performing spaces. As these planes ascend, they cantilever and shelter the cracks where interaction happens.

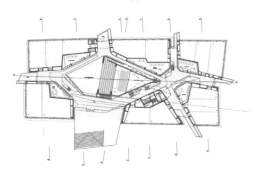

DAVID NILAND „ This project has a lot of spirit. „ That's why you're getting the input. It's as „ if you're trying to get in touch with God, or „ something like that.
{Laughter}
„ But some of what you don't show could be „ examined more closely. To speak more specifi- „ cally, if there's a correlation between what's „ expressed overhead and what's below it?
CARLOS FELIX RASPALL-GALLI „ No.
DAVID NILAND „ Why not? Because then you could „ have a relationship, and find that you might „ get continuity between what was up there...
CARLOS FELIX RASPALL-GALLI „ I know that it's a „ question about glazing the structure of the „ roof, but in themselves the structural ele- „ ments are quite relevant because they have „ that contact where they…
DAVID NILAND „ Are you certain that the order is „ there that sustains exploring the idea?
CARLOS FELIX RASPALL-GALLI „ I'm sorry, I didn't „ understand the question.
ED MITCHELL „ Let me answer the question: yes.
{Laughter}
DAVID NILAND „ The striations are in the section „ drawings, and those are representative of the „ structural elements. You have a reciprocation „ on the roof. You have an opportunity to get a „ correlation between what's above and what's „ below, and that, in turn, might give you a „ few clues about getting specific with your „ intuition of glazing, so it doesn't just cover „ all that area.
ROBERT CAMPBELL „ I just want to throw in a quick „ comment. We all like this project, but I read „ the program on the train coming down here and „ this does not say very much about the kind „ of building that could fit different purposes „ at different times as the city evolves. This „ is very much a fixed thing that's going to be „ what it is.

DOUGLAS GAUTHIER „ No, I would disagree. I think „ one of the best things about this project is the „ pure robustness of the models, the robustness „ of the diagrams, the robustness of the systems „ coming into play. It seems to me that this „ project has the robustness--if you actually „ started to read these things according to some „ of the green technology and the water movement, „ and you indicate lightly that you're going to „ put the glazing at different levels because of „ the sun--it's a very, very beautiful project. „ But I saw the same robustness at midterm. You „ should have spent the time from midterm to „ now developing and supporting your argument „ in these other tertiary examples, of how this „ thing could have turned out. This thing could „ have been drawn to death. The drawings and the „ models are beautiful, but they're short of the „ things that could really, really argue for the „ robustness. Because I think this project is „ not necessarily a school: it's a school when „ it wants to be a school; it's a market when it „ wants to be a market; it's a theater when it „ wants to be a theater; and I think that's the „ pure heft of it.
ED MITCHELL „ One of the things you don't see is „ that he was using Grasshopper and modulating „ the depths of the surfaces, so he was also „ looking at this piece here.
PATRICK HICKOX „ I think if you had pushed it „ down to the ground, the circulation would have „ been very, very beautiful, even though it's „ designed for maybe a tropical climate.
MARK WAMBLE „ It's almost as if you recreated „ the city within the building, and then it has „ a self-similar relationship to its fabric. And „ if it can't be empty, then that suggests a dif- „ ferent relationship between the object in the „ middle and the six boxes. So that may not be „ all that useful, but I think it's a beautiful „ project so I'm trying to rationalize it.

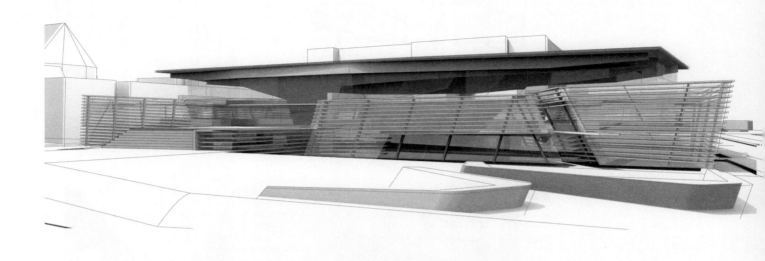

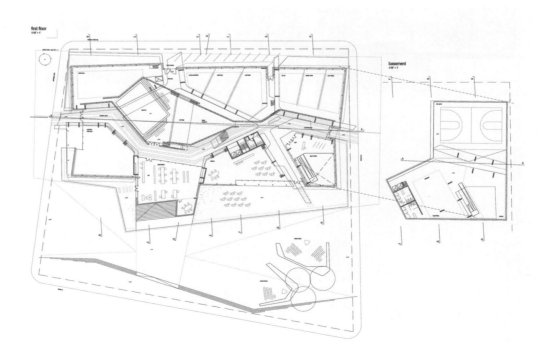

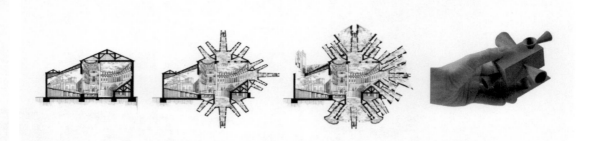

II

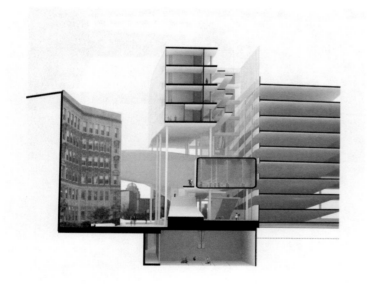

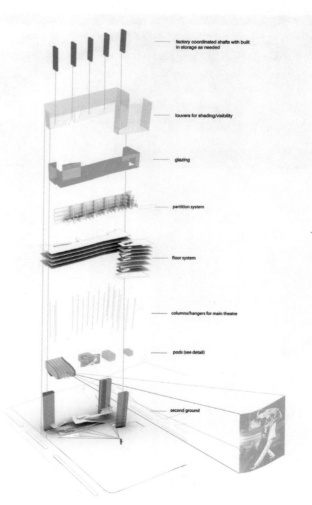

factory coordinated shafts with built in storage as needed

louvers for shading/visibility

glazing

partition system

floor system

columns/hangers for main theatre

pods (see detail)

second ground

III

FRED KOETTER

ED MITCHELL

ROBERT CAMBELL   DOUGLAS GAUTHIER   PATRICK HICKOX   DAVID NILAND
KAREN FAIRBANKS   BRIAN HEALY   FRANK LUPO   MARK WAMBLE

ED MITCHELL „To put it simply, the main space of „ the theater is a central urban square, which „ is a whole bunch of big doors that can be „ opened up to the second level, which can be „ opened up again into the closed theater spaces „ of the specific small performance theaters „ that it attaches to.

DOUGLAS GAUTHIER „But what we also saw at mid- „ term was a bit of a Hejduk project, where there „ were these elements which were operational, „ and those were specific programs which were „ attached to specific rooms, which did specific „ things for the relationship to the school, and „ then together created--the same way Hejduk's „ objects created a new urbanism.

NICHOLAS GILLILAND „I think that's still pres- „ ent, because the drawings you see on the dark „ board here are those highly defined volumes „ that could be almost prefabricated, although „ they have an existing form.

BRIAN HEALY „But the difference I have, is if you „ look at the plans it's like a castle plan; it's „ poche in the rooms--the rooms, the rooms are „ highlighted, so the spaces are foregrounded in „ the plan. And in the model, it's the frame it- „ self that's in-filled with shapes, so spatially „ it's such a fundamentally different thing that „ the dominant void of your room is just an „ absence of a frame, as opposed to a room. It's „ a nice idea that it's a machine that could be „ transformed by the students, but you're making „ it sound more like it's a big family room in „ the middle of the building.

PATRICK HICKOX „It certainly is rather like a „ courtyard, and with the exception of how it „ pops through the roof there it's a lot like all „ the other things. You've created a structural „ system, not exactly free, but with immense „ flexibility, even though you've got all these „ classrooms that are virtually identical and

„ they could all be squeezed together, you don't „ need all that circulation and everything, but „ that's just sort of diagrammatic.

KAREN FAIRBANKS „I'm really glad I missed the „ midterm.

{Laughter}

„ I'm glad I missed the midterm because I think „ this project has a lot of really interesting „ things going on. I'd like to question the scale „ of that large space in relation to everything „ else. Just formally, that thing really does „ take over as this forced layer between things; „ not so much the object itself. It's changed a „ lot from that model. This model, everything is „ wrapped around that space, that volume in some „ ways is between everything else that's going „ on daily. And that's the one big event space. I „ love the idea that you describe the site not as „ something that you traverse, but you describe „ in terms of loading, set-making--a big space „ to just make stuff, and to bring materials in „ and out. I'm not sure yet about the scale of „ that; the vastness of that space, and what „ controls the floor.

MARK WAMBLE „Your project is straddling two „ different models that are difficult to resolve, „ although there's a clear struggle to do so. I „ think one, which you mentioned earlier about „ the Hejduk model, is an interesting one. I „ hadn't seen it originally, but I think it's in „ conflict with the other one, which I think your „ language has paid homage to, which is the Ce- „ dric Price model. But I don't know that those „ are ever resolvable, because one is talking „ about signification and the stability of pro- „ gram and then the flexibility and the life of „ the school in relation to that flexibility--a „ battleground against that stability which I „ think would be a problem in a performing arts „ high school.

II
TEATR LABORATORIUM
NICHOLAS GILLILAND

City/School: the performance begins on a dormant lot at the edge of down-town. Buses, workshops and basketball courts set the scene: a school whose framework simultaneously links to and internalizes the city. Escalators, gangways and courts extend the public realm upward into a network of spaces for discussion and improvisation. The volumes of traditional performance nest within; classroom modules infill the voids as opportunities arise; operable wall panels allow students to create acoustic continuity or rupture between these figures, constantly folding and redoubling the limits of the perfor-mance. As the positions of spectator and performer are constantly mirrored, disciplinary frameworks find concrete expression. City and institution coalesce in performative experience.

DOUGLAS GAUTHIER „I think David's question is „ a good one, and I'm going to ask the same „ question in a different way. If this were a „ museum structure, is this a white box, or is „ it not? What is the motivation? It seems like „ there's a certain set of classrooms getting to „ the urban scale, but then there's not that sort „ of going into it with a section or perspec- „ tive idea to define the relationships of the „ body, the eye, the city, the performance, and „ all that. You need a little more forethought „ about what you're saying to set up this set of „ relationships.

PATRICK HICKOX „I could see the generic version „ of this being something easily prefab, so that „ that could be a model for schools.

ELIZA HIGGINS „That's the way that I've been „ thinking about it, that this could be applied „ to other schools. And it doesn't necessarily „ have to be a performing arts school, but it „ allows for specialization to occur by saying „ that there's a range of functions. I am trying „ to set it up so that it is architectural. In „ terms of the junk space or the gallery spaces, „ I'm actually doing…

ROBERT CAMPBELL „In this neighborhood, it's all „ junk space.

{Laughter}

KAREN FAIRBANKS „There's a really important „ break in the public line and the rest of the „ school. One of the questions I would ask about „ this project is about the idea that you learn

„ in a certain way in one class, and then in „ a different way in another class, and then „ there's a different type of learning in the „ performance spaces, and so in terms of the „ urban gesture and inviting the public in, and „ trying to find that line, I think your project „ has a clear idea about that. In terms of the „ rest of the ways learning engages the stu- „ dents, and especially engages the community, „ it's a little less clear to me. I think it has „ to do with hierarchy in this project, and how „ you differentiate between the spaces.

ROBERT CAMPBELL „That's why I was asking about „ junk space. This is junk space, between these „ buildings and here--that whole zone. And so „ I think the question about language is ap- „ propriate, because it's a little too precious. „ What kind of language would allow you to oc- „ cupy this junk space? Could it be more of a „ background?

MARK WAMBLE „The setup is that there is perhaps „ a proto-component to this. In other words, you „ are approaching the project giving yourself „ an additional design problem, beyond context, „ beyond functional distribution of program, „ that you want it to be prototypical and re- „ locatable. That automatically begins to bias „ the language, bias the program, and separate „ it out. All that makes a lot of sense. You „ have the parts that can be lifted to some „ degree, and you have the parts that are more „ specialized.

III
IN-BETWEEN
ELIZA HIGGINS

The Boston Performing Arts School creates a new pedestrian and vehicular gateway to the city's developing Theatre District and acts as a beacon to theatergoers in an otherwise scattered urban streetscape. The main classroom bar hovers above the street, creating a new path into the district, engaging the performance-based landscape. The street level path peels upwards, forming a secondary landscape which connects performance spaces or pods that are suspended from the bar above. With this shift in landscape and program, the spaces in-between gain importance, creating informal but active zones for watching, video projection, gathering, and practice.

511A

SCOLARI STUDIO

The theme is a small archaeological museum holding three objects of the Minoan civilization with living quarters for three to four people in an annex situated on the extreme limit of the Minoan caldera on the island of Santorini. Limit does not signify simply "on the edge of" but is a state that demands a comparison and resolution of two topographical and conceptual conditions, in order to find a single solution. The explosion of the volcano on Santorini (the ancient Thera) in 1600BC was in all probability responsible for the disappearance of the Minoan civilization, the center of which was Knossos on the island of Crete. The museum is therefore symbolically also the "museum of the catastrophe."

    The project is carried out on the island of Santorini. On our way there, we will visit Crete in order to see the Palace of Knossos, an expression of the labyrinth principle which, according to tradition, Dedalus had learned from the Egyptian builders of the labyrinth situated in front of the pyramid of Amenhamat III at Hawara, one of the wonders of the world according to Herodotus.

    We shall also work on plans for a device for producing wind and solar powered energy, which is formally integrated into the project. In addition, students produce a 1:1 scale prototype of a chair and a door handle for the museum. The latter objects enable us to make an evaluation of the difficult relationship that exists between representation and construction.

I
MUSEUM
PATRICK LUN,
H.I. FELDMAN NOMINEE

Located on the island of Santorini in Greece, this project anchors itself to one of the basaltic fissures found along the trail from the city of Oia to the city of Fira. The museum's circulation stems from the path and then breaks into multiple different, yet continuous, paths. This allows for a varying degree of interaction with the building passing by; visiting the museum; or staying and studying indefinitely. All of these paths allow for circuitous movements through the building that might meet upon themselves, but never overlap. Where the labyrinth uses a set path to stretch the experience of space and time within two-dimensions, this museum to the Minoan civilization takes a single path and folds it in three-dimensions to stretch space and time as well as create different kinds of spaces.

ARIANE LOURIE HARRISON „ The drawings suggest „ a question: why not mine the richness of the „ actual landscape in your representation? I „ think these three-dimensional elements are „ quite rich, yet I actually find your represen- „ tation quite thin--not engaged in the powerful „ language of the site.

PETER EISENMAN „ Patrick, when I look at your „ building, it seems to me that it should have „ poche in plan, some thickness and thinness. It „ looks cut out of a rock, but the plans are just „ straight walls and there is no sense of poche „ or going into the landscape, which you read in „ the elevation.

STANLEY TIGERMAN „ If you had found a way of cut- „ ting through the actual rock, and then found a „ way to document it, it would become architecture. „ Why do you have to build something, if you had „ actually inhabited the very thing there?

PATRICK LUN „ I think it was always a question of „ how much do you engage the basaltic fissure and „ how much do you leave as a monument unto itself.

JOSHUA ROWLEY „ You shouldn't mind coming into „ contact with it as much as necessary, or as little „ as necessary. But you do need to respond to it.

ED MITCHELL „ I think it would have been nice „ if you had pivoted the walls; you could have „ delayed that view for a little bit. So you're „ slowing down and getting glimpses that are „ powerful as a meaningful gesture on site.

ARIANE LOURIE HARRISON „ So right now your „ building is set next to that basalt wall?

PATRICK LUN „ Yes.

STANLEY TIGERMAN „ So is it in competition with „ the basalt wall?

PATRICK LUN „ In retrospect, I think it is a bit,

„ although it was never my intention. My inten- „ tion was to let the basalt make its entrance, „ make itself known, and then you walk through „ the building knowing that you're passing it.

JOSHUA ROWLEY „ Regardless of your decision to „ have a straight wall, you did have to select „ the negative space between the wall and the „ building. In a way, by not addressing the wall, „ you have actually made a bigger decision by „ choosing the shape of that negative space.

STANLEY TIGERMAN „ What you've really done is „ open up a discussion which expands architec- „ ture within its normal conventions that we're „ used to using and criticizing. With this sug- „ gestion, it opens up another discussion about „ where architecture can go; your project is „ pregnant with possibilities. Without it (your „ project), I'm not sure that any one of us would „ have been able to come up with that as an „ idea by itself.

LEON KRIER „ I think it's incredibly interesting „ and poetic, and the most interesting view is „ actually from below, which you don't show. „ I think you could have carried your logic „ through, technically and tectonically, to do a „ stone building.

PETER EISENMAN „ I don't think you'd like it as „ a stone building, since the whole island is „ stone and the concrete stands against the „ stone.

LEON KRIER „ It's a beautiful thing, but it is „ very linear. And as you go through there is „ no real event within the building. If you have „ such a long developing procession, maybe you „ need something more. It ends with a whimper „ rather than with a bang.

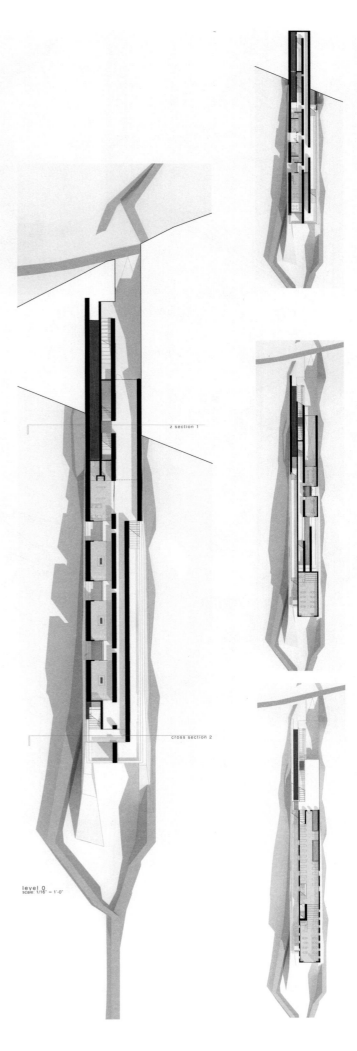

z section 1

cross section 2

level 0
scale: 1/16" = 1'-0"

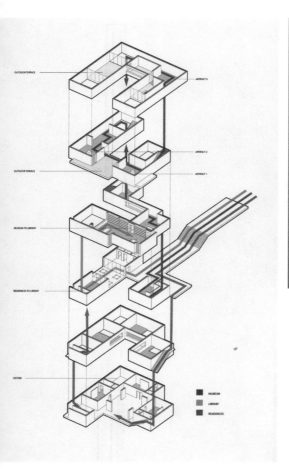

II

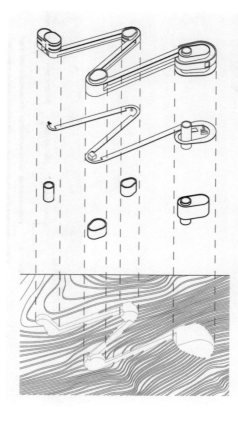

III

LEON KRIER „ I think it was an interesting exercise to draw, in your elevations, the different churches next to the building or the houses. Then this becomes an enormous object. It looks small, like a house, but it is an immense building. The question then is, does the program really lend itself to such an enormous architectural statement?

PETER EISENMAN „ The scale of this building, Leon, to me, is far smaller than the one that we were just previously looking at.

STANLEY TIGERMAN „ Why did you select a cube?

JOSHUA ROWLEY „ This is probably the only cube on Santorini.

MIRIAM PETERSON „ I had a scheme with a smaller cluster of buildings, and after visiting the site, and seeing it from the water, I wanted the building to make an impact from a distance. A platonic object on an enormous landscape, to me, suggests the sort of monumentality that I found to be interesting.

STANLEY TIGERMAN „ Did you ever think about the scale of the architectural object in this program? Not to challenge the program, but to think maybe they would occur in diminution?

ARIANE LOURIE HARRISON „ That is where the siting in comparison to the church begins to matter.

PETER EISENMAN „ I have a question for you: I don't see the relation of the chair to the object in this project.

MIRIAM PETERSON „ My chair is not related to the building.

STANLEY TIGERMAN „ Does the Barcelona Chair relate to the Pavilion?

PETER EISENMAN „ I just asked the question.

(Laughter)

STANLEY TIGERMAN „ The existence of the word 'labyrinth' makes one look for a predecessor. That's reinforced by having these archaeological pieces, and there would be value to that. What is nice about the chair is that it is autonomous in the same way that the Barcelona Chair is not related to the Barcelona Pavilion. I was concerned about the labyrinth. I don't know that it is useful. You went in

another direction; you tried to do something autonomous. You get it when you see the chair, which is obviously derived from the object, which is already autonomous.

MASSIMO SCOLARI „ She started with a sculptural model and then investigated how the sculpture could become architecture. Then we discussed transforming a sculpture into architecture.

ED MITCHELL „ What is the difference between those things?

PETER EISENMAN „ Yeah, why isn't the sculpture architecture? I think that is architecture.

MASSIMO SCOLARI „ Yes, but she didn't find that enough to articulate it to be architecture.

ED MITCHELL „ But it hasn't dealt with the problem of interiority, addressed it specifically.

MIRIAM PETERSON „ That is the issue in the difference between the sculpture and the architecture that I have not solved yet.

MASSIMO SCOLARI „ The process that I found very interesting was that she was able to articulate the labyrinth idea into a cube, which is incredibly complex. Transformed into a building, I think it was about process, so I was very pleased with this.

LEON KRIER „ I think despite it being very interesting, I think the most important thing about architecture is that it must be appropriate. You must make it powerful for what it is and when. If you do not, the symbols don't come where they should. It is not just enclosure; it is also sitting on an enormous landscape where you have big windows. On the other hand, where you want these views, not just the central views but the corners, it is very interesting.

PETER EISENMAN „ Leon, let me ask you a question. You said that architecture must make sense?

LEON KRIER „ No, if you want a powerful impact you need the effect to be at the right spot, at the right moment.

PETER EISENMAN „ Was Borromini at the right spot when he did Sapienza?

LEON KRIER „ No.

PETER EISENMAN „ No, he wasn't. But the effect is something.

ED MITCHELL „ The best thing you did is this chair; it's really interesting. Clearly, something about how you make the chair is informing the architecture. The building looks like you stuck objects into that winding line.

PETER EISENMAN „ When you produce forms like this, they either have some iconic or some symbolic resonance. In other words, why these forms as opposed to any other?

LEON KRIER „ But they have a reference; you could easily see how they could be about the vernacular of Santorini, with the white elements.

PETER EISENMAN „ They look like Modernist Expressionism of the Mendelsohnian Einstein tower era. I'm just asking a question, because I'm prone to like forms like this. I'm trying to bring out what seems to be an obsession with those forms. What is that?

JULIANNA VON ZUMBUSCH „ I think that at a certain point the diagram overtook the building.

STANLEY TIGERMAN „ That's fair, because you are trying to traverse that hill and that knuckle, which is a cam, where those things occur.

PETER EISENMAN „ But the trouble is when they start to look like something else they lose what you are talking about. When they start to become icons, that is a visual simularity to something else and is when the trouble hits.

JOSHUA ROWELY „ Maybe the way to explain them is to not necessarily rely on shelter.

STANLEY TIGERMAN „ Absolutely.

JOSHUA ROWELY „ We talked about protecting things that don't need protection and I think the people have relied on the idea of another cataclysimic event coming. Maybe it would be better to impose some larger views as oppsoed to imposing shelter. Maybe it isn't so iconic and it loses some vocabulary.

MASSIMO SCOLARI „ I think that's a nice idea, to have separate pavilions each with one function and traditionally the way you order buildings is that typologically you have undivided space and divided space. But these suggest that they are undivided spaces, with a singular purpose. One for dining, one for living, one for

exhibiting. And yet, every one of your buildings is inside with incredibly complicated interiors and I think that for an incredibly simple proposition it's too much.

STANLEY TIGERMAN „ It's so interesting, because of the cam shaft asymmetry there is a place for the stair. The rest of the space you just leave as a room. Why do you bother with the other interior subdivisions?

MASSIMO SCOLARI „ Also, when you have these round forms it's good to have something not round to contrast.

JULIANNA VON ZUMBUSCH „ I think some of the complexity that is read into the forms is part of the path that is entering the buildings and is doing the wrapping. I think it's intended to be simpler than it is.

ARIANE LOURIE HARRISON „ I wanted to ask you a question about your intuition. You made a very large formal change from your midterm. You had a scheme that was more sensitive formally to the topography; you changed it in a way to make it really contrast. I don't understand the logic or the intention with what you are trying to do with this round form.

JOSHUA ROWLEY „ Did any of the exisiting churchs affect this?

JULIANNA VON ZUMBUSH „ No.

ED MITCHELL „ I thought there was a formal proposition in the chair—where the tension that happens between parts makes a linear element that has to resolve a corner. You're getting things that are solid at the voids, and that shape, the chair, picks up and it's very nice. You go to this thing, and anything that is the landscape is not in play with the architecture. There is a line that's happening and there's no relationship. If the void spaces made between the ramps started to inform the building logic, I think you would have a better project. I think the student has to make a claim as to where there formal project lies, otherwise we could cite all kinds of architecture—but it's your project and you have to lay claim to it as a designer.

II
THE MONUMENT AND THE VOID
MIRIAM PETERSON

The concept of the Labyrinth is derived from Vincent Scully's description of the Palace at Knossos which is not as a tortuous maze but as a series of distinct paths: the ceremonial, the private, and the sacred. The project—a small museum for three artifacts—is a monument to both the Minoan civilization and the event of the eruption of the Volcano at Santorini. The basic cubic form, voided at the core, casts a monumental architecture with a small program against the sublimely monumental scale of the caldera edge on which it sits.

III
MUSEUM FOR THREE ARTIFACTS
JULIANNA VON ZUMBUSCH

This project responds to the violent eruption that transformed Santorini in the seventeenth century BC, burying the existing civilization. By dispersing the program into four loosely connected buildings, a pattern emerges between concentration on the landscape and on artifacts from the time of the eruption. A covered path wraps around the buildings, which descend down the cliff created when the central portion of the volcano exploded. This act of descent is symbolic both of reclaiming the barren landscape and of the quest for knowledge, which is related in the library and museum program. The chair and the door handle were designed in dialogue with the building in that they also embody the notion of a continuous system, or line, exposing fragmented pieces.

513A

ATWOOD/SCHWARZ STUDIO

Las Vegas, America's entertainment capitol, is once again changing its face. Gone are the boxes and parking lots of Learning from Las Vegas, razed and replaced by 5,000 room resort casino towers accompanied by custom-built theaters offering musical and theatrical stars. The casinos remain, but are now surrounded by celebrity chefs plying their trade around the clock among vast collections of high-end retailers imported from Madison Avenue and Rodeo Drive. Once a gambling destination, Las Vegas now produces the majority of its revenues in non-gaming ventures. All of this is good news for architects, who have been called upon to offer the next generation of spectacular experiences. To learn these new directions, we will need to conduct research.

We are self-consciously following in the footsteps of the 1968 fall semester, when Robert Venturi, Denise Scott Brown, and Steven Izenour took eleven students to Las Vegas to look at the Strip. In opposition to the Modernist's tabula rasa urbanism, they insisted that 'there is a way of learning from everything.' Their research influenced a generation of architects, and catch phrases like "main street is almost all right" came to represent not only an acceptance of American development patterns, but an interest in working with its materials: billboards, symbols, and streets. Their work focused on the strip typology, mining it for ideas and development patterns which were influencing the American landscape.

Throughout the semester, guest critics are brought in to help evaluate and guide decision making, peppering the students with points of view ranging from entertainment moguls, casino presidents, developers, architects and cultural historians in an effort to guide our thoughts and responses to Las Vegas's rich cultural and architectural history.

The semester concludes with collaborative work on a book that collects the studio's earlier research and drawings. These graphic materials are accompanied by guest writers. We hope to stage an exhibition showcasing our research, arguing for a reinterpretation of The Strip typology and demonstrating several approaches for urban development in the twenty-first century.

I
ENCLAVE
PATRICK MCGOWAN & TOM TANG,
H.I. FELDMAN NOMINEES
On the corner of Flamingo Boulevard and Las Vegas Boulevard, our site is centrally located along the Vegas strip. With its proximity to Caesars Palace, The Flamingo, Paris, Bally's, and the Bellagio, this site is arguably the most valuable property along the Las Vegas Strip. Our approach to the site stems from recognizing its pivotal role in joining together the 3 adjacent Harrah's properties. To negotiate the complex requirements of the site to connect its neighbors but retain its own identity, we developed the project with the concept of an enclave.

An enclave is a territory entirely enclosed within another territory. The enclave retains identity, but draws its resources entirely from the territory around it. Likewise, our 50 story hotel must negotiate pedestrian flow from its adjacent resorts, but also retain its own brand. Furthermore, to capture the charged corner between Las Vegas Boulevard. and Flamingo Boulevard, our tower contains in its base an ultra-sports bar with stadium seating and a performance theater, both viewing activity of the strip and contributing to its intensity.

JOEL SANDERS „ Is the plinth a pre-existing condition?
PATRICK MCGOWAN „ There are a few reasons for the plinth. The first is the bridge connection that brings people to plus twenty feet. The other condition is the master plan which also bridges across at plus twenty.
JOEL SANDERS „ Is it then a response to your master plan or to a typical Las Vegas master plan?
PATRICK MCGOWAN „ It's a combination of both, in that both use an elevated plinth condition.
DAVID SCHWARZ „ What the solution is there is to create an urban-friendly, or rather urbanistically appropriate, sidewalk street level, while at the same time creating a walkable enviroment to run East-West.
ROBERT A.M. STERN „ I have a question: what would happen if your client said to you, 'There's a lot of corners in your building,' because corners are quite expensive in architecture. How would you handle that awkward moment?
PATRICK MCGOWAN „ I would say if you're already spending the money to build at this location in Las Vegas than you should go ahead and make an icon. This is an icon; this is the first thing you will see when you arrive from the airport or the highway. If you want to save money be reducing those corners, than it would hurt in the long run.
ROBERT A.M. STERN „ I would commend you on taking the high road and turning the question around, but I don't think your building is an icon by world standards. The better defense would be what Leon (Krier) mentioned earlier--you can earn more revenue from the unique corner rooms as the rooms migrate to interesting locations to achieve diagonal views.
PATRICK MCGOWAN „ But the question of icon is an interesting one because it's a different animal elsewhere in the world because you are dealing with a lot of pastiche. The beginning of this conversation started out with the discussion of architecture's role for the future. There are multiple ideas here about activating the façade and making this a 3-D billboard.
ROBERT A.M. STERN „ But it has to do with composition. Most icons are well composed in the round and are point markers on the skyline. When you have a slab form, it's already not as iconic as other projects like Bilbao, Wright's Price Tower, et cetera.
DEBORAH BURKE „ I want to come to their defense, because I like this project. They have addressed some of the many important questions that have been raised today, from the corner rooms to the problem of the oversize plinth and the megastructure. It takes the smallest piece of the client's property that touches the strip and says put all your money here.
DAVID SCHWARZ „ I think the question of icon is an interesting one because--because it isn't you who decides it's an icon, it's the architectural historians. You can decide to make a landmark, however, which is a much easier thing to make than an icon.
PATRICK MCGOWAN „ What are the qualifications of a landmark?
DAVID SCHWARZ „ Something that marks the land, it's that simple.
PATRICK MCGOWAN „ So is it just height?
DAVID SCHWARZ „ You can do it with height, you can do it with scale, or with an orange and yellow façade {pointing to the rendering}. So if on the underside of your soffit you're making something kinetic, it provides an identification of place or a way to be described.
ROBERT A.M. STERN „ If you really want to make an icon, in my view, whether it's based on precedent like the Empire State building or the Chrysler Building, it's because they have dramatic silhouettes and because you can see them from all around the city. Their shape leaves a lasting impression.

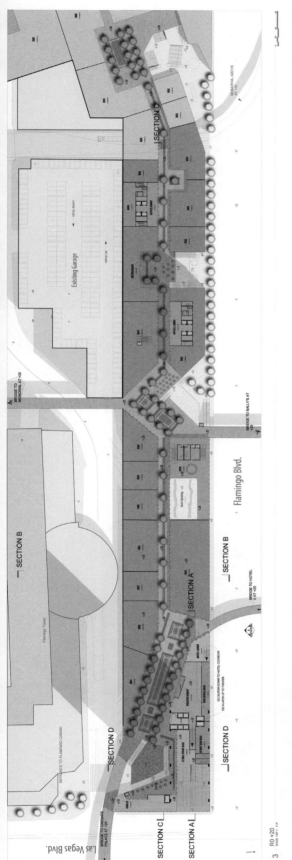

SECTION D

SECTION B

Existing Garage

Flamingo Tower

SECTION B

Flamingo Blvd.

SECTION A

SECTION D

SECTION C

SECTION A

Las Vegas Blvd.

3   R0 +20

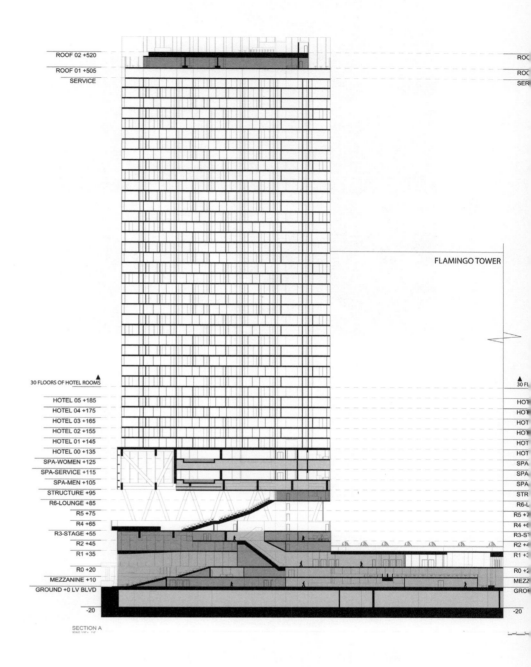

ROOF 02 +520
ROOF 01 +505
SERVICE

ROO
ROO
SER

FLAMINGO TOWER

30 FLOORS OF HOTEL ROOMS

HOTEL 05 +185
HOTEL 04 +175
HOTEL 03 +165
HOTEL 02 +155
HOTEL 01 +145
HOTEL 00 +135
SPA-WOMEN +125
SPA-SERVICE +115
SPA-MEN +105
STRUCTURE +95
R6-LOUNGE +85
R5 +75
R4 +65
R3-STAGE +55
R2 +45
R1 +35
R0 +20
MEZZANINE +10
GROUND +0 LV BLVD
-20

30 FL
HOT
HOT
HOT
HOT
HOT
HOT
SPA
SPA
SPA
STR
R6-L
R5 +7
R4 +6
R3-ST
R2 +4
R1 +3
R0 +2
MEZZ
GROI
-20

SECTION A

KANYE

II

GAMING   RDE   HOTEL   CONDO   CARPETED MEETING SPACE   INTERIOR PEDESTRIAN SPACE

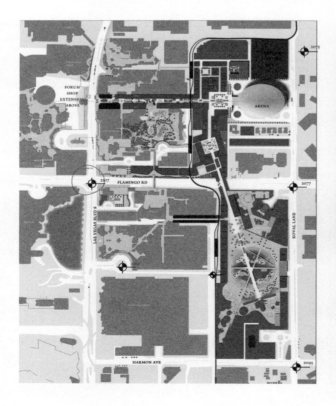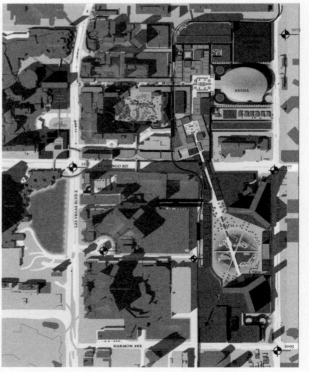

III

JOSHUA ROWLEY „ That's what I was asking about before--that's your main idea, regardless of how the architecture seems. When I am in a courtyard I don't have to leave the semblance of having a good time in one area before I am in the next, before I think about it. In a way you are utilizing the area of your plan more than you tearing it up and having people commit to one destination at a time.

JOEL SANDERS „ But isn't the idea that you could lift these Modernist buildings off the ground to see a continuous porous landscape that is a series of interconnected places each with their own character? Such that they aren't courtyard specific--they aren't isolated traditional courtyards, but are a continuous landscape that operates from one end of the project to the other? That is, in my mind, a very promising idea but I want to understand why there is such a disconnect between what you say and what you're showing us.

DEBORAH BURKE „ The other problem is that they are making an argument about perimeter that your plans don't really recognize. Your double-loaded corridors don't speak to your position about perimeter, meaning the internal buildings can have double loaded corridors, based on your argument, but the external ones cannot. I'm not arguing for single loaded corridors, I'm saying that on either side of the hallway you need a different strategy.

ROBERT A.M. STERN „ It's a matter of architectural language. That, I think, is the problem. It looks ministerial, like a hospital, I could go on and on. If you had conceived of a building beyond the bondage of utilitarian Modernism, and tried to think in terms of an environment, you would have had a much better space.

ED BASS „ I would like to add something. I think the most interesting idea you have is that you're going to have a whole series of court-yards and you have thought out how your pro-grammatic elements fit within the courtyard and interconnect in an intriguing way. But to be in a courtyard surrounded by a corporate build-ing is to ruin the magic of the courtyard. If this is to be a twenty-first century Las Vegas building, with micro-controlled climates and so on, then why don't you think of creating the courtyards in Las Vegas style? Maybe you have a series of low buildings like Yale Colleges, maybe they look like they're out of a science fiction movie, but you are creating courtyards with low rise perimeter buildings.

DIANA BALMORI „ I think to add to what Ed was saying, the courtyards are incredibly depen-dent on the wall around it.

ED BASS „ And the experience inside the hotel room has absolutely nothing to do with the shape of the building on the outside.

DAVID SHWARZ „ I don't think it's the height of the building that is the problem; I think it's the architecture that's the problem.

DIANA BALMORI „ Exactly, that's why I was articu-lating the character of the courtyard wall.

JOEL SANDERS „ We are all talking about court-yards, but it seems the thing that is at stake here on the one hand is more traditional court-yards being bounded and each with their own function and on the other hand, the sequence of spaces that might link these traditional courtyards. Maybe I am misreading the project but what I hear you say is that these aren't courtyards, and this is a continuous blurred landscape that has potentially porous junc-tures between them. Although the tenor of the jury is criticizing the components of failed Modernism in your project, the thing for me is that you haven't explored the precedents of Modernist floating slabs and open ground projects that might give you clues as to how this works.

II
THE SECRET
CHENG HUI CHUA & ZAK SNIDER

Las Vegas is undergoing a transition with the constantly evolving visiting demographic. Competition has tran-scended home soil, and international attractions are contesting for the limited pool of rollers. This project speculates on the future trajectory of activities on the Strip, investigating a scenario whereby land along the Strip is fully saturated and developers are forced to build off of Las Vegas Boulevard. It situates this problem on a real site, acquired and owned by Harrah's Entertainment, as a starting point for exploring a coherent campus masterplan, and eventually leading to the design of a 3,000 room resort. Off the strip, the immediate context in-cludes parking garages on three sides-- yielding a new resort strategy that compresses the typical tower-podium relationship into a more integrated, inward-looking series of courtyards, each of which is specifically branded for its programmatic activity including casino, pool, and ultra-lounge. This allows new programmatic types and rela-tionships to emerge between spaces, blurring the boundary from exterior to interior, and enabling one to gamble in a bikini, or dance in a club from a hotel room balcony.

ERIC KRANCEVIC „ From our ongoing semester-long analysis of successful urban spaces that have retail, dining, and entertainment, we have the understanding that people go where other people are.

LOUISE LEVI „ For most places outside of Las Vegas, the life, and potential money to be made from retail environments, is in the streets. What we found was unique about Las Vegas was that some of the most vital public spaces are pri-vate interior environments. We aim to connect into the grid of those public interior envi-ronments while creating an exterior public pedestrian environment that links all of Harrah's campus.

TOM TANG „ We love these vibrant interior streets. The modern Las Vegas visitor is promiscuous.

ROBERT A.M. STERN „ In the daytime hours, or…
{Laughter}

ERIC KRANCEVIC „ We would like to have more fluid transitions between the Harrah's properties.

TOM TANG „ Our goal here is to take these suc-cessful, profitable, interior spaces around Harrah's campus and link them together with a series of cross sections through different boulevards that primarily have retail and din-ing at the ground and balcony levels.

LOUISE LEVI „ We are presenting a plinth project as our architectural solution for two reasons. The first is a thirty-foot difference between the strip and the pedestrian walkway. The second is the arena, which we are putting on axis with the entry into the new forum shops, which is entered through the concourse level at grade thus allowing the pedestrian to feel privileged within the space in a way that we hope will be a spectacle that is unique to Las Vegas.

ERIC KRANCEVIC „ The linked streets are one of two strategies that we are using. The other is about creating spectacle and a monumental scale. To give you an idea of monumental scale in Las Vegas the Bellagio Fountains are a good example. It's important to provide something unique for visitors to draw them through the depth of our site.

LOUISE LEVI „ More specifically, this public plaza outside the arena of our proposal can be acti-vated twenty-four hours as both a public forum following entertainment events in the arena and by day as a convention center through shared connections with The Sands convention center.

III
HARRAH'S MASTERPLAN
ERIC KRANCEVIC, LOUISE LEVI & TOM TANG

From our analysis of retail environ-ments, we have come to understand that people go where people are. Crowded environments are profitable environments. For most places, this means that life (and money) is in the streets, but in Las Vegas some of the most vital pub-lic streets are interior environments. Harrah's rocks--we love many of the vibrant streetscapes created in the in-teriors of the resorts--places like the forum shops, or the street lamp-lit "boulevards" in Paris. We aim to add to the existing strength of the Harrah's properties--these interior, crowded, profitable spaces--by linking them with a pedestrian boulevard that has a twenty-four hour mixed-use environment with retail, entertainment, and dining on the street and balconies and office space above.

CHENG HUI
ZAK SNIDER

ERIC KRANCEVIC
LOUISE LEVI
TOM TANG

101

DIANA BALMORI   RACHEL GRUZEN   SANGMOK KIM   JOEL SANDERS

AMALE ANDRAOS   BARRY BERGDOLL   DAVID HAYS   MARION WEISS
SUNIL BALD   BROOK DENISON   ANURADHA MATHUR   DAN WOOD
     KELLER EASTERLING   CHARLES WALDHEIM

BALMORI/SANDERS STUDIO

515A

While a book could be written about how architects have resolved the line where a building meets the sky, this studio looks instead at a similar defining line that until recently has received very little attention: the Interface where building and land, architecture and landscape, meet. We interrogate the issue of interface through a real scenario--an IT campus in New Delhi. Rai Foundation plans to build an IT Campus on a 28 acre site formerly occupied by abandoned textile mills on the outskirts of the city. This parcel will be transformed into a Free Trade Zone, a temporary home for a constellation of international telecommunication companies who will lease space for seven-year periods. The mixed-use program must meet the needs of a new breed of globe-trotting professionals: how to create a vital enclave that integrates state-of-the art office and research spaces with housing and recreational facilities in a campus-like setting that forges links with the local urban context.

Our work this semester requires us to shift back and forth between two scales: the comprehensive scale of the Site and the smaller scale of the Building that articulates the juncture where nature, enclosure and the human body meet. The studio requires students to create concrete proposals that identify a strategy for using sustainable design principles to weave together structure and materials with the goal of staging provocative ways that human activities can unfold in the interface between interior and exterior, nature and architecture.

I
ADAPTIVE PATTERNS
KRISTIN MUELLER & YIJUAN QUIAN,
H.I. FELDMAN NOMINEES

The project utilizes the equal distribution of solid and void existent in the pattern of the jali screen, deploys it at a new scale that allows landscape and building to have a permeable relationship, and allows the program, site, and ecological issues to influence and manipulate this relentless pattern into a responsive interface of landscape and architecture, inside and outside, public and private. The differentiation occurs through a figure - ground reversal, strategic voids for sun and wind, a geometric and spatial pattern analysis, and a program analysis (focusing on a comparative study of office and retail space). It draws on the precedent of the traditional Mughal gardens of India and attempts to render a new, inhabitable and highly responsive architectural solution.

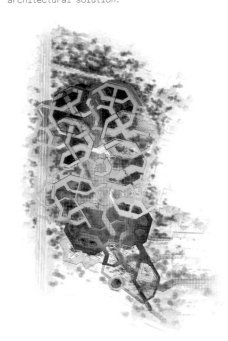

MARION WEISS „ The thing I see is that you haven't „ looked at the prototyping effect that you're „ hovering very near, which is this kind of „ extruded mega-structural upper-level pathway. „ I think the question is then how much and „ how far. In effect you have been very delicate „ about the reference to megastructure, you've „ been only talking about the reference to a „ jali screen, or a tapestry, but in fact you've „ created a heroic volume that's inhabitable. „ So I think my question is, once you've created this, do you then find it has solicited a „ conversation that you need to enter? A con„ versation which goes back to megastructural „ fantasies, thank God so few got built, but you „ want to look at the ones that did get built, „ right? I'm quite fascinated sitting here, but „ you kind of need to know where you reside „ in this whole architectural conversation once „ you've gotten there.

ANU MATHUR „ I think what is being asked is the „ position vis a vis architecture. You start with „ a jali screen; you just keep taking the jali „ screen, producing it, cutting it. I think the „ idea would be what the jail does, in that it „ completely brings the outside inside in a very „ different relationship from the vertical. Is „ that the position you're interested in, some„ thing that enables?

KRISTIN MUELLER „ We did consider having a dif„ ferent experience on every level, and then „ having these cutaways on the terrace so that „ it disappears at this point in a different way „ than it does on another level.

ANU MATHUR „ If that's your position, that the „ building almost dematerializes, and you „ are inside and outside but never actually „ looking at the building, then you're looking „ at it like a megastructure. When I first walked „ up I thought 'Oh no, not another octagon proj„ ect.' But the way you talked about it, it was „ very seductive.

SUNIL BALD „ I think it's an interesting moment „ when the graphic begins to become volumetric, „ that moment when coupling occurs. I find it an

„ interesting moment because you are making a „ choice there. Maybe not much of one, because „ you want the figure to remain, but in order to „ do that you actually create another figure. „ You take the pattern and you imbue in it a „ different kind of organizational paradigm that „ can be translated from the two-dimensional to „ a three-dimensional thing.

AMALE ANDRAOS „ Every time you are relying more „ on testing and performance and calibrating. „ This is more promising as soon as you start „ losing the figure and using performance and „ program and relationship to urban conditions.

DAVID WOOD „ I agree, and to add an emphasis, „ obviously when you look at the plan those „ shapes are not helping the experience on the „ inside, which is really an office, right? The „ thicknesses that you talked about aren't re„ ally inspiring different spaces. I think that's „ a good starting point, to really look at it „ objectively as how could this office be better.

BERRY BERGDOLL „ When you were deep in this, did „ you ever become curious about other archi„ tects whose work was kind of obsessive, and „ about creating a system and pushing it to the „ limits?

JOEL SANDERS „ For better or for worse, and I „ think it is for the better, these two took this „ idea to the limits but also showed it could be „ pliable and flexible. I think they had to begin „ to understand the Graphic Standards typical „ office dimensions, but ultimately it's about an „ indoor-outdoor relationship.

DAVID HAYS „ The question is, if you were to „ keep pushing this forward, would those figures „ disappear, or would they persist? and if they „ persist, why?

MARION WEISS „ But that's where I found it was „ a system that had a self-sustaining autonomy „ that had the capacity to be translated into „ something that could be scaled at a very „ different level that could be volumetrically „ revelatory. I think that is something that you „ have done, you've mined it, you've scaled it, „ and you've mapped it.

KRISTIN MUELLER
YIJUAN QUIAN

OFFICE

RETAIL

ping pong

I

<u>DIANA BALMORI</u>   RACHEL GRUZEN   SANGMOK KIM   <u>JOEL SANDERS</u>

AMALE ANDRAOS   BARRY BERGDOLL   DAVID HAYS   MARION WEISS
SUNIL BALD   BROOK DENISON   ANURADHA MATHUR   DAN WOOD
          KELLER EASTERLING   CHARLES WALDHEIM

II

II
SHORT CIRCUIT
JASON KIM & TRISHA SNYDER

This project began with questioning
igure ground as simply the binary opposition between building and landscape
and between public and private. Our
initial exploration led us to examine
shadow as a means of creating a new figure on ground that is represented by
both landscape and building. The notion
of creating conditions generated by
both building and landscape serves as
the interface between them. The figure
is a direct reaction to the environmental conditions found on the site and
creates protected pockets along the
linear path of the project. Those pockets are then connected to one another
through a series of short circuits
through the landscape.

MARION WEISS „ This is to be admired, on so many
„ different levels. I find that the smartness
„ of your berm protecting both from winds and
„ sound--you create one sort of back side so the
„ interior is nuanced, so there's not just one
„ courtyard, it's a selection or variation of
„ them. I think there's immense invention here.
DAN WOOD „ The incredible creativity, on one
„ side, and the interest in life, and program,
„ and then on the other hand, a complete lack
„ of self-criticism or a complete love for this
„ shape. Because the shape is not working with
„ the idea. How did the idea of the hotel, for
„ example, impact the shape?
BERRY BERGDOLL „ And actually an earlier step,
„ which I would just add onto that, where the
„ diagram became the building form, I was just
„ waiting for the penny to drop, for you to
„ say what was the factor that conditioned the
„ shape. There didn't seem to be one.
DAVID WOOD „ Exactly. And I think you actually
„ prove that it's not the right shape.
MARION WEISS „ Can I help them out here? Because
„ I want to argue for this kind of shape.
BERRY BERGDOLL „ This kind of shape? I agree.
MARION WEISS „ There is a long history, but all
„ those histories first started with the idea of
„ something that had continuity. That's why I
„ said something about cars: Corb had the idea
„ of movement on top; Edgar Chambless, with his
„ 1812 train tracks with cultivation on either
„ side and habitation in the middle. You are so
„ darn close to getting yourself right into the
„ train tracks, but you missed it. This could
„ have been something that had a chameleon-
„ like capacity to link it in a stealth-like
„ way, delicately, with fragile frameworks over
„ there, because you have something truly robust
„ there. And then the reason you make it as
„ long as this is that everybody needs natural

„ light, and so on and so forth. So you haven't
„ answered…
DAVID WOOD „ And that doesn't answer why you
„ make one drawing and stick with it the whole
„ semester.
SUNIL BALD „ The way you framed it was in terms
„ of it's response to the sun angles on the
„ site. So there's a relationship there you
„ set up in terms of the site or the ground as
„ being somewhat passive, and the building as
„ being the thing that actually, through shade,
„ extends its presence and actually activates
„ that zone by making it habitable. That's where
„ I think that that model is really amazing
„ and interesting, because there is more of an
„ ambiguity about what is forming what. I think
„ there might be an opportunity when you go back
„ to your final plan, because it doesn't inform
„ how you use landscape to then break down the
„ relentlessness of the form, like entry and
„ zoning, which become things you take clues
„ from when you overlay them.
DAVID WOOD „ I think it's type. It's a type that
„ is incredibly malleable, which could have done
„ a lot of things. I'm not questioning the type.
„ I'm questioning the shape that the type takes.
„ I feel like this created six courtyards, and
„ three of them got filled in by you. It's an
„ interesting approach, I would just try more
„ options. You should be taking other factors in
„ when you are drawing other approaches.
BROOK DENISON „ You could introduce criteria to
„ test them out and say, 'Well, here is the shape
„ that solves everything.'
MARION WEISS „ Then the question is--everything
„ has been done planimetrically. And you have
„ stacked your plans. I think your tools, if
„ you shift and adjust them, might give you
„ something more synthetically akin to the thing
„ you've found.

JASON KIM
TRISHA SNYDER

PETER EISENMAN   MICHAEL WANG

HENRY COBB   LUIS FERNÁNDEZ-GALIANO   FRANCISCO MANGADO   STANLEY TIGERMAN
KURT FORSTER   JEFFREY KIPNIS   INGEBORG ROCKER   ANTHONY VIDLER
     KEITH KRUMWIEDE   MASSIMO SCOLARI

517A

EISENMAN STUDIO

The relationship between part to whole, and subject to object, determined, up until 1968, the synthetic project of architecture and the formation and naturalization of the Cartesian subject, respectively. While the parallels between these discourses are of utmost importance to our understanding of both the conception of architecture and its practice today, this studio also focuses on the political and ideological implications of these relationships-- examining, simultaneously, our contemporary condition of "lateness" alongside modernity's darkest manifestation: the Third Reich.

At the intersection of these concerns, the studio focuses on the design of a "doku- mentationszentrum" dedicated to the history of National Socialism. Slated to be built on the site of the former "Braunes Haus" (the "Brown House," so named after the color of the Nazi uniform), which housed the offices of many high-ranking Nazi officials, including Hitler, the Center will operate as an exhibition and educational facility focusing on, especially, the role of Munich, the birthplace of National Socialism, as a political, administrative, and representational center of the Third Reich. Twenty years in the making, the plans to construct a memorial building arrive amidst criticism concerning Munich's history of whitewashing its Nazi past. The site, near the palaces of Ludwig I of Bavaria, was, during the Nazi era, part of a complex of ceremonial and monumental buildings commmemorating Munich as the birth- place of the party and solidifying its role as a center for Nazi art (where, infamously in 1937, modernism was labeled "degenerate" in the exhibition "Entartete Kunst" and contrasted with the exhibition of Party-approved German art held in the neo-classical Haus der Deutschen Kunst.) The design of the Center serves as the medium for the integration of those design strategies identified in the studio with lateness (i.e. problematic symbolism, internal disciplinary issues, etc.) while simultaneously questioning the ethical imperative of such a monument. Here, perhaps, Hanna Arendt's conception of the "banality of evil," suggestive of the ultimately antispectacular flows of power that undergirded the most spectacular of regimes, carries architectural implications as well. Indeed, a "dokumentationszentrum" dedicated to the history of evil can be anything but iconic of that evil, but at the same time it cannot ignore the mere presence of its program. Following Loos, the studio attempts to uncover those strategies, revolving around the re-articulation of the part-to-whole relationship, that offers an anti-spectacular solution to this ambivalent, yet imperative, task of the monument. The specific programmatic requirements of the center were articulated by the project organizers in the middle of August and constitute the program brief for the studio.

I
THE REAL AND THE SYMBOLIC
PARSA KHALILI & MATT ROMAN,
H.I. FELDMAN NOMINEES
Building from the premise that the work of Adolf Loos represents a moment in architecture caught between 19th century eclecticism and 20th century modernism, the project developed from a series of formal operations on what we perceived as real, imaginary and symbolic arti- facts on the Brown House site in Munich. In order to overcome Nazi rhetoric, the darkest manifestation of modernism, these operations of multiplication and repetition dislocate the symbolic value of the two Ehren Temples, in particular, and disrupt the existing pre- and post- Nazi axes in the city. This re-figuring of the urban landscape is analytic in its approach and critical in its re- lationship to history and contemporary architectural issues of composition and index.

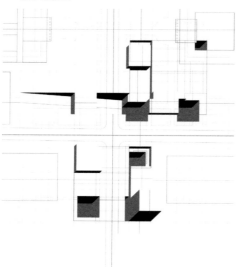

PETER EISENMAN „ We've seen five different proj-
„ ects, and it doesn't matter necessarily the
„ quality, it's what were the ambitions, the
„ critical ambitions of the projects in the stu-
„ dio. I opened the discussion by saying one of
„ the 'monkey wrenches', as we call it in studio,
„ was a Nazi museum. To this day, I cannot figure
„ out how one makes a critique of a Nazi museum,
„ of the history of Nazi architecture. Why would
„ one make an auratic project, to the aura of
„ something that is already auratic? And so the
„ question is, what alternative method, given
„ the Neoclassical site, given the whole thing,
„ what alternative project could you think of in
„ the studio? And we've seen examples. I don't
„ want to defend the studio. I think the studio
„ has been enormously interesting. I don't know
„ what the answer to the question is, but the
„ fact is that the studio is not about answering
„ questions, but proposing other questions. I
„ think a project without index--in other words,
„ this is a project that I would consider to be
„ a post-indexical project, alright? Is it pos-
„ sible to have a mental, post-indexical project,
„ dealing with what I call partial figures, et
„ cetera? I think that that is, without speaking
„ for you guys, where this project is. I think we
„ as critics ought to judge it on that basis.
JEFFREY KIPNIS „ In that case, the use of tropes
„ of abstraction, and the way you have abstracted
„ the figural out of the basic geometry to make
„ the tropes more…
STANLEY TIGERMAN „ I think the reason that every-
„ body got wound up and became emotional is because
„ this is one of the projects, and actually one
„ could argue it's the only project, that presents
„ an architectural alternative to the Classicism one
„ finds in front of the Königsplatz. So you choose a
„ Modernist alternative which happens to be timed

„ precisely with the documentation of 1918-1933.
„ Then the question is, is the Modernist approach
„ to housing the archive of the documents of the
„ Nazi in those kinds of buildings? I think it is.
„ What's interesting about it is that architecture
„ itself stands in such contradistinction to the
„ documents and to the Neoclassical four-square
„ axes that I think it's extraordinary.
PETER EISENMAN „ Also, contradistinction internally.
STANLEY TIGERMAN „ That's actually very unique.
„ That actually takes this thing and turns it
„ into its section.
ANTHONY VIDLER „ And that's why they did Loos.
STANLEY TIGERMAN „ It's also interesting that we
„ end up with a Modernist scheme facing up to
„ the Classical that precedes it--where archi-
„ tecture actually does challenge the doctrines.
„ And to see this Loosian section is actually
„ quite extraordinary.
HENRY COBB „ It's true that because this project
„ is so complicated it raises a question: when I
„ look at the project, I'm not disturbed enough
„ by it. I think the only place where I begin to
„ imagine it might be disturbing is when I get
„ inside those boxes, and what you've called the
„ Loosian project begins to take effect.
KURT FORSTER „ Isn't the tragedy in the fact
„ that they did have such a constitution?
„ That Nazism emerged from a highly reformed,
„ democratic society? So the last questions I
„ have--everybody paid their compliments and I
„ happily subscribe to their compliments--are
„ ultimately about this historic moment. The
„ longer I look at this, I am confronted with
„ two dilemmas. The first is, do you have to act
„ like they did in order to make your project
„ get across? Do you have to make this physical
„ intervention to carry across what in the end
„ will be a weak symbolic message?

PARSA KHALILI
MATT ROMAN

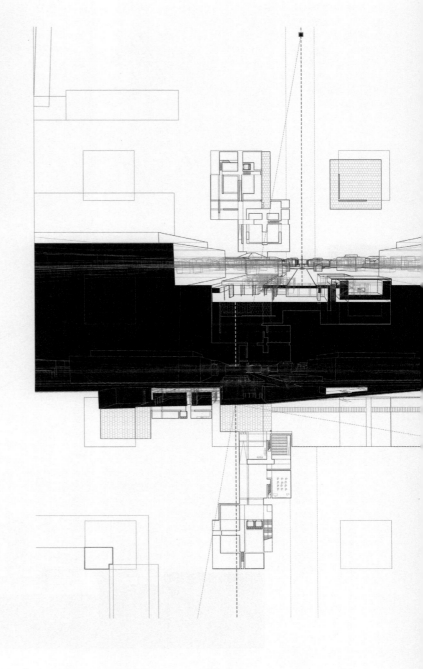

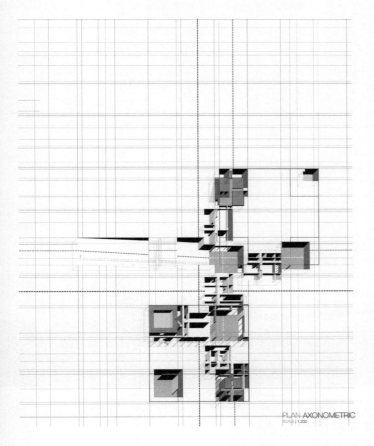

PLAN AXONOMETRIC
SCALE 1:200

I

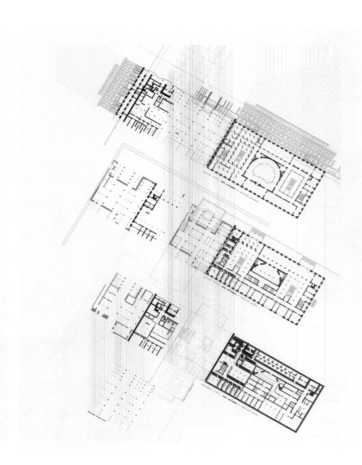

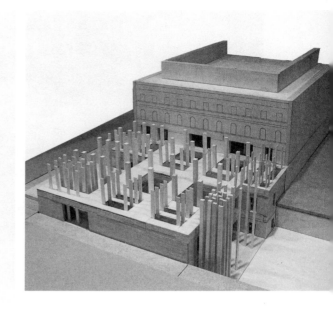

II

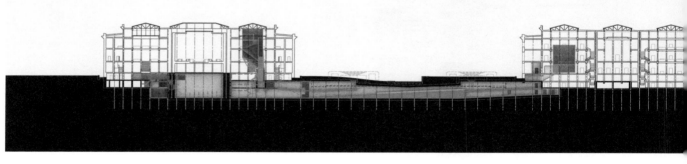

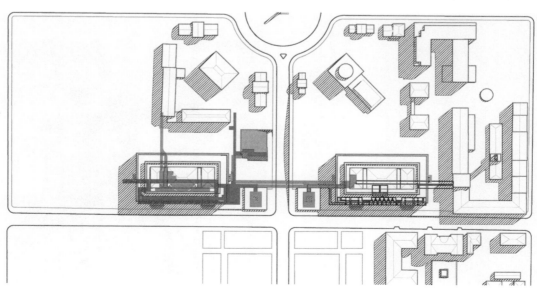

III

PETER EISENMAN   MICHAEL WANG

HENRY COBB   LUIS FERNÁNDEZ-GALIANO   FRANCISCO MANGADO   STANLEY TIGERMAN
KURT FORSTER   JEFFREY KIPNIS   INGEBORG ROCKER   ANTHONY VIDLER
KEITH KRUMWIEDE   MASSIMO SCOLARI

HENRY COBB „ The distortion of the columns is one of the things I find most attractive about this project. I see that as the final and most important step in the game that is being played here.

KEITH KRUMWIEDE „ But I wonder if it's that you're too close in the relationship between the old and the new?

HENRY COBB „ The cutting off of the columns is, to my mind, the idea that this project moved to Berlin before it was finished, and therefore it was left unfinished here. The distortion of the columns has to do with the distortion of value systems, the distortion of--whether you call it the Classical language or otherwise this idea is so fundamental to the Nazi project that I find this very moving in that sense.

LUIS FERNÁNDEZ-GALIANO „ I think that the distortion here is not well composed, and let me say why. This is an extruded building, compositionally, but the building is pushed on two sides. That causes the problem of the corner, which has not been solved.

PETER EISENMAN „ Luis, let me ask you a question that Tony and I were just talking about, about this so-called, in quotes, 'Eisenman Studio.' Had they moved the building, because this building would fit on the Brown House site, they never would have won anything because the building depends not on its size being the same as the Brown House, but being where it is. The authorities would never have let us build on those façades; those two buildings are sacred buildings. Because we would have done a Brown House building, and we would have lost. And that's precisely the strength of this project, that it critiques the purity of these two end façades, it critiques the symmetry, and it does all of the other urban things. It requires itself to be right where it is.

KURT FORSTER „ But then the question that continues to haunt me here is, is it possible to work purely with the deformation of elements, like the thinning of the post to a pilaster? Or, is it enough to make something redundant by repeating it where you wouldn't expect it? A Classical order of elements in space can assume these entire subordinate but very important end defining qualities for your project, through only the act of their deformation and redundancy.

ANTHONY VIDLER „ Well, it could be done with spacing. But I have to say that the reason that we're around this project with such passion is that it's an exceptionally good project. As a student project, to produce this level of sophistication through the first moves and then to try and complicate them by making them representational in relationship to the building that you have--to ruin in order to make the point about the building that you're building--I think there you have succeeded enormously.

INGEBORG ROCKER „ I want to respond to the comments about what language would be the adequate one here. It seems to me that you purposely use a conventional language, and I think you do this as much as you also use a systemic idea. But I think you do this in order to lodge a critique of that very logic, which is going to be exhibited here. Through the techniques and materiality of architecture, in this particular project, it is acceptable.

JEFFREY KIPNIS „ I think you should come away from this project knowing that you have made progress on column modulation. In other words, if you walk out of a project knowing what you have to do next, that's the reason you're in school. The intuitions are the modulations of the columns.

FRANCISCO MANGADO „ At first, I was thinking that your approach was quite sensitive in the sense that you are making the most of these two buildings and making the most of these tunnels. The building is quite attractive, subtle, and reasonable. In the end you make the most of all of these elements, but in my opinion, what has happened is that it's not too ambitious, this solution. It's too simple, perhaps, working with this system, trying to create a more intensive relationship with these buildings, creating the kind of surprises you need.

ANTHONY VIDLER „ I think that the tension is in these structures underground which are totally interconnected and linked to each other. And what they want to do is not build a separate memorial to Nazi documentation but a network which implicates all these structures.

KURT FORSTER „ The idea of a hidden tunnel into buildings themselves--in a sense, this is like a vertical tunnel. Actually you go through all of this in a separate sphere, in a totally separate conduit, which works in the vertical where you need it, and in the horizontal where you move from one building to the other. So you sort of tunnel into the body of the existing buildings.

JEFF KIPNIS „ What's being said is correct and therefore it's bothering me. This is a very good example of the kind of intelligent and poetic display given the archaeological circumstances, with no critique of the question of history, no critique of the circumstance. In other words, it's very smart about how it displays things, but it seems to be utterly out of touch with the studio in the sense that there is no critical or speculative project.

ANTHONY VIDLER „ Revealing--it is not critique?

JEFF KIPNIS „ We know the archaeology of revealing it, in particular we know the archaeological situation underground. I think it's a really good building. It's just very hard for me to hang any architectural merit on it.

STANLEY TIGERMAN „ Let me add something to that. I was talking to Peter just before the review about the role architecture has. It's difficult to critique the material, on one level. What can stand in contradistinction is the building. What is the critique of the material that is on display?

INGERBORG ROCKER „ I think there are too many overlaps, a few too many ideas. You could say that by taking the functionality of the corridor away, by avoiding those actual moments of transition into the existing buildings, the critique is achieved. For me that is the only moment that you critique the material.

ANTHONY VIDLER „ I would appreciate that. I think this is one of the best things we've seen. I really think it has a palette to it, energy to it, a diagrammatic clarity to it, we can argue whether it is transparent or it's not transparent. The using of those tunnels and the blocking of them, the organization of them, and then the way they do take over what they were there to take over in the first place but in a different way.

JEFFREY KIPNIS „ But is it critical?

KURT FORSTER „ It is very critical because what this says is that you enter into this past only by going behind the scenes, which refers to the access denied you. Now you extend that exclusive, behind the scenes approach to the buildings themselves. So you don't have to move anything in the buildings, and yet anybody going in to them will inevitably have to reckon with this fact that he was inside the building and he was not in the past.

II
NATIONAL SOCIALISM DOKUMENTATION-
SZENTRUM IN MÜNCHEN, GERMANY
NICHOLAS CARUSO & ALEX MAYMIND

Our task was to analyze and then work from the existing historical context of Nazi-era Munich in order to create an architecture that is conceptually neither historicist nor nostalgic but is motivated by the memory and history of a highly-loaded site. The Fuhrerbau, a Troost-designed 1930s existing but suppressed building, one Ehren Temple now in a state of ruin, and an assigned site recast as void became motivated forces that formed the logic and geometry of a deformed and modulated column grid. The columns and the modulated grid determine openings in the floor plate, exhibition layout, and openings, creating a high contrast between the vertical expansion and horizontal compression, and the related experiences of the documents versus the banality of the grid.

III
RÄUME OHNE EIGENSCHAFTEN
NS-DOKUMENTATIONSZENTRUM, MÜNCHEN
CODY DAVIS & DANIEL YODER

Reserving our capacity to act from judgment, we have chosen an intervention forsaking violence, formal didacticism, or moralizing exhibition. Ours obliges the visitor to confront the curiosities/atrocities originated on this site by emphasizing spatially not only what exists and has been exhumed but also by revealing that some things can never be shown.

The project, shaped by circulation, unearths the disparate pathways that previously linked exclusively separate systems in a larger highly compartmentalized organism. Through a series of connections, unlike any this building has heretofore hosted, occupants continuously shift between the physicality of the existing and an absurdly compact underworld.

CHRISTINA CHU

PEGGY DEAMER   STEVEN HARRIS
KENNETH FRAMPTON   CARLOS JIMÉNEZ
LUIS FERNÁNDEZ-GALIANO

FRANCISCO MANGADO

SERGIO KEIRNAN   FERNANDO MUT OLTRA
CESAR PELLI   JUAN MIGUEL OCHOTORRENATO

519A

MANGADO STUDIO

The effects of mass tourism pose a significant architectural challenge to a large extent of the Mediterranean coast. The sudden increase in population density has facilitated economic growth, but it has also resulted in a disorderly and visually chaotic urban environment. Although this growth has enriched the social structure and economy, it has come at the expense of vernacular architecture and planning, which have been displaced by vast areas with a shortage of civic services. This subtraction of urban amenities is best witnessed in the territory between the beach avenues and inland development.

Now that this growth has stabilized, there is an opportunity to confront the disorder of these architectural and urban transformations. In the past few years, Spanish Mediterranean authorities have initiated a large-scale restructuring process. These political initiatives prompt the question of the degree to which architects can influence urban transformations with individual buildings. Or should they now address more of the environmental and infrastructural context? In other words, does the necessity of circumstance merit a re-envisioning of the architect as generalist?

The studio develops a project that first takes on a brief urban design project (a public park and network of pedestrian streets) and then a specific architectural intervention (a mixed-use hotel). The chosen site is Gandia, a city of the Spanish Levante (a region located in Valencia), which is committed to the transformation process described.

I
RE-MIXING GANDIA
ISAIAH KING,
H.I. FELDMAN NOMINEE
This proposal uses a mixed use hotel as an anchor on an underused park to foster a re-mixing of the public and private through new civic and commercial spaces located within the park. The hotel, placed at the crossroads of the beach city, nature preserve, and the old city, creates a large public space that acts as a meeting place for activities and groups from all three areas. As a piece within a larger urban plan for a connecting greenway back to the old city, the hotel becomes an important node, offering an alternative to the beachfront focus and enlivening the less popular backside of the linear beach town.

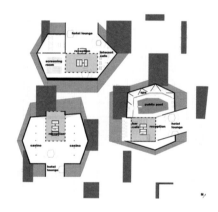

CESAR PELLI „The road is very difficult to cross. „ The circulation is too convoluted. It's a „ shame; there should be a really nice walk to „ get there.
ISAIAH KING „The intention was to use the park- „ scape as a way of circulating people down „ to the beach and not as a direct shot right „ across the road.
CESAR PELLI „But if you are trying to get to „ the beach in a hurry, you aren't interested „ in participating in this lengthy, picturesque „ circulation.
ISAIAH KING „Well then I think this hotel oc- „ cupies a slightly different status in this con- „ text. There are plenty of hotels already right „ on the beach. There need to be other reasons „ to come here than only the beach.
CARLOS JIMÉNEZ „I think that what Cesar is „ implying is to be more refined with the issue „ of circulation, because it is critical. I do „ very much like the way the park works here--it „ sets up a type of plinth for this area, and I „ like the way it relates to the marshland. The „ question is, with the circulation, is there „ another way of articulating this carpet that „ rolls out to the sea? I don't want to redesign „ your project, because I like so much of what „ you've done. You haven't allowed the building „ to conform to the orthogonality of the other „ buildings around it; rather, you've decided „ that this area away from the beach is actually „ incredibly interesting, and so you came up „ with a new building form to maximize the types „ of views to everything around it. It really „ creates some very nice and different moments.
LOUIS FERNÁNDEZ GALIANO „I really do admire so

„ much of what is going on here. What I think is „ important is to pay attention to some of these „ details, to weigh them into some logic. It's „ one thing to create this really compelling „ landscape; it's another to then think about „ all the ways that it can start to work with „ shading and privacy. It's where you're head- „ ing. It's crucial though--we have seen so many „ of these failed hotels or parks that never „ really considered the specifics for how the „ space is animated and used.
CESAR PELLI „Why does the hotel widen in the „ center?
ISAIAH KING „It's a way to negotiate this plat- „ form. It actually pulls the section and cre- „ ates larger indoor public spaces with natural „ lighting on both ends.
KENNETH FRAMPTON „I think that, although your „ scheme has many virtues, I think you should be „ aware that the program that was given to you „ really encouraged you to create some sort of „ hybrid building--it's a hotel plus something „ else. And I think that most people have really „ steered clear of trying to be inventive about „ this. I think it has the greatest impact on „ the hotel's public spaces. Even when you look „ at your section, there seems to be no sort of „ schematic inflection in those spaces; they all „ seem very safe. There is really a potential „ there. It might also just be a problem with the „ complexity of the studio.
STEVEN HARRIS „There is a slightly odd formal „ rigor to it, where the angles are all the same. „ On the one hand, it gives you formal consis- „ tency. On the other hand, it really wants a „ risk. It wants a tease.

ISAIAH KING

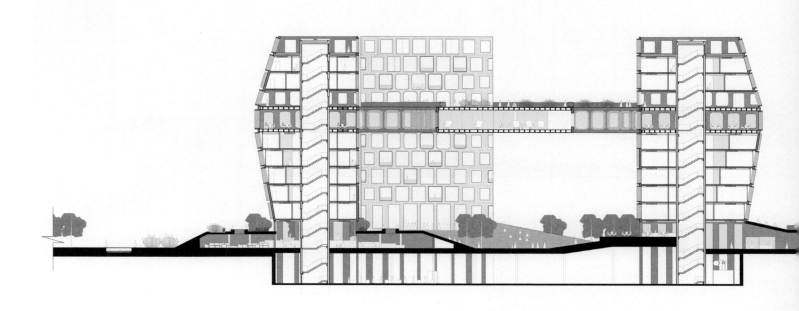

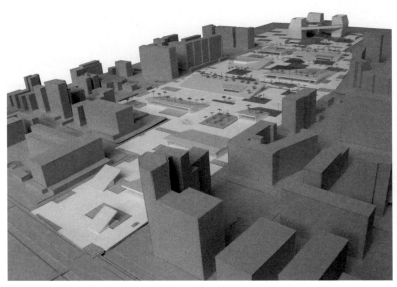

II

III

CHRISTINA CHU

PEGGY DEAMER   STEVEN HARRIS
KENNETH FRAMPTON   CARLOS JIMÉNEZ
LUIS FERNÁNDEZ-GALIANO

FRANCISCO MANGADO

SERGIO KEIRNAN   FERNANDO MUT OLTRA
CESAR PELLI   JUAN MIGUEL OCHOTORRENATO

CARLOS JIMÉNEZ „What was the intention with the „ form of the topography? FELICIA MARTIN „The idea was to pull people back „ from the beach, through the site, to give them „ a small pinch of the larger scheme. LOUIS FERNÁNDEZ GALIANO „Well I think it's pro- „ portionate, I think it's elegant--I think it's „ a very good project. STEVEN HARRIS „Yes, but I think that there's „ another way of going about it. The ball courts-- „ the place where there is a latent ritual. CARLOS JIMÉNEZ „Right, you could imagine con- „ certs here, you could imagine all sorts of „ things. STEVEN HARRIS „Exactly, and it makes it possible „ to be so much more specific about what all „ these smaller elements are doing. LOUIS FERNÁNDEZ GALIANO „Because right now, it's „ like, 'should I move them up, should I flatten „ them down, et cetera. It's a little gratuitous, „ the way you're playing with it. I think that „ there's an opportunity to make something that „ has that so-called 'latent ritual.' KENNETH FRAMPTON „I agree with these comments, „ but what troubles me is still the hotel. These „ forms suggest a sort of morphology integrated

„ with the movement through the park, and then „ suddenly the bar of the hotel running across „ is like another concept of the world entirely. „ One of the really attractive things is this „ rhythmic directionality, and this building „ counters it. CARLOS JIMÉNEZ „Do you suggest that the build- „ ings want to remain outside in some way? KENNETH FRAMPTON „Yes, because now these build- „ ings are answering, in a very conventional „ sense, 'What is a Mediterranean vacation „ hotel?' But the landscape is about some other „ poetry altogether. STEVEN HARRIS „There's such potential to carry „ this logic into the hotel. Right now, nothing „ is going down; everything is being lifted. If „ you excavated the way that you were building, „ it would create this sort of reciprocal space „ between them. CARLOS JIMÉNEZ „I think that that is what I „ was advocating. I do like the repetition a „ lot, and I think the way you've colonized the „ entire site is really interesting. The room „ for the ever so slight variations among all „ of these pieces is where the essence of the „ project development lies.

II
PLINTH REACTIVATED
FELICIA MARTIN
Gandia, a Spanish beach town developed for tourism in the 1970's, is a ghost town during off-season. The prevalent existing typology of the hotel atop plinth creates a privatized and homog- enous experience of the groundscape. This project is a critique of the condi- tion of the plinth. A series of trans- formations are made to the plinth: the plinth is inverted and becomes a surface occupiable from underneath and above. These transformations reactivate the ground plane, create space for civic and public programming, and allow for a richer and more varied space that pro- vides an alternative to the coast line.

KENNETH FRAMPTON „I want to ask you a question „ right away. What type of landscape do you „ envision these forms as? What example of „ modern landscape can you give to explain the „ type of space you are trying to create? MIEKO OKAMOTO „Well I was interested in a way „ that the landscape might grow out of the „ building. It might seem contradictory, because „ there seems to be a complete disjunction, but „ I am interested in the visual as well as the „ physical connection. KENNETH FRAMPTON „Why I ask that question is „ that there is obviously an enormous amount „ of information possible in these circles. „ Certain of them are like these livable „ mounds while others are like circular pools „ of water; which leads me to questions about „ shape. Although the project is very organic, „ it's also extremely abstract in the sense „ that it makes you wonder, if I wanted to go „ to the beach, how strange a way I must take „ to actually get there. From another point of „ view, the circles of water are very limited „ and contradictory to the image of a flowing „ canal that we usually associate with this type „ of landscape. So with all of the geometries „ that imply a sense of organicism, nothing „ is actually as free as you might assume it is. CARLOS JIMÉNEZ „I think that's where the formal- „ ism traps you. There are many things I like

„ about this scheme, but I think the random „ placement of some of this prevents you from „ developing some tangencies, but also some „ concentric moments. My favorite building is „ the elliptical, because it's slipping away and „ it is more complex--it becomes richer. LOUIS FERNÁNDEZ GALIANO „She's obviously very „ talented and she's presented some models that „ are exquisite. But I do not think you want „ to be an architect yet, because all of the „ architectural decisions have been avoided. As „ an artistic project, it is stunning. As an „ architectural project, nothing works. CESAR PELLI „Don't listen to him, we like you „ as an artist.
{Laughter}
FRANCISCO MANGADO „But this does allow you „ to project so much into what could happen „ here--for instance, these delightful raised „ walkways and the rest. KENNETH FRAMPTON: „And there are issues that „ arrive, and not to use such an out-of-fashion „ word, but phenomenologically speaking, there „ are so many different conditions that can occur. „ For example, water running through the site „ versus water contained in the pools. The ques- „ tion of the differences of experiences between „ the subjects is perhaps what will give you the „ conviction to move this from an artistic to an „ architectural production.

III
BOARDWALK URBANISM
MIEKO OKAMOTO
The geometric properties of the circle are exploited to create elevated pedes- trian connections between the beach and the farm, provide fluid visual and physical transition from one program to another, and draw liminal boundaries between the building and its urban setting, the rooms and the hallway, right here and over there.

GEORGE KNIGHT   DEMETRI PORPHYRIOS

THOMAS BEEBY   LEON KRIER   ALAN PLATTUS   JAQUELIN ROBERTSON
KENT BLOOMER   BARBARA LITTENBERG   ALEXANDER PURVES   FIKRET YEGUL
DIANA KLEINER

514B

PORPHYRIOS STUDIO

The studio studies the tradition of Hellenistic, Roman and Muslim baths from a typological, morphological and cultural point of view. Principles and cultural ideas are drawn and students are asked to design a present day spa-centre that may be informed by historical precedent. Students visit Marrakech to study relevant architectural and urban design examples.

I
MEKNES WOMEN'S HAMMAM AND
RESOURCE CENTER
LAUREN MISHKIND,
H.I. FELDMAN NOMINEE

The project is imbedded in the carved Meknes medina. It attempts to address the social and spatial requirements of the program and site by focusing on three main points: interiorizing the density of the medina by linking programmatic zones with corridors and sightlines as connective tissue utilizing the indigenous building type, with the court serving as the social and organizational center and perpetuating the blurred line between the public and private sphere through the use of the roof as a congregation space and multiple entrances to suggest a continuity of urban traffic across the site. There is minimal focus on the exterior walls, except to illuminate access points, thereby limiting the legibility of its orientation. Barrel vaulting is employed across the site to announce its civic function and mirror the syncopation of the urban fabric.

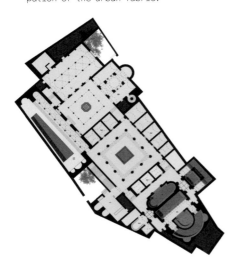

FIKRET YEGUL „ Water on both sides. Water inside water. There's a bath in North Africa that uses that theme. There's a pool and a pool, water inside water. So that reminded me of that. It's a wonderful ambulatory swimming area, and an interior more intimate pool. This is in Algeria--gorgeous.

ALAN PLATTUS „ There's a kind of amazing 'aha' moment, when you're headed for the main courtyard, and you look off to one side or another, and there are these incredible slices through the whole thing which then open up on both sides in different ways so that this moment here--that solid wall versus that screen wall--is a little bit like what that water moment could be, where you're always in one room, sort of looking through to the next, and there's a degree of transparency about it that's potentially fabulous.

JAQUELIN ROBERTSON „ It's a great device. And you see it, and the first time I saw it, it was so dumb, and you've got it in this beautiful long courtyard, you've drawn this very beautiful section, that's fabulous here. There's this light against this wall, and light bouncing off that wall, it's going to come onto the pool; light hitting the water is going to bounce images of the water on the wall, and you'd look at it and say, yeah I got it, and I've never seen that before. So it--this is as good as you can do. In the summertime, you're going to get light in the morning hitting this and bouncing down onto the water…

FIKRET YEGUL „ And making all these wavy patterns on the wall.

JAQUELIN ROBERTSON „ You're going to get that highlight hitting the water and being reflected up on the walls, and it's magical.

FIKRET YEGUL „ I want to say something about the program. If I were part of the program, one of the things I would have asked for would be a general lounge for after bathing. The idea being this: the caldarium, the laconicum, the halvet, the hot areas--you really get tired there physically. Because if you've really taken a Turkish bath or an Arabic bath, a Roman bath, the high degree of heat, the steam, it's a nice kind of tired. Then afterwards, all your muscles are relaxed, you want a place where you can have a cold drink, or a cup of tea or something like that--and of course I didn't invent this, this is traditional in Roman baths and Turkish baths. So after they've bathed they don't just quickly go back to the apoditerium and put their clothes on and out of the door, because that would also be against health, you know, they'd catch cold. So someplace here, a lounge, where they could just loll around, chat a bit, lie on couches, you know, something of that sort--you probably saw those in Cairo, in Arabic baths, that sort of cool area after the hot baths.

DIETRICH NEUMANN „ What about that central courtyard? Could that work?

FIKRET YEGUL „ That central courtyard might work.

JAQUELIN ROBERTSON „ That central courtyard here is so beautifully scaled, and it steps down to the pool. Which is perfect. And it gives you that long shot into Never Never Land. And it happens exactly at the right point after you enter. Because you enter, take a right turn, go up the steps, see the steps, your head whips this way and sees the steps going up and then goes through and then has the long axis. So the second floor is announced, and you could even take a piece of this wall away so that you see that step going up.

BARBARA LITTENBERG „ Would you make us a roof plan?

JAQUELIN ROBERTSON „ She's got one.

BARBARA LITTENBERG „ Because it seems to me this stair might lead up to a sundeck.

JAQUELIN ROBERTSON „ It does; it's even better.

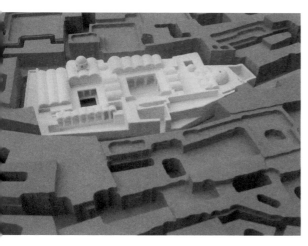

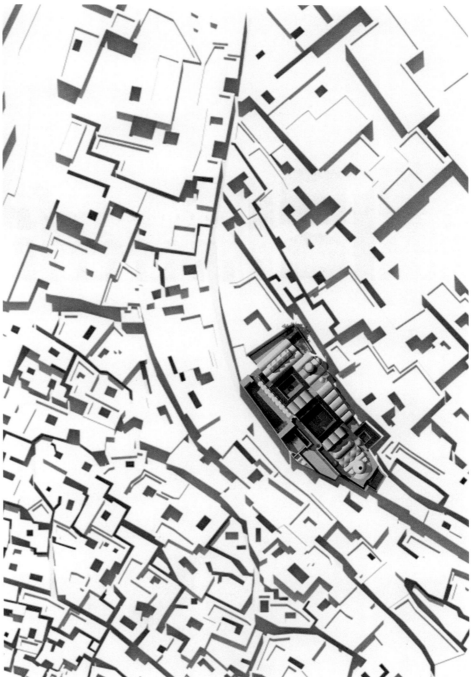

I

II

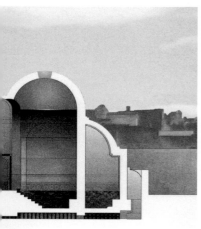

III

THOMAS BEEBY LEON KRIER ALAN PLATTUS JAQUELIN ROBERTSON
KENT BLOOMER BARBARA LITTENBERG ALEXANDER PURVES FIKRET YEGUL
DIANA KLEINER

FIKRET YEGUL „ A question I would like to ask „ first is, by making this bath in Puerto Rico, „ not in Marrakesh, you made a very significant „ decision, a change, and I cannot--I do not „ want to accept that because you're from there. „ That seems it would be too simplistic. Are „ there some deeper reasons why you put this „ bath--and you went to Marrakesh--in Puerto „ Rico, in a busy square, across from the city „ center?

KENT BLOOMER „ Just in relation to the tremen- „ dous humidity of the Caribbean, Marrakesh is „ incredibly dry, and the fact that you have the „ water right nearby…

LEON KRIER „ In your case it would help to have a „ few three-dimensional drawings. Because it's „ very beautifully drawn, but we don't really „ get into it. If you had a few sketches showing „ the courtyards and so on--it's a nice project.

ALAN PLATTUS „ I quite like it. Typologically, „ it reminds me of the way that theaters, movie „ theaters in American towns relate to main „ streets. You get this kind of compressed en- „ trance, off in the midst of a commercial row, „ but then you penetrate it from the middle of „ the block, and the big space is the lobby, „ and then the theater itself opens up. In a way „ the only thing I'm missing is, I feel like I'm „ getting in to the sequence of the bath too „ abruptly. If it's on the main square of the town, „ I'm looking for a little more spatial relief „ before I get right into the impacted business „ end of the baths. I'm not quite sure how to do „ it, but it may have to do with using some of „ the adjacent spaces and elaborating the se- „ quence. I'd almost like to go all the way around „ to where your café is, and find the axis that „ way, and then come back all the way across „ the site.

BARBARA LITTENBERG „ You know what I was won- „ dering, I'm thinking, this is a big public

building, the big spaces are up on the second „ floor, and the whole underbelly is filled with „ market stalls, why couldn't the whole building „ be upstairs? I don't give a damn what he did, „ it's a fantastic piece of urbanism, all wrapped „ up. If you had taken the whole thing, put „ it up fourteen, fifteen feet, then you'd carve „ in from the top and you could put Marshall's „ in, you could do whatever you want underneath „ and then you could wrap it. What you want is „ something viable, given where you've put it. „ So I think in your case, the argument that you „ didn't want it to be too showy on the street „ doesn't hold.

JAQUELIN ROBERTSON „ I think the small scale is „ to his credit; I'd just like to see it.

BARBARA LITTENBERG „ But you can make a big thing „ small-scale. You can cut it up into as many „ pieces as you want--and the model for that „ kind of urban piece building is the basilica. „ The more I look at it, the more I think it's „ really a brilliant piece of urbanism.

ALAN PLATTUS „ The bath that works exactly like „ yours today is the Roman bath at Bath, where „ you have the street, and you go through the „ door, and then you find yourself in the space „ looking down. But I think what's brilliant and „ then unrequited, everybody's saying, are that „ the urban possibilities of this, transposed to „ a site like this--it's going to interact with „ the city in a different way if you let it. And I „ don't have a right answer, I think it's inter- „ esting, this idea, as Barbara is saying, that „ you would put in a Palazzo della Ragione with „ a ground floor market and then the big meeting „ room, if that's the cognate thing, above. But „ I also like my idea that the movie theater is „ buried in the block because in a way the bath „ is private--it's not a law court. It's more „ private, where you retreat from the public „ space. It's a more intimate kind of space.

II
PLAZA DE ARMAS SPA COMPLEX
ANGEL BEALE

The site chosen for the Spa complex was Old San Juan, Puerto Rico, the colonial city established in 1509 by Juan Ponce de León for Spain. The site is home to several historic buildings including the second oldest Church in the new world and the San Jeronimo Fortress that saw wars among European navies. Within the colonial city the spa will be placed in front of the central square, "Plaza de Armas", facing City Hall. Currently the site holds a two level Marshals and an eight level office building. The pro- posed complex will replace these, re- storing the character of the city to its Spanish heritage. At the same time it will help to eliminate big box retail as well as the offices that contribute to heavy congestion in and out of the city. Even today entry into the city is by two small roads left over from the city's defensive organization, making it sen- sitive to fluctuations in traffic flow.

The spa will be two stories, reflect- ing the two stories of city hall across the plaza. Several additional programs will surround the spa in order to produce a variation of façade typol- ogies. This will keep the bath from becoming a monolith on the square. Sur- rounding programs will include a Beauty Salon, a small hotel, 3 shops, and a café. The style of the spa itself is influenced by Moroccan architecture to maintain dialogue with several original Spanish structures that call out Spain's history of Islamic rule.

FIKRET YEGUL „I think if you would have ex- „ plained this area not so much as a private „ part of the bath, where you need to be naked „ or in bathing clothes, but rather what I see, „ or would like to see in this, is an almost „ public square.

JAQUELIN ROBERTSON „Well it is. It's a public „ water square.

FIKRET YEGUL „Well if it is a public square then „ I can understand. And by the way, look at the „ scale. This is about forty meters by thirty- „ five meters or so. That's huge. It is the square „ you were talking about. And it organizes, in „ this very orderly fashion, a bath, another „ bath, and in between the treatment area. So „ it would be alright to come in here with your „ street clothes, and go in and change here, and „ then go here.

JAQUELIN ROBERTSON „But this entry is a kind of „ throw-away western space that you almost never „ see in the Middle East. It's neither one nor „ the other. Either this is a high wall and these „ are bigger and this is--my guess is that these „ have to be enclosed and have to be places that „ you can go out into in privacy--and that it „ wants to have nothing to do with the street.

FIKRET YEGUL „No, it just has to be private.

JAQUELIN ROBERTSON „This low wall stuff, you „ can't use this.

BARBARA LITTENBERG „ It looks like an American „ museum. It has this little sculpture garden „ out in front.

JAQUELIN ROBERTSON „ It then questions how you use „ this piece. You could say this is a drive-in, „ where you can drop people off, so I can get in „ from both ends, which is okay, but these things „ want to be part of this world. Because they're „ more intimate, and you don't want to be look- „ ing into them from the street.

KENT BLOOMER „Are they not available to people „ on the street? I mean, is this not public prop- „ erty? You know it's funny, the comment that „ Karen made, that really still reverberates, „ that the amount of public space is one foot- „ print per person multiplied by the population,

„ did you hear her say that?

JAQUELIN ROBERTSON „In Cairo, yes.

KENT BLOOMER „So what's wrong with allowing a „ little more? That's my question.

JAQUELIN ROBERTSON „No, if you could stop here „ and have tea…

KENT BLOOMER „Or just walk in, and walk out.

ALAN PLATTUS „I have to say, I hate all that „ stuff. That's a category mistake, it's this kind „ of Western-style lobby, if you entered right „ into the courtyard and then everything--all „ of those service functions like the front „ desk--are off the court. So instead of doing „ this, if you pretty much came right into the „ courtyard, it would also free up a lot of space „ on that side, either to extend the garden or „ to slide this stuff around and get the women's „ bath, the men's bath, and the shared facilities „ all working off the courtyard rather than off „ this axis. George (Knight) and I were having „ an important conversation, which is that these „ rather beautiful spaces--that's the big court- „ yard, right? In these it's not so big, it's „ tall and shaded, and much more intimate than I „ suspect it is given the dimensions of it.

JAQUELIN ROBERTSON „ How tall is that? You sit „ overlooking the water, in a double colonnade.

FIKRET YEGUL „It's quite beautiful.

KENT BLOOMER „Beautiful. It's absolutely beauti- „ ful. Who else has made these light studies? „ Those are the best light studies I've seen all „ day, I've kept my mouth reasonably shut, but „ the ornament and the treatment of walls--I do „ think you have to be commended for your light „ studies, for your explanation of light and „ dark, for what George and Alan picked up in „ their conference about the size of that room „ which is shown in that drawing. The same kind „ of investigation is going on in these sec- „ tions; I think that's spectacular, actually.

FIKRET YEGUL „I think this is also one of the few „ projects that has achieved a sort of density „ of ornament, if you like, an elaboration, and „ to me that's very effective in a way that you „ seldom see.

III
THE EMBEDDING OF ORDERS
TERRENCE CHEW

Situated in a bustling urban quarter of Marrakech and directly adjacent to the Djemma el Fna, a UNESCO-celebrated city square, the project is set amidst the bazaar and the ancient city walls of Marrakesh's Medina. In order to accommodate the intimate nature of the spa program, the proposal calls for a breakdown of the large site-block and the introduction of small retail blocks akin to those in the adjacent souks. The project embeds itself within this pseudo-organic configuration and estab- lishes its own spatial order through a series of courtyards, each of which is uniquely defined by program and by nuanced ornamental strategies.

TIMOTHY NEWTON

JOHN PATKAU

CYNTHIA DAVIDSON   MERRILL ELAM   CARLOS JIMÉNEZ   WILLIAM SHARPLES
PEGGY DEAMER   KENNETH FRAMPTON   ARIANE LOURIE HARRISON

516B

PATKAU STUDIO

This studio focuses on the essential and formative contribution that material issues bring to an understanding of architecture. Architectural design studios frequently focus on the "who, why, what, where, and when" of a project. We consider these things; they are the base data from which the design of every building is formed. However, they are not our principal focus. We concentrate on the "how," how a building is actually made; for while a work of architecture can be broad, multivalent, and even self-contradictory in its cultural engagement, it is nevertheless highly specific in its material resolution. This studio suggests that it is possible to understand material inquiry as truly generative, that issues of construction contribute both enduring value and meaningful invention to architecture.

We address the design of a specific building on a specific site via focused inquiries regarding scale, geometry, topography, structure, material property, assembly, craft, construction, and fabrication process.

More specifically, Horse Island is one of a number of rugged granite islands which make up the Thimble Islands in Long Island Sound not far from New Haven. It is owned by Yale University and maintained by the Peabody Museum as an ecological reserve. As part of the museum outreach program Horse Island is the site of a number of university and public uses.

A small field station is planned which will combine a university meeting retreat with an environmental education center which focuses on the geology and biology of Long Island Sound. The meeting retreat continues past use of the site as a secluded location for important gatherings for both university and organizations such as the United Nations. The environmental education center continues use of the ecological reserve for university field work as well as public education.

I
EMBEDDED RUIN
ZAK SNIDER,
H.I. FELDMAN NOMINEE

Located on Horse Island in Long Island Sound, this ecological field station and meeting hall engages the building as an armature to capture and study landscape. Landscape spaces take advantage of subtleties in territorial definitions, distinguishing them from traditional architectural and urban spaces. As a strategy, it allows for a more complex and nuanced order of spaces to emerge. Stretching across the narrow throat of the island, the device of the curved wall is used to draw visitors along a cinematographic unfolding of space, create a free section for landscape undulation, and remain formally sensitive to the curvature of the land. The sectionally varied paths through the building allow moments of privacy and re-emerging spaces of congregation.

The construction process aims to minimize material by varying the depth of the weathered steel wall thickness according to structural load, thereby producing a reveal and greater level of surface articulation. Voids in the steel, mapped from the structural depth of the folded steel enclosure, produce a varied pattern enabling species to nest, facilitate decay, and allow the building, as ruin, to recede into the landscape of the tree canopy.

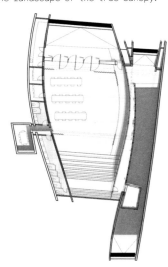

WILLIAM SHARPLES „Well I'll commend you on your presentation; I really enjoy looking at the work. The penetration through the pattern, the filigree--I like it. You can imagine all the legibility you can create, from light, to the idea of critters living in it, to how it will be engulfed by the island over time so there's kind of this ruined quality about it. But when I look at the end of the perspective, what I'm not clear on is--this is steel plate in your model, this is pretty thin steel plate, and it's broken into two separate frames, and in this drawing they're actually composed as a singular, I would say, in this case, a wall, not a plate. That scale difference, for me, is bothersome. I mean, it looks like it's a foot thick here. That's very different from what I read--I read filigree, and I think, touching steel plate, especially if it's, two inches thick like Serra or something, or a thin plate that you can actually hit or throw a stone against--it has a very different reading.
JOHN PATKAU „That's a very subtle issue because in order to achieve the structural capacity that it's going to need to achieve, these plates, these walls are going to have some thickness, and I think the perspective demonstrates that you can easily go too far and they can become too thick. One of the things that troubled me was the disjunction between the dark model and the light color of the perspective, and I was worried of the darkness giving the building a more aggressive kind of character and wondered whether it wouldn't be better as a concrete structure. But then you would get into this thickness thing, and I think that would be a problem too. So it seems to me that the balance would be to make it out of steel but keep it thin, but not to get it to be that dark thing, because it tends to take on a more aggressive character rather than the light filigree; you almost, I think, want it to be like the light renderings, monochromatic like the trees, like the surrounding forest.
CARLOS JIMÉNEZ „Is it more enjoyable, perhaps, to traverse through than to be cuffed in? These images are so wonderful, you can go up to different levels, you can inhabit the roofscape, you can be underneath the paths, and so on and so forth, so there's constantly an experiential turnover, like a conveyer belt that begins at one end, and perhaps the scientists are more discriminating and that's why the spaces are very simple. You know, I come from a country where rainforests are very popular, and they have invented these incredible canopy pieces where people hang from the canopy to look at the flora, fauna, and everything below without touching it, and there's something here that reminds me of it--that drawing particularly, the piece that moves through the site, and that's why I was very perplexed when you said that everything is the same material throughout. I expected that, like one of those inventions, there is an outer shell, there is a structural shell, and here there is a layered shell that is lighter, of a different materiality. I wonder if you were carried away by the model and its fabrication and abandoned the section.
PEGGY DEAMER „I'm going to throw something out here, which is that the cutouts of the filigree, which are claiming a little of our attention, are a real problem. Because my reading of what you've done is, with very simple moves, you've made a lot of interesting, complex spaces in section--in this bridge, in the tunnel underneath it--what is inside, and what is outside, where we arrive, where we end--it's just so beautifully measured. That all happens in a very un-self-conscious way. And so the self-consciousness of the pattern I just think is too bad. And I actually think it's a red herring. I think that the fact that it's the only thing we're talking about should be an indication to you that maybe the energy is in the wrong place.
KENNETH FRAMPTON „The presentation is excellent, and also the verbal presentation. But when you start to look very carefully at the spaces, and their relationship to the two sides of the island, you have this uneasy feeling that these spaces are not--they're like the consequence of the idea, they're not desireable in themselves. The project is more interesting as a route through, but there's nowhere in the route, I think, one would really want to stay. So, that's where the trap lies. And all this steel, not just one layer but two you have to have two layers, in order to simulate somehow or another, trees? Then the whole proposition becomes heavy, I mean, heavy literally. And that brings me to a point--this is too bad but I'm going to say it. I personally think Herzog and de Meuron, Rem Koolhaas, Bejing--is unethical art. Using steel in this way is completely and totally unethical! Because steel, in terms of energy, in terms of money of course, is the most expensive stuff.
WILLIAM SHARPLES „This is reclaimed steel by the way.

{Laughter}

KENNETH FRAMPTON „Anyway, I do think these issues come up. It's amazing how difficult it is to really value material, not only in terms of its literal economic value but in terms of its poetic value.

I

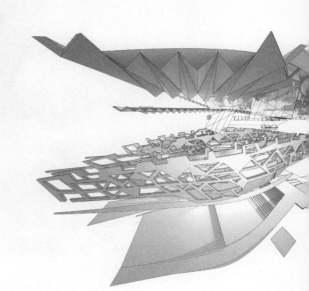

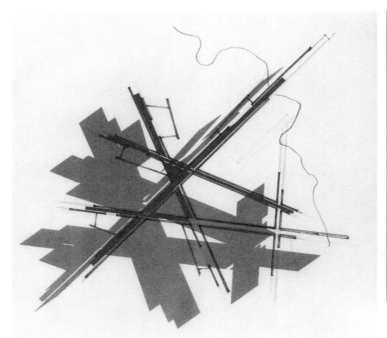

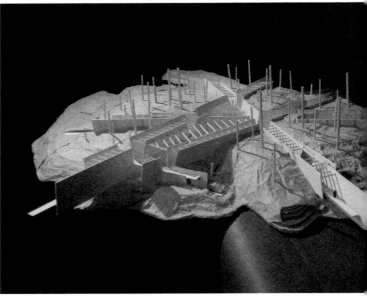

II

III

II
TENUOUS/TENACIOUS
MARK GAUSEPOHL

This structure conveys the nature of the connection between the bedrock and the vegetation of Horse Island. A seemingly tenuous attachment by the vegetation, on and in the island bedrock, is spitefully contradicted by the reality of a tenacious hold. The design of this remote occupation dwells in that contradiction.

This dwelling occurs in a small yet severely exposed segment of the extensive network of crevices and glacial scars which exist in the bedrock of Horse Island and the sea floor.

IV

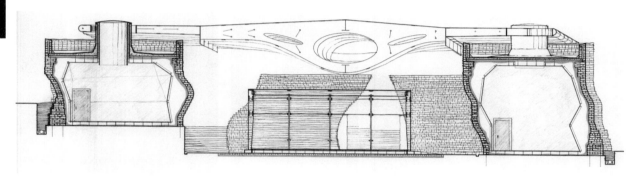

V

III
HORSE ISLAND FIELD STATION
REUBEN HERZL

The Horse Island Field Station is located on uninhabited Thimble Island. Its total area oscillates between eleven and seventeen acres, depending on whether the tide is high or low. The station is sited on the most topographically varied portion of the island. Since the building is located on the narrowest part of Horse Island, it can easily stretch between the northern and southern ocean views. In order to address the flexible usage of the building, the large floor plate contains very few walls and no columns. The exterior spaces have large canopies that provide shelter for outdoor summer events.

VI

VI

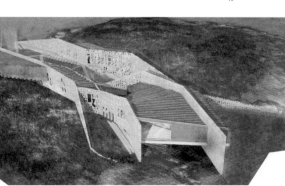

VII

IX

X

IV, V, VI, VII, IX, X
HORSE ISLAND PROJECTS
ROBERT A. COLE, ERIC KRANCEVIC, MWANGI GATHINJI, MARIANNA MELLO, KRISTIN MUELLER, SAIFULLAH SAMI & JULIANNA VON ZUMBUSCH,

KATHERINE CLARKE   LIZA FIOR   ANDREI HARWELL

PEGGY DEAMER   KEITH KRUMWIEDE   GREG LYNN   KEVIN OWINS
ARIANE LOURIE HARRISON

518B

MUF STUDIO

London declared that the 2012 Olympic site will be a legacy for East London: the legacy is to emerge from the remains of the games as a new piece of city with neighbourhoods and infrastructure. This legacy is in the main to be delivered by developers and private investment as a low risk strategy. For political reasons, risk avoidance has been an important theme for these Olympics.

The elimination of risk demanded the re-use of a tried and tested model. But there is no pre-existing model because the situation, the site, the real place of the Lower Lea Valley where the Olympics is sited, is specific only to itself. Only by holding everything that is known about the site at arm's length can the fantasy of the elimination of risk be entertained.

The paradox of the arm's length approach is that it actually precludes any accuracy: to test the relevance of the emerging design in relation to a place requires an interrogation, a testing of both place against design and vice versa. Detail informs the strategic moves.

These interesting times mean that certainties have crumbled, but the legacy has been promised and therefore must be delivered, albeit more slowly, and in order for the double blight of fallow sites to be avoided, temporary site uses must be found. 'Temporary' in this context can mean thirty years.

Students are asked to contribute to creating an alternative Olympic legacy. Each student produces a proposal for an alternative temporary use for a portion of the wider Olympic site. The students work between proposal and critique, detail and strategy, and the tactical and the material. The student draws on the example of New Haven to exploit the coincidence of the Yale Bowl and park which are the same footprint of the Olympic site alongside the effect of stalled developments as a means to explore both scale and the methodology of moving between acquired and received knowledge, and between the arm's length and the up close and personal.

I
SPLICED TYPOLOGIES
BRYAN BERKAS,
H.I. FELDMAN NOMINEE

The new Stratford International Train Station is poised to become a significant intermodal transportation hub and entry point for the 2012 Olympics and the regeneration of East London. This design, extending the train station laterally into the city, activates otherwise unutilized space for occupation by constituents of East London that are not officially connected to the Olympic Games, establishing the presence of the community when it would otherwise be overlooked. Recognizing the programmatic variation in the traditional iron-and-glass shed form in precedents throughout the London region, from train sheds to markets, botanical gardens and museums, temporal activities are spliced into the intermediate spaces between the fixed programs of the train station, tube station, and the surrounding developments and Athletes' Village.

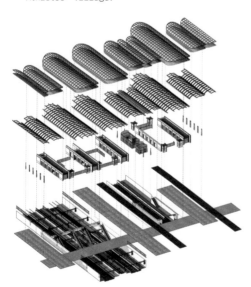

PEGGY DEAMER „In some way it really just does make a lot of sense that the biggest gift you can give is to make it beautifully designed, well respected, somewhat traditional, in the sense that its monumentality says that this city cares for this space and you can have a lot of people but if it doesn't have a lot of people it still doesn't feel empty. And so the legacy is just a great train station. I actually admire that in studying this, you went for the thing that's not going to display your virtuosic, stylistic architectural skills, and just went with something that I suspect would really work, really well.
GREG LYNN „You don't think this is stylized?
PEGGY DEAMER „Totally stylized.
GREG LYNN „Okay, good.
PEGGY DEAMER „And he opted for a style that we're not going to like, and stuck with that.
ARIANE LOURIE HARRISON „I think that this was intriguing, and engaging, kind of smoky, gritty; I actually thought here in the renderings you were getting at a sort of dusty--really getting obsessive about a lot of the train details that I thought, for me, was a kind of aesthetic dimension that you were layering onto this. One of the things I wanted to ask is, there are some strange moves about how you finish or don't finish things off, and I think that probably breaks apart for me. You have very strong profiles against patterns, but then you have completely not credible moments.
GREG LYNN „But the thing that I find very weird-- I understand that you're playing with a style of architecture--you're trying to find the right style, let's say. Those images are very strange. Because where the vault springs down, it's like something you find in the base of Grand Central Station, which is carrying immense loads. Okay, but then from the vault up, it's this very smoky, lightweight, perforated steel. And it's just that in terms of construction, but also just aesthetics, it's wrong. There's something very wrong about it. Where you're going to bring the towers down, I could

see it getting all heavy like that, but where there are no towers I could see it getting lighter. I mean, you have to know how weird it is to have this line of 25 arches in a row. It really feels subterranean, like down in Grand Central, but then you find out it's more like a breezy space, where it's this light steel thing up on a plinth. Planning-wise, it's great; the section is great. It's the language that seems a little bit schizophrenic to me.
KEVIN OWINS „On that point, because you showed St. Pancras, and Pancras is an engineering station, I get the whole diagram picture, and then your explanation--it was all about lightness, it was actually minimalism that's Victorian minimalism, it's structural. And I share the same issue, that that base and its massiveness, and the weight of that--I find myself betwixt and between on those. And I think the pattern of the roofs is romanticized, looking at the railway from a British, London railway station--it has all the references of Paddington, and St. Pancras, and King's Cross--absolutely. It's just that I find the two unconnected.
KEITH KRUMWIEDE „But there is something to be said for developing a language--it looks like Renzo Piano collaborated with Demetri (Porphyrios), in some way. And you've got to figure out what that would mean; I think part of it is recognizing the distinctions between the bays, like Greg pointed out. So you have these bays that are basically functioning as the possible future base for a tower, though at the end of the day I have a hard time believing it. But these end bays, whether it's the one that's up on the road or the one that's on the street--the possibility of actually letting the vaults, or the language of the steel, come down there--that that is a lighter moment. How does the arch actually relate to the production of the atmosphere in that space, rather than your structural or tectonic idea, or bring them together? But I think it's incredible work.

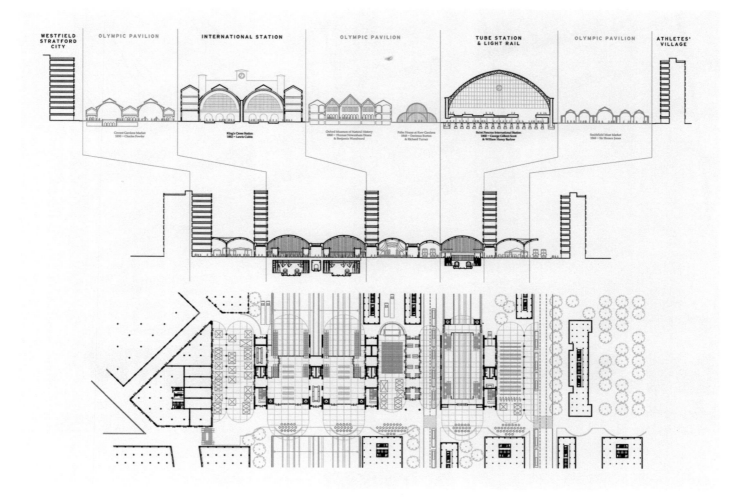

Covent Gardens Market
1830 — Charles Fowler

King's Cross Station
1852 — Lewis Cubitt

Oxford Museum of Natural History
1860 — Thomas Newnham Deane
& Benjamin Woodward

Palm House at Kew Gardens
1848 — Decimus Burton
& Richard Turner

Saint Pancras International Station
1868 — George Gilbert Scott
& William Henry Barlow

Smithfield Meat Market
1868 — Sir Horace Jones

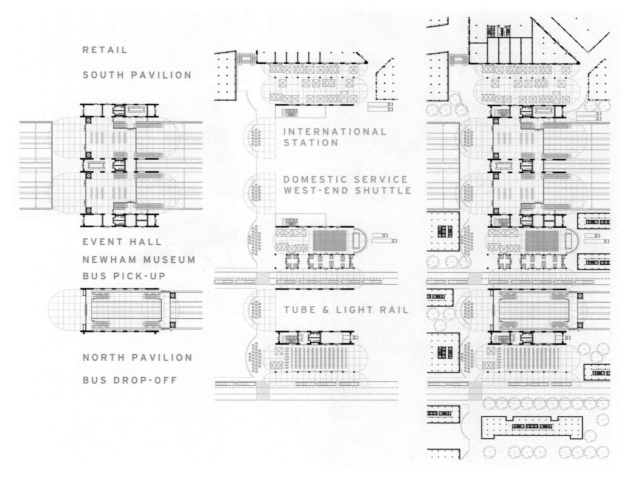

RETAIL

SOUTH PAVILION

INTERNATIONAL
STATION

DOMESTIC SERVICE
WEST-END SHUTTLE

EVENT HALL
NEWHAM MUSEUM
BUS PICK-UP

TUBE & LIGHT RAIL

NORTH PAVILION

BUS DROP-OFF

I

II

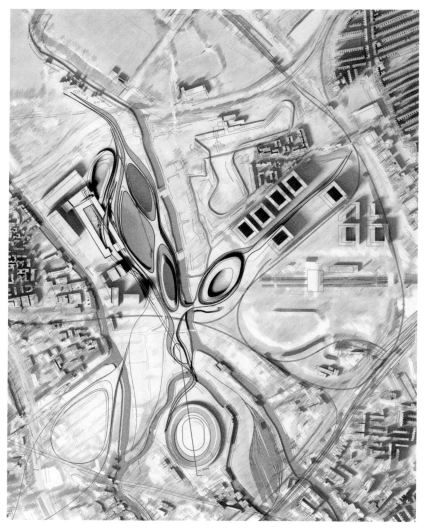

III

KATHERINE CLARKE   LIZA FIOR   ANDREI HARWELL

PEGGY DEAMER   SELINA MASON   ROWAN MOORE   ELIHU RUBIN
GREG LYNN   ED MITCHELL   KEVIN OWINS   STANLEY TIGERMAN

KEVIN OWINS „It's a piece of obstruction which at
„ the moment sits in the middle of nowhere. So
„ who's responsible for it? I think it's a very
„ interesting strategy; I just ask the question
„ in terms of the local markets which have been
„ drawn into the Olympics for the games and then
„ transition back. Or in terms of the games, the
„ environment that's created here is surely one
„ of the things that should be embedded into the
„ Olympic Park, which is that market culture that
„ we have in this area. Is this the whole thing?
„ Is the whole thing removed for the games? How
„ does that transition take place?
DEXTER CIPRIAN „Well, I think an event the size
„ of the Olympics will probably not happen very
„ often. So the upper part of that will go away,
„ and some of it will stay so that it's laid out
„ for future events.
GREG LYNN „As I understand those markets, they'd
„ have a storefront in many cases, and you'd
„ load all your stuff into that storefront, and
„ basically expand and contract your storefront
„ into the street. And the one thing that I'm
„ not clear about is how the Olympics and the
„ market coexist and how it would be interesting
„ if they coexist. Whatever it is you can get
„ at the Olympics, or three weeks before the
„ Olympics, I was thinking that plenum could
„ be the place where you just lift everything,
„ jack everything up off the ground floor, and
„ let everybody buy their jerseys and stuff.
„ It's a little redundant, with that cover under
„ there too. Once you've got the wrapper on the
„ stadium, you don't really need the screen over
„ the top of the market anymore, because you've
„ got the underside of the seats. So that kind of
„ stuff could be solved…
DEXTER CIPRIAN „Part of the attempt was to
„ bring this down to a human scale from such an
„ enormous scale.

GREG LYNN „But you'd want it at human scale for
„ the Olympics.
KEVIN OWINS „That's why I would say, I would
„ applaud this approach, if you look at this
„ in the context of the Olympics, especially
„ in relation to Beijing, for the experience of
„ people on the ground. The level of intimacy
„ was not there. So to bring that dynamic right
„ into the heart of the city, that's as close as
„ you're going to get to an urban gesture.
PEGGY DEAMER „I think it's a great project. But
„ then I get--I want to see more, and I think it's
„ something with the architecture--I want you to
„ go farther, to say whether it is just branding
„ or advertising, or is it a stall in some way?
„ So for example I look at this and I think,
„ this is probably not just a Plexiglas screen,
„ it's an LED screen in itself. Your materiality
„ is different from the structure, and then when
„ that's brought into material scale, maybe that
„ LED is not just one panel. What do I do with
„ this screen? Can I take this screen off, or is
„ this attached at the back or--I get interested
„ in all the very specific things that come up
„ when it's such a supposedly simple thing.
GREG LYNN „I think the word 'screen' is a great
„ architectural idea, that has a great message
„ to it. Like with the two perspectives, those
„ are your strongest drawings. The one, where
„ you say, look, I can do one thing that's a
„ stadium-scale thing with the images like this,
„ and then the other scale is a patchwork of
„ smaller elements. I think that architectural
„ idea, which gives you those two scales and
„ constituencies, could work more in the land-
„ scape at the stadium scale and all that. I
„ think in a funny way, you're looking for that
„ miracle solution to get the market into the
„ stadium, which is like the miracle solution
„ for everything.

II
OLYMPICS
MYTH BRAND & POLITICS
DEXTER CIPRIAN

The site for the 2012 Olympics in London
is a highly contentious one, with many
players fighting for their voices to be
heard. This is a reality hardly existent in the many forms of branding.
These, rather, portray a myth of hyper-
inclusiveness and agreement as embodied
by the mantra "everyone's 2012", reminiscent of the propagandistic campaign
to get Londoners to "fight for your
Britain" of the 1940s. The proposal
seeks to demystify the branding of the
Olympics, and politicize it by occupying the very space where the myth takes
place, and infiltrating it with local
markets. In addition, the wrapping
of the stadium is used as a platform
for both global and local businesses
to advertise themselves. In effect, the
rhetoric of 'everyoneness' ceases to
be a merely aestheticized image for
a better public image, and becomes a
political reality.

ED MITCHELL „I have a question because the
„ drawing sort of triggered something you're
„ surfing around that might be interesting. In
„ some of the bids, and I'm thinking particularly
„ about New York, these middle range facilities
„ were actually a real boon for the city because
„ they had none of them in New York, no venues
„ that could seat three to five thousand people
„ for community activities. And if you located
„ them strategically within the city they made
„ sense to organize neighborhoods. So what I
„ thought you were going to say is, here's a
„ neighborhood in attraction to these middle
„ range facilities--this is big scale stuff.
„ This is a shopping center that's gathering
„ another neighborhood that's divided by a ca-
„ nal, but then in the seam in between, which
„ is the park, they all meet up. So I think your
„ sections, then, are cut in the wrong places;
„ I'd rather see a section through the neighbor-
„ hood, through that periphery of buildings and
„ into the green zone that shows that all these
„ things are linking up. So if you do your pep-
„ per around there and link these different com-
„ munities together so that they actually have
„ a seam, program it in a way so that they're
„ taking advantage of it. And I actually think
„ you would want to program, nominally, one of
„ the other middle venues like the velodrome
„ or something as a sample of the kind of thing
„ you're talking about. Then these communities
„ are probably split by that territory or, actu-
„ ally, tied together, and then they're negotiat-
„ ing at a narrower seam of the park through
„ your intervention.
ELIHU RUBIN „It seems, and I think it's suc-
„ cessful in a different way, but it's not so
„ much taking legacy from the Olympic site out
„ into the neighborhoods but actually taking
„ program from the neighborhood and seeding it
„ back in. Your intention, because of the visual
„ continuity between the two, is to say, it's
„ from the neighborhood into the site that these
„ installations continue, and maybe with these
„ other kinds of navigation devices neighbor-
„ hood people feel comfortable moving into it
„ because it's now become an extension of the
„ neighborhood. And then my question is, why
„ does it need to move as it seems to do, from
„ the smallest pieces on the outside to the

„ largest pieces on the inside? It seems like
„ that becomes too much of a scheme as op-
„ posed to thinking individually why some of the
„ larger pieces can't be on the outside and some
„ of the smallest pieces in the very center. But
„ I'm assuming because you've analyzed specific
„ places that it makes sense for smaller ones to
„ be here and larger ones to be there.
PEGGY DEAMER „So the strategy is that once you
„ get to this main path, that oval then takes on
„ a certain typology. So we could concentrate on
„ the particular site right here but because of
„ it the typology develops around the ovoid.
YIJUN QIAN „Basically the running track is over-
„ lapped with the greenhouse area.
LIZA FIOR „And develops at this point an inten-
„ sity of all those routes.
STANLEY TIGERMAN „The single, strong overarch-
„ ing thing is your track going through there.
„ That's actually pretty interesting.
LIZA FIOR „He's making it more interesting.
STANLEY TIGERMAN „Oh, so it doesn't have the
„ grid on it? Because I would hope it does.
LIZA FIOR „It could, yes.
STANLEY TIGERMAN „Does it?
YIJUN QIAN „Yes. This covered area has a visual
„ connection…
LIZA FIOR „Yes, it's about privacy.
PEGGY DEAMER „Can I just say one thing? The part
„ of this that I really appreciate is that you
„ take on this problem of private gardens that I
„ guess is controversial. How you take this prob-
„ lem of hybridization and make a public project
„ out of it--it's a complicated system that is
„ very sophisticated. I really appreciate that.
KEVIN OWINS „I think you take it head on. The
„ allotments…
GREG LYNN „I think the language of perforated
„ sheets is very interesting. I think the idea of
„ little tomato gardens and little dots all over
„ the place is very interesting. I actually--
„ I'm having a hard time reconciling chopping
„ through the media center, which seems like
„ a very alien gesture to the ability to have
„ these flexing perforated sheets, and then the
„ garden. I don't know, I would almost say that
„ whatever is in the new center, whatever is on
„ the ground up there with the green gardens,
„ that that language of perforated surfaces,
„ like that, could do a lot more work.

III
FARM AND TRACKS
YIJUN QIAN

By drawing analogies between New Haven
and London, the "Farm and Track" proposal aims at creating an expandable
interweaving network on the site, which
allows three activities to happen
simultaneously: commercial, gardening
and research. Moreover, a system of
interlocked loops of running tracks is
introduced as the physical linkage of
those programs. Connecting the newly
developed East London business hub
Canary Whalf and the Olympic stadium,
the running route stretches from the
south Thames River bank to Stratford
City in the East London. By focusing
on the area of the Media Center, together with its neighbored multi-storey
parking garage, commercial activity
is introduced and a pedestrian corridor
is placed between the Media Center
and the green house.

JOSH EMIG   KONRAD GRASER   <u>WILLIAM SHARPLES</u>

CONSTANCE ADAMS   MICHAEL BLUM   DOUGLAS GAUTHIER   CHRIS SHARPLES
SUNIL BALD   VISHAAN CHAKRABARTI   JOHN PATKAU   MARTY STEIN
ANNA DYSON   GREGG PASQUARELLI

520B

SHARPLES STUDIO

Similar to the airport, the spaceport has the potential of operating at multiple scales. As a place of global and extraterrestrial connection--an ecosystem operating at multiple flow scales, space scales, program scales--the spaceport should assume an important public role of the new metropolis. Are spaceports to remain peripheral to major urban centers, as they have for the past four decades? Or will they become self sustaining urban centers of their own? These changes will have profound impact on how we think about our spaceports, not only as instruments of travel but as destinations in and of themselves--less as unidirectional infrastructures and more as multifunctional environments--making them not only an important gateway to our cities but also a possible catalyst for re-forming the city.

As a point of departure into this new typology, the studio utilizes the research, analysis and design explored last spring semester in the development of a next generation airport as its frame of reference. It develops a program and architecture for a spaceport that will support suborbital and orbital commercial space flight. The studio explores and critiques historic and existing air travel narratives. Students utilize contemporary methods of modeling to forge innovative paradigms in order to revitalize existing space travel infrastructure and to critique a programmatic menu unique to this infrastructure. Particular emphasis is placed on seeking out current and next-generation aviation and ecological models with the desire to inform the evolution of these new formations.

We pose questions such as: How can current and future innovation in space flight assist in creating new models of travel and experience? How can earlier models of passenger air travel be critiqued to offer possible suggestions of similar experiences for suborbital and orbital space flight? What role will public policy, regulations, and governmental agencies, such as NASA or the FAA, have in fostering or limiting this commercial initiative? What are some possible economic models for regional spaceports? Are they viable? How will this emerging market sector affect urban and regional economies and ecologies?

The studio focuses on three hypothetical sites for spaceport platforms and draws in other programs and infrastructures which could support and sustain innovative growth within the spaceport complex.

I
SPACEPORT CALVERTON
<u>ELIZA HIGGINS & ISAIAH KING,</u>
<u>H.I. FELDMAN NOMINEES</u>
This project rethinks the train and air infrastructure on the Eastern seaboard, proposing a new air/space cargo hub that relieves New York's existing airports and creates new types of jobs in the region. The spaceport is paired with a proposed high speed rail line linking east coast cities and creating a new means of shipment and travel.

The Spaceport converts an existing Grumman airport in Calverton, Long Island into an air/space cargo hub. Touching the site lightly, the cargo port is a transfer center between land and air linked to sorting infrastructure around the region by high-speed maglev rail. The spaceport also functions as a point-to-point space travel hub for business passengers to major world destinations, space hotels, and the international space station. Passengers are delivered by a maglev space train terminal that connects major East Coast cities.

The spaceport utilizes its scale to generate wind and solar energy, acting as a test bed for ecological technology research. The spaceport's roof is formed into an airfoil for wind collection and creates an armature for testing solar energy technology. The roof creates a filigree, screening the air and space planes from weather to reduce delays from ice build up and inclement working conditions.

GREGG PASQUARELLI „I mean, look, there are some really beautiful moves and it's a really interesting research project, so I don't want to get hyper-practical on it. My biggest problem is that it's in Calverton.
WILLIAM SHARPLES „Well that's my fault.
{Laughter}
GREGG PASQUARELLI „No, it's not that. I like the whole sort of piggybacking on other systems as a way to--I think Anna (Dyson) brought up a really good point in the beginning about the social implications of what you're doing-- what's the kind of investment, what are the other sort of positive externalities that spin off from doing this?--and the point is that Long Island is unfortunately, or fortunately, a spur to a dead end. Why would you put it all the way out? I would almost see this stacked. It would just seem to me that if you put it between New York and Boston on whatever that route is, it would be a more centralized location.
VISHAAN CHAKRABARTI „You think it's a better use for New Haven?
{Laughter}
GREGG PASQUARELLI „That was what I was trying to get to. Exactly. But there's such an unbelievable amount of infrastructure, and I think that that's what everyone is getting at--that the believability isn't that the train actually looks like that, or it can actually clip on or off--they're all good ideas in the research you did. But for me, it's got to get a little bit tighter in terms of--what are the other things I'm getting from this massive investment that works not only for the few who work for the spaceport? And the thing I like the most is, you get a greater efficiency from the existing airports, so instead of having to build a ten billion dollar cargo port/passenger port somewhere out in New Jersey, I'm building a one billion dollar space port with this very efficient and not-that-expensive roof that deals with only twenty passengers per day, but ten million cubic yards of cargo, and then it's really easy for me to expand Newark, LaGuardia and JFK. But again, my only point is, it seems like it's out on the end of Long Island, which seems like the wrong spot to put it.
VISHAAN CHAKRABARTI „But do you think that though?

„ Is it a fourth airport from that perspective?
GREGG PASQUARELLI „It's not a fourth airport, it's just a cargo port. Like when the cargo ships went out and there was a hammock on the back where someone got a ride to the New World on the back. This is kind of the same thing.
VISHAAN CHAKRABARTI „What's interesting about the passenger business model is that it's relying completely on the cost of the flight. Because there's no other revenue generation that's really going on. Constance (Adam's) point about, well, wouldn't the airport experience be much nicer, the normal airport experience, if you get on and then transfer directly to your gate? It would be nicer for us, but it would also mean that the airports would all go out of business. Because the airports all survive on their retail. They're just big malls, right? And one of the interesting things about your port itself is that it has no opacity. There's almost no program. It's just a shed. I don't know if you looked at the airport in Jeddah--if you haven't, you should look at the airport that Bunschaft did for Jeddah. Because it's basically just this series of these big fiberglass tents that sit out in the desert. Because Jeddah is a very small regional airport that once a year, because of the Hajj, expands into the busiest airport in the world. And so there's almost no program in the airport. So from that perspective, instead of looking at it as a fourth airport that should be centrally located…
GREGG PASQUARELLI „No, that isn't what I was saying. I'm saying that you don't have to build a fourth airport if you build this.
VISHAAN CHAKRABARTI „Yeah, but I'm not sure that's what it's trying to be.
GREGG PASQUARELLI „No, it's something else: it's a cargo port, that just a few people use for space every once in a while. By doing this, you don't have to build a fourth airport.
CHRIS SHARPLES „But the point you're making is, find out how much new space you're now making at JFK or Newark when you get rid of the cargo.
GREGG PASQUARELLI „But just before we get off this, it's also a great roof. It's a great shed. And I like the way you just plug all of the stuff in, and Jeddah is exactly right.

126

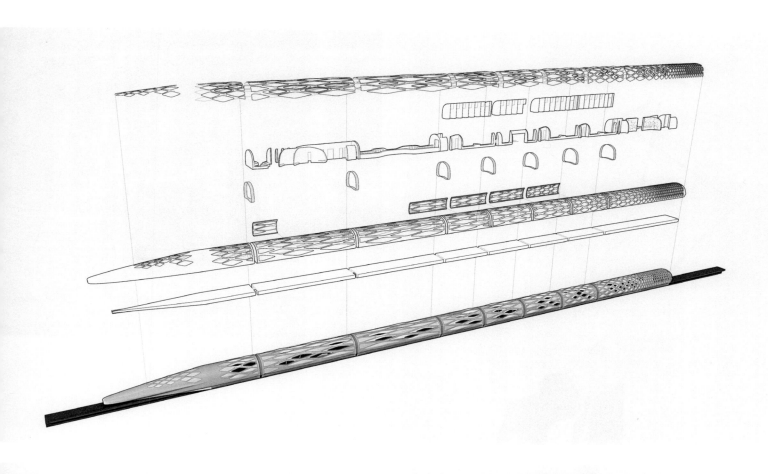

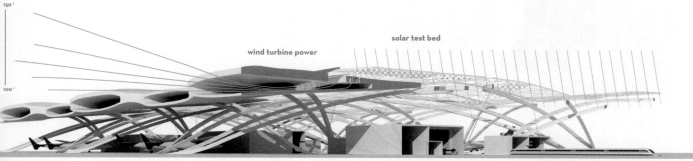

150 '

wind turbine power   solar test bed

100 '

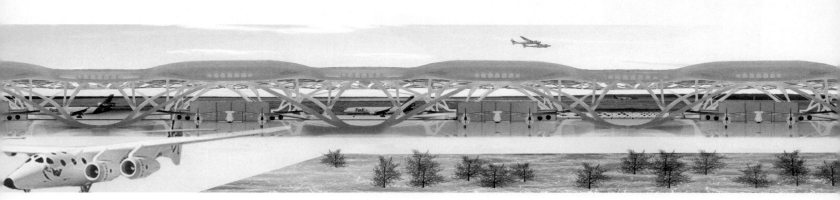

II

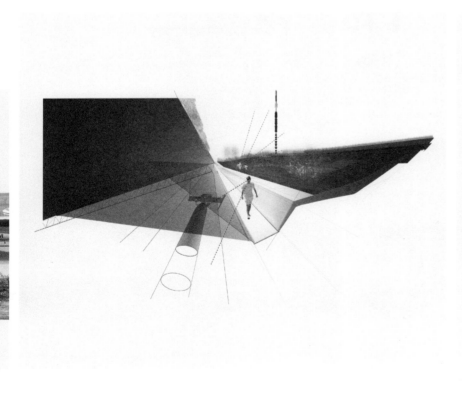

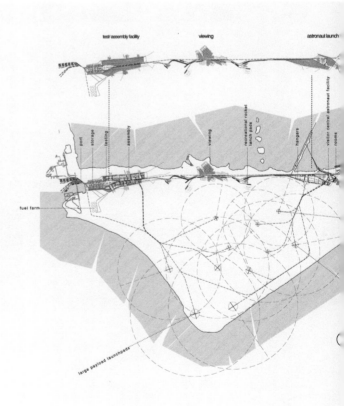

III

JOSH EMIG   KONRAD GRASER   WILLIAM SHARPLES

CONSTANCE ADAMS   MICHAEL BLUM   DOUGLAS GAUTHIER   CHRIS SHARPLES
SUNIL BALD   VISHAAN CHAKRABARTI   JOHN PATKAU   MARTY STEIN
ANNA DYSON   GREGG PASQUARELLI

DOUGLAS GAUTHIER „It was a very long presentation, a lot of ideas, but I'm actually going
to compliment you, you kept us in it, even
with us sort of jonesing for you to go faster.
And the drawings tell a very good story; the
drawings are quite beautiful. The first question I see when I see your historical work
is, that's what the future used to look like;
what is the future going to look like? And
I think you're caught in that a little bit.
So the beauty and seduction level of these
drawings is very, very exciting, but—it's all
possibility is I guess the conclusion of your
presentation. What I don't understand on the
site or in the masterplanning, which is what
it is right now, is, what are the limits? In
some ways the limits seem like they're in the
landscape or these implied aerials; I liked
when you started talking about the 2600—the
distances of the rocket launches, because it
seems to me like that kind of information,
the constraint information, could provide that
tattoo, or that field of information, that pure
data, because in some ways it's a data collection. As much as I like the image, it has to
make that data present. I think you need to
bean-counter-it-up slightly in order to understand how that data exists in the landscape.
What are the percentages of people to payload,
what are the weights, what are the scales? I
know these are very large things and you're
probably dealing with them, but it seems to
me that that set of limits—because it's a
beautiful set of possibilities and then it's
a sort of intuitive masterplan, and it doesn't
do justice to the amount of information you've
brought to the table.
SUNIL BALD „Well I think maybe taking an approach like that would allow you to, say,
take some of the organizational, quantitative
aspects of your project and begin to fold them
into a narrative, rather than—right now these
two types of research are so in contrast with
each other. You have these moments, and there
are quantitative aspects, I guess, within each

of these moments in terms of populations and
people flying in the sky and so on, and there's
this sense of immediate moment and then depth;
all your perspectives, they do have that sense
of horizon in them. In these things there's an
imaginary that you're beginning to construct,
but these drawings—the way of organizing that
imaginary within a context, or a site, that
has dimensions and up and down, even if that
site is kind of no place—you guys are trying
your hardest to actually find something on this
site. You know, you come up with a little mound
as a way to contextualize things to a certain
degree, but it's not as convincing as some of
these other things. So then, how do you begin
to either weave that organization into the
narrative, or how do you site these narratives
relative to each another as a first step?
JOHN PATKAU „Is your site subject to the flash
flooding you were referring to?
ANDREA VITTADINI „Yes, in this area, but most of
all, all the way west.
JOHN PATKAU „But you're not worried about the
building being subject to flash floods?
ANDREA VITTADINI „Actually, we want it to catch
the water.
JOHN PATKAU „I see.
CONSTANCE ADAMS „But it's going to evaporate,
with the steady wind across the site.
NICHOLAS GILLILAND „It's not exposed. That's the
thing—it's an enclosed volume.
ANNA DYSON „Even as an enclosed volume you'll
deal with evaporation, but you'll try to control it through condensation.
CHRIS SHARPLES „So are there any precedents out
there where water is being used in this way
to deal with very tight tolerances? Instead of
trying to pour a really flat floor, and put rails
on there? Is there any kind of precedent?
CONSTANCE ADAMS „So you actually have locks
inside this canal?
NICHOLAS GILLILAND „In the terminal, at the end.
CONSTANCE ADAMS „So the size of the rocket is
going to determine the maximum size of your assembly. That's going to limit you, right there.

Ⅱ
ROCKET, INC., APPLIED RESEARCH
IN THE WHITE SANDS DESERT
NICHOLAS GILLILAND
& ANDREA VITTADINI
Aerospace research and rocket manufacturing are superimposed along the
length of an underground manufacturing
channel, linking existing horizontal
launch facilities to an inhabited hill
four miles south-east in one continuous
infrastructural axis. Maximum efficiency
and sustainability drive the spacecraft
through the assembly process and toward
the launch-pads. Water forms a connecting thread which organizes both space
and processes. Harvested from seasonal
downpours, its self-leveling characteristics resolve issues of precision
assembly while complementing themes
of environmental autonomy. The channel
organizes landscape through linear geometries as tattoos in the sand. Solar
panels, wind farms, runways, launch pads
and power lines: technical elements
become territorial markers, collapsing
function and language into one entity
visible from space.

VISHAAN CHAKRABARTI „Speaking up for some of
the planners in the room, I actually think
there's a compelling set of ideas here, and a
notion of these buildings as pieces of landscape. Because it's kind of the last thing
you would think of. I mean, given the weight
of the technology, the notion that this whole
thing is a landscape experience is really
an interesting idea. There's something about
the way this roof is made that's critical to
the idea. Generally, I think there's a good
set of ideas here that are somewhat poorly
presented in that there's not enough shift
in scale. You need something that's far, far
more focused in, and like Gregg (Pasquarelli)
said, some kind of a sectional cutaway and
something that really explores the nature of
that roof, because the roof is the building.
Fundamentally, the roof is the moment where
the public gets to interact with all of this
stuff that's happening below it. And it could be
something much richer. Even when the question
was asked about where that perspective view
was taken, when you look at this, the public
is in the rain gutter. There's something really odd about the way that's developed. But
I think the fundamental idea of it pushed
away from the ocean by the city, with these
launchpads out there, is a pretty compelling
parti for the plan.
CHRIS SHARPLES „I think it also says something—I
don't know if it's a generational thing, but
it's very different from the VAB (Vehicle Assembly Building at the Kennedy Space Center)
and the whole heroic architecture. That there

in the landscape—it's massive, and here it's
so camouflaged; it's an interesting ecology. It
sort of comes back to what Anna (Dyson) was
saying about how it really does operate as a
unique ecology at many different scales.
CONSTANCE ADAMS „I think from a master planning
point of view, too, the next step might be—the
point has already been made that you turned
away from this. So in a way, you're showing the
wrong end of it. As you know, you're talking
about the public coming out to watch launches,
all of this, from Port Canaveral down is sort
of the world of Cocoa Beach built around the
Apollo missions, and the excitement of all of
that. And Ron Jon built this great big resort
right at that corner there at Port Canaveral
just recently, a couple of years ago. So in a
way, if you had found a way to join back to
Cocoa Beach, back across the port, how does
that part of the procession take place?
MICHAEL BLUM „Is it about camouflage? Or is it
about celebrating this?
WILLIAM SHARPLES „Who said camouflage?
CYRUS PATELL „It's not about camouflage.
VISHAAN CHAKRABARTI „It's not about camouflage,
it's about celebrating. When you see it rendered
at this scale it can be misinterpreted. But if
I had to pick, I would've picked camouflage.
Because you want to see that interaction on
the different levels: what do I see, what can I
see, what parts of it are celebrated, how does
it connect to the landscape? I think it would
be really amazing to see these sort of dunes in
the water and the reeds, and then rockets under the surface—that would be sublime, right?

Ⅲ
A SECOND ECOLOGICAL LAYER:
SPACE FLORIDA
CYRUS PATTELL
The site is part of a continuous stretch
of rich wetlands and is an active launch
site. Understanding the process of re-
mediation, the approach was to concentrate on the eastern edge of the of
the cape, using the roof of the 'built'
to form a 'second ecological layer'
and leaving the rest of the site a field
of launch-pads. A complex rail system
would serve the city with multiple nodes
and form an extensive network within
the site itself.
   The resulting part is two structures
at the ends along a central 'chasm'
fed by rail. One is a commercial rocket
test/assembly facility that opens up
to an extension of the existing port.
The other caters to human aspects of
space flight—space missions and exploration, tourism. Between these is a well
articulated system of walkways, viewing
platforms and smaller launch-pads for
school children to launch small rockets.
This system extends beyond onto the
roofs of the buildings. The roofs of the
roofs of the buildings 'crease' to form
pedestrian paths allowing views of its
inner-workings ,and at the same time,
maintain necessary separation.
   The 'egg-crate' roof allows a variety
of planting depending on the depth,
realising within it a rich ecosystem
and replacing what it has been lost by pol-
lution below.

LARRY BOOTH   KARSTEN HARRIES   DIETRICH NEUMANN   SARAH WHITING
PETER EISENMAN   GEORGE KNIGHT   STEVEN PETERSON

522B

BEEBY STUDIO

The School of Architecture at the Illinois Institute of Technology in Chicago is planning to construct a new building next to Crown Hall in order to satisfy the unprecedented growth of the school over the last decade. The required space needs will have to be accommodated within a building envelope proposed by Mies van der Rohe in his final campus plan of 1940. The foundations for a structure at this site were completed at the time of the construction of the Chemical Engineering and Metallurgy Building in 1946 and subsequently buried shortly thereafter due to inadequate funding.

The school's spatial needs have currently expanded well beyond the confines of Crown Hall with students now occupying 3 buildings. The faculty and administration of the school would prefer to see it housed in one structure again with Crown Hall becoming a museum and exhibition space dedicated to architectural exhibits and the Mies van der Rohe archive.

The studio is structured to consider change in relation to architectural thought. Both the "Shape of Time" by George Kubler and the "Anxiety of Influence" by Harold Bloom deal with issues that relate to creative responses to brilliant artistic ancestors. Each student in this studio is expected to be conversant in the architecture of Mies van der Rohe by the end of the semester. In addition the origins of Mies' architectural legacy are a source of discussion. These topics include the architecture of Chicago, the architecture of Karl Friedrich Schinkel and Peter Behrens as well as contemporaries of Mies van der Rohe such as Gerrit Rietveld, Theo van Doesburg and Piet Mondrian. Finally, the student union of Rem Koolhaas is discussed in its response to the architecture of Mies van der Rohe.

I
NEIGHBORING MIES
SEHER ERDOGAN,
H.I. FELDMAN NOMINEE

Considering an addition to IIT campus in its post-Miesian state, the project aims at implementing the architectural language Mies has developed while finding opportunities for subtle deformation. With the recent additions by Koolhaas and Jahn, the IIT campus no longer retains the stillness of the Miesian master plan, and the current dynamic should inform the new school of Architecture in establishing a new vibrant node on campus.

With the urban siting in mind, the volume is elevated off the ground to maintain the open space and the entry is suggested by the cantilever of the auditorium. As a result, the procession becomes an attenuated experience where the entry begins in advance of the physical perimeter of the building and continues through its newly activated, materially articulated underbelly. At the scale of the building, the homogenous measures of universal space are recalibrated to acquire certain nuances, where the "still body" slightly flexes its muscles and the "central courtyard" becomes an externalized element to test the limits of spatial fluidity through Miesian terms.

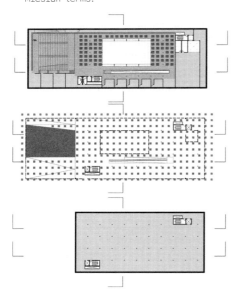

ROBERT A. M. STERN „Why do you have to raise the building at all?
SEHER ERDOGAN „Mies elevates his buildings in a strange way, which intrigued me because it creates this ambiguous relationship of the body to the ground. Like the Farnsworth house.
ROBERT A. M. STERN „Elevated because it flooded underneath!
SEHER ERDOGAN „Well, I also have an open space that I want to maintain, visually, and it was an experiment to try to make something positive out of something that is categorically not done.
ROBERT A. M. STERN „Certainly, many of us are impressed by this project. The concept and the execution--it's very intelligent and inspired work. You should be complimented. I have two reservations, which I think can be addressed, one of which you are stubborn about now, but I know you're going to see how right I am.
{Laughter}
The underside of this building would be grim beyond all measure, because of the lack of light, the wind, the inability to grow things; not enough people in the whole IIT could enliven it. The other is that I just think the building is too big. In reality, value engineering would take care of that for you, but I think conceptually--well, it's like a great big battleship coming in to poor old Mies, and he doesn't deserve the rough treatment.
STEVEN PETERSON „I agree, and I think this is a marvelous project. The other question is, do we want to try to turn this around? So it rises up and...
PETER EISENMAN „Eats Crown Hall? No.
{Laughter}
LARRY BOOTH „Yes, it's a wonderful project, it's very well presented both verbally and graphically, and it has, really, very many interesting things. It's a beautiful plan, the floors being eccentric, the ramp going around outside, I could go through all of these things that you did casually and asymmetrically, and then you have these two big spaces as you show in that section; I think it's just terrific.
PETER EISENMAN „I am going to get off my Simon Cowell mode and say that this is a terrific project, the plans are stunning. I wish you

hadn't said a word, because I would hope that these critics are astute enough to understand your project so clearly presented without even saying anything. The model is stunning. I agree with Stern that it's a little out of scale, but so what? My only comment is, why do you need the little remnant? I meant "rem" in the double sense of the word. It was a joke.
{Laughter}
I look at this section, and I really wonder if we need that little tweak at the end that has nothing in the plans which suggest it.
STEVEN PETERSON „As stunning as your project is, I think it's a little kink that really isn't necessary, and I think the cut is spreading its jaws and gobbling up towards Rem's building. There's so much clarity here that I don't think you need it.
KARSTEN HARRIES „It occurred to me as you were describing this that you've got it the other way around. You've got a perfectly good structural system that suggests that you don't really need this truss at all; you only need it because you've got this jaw which you lifted up with a double cantilever. Personally, I think that jaw would be wonderful if you had columns under it and you could walk under it...
ROBERT A. M. STERN & PETER EISENMAN „{Protests and moans of disapproval}
{Laughter}
ROBERT A. M. STERN „I think about the lighting on your ceiling. The square light is a very dangerous kind of lighting idea, because it will always give you shade/shadow, lightness/darkness in a component.
SARAH WHITING „But the squares actually speak to something else. I love the project, absolutely, but I really have a problem with the squares in the ground plan and the squares in the ceiling, and I don't understand where that came from. It's a way of countering the directionality, and the fact that you made it so pronounced in the plans is very telling, but it obliterates the beauty of the ground floor plan. In terms of lifting the building, I understand the pragmatic argument that Bob raised, but I think you could have dropped more down and had a more developed landscape, through the architecture, as opposed to the squares.

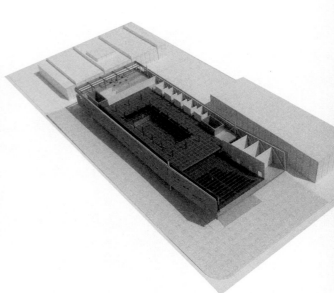

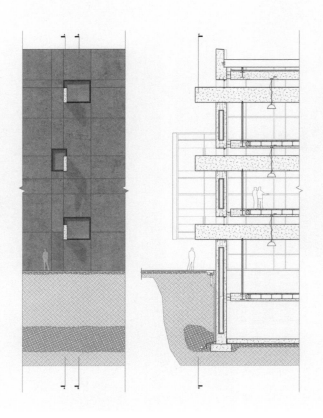

II

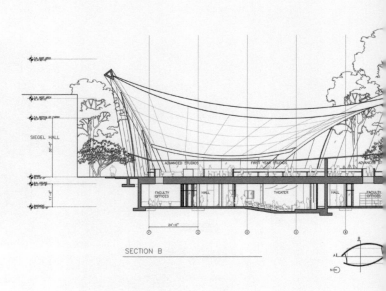

SECTION B

III

LARRY BOOTH   KARSTEN HARRIES   DIETRICH NEUMANN   SARAH WHITING
PETER EISENMAN   GEORGE KNIGHT   STEVEN PETERSON

SARAH WHITING „I think you've understood the problem quite well. But you're saying that you want an ambiguity in the relationship of the emergent lines and the compositional figure, and I think that is disappointing because it's that desire for ambiguity that is the sort of relinquishing of your project—it's like, 'I'll have a little bit of everything and then it'll be good,' or 'it has to speak to everything and then it'll be better,' as opposed to taking this band of analysis and really saying 'I'm going to create a figure that manages to make these lines manifest, and they're going to constantly compete and I'm going to count on the world at large to try to give some meaning to them.' It is true that the figure gets lost, the figure of the five boxes, but it's also that combination that gets lost. You give up your control over it.

KARSTEN HARRIES „What came first when you were working on this project? I think the sort of Reitvelt vocabulary—that I think is a wonderful idea. So what came first, this idea of planes, or the way of generating a volume through these five boxes?

MATT ROMAN „They were pretty much simultaneous. There is an idea of planes intersecting these volumes.

DIETRICH NEUMANN „Well, it's been said; there's just too much going on. In a way, this is one of your very nice ideas, to explore these (beams) as holding something from above. This, I think, is what punches through the windows, makes it public, and then you play with it and hang the trellis from it. If that had been the governing idea, I think it would have been enough to generate something wonderful. And I think we can blame Peter for some of what's going on in here. There is too much going on, but there is clearly some Peter Eisenman mixed in with the Rietveld.

PETER EISENMAN „I get blamed for many things.
{Laughter}
THOMAS BEEBY „Can I just say one thing about the studio here? The studio is interested in the

relationships with Mies, but it also asked them to produce a finished building. Very rarely does one get asked to do a finished building here. So I think the detail he pursued from the very beginning—and the integration between the overall planning and the details is very hard, and I think what he pursued is very interesting.

PETER EISENMAN „Let me ask you this. I happen to like this plan; of all the plans I've seen today, it has a certain modesty, it has a certain calmness, et cetera. Then I see this up here in the scale related to the context, and because it doesn't have this serenity, because it has these things that shoot off in different places, it loses what I see in this plan. Something between the scale of the plan and the building went awry. I don't think it's the resolution of a building, Tom. I think it's something about the over-articulation between volume and plane.

THOMAS BEEBY „Having observed this, one reaction to Mies was that simplicity seemed a problem. Everyone was trying to escape simplicity.

ROBERT A.M. STERN „But Mies is not simple. He's very complex, and I think that if the students—well, I guess I'm a little critical of you, Tom, because if you can't get the students to see how complex and amazing that is, then I think it's too bad because then it's no longer a problem of reacting to Mies, it's just a problem of making a building. I really don't think that this project has anything to do with grappling with an incredible environment that this man created in this particular place.

SARAH WHITING „Everyone is looking at you saying 'here's where your project is, you need to edit out this or that and then your project gets better.' Dietrich pointed to the way that the beams works and the details work and you turn that into the project, Peter pointed to something else, and I think for me it still goes back to the point of complexity for complexity's sake. There is that sense that that will make the project.

PETER EISENMAN „Trisha, I have to ask you about siting. Since we would not notice the stylistic differences in your building, why is it off-axis with the other buildings? Is that to ensure that we notice what is different? It does not mean that it is bad, I just want to know why.

TRISHA SNYDER „I was interested in the way that you approach Mies' buildings: it's never on axis, even though the plans are often axial. You're entering on the side of the weird third bay of the building and then you're wandering around. All of Mies' buildings at IIT, with the exception of Crown Hall, are approached indirectly, not straight-on.

LARRY BOOTH „That's a rectangular structure, running on the grid of the campus, with this eccentric flying roof over it. Wouldn't it have been better to have that plan, more or less, visible upstairs, so that you saw the conjunction of the grid with this thing flying over at an angle? There is a third idea, which is this flowing thing that isn't related to the roof or the basement below. It is like an imposed formal order that I think is getting

the scheme to be confused.

SARAH WHITING „On the site plan, Crown Hall is an object, but if you look at the way it sits on the campus, it is very much in conversation with the fabric of the other structures. The Commons, as it's been redone by OMA, has another way of responding to the campus. You're doing something so different. What does that offer to the campus?

TRISHA SNYDER „There's a growing group of architectural buildings here that don't necessarily relate to the rest of the IIT campus.

SARAH WHITING „But the other two do so much.
ROBERT A.M. STERN „But families usually have relationships.
TRISHA SNYDER „Not always good ones.
{Laughter}
STEVEN PETERSON „She is related to Rem, quite clearly. In the little model it looks like a moved-over version. It's turning itself to the student union. I think you've got a lot of mutually-exclusive ideas, and how you relate them is difficult. I think there are many beautiful, poetic things in this, but it's that relationship that still needs to be there.

II
MORE IS MIES
MATT ROMAN
According to Mies' "rules" of modernism, which simply extend and abstract the classical relationship of part-to-whole, adjacencies between buildings in the master plan for IIT are precisely figured to avoid stresses or pressures in the composition. My ambition is to overlay two historical and contemporary disciplinary projects: one is a problem of composition, which follows from a Beaux-Arts tradition of arranging spaces and forms; the other is an interest in indexing internal and external information so it becomes legible in the project. In this way, I consider a more charged relationship between figure and ground and building to building. Moments of "awkwardness" might be exposed and expressed in this scheme as a means to draw us away from classical (and Miesian) traditions of resolution and synthesis at a variety of scales.

III
MIES & THE LONG SPAN
TRISHA SNYDER
Mies's objectives were not so dissimilar from the master spanners of the 1950s and 60s—Nervi, Candela, Isler, Trojja, Maillart, etc. Each aimed to create efficient, long-span structures using new materials and technologies of the time. Each used principles of symmetry and repetition, but while the engineers created sculpture, Mies produced rectangular boxes.

Advancements in tension fabric structures began in the 1970s but it is only since the 1990s that we have started to seriously consider fabric as a building material to be used in permanent structures.

I propose to explore the structural language of fabric just as Mies experimented with steel and glass. From the first buildings on the IIT campus to the Commons Building to Crown Hall, Mies becomes increasingly interested in universal space and we see an increasing disjuncture between the structure of the main space and the structure of the service spaces which are eventually relegated the basement in Crown Hall.

A fabric structure spanning the ground level studio space is rotated off of the twenty-four foot campus grid, finally freeing the universal space from the gridded service space below. The independent structural systems of the upper and lower levels are exposed and celebrated.

THOMAS AUER   KATE JOHN-ALDER   KEITH KRUMWIEDE

LJILJANA BLAGOJEVIC   DOLORES HAYDEN   ALAN ORGANSCHI   SARA STEVENS
KEVIN DALY   DENISE HOFFMAN-BRANDT   ALBERT POPE   STANLEY TIGERMAN
TIM LOVE   JOEL SANDERS

KRUMWIEDE STUDIO

524B

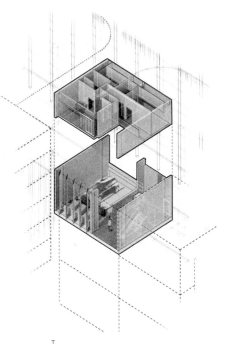

Over the course of the last 15 years, housing in the United States--which essentially means single-family houses--has been driven by ever increasing levels of excess. It is now common knowledge that the house doubled in size between 1950 and 2000, and in the first years of this century, during the expansion of the bubble, houses grew even larger as builders sought every available dollar liberated by the free flow of credit. Now, obviously, the housing bubble has burst, and the costs, both economic and environmental, of building and operating detached and distant dwellings are no longer tolerable. Limited by long-held cultural and technological assumptions, conventional housing practices and products hold little promise of a sustainable solution to the environmental and economic crises we face. It is the confluence of these crises, however, that exposes an opportunity to rethink the function and form of American housing in a manner that could actually have an impact and an application. This studio explores this opportunity.

In order to achieve substantial, and marketable, changes to housing, it is important to seek deeper levels of integration between the economic and cultural conditions of contemporary dwelling and the social and ecological demands of the contemporary metropolis. Any new housing proposal must synthesize multiple priorities (from needs and desires of varied human and non-human agents to vital urban ecological demands) and scales of operation (from building details to urban systems). Rather than the typical parasitic relationship between houses and infrastructure, this studio, in its attempt to redefine the concept of dwelling in an American context, seeks a new symbiotic relationship between housing and a reconfigured public infrastructure that enhances urban ecosystem services. We investigate whether it is possible to connect the verdant views, spaciousness, and luxury thought to be available only at the end of a cul-de-sac to the higher densities and resource efficiencies necessary for sustainable social urban development.

The challenge of the studio is to design dwellings that appeal to the newly green-seeking, likely downsizing homebuyer who still aspires to some part of the American Dream epitomized by the single-family house. In doing so is necessary to qualify and quantify the components of the single-family house, reconcile them with changing demographic trends and environmental goals, and redeploy them in new urban configurations to produce dynamic, ecologically integrated communities. The goal is to offer new insights and directions at a time when fresh alternatives to the housing status quo are desperately needed. The projects therefore must be plausible, persuasive, and packaged to engender desire for a new form of dwelling--of living--that recasts the American Dream as the pleasurable ecological inhabitation of the city.

I
TEXAS DOUGHNUT REDUX
EMILY ARDEN WELLS,
H.I. FELDMAN PRIZE RECIPIENT

Houston, similar to many other Western cities, is dependent on the car. The car not only embodies a sense of identity, but people spend a significant amount of time in their cars--mobile homes away from home. It is this symbiotic relationship that brought my attention to the Texas Doughnut, otherwise known as the Texas wrap. In the effort to maximize the benefit of being able to park on the same level as one's unit; I have brought the parking directly into the unit. Conceptually this merges the suburban garage and the apartment unit, as well as the cul-de-sac and the parking structure. Trees planted between the parking garage and the apartments create a buffer for light and noise, and also act as a backyard: each car drives through the tree canopy and into its unit. The doubling of the doughnut requires elevated bridges to connect the apartment buildings; and creates a lush urban canyon that is grown over with plants and vines.

By inverting the logic of the Texas Doughnut, it creates an opportunity to create courtyards for the tenants. Each unit is cross-ventilated and employs different strategies for solar blocking such as louvers and operable screens that minimize air-conditioning demands. Units have private yards and the ability to open completely to their respective privatized open-spaces. Because the parking is brought directly into the unit and each unit has its own garden space, the ground plane is multiplied and elevated, giving each tenant their piece of terra-firma. By bringing many of the benefits of suburban living to the Texas Doughnut, I hope to decrease the demand for the car in a neighborhood district, increase density, increase a sense of community, and re-define relationships between the city and the car.

KEVIN DALY „I think the question is whether „ or not you solved the problem that needed „ to be solved. I think you've made a series „ of really interesting propositions and really „ interesting observations about Houston, and „ I think the degree to which the housing is „ worked out as a complex series of interior „ spaces is spectacular. But what you set out to „ do is to take this ubiquitous builder's form „ and multiply it by itself. You've increased „ it by an order of magnitude. But you also, „ by doing that, exposed its shortcomings. And „ so, not to imply you're being disingenuous, „ but I think the degree to which this is a „ real proposal, versus the degree to which it's „ a rhetorical piece that is an evaluation of „ development and builder practices--I think „ you need to come clean about that. Because if „ it's really, truly, an innovative thing, then „ I think we do have to compare it to the Unité, „ and look at other different forms of housing, „ and organizations of parking with respect to „ housing, and contextualize it in the spectrum „ of other housing investigations.

ALBERT POPE „Well, I don't know, I think there „ are positive examples. I think Stanley Saitow-„ itz has done some really interesting--basi-„ cally, they're donut buildings. They're Texas „ wrap buildings, but they're in San Francisco „ and they're quite urbane. And they solve the „ same sorts of problems. But it's an issue of „ whether or not this is a real proposal or „ a kind of inquiry--a self-directed one, and „ very, very thorough--and you need to receive „ a huge amount of acknowledgement for doing „ that. The degree to which you've taken the „ premise as a very sincere premise, and pushed „ it, is really impressive.

TIM LOVE „I don't think it's that far off though. If „ you took one half of your project and you lined „ the edge that has the green wall on it with that „ upper garage, with a long, skinny, single-edge „ bar building, so that only the drums of the „ parking garage--the rhetoric of parking--was „ exposed, rather than the whole flank of the „ garage, that seems like a better rhetorical „ balance of showing and hiding the auto as an „ image, than having the whole flank exposed.

STANLEY TIGERMAN „There are a lot of redesign „ possibilities. It could've been lower, as „ is. That thin green line could have actu-„ ally been spread apart to be units. But I „ want to say something else. I think--because „ I saw her midterm review--she is obviously „ capable of massive amounts of work, giving „ up the lie of the Ivy League student going off „ to the Bahamas. Irrespective of that, I just „ don't buy into 'this is illogical'--whatever. „ She's trying something that's--it's truly an „ investigation.

ALBERT POPE „I think the innovation--perhaps „ what attracted you to the type--is that new re-„ lationship to the car, that you could actually „ have a garage on the fourth level, drive into „ your house. And I think that's the innovation „ that's clear here, in this unit plan and in this „ unit plan, and the surreal nature of shuffling „ the ground plane. The ground plane is no lon-„ ger on the ground. It's now on the second floor, „ the fourth floor; that could have, maybe even „ in a more modest way, informed the rest of the „ project. For example you didn't use the roof „ terrace. It would be an enormous opportunity „ to investigate that strange relocation of the „ ground plane up to a higher level. Be a little „ bit more adventurous in moving that ground „ plane around, and realizing that that's really „ the source of your interest in the type, that „ you can take these types that are normally wed „ to the ground, like the garage, and begin to „ shuffle it in an urban building.

DENISE HOFFMAN-BRANDT „I would say this: don't „ call it a garden for God's sake. Clean up your „ rhetoric. It's a parking lot. This is a stacked „ motel. I love cars. If you had talked to me „ about how you're creating a parterre of the „ parking tracks as a solid versus an aggregate „ material which was going to collect the runoff, „ and that the thing acts like a parking lot, „ which is what it is, and at the same time „ performs as something else, it's an entirely „ new condition. The minute you tell yourself „ it's a garden because you put a green screen „ on it, you reduce it in your mind and you make „ yourself unable to get beyond it and see the „ really cool thing for what it is.

EMILY ARDEN WELLS

I

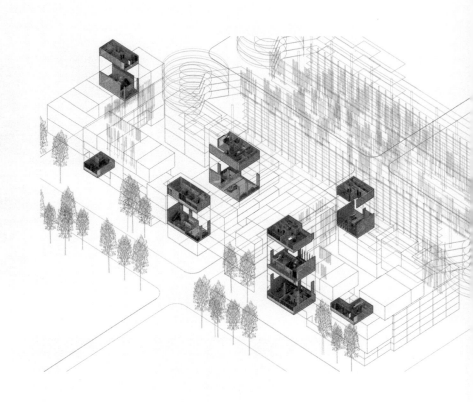

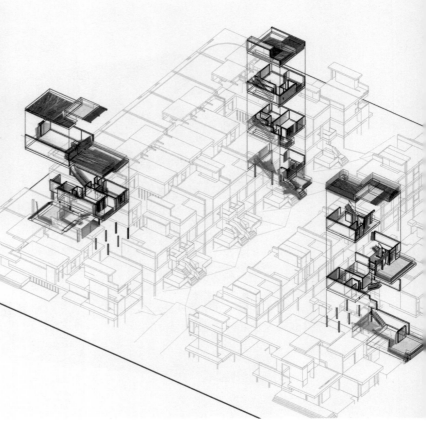

I

Section and Elevations
1/64" = 1'

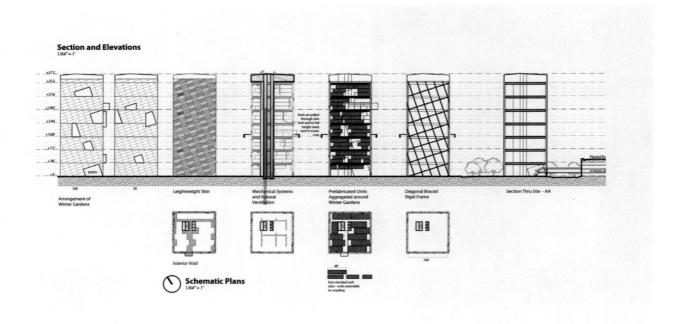

SW   SE

Arrangement of
Winter Gardens

Leightweight Skin

Mechanical Systems
and Natural
Ventilation

Prefabricated Units
Aggregated around
Winter Gardens

Diagonal Braced
Rigid Frame

Section Thru Site - AA

Interior Void

Schematic Plans
1/64" = 1'

four standard unit
sizes - units amenable
to coupling

II

THOMAS AUER   KATE JOHN-ALDER   KEITH KRUMWIEDE

LJILJANA BLAGOJEVIC   DOLORES HAYDEN   ALAN ORGANSCHI   SARA STEVENS
KEVIN DALY   DENISE HOFFMAN-BRANDT   ALBERT POPE   STANLEY TIGERMAN
TIM LOVE   JOEL SANDERS

DENISE HOFFMAN-BRANDT „I would like to see the criteria for your opportunism. Because what I like about it is that you're taking advantage of surgical opportunities, but you're not really clear about the criteria for your decision-making and it goes into amplifying the variety of possibilities here.

TIM LOVE „It might just be available land. There might have been a map of a whole block, a half-block, a quarter-block, it might have been a table of them, and this works for all five of those conditions. But it's optimistic, just the way it's developed by mapping the number of acres. And that's more the spirit of how I see your project than the spirit of being a piece of a master plan; it would be more like a system in a way.

ALBERT POPE „That's the beauty of it: to take an aggregate unit and play it out as what it does in various different scenarios, but embedded within the aggregate itself is an anticipation of enlargement, the superblock, and larger entities that can occur as you play out that scenario; not fixing a master plan, but allowing this aggregation. For example if there were more scale variation, and there were--I'm just shooting from the hip--there were more difference between this and this, then this could anticipate a larger grouping. It doesn't have to make the larger grouping, it functions as an aggregate unit in itself, but it anticipates any number of scenarios--the possibility of larger organization without losing the qualities of the aggregate.

STANLEY TIGERMAN „I think it's a problem of the studio. Because the ability to read, in your own conceptualization, areas that could require--that could benefit from--an idiosyncrasy that isn't part of the program at all. I mean, the area is so vast that there are more or less important areas. You'd have to go

beyond the problem that was posed, which was about housing that was environmental and ecological, et cetera. And to be able to do that, you have to have within you the ability to read your own work. It just wouldn't be housing. There's some absorption that allows for that amount of housing, then certainly a small-scale--some damn thing--would show up. But you have the mentality to go beyond the program. And there's another thing. This project highlights the problematics of designing a unit, and then plugging that into something. Another approach to a project like this actually starts with a document like that, and you try to figure out what the points of entry are, or the pressure points, and then you decide the more idiosyncratic stuff, as opposed to trying to force this condition. Because you're absolutely right: at some point, it'll be infeasible. You can't always carry on a project of this magnitude with these three types. So I'm saying it's another strategy, and whether or not you did it, as long as you walk out of here knowing that that's another possibility for approaching a large-scale project like this, that's something.

TIM LOVE „To put it another way, you've reframed the studio, clearly.

LJILJANA BLAGOJEVIC „There's an idea here which is beyond reality in a way, it's an idealized situation. There's an almost resort-like feel to this which misses the harsh reality of Houston and this particular area which may have actually radicalized your ideas in terms of what the urban face is, and so on. Because this is a conflict as well, and that doesn't show, although you did a very systematic--I want to commend you, you have a very systematic and very clear way of presenting your ideas--you needed some conflict there. Radical urban ideas maybe could have helped.

II

DENSE-CITY HOUSING
REBECCA BEYER

My goal has been to reexamine the single-family house in Houston, and in general, by maintaining the same density of units per block as practiced by developers, but by creating different kinds of solid/void relationships at different scales, from the unit, to the block, to the district, with a more interconnected relationship between inside and outside at each of these scales. Though the privacy that people desire in a single-family house is maintained, there are more opportunities for interaction between the different types of residents, from the open parking area to neighboring porches and terraces to the new pedestrian streets between units. Inherent in this proposal is a reexamination of the American dream in a dense and urban, post-bubble housing development.

ALBERT POPE „You didn't really make a case for the vertical, you just said that you plugged it in, and then you went back and talked about other things. I mean, you probably have the best project and worst presentation ever.

{Laughter}

The basis of the project, which I think is very laudable, is that you take forty-five percent of the volume out of one condition, which solves an energy problem, and creates this contingent space. It's the old porch space, the screened-in porch, that you're offering. The idea that you could overlap shared space, which is united atmospherically and climatologically with this forty-five percent that's been excluded from the envelope--that's interesting. The climatological and social are merging, and that's something that you could promote. I somehow think that you sort of let that fly. If you look at the grass land versus the grid, there's an interesting juxtaposition that you can find between open space, which is essentially unstructured, and the built space, which you're describing as gridded. And the edge between those, where those meet, is where you put the vertical element. I think what probably makes more sense is that you use the tower to create more open space within the grid, so that the grass land can be traced on the grid. I don't think you want to block off that edge between the canopy of the forest and the grass land. Instead of locking up that edge I think you actually want to increase that edge by pulling the grass land into the grid, and that would be the job of the tower. It would give the tower a role.

DOLORES HAYDEN „I think there were two basic assumptions you made right at the beginning, that locked you into a certain set of layered decisions. The first was, you said you were going to push the parking to the edge because you thought that would make it more urban. And you have to ask yourself what urban means, and what urban means in Houston, and whether or not by pushing the parking to the edge you've

constricted what your possibilities were. So the space that you gained in the reduction of unit sizes, you have then assigned to four units to really negotiate over. And I think that's the second assumption. You would really have to ask yourself, is there research of any kind that suggests that people in four units want to negotiate over open space?

JOEL SANDERS „But I'd like to believe that you could respond to that point, which I think is so important, if you had better developed, at a larger scale, the nuances of your project. I'll just step back and say that I think a lot of people have recognized what I think is the richest thing about your project, and perhaps about the studio: this provocation to somehow bring together the things we don't often do, which is let's say the environmental and the formal and the social, and their rich promise. But I think, and you asked the question, will these negotiations work? And I feel unable to respond to that, because the scale and the manner of your presentation is never to allow us to jump in scale and understand the kind of life, the climate, the social activity, the membranes, the sections, the kinds of sliding doors--it's all about these nuances.

KEVIN DALY „You also dropped this huge bomb at the front, saying one of the problems is the ability of developers to transfer ownership at this very early stage in the building. And you propose that maybe that has to change, so the point at which they no longer own things is much later in the life of the building. I think that would really substantially change the way you build stuff. I mean, if you were a developer or contractor and you have interest fifteen years into the deal, I suspect the detailing would be a little bit different. So now in this banking crisis, in the process of actually legislating against the ability of builders to offer financing, one of your counterintuitive insights into this is that maybe it ought to be a requirement, and I think that was a really interesting observation.

III

HOUSING AGGREGATIONS
CHRIS STARKEY

Analysis of two distinct types of development on-site, (high-density single-family and multi-family rental) rooted long-term social and environmental performance failures in the lack of planning as units aggregate. Designs for both densities are proposed that decouple building systems from living space, create negotiated common space, are adaptable to living conditions that change through time, and manipulate vegetation and passive conditioning techniques. Interior space is extended with exterior space allowing the home to expand or retreat with the seasons. Good neighbors negotiate their relationships in exterior spaces: sharing, isolating, expanding and contracting. As these spaces aggregate they mass into hollowed building volumes whose skins and voids are dynamically adapted to a community.

MED INDEPENDENT RESEARCH

The proposal submitted with the admissions application is the basis for each student's study plan which is developed in consultation with faculty advisers. Independent research is undertaken each term under the direction of a principal adviser for preparation and completion of a written thesis. The thesis, which details and summarizes the independent research, is to be completed for approval by the M.E.D. committee by the end of the fourth term.

I

This thesis traces the influence of conceptual and performance art within the intellectual and artistic development of Bernard Tschumi during his formative years in the 1970s. Through a close interpretation of his drawings and manifestoes, I will argue that the concepts of notation and score were central to his architecture in that they dislocated the traditional architectural drawing--the plan, section, and elevation--from its reinforcement of a socio-economic project and uncovered a movement and sequence that conventional modes of representation exclude. These shifts in methodology construct an alternate view of the modernist object, not to displace the visual, but to use experienceand perception to reveal an unbounded narrative structure of architectural space.

Central to this thesis is that Tschumi's work leading up to his Manhattan Transcripts (published in 1981) must be understood outside of architectural canons and instead be situated within the historical and cultural contexts between London and New York. Tschumi's pedagogy at the Architectural Association and his collaborations with performance artist RoseLee Goldberg establish a framework to explore a new relationship between theory and its spatial praxis. In addition, this research will look at the role of Peter Cook's Art Net gallery (1973-1979) as an enclave of an alternative, conceptual architecture of London against the perceived rigid formalism of the New York Five. Here, the work of Peter Eisenman and the lineage of Colin Rowe will be used as a counterpoint to critique the radical articulation of Tschumi's self-proclaimed transgression.

Ultimately, this thesis will make a plea for architecture that is not based on formal manipulations but on the infinite possibilities in the participatory nature of architectural and urban space. At a time when architectural discourse is dominated and standardized by parametric and morphological technologies, this research could not be more relevant. Tschumi's early projects will highlight an alternative pathway where architectural representation, as the embodiment of architectural ideas and concepts, can be used to test the very limits of architecture.

II

My thesis tracks the dialogues between architecture and the minimalist arts. It is primarily concerned with maintaining critical ideas that fostered the discussion.

At the forefront of this project is the term "topology," which, divorced from mathematics, emblematically functioned to account for the inherently social relationships embedded in the minimalist project. Theoretically, I do this through following art historian Eric de Bruyn's seminal text Topological Pathways of Postminimalism, which, in an account of artist Dan Graham, raised the stakes of minimalism by underscoring its political implications. In following this category through works of art and architecture, the thesis makes a case for the critical efficacy of minimalism by underscoring the political dimensions of agency it fostered when implemented within the built environment.

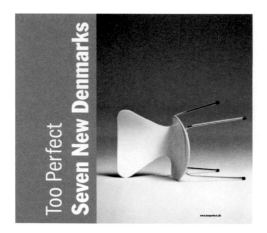

III
DANISH BY DESIGN
IBEN ANDREA FALCONER
Architecture, Nationalism & Promotion

IV
CITIBANK
OLGA PANTELIDOU
The Bank that Never Sleeps

III

In 2004, a group of young Danish architects collaborated with Bruce Mau to create an exhibit entitled "Too Perfect: Seven New Denmarks." The goal was to "rebrand" Danish architecture. The exhibit displayed seven projects that address current issues such as housing, energy, land use, and childcare. The projects were purposely over-the-top and bombastic, rejecting the idea of Danish architecture as modest and craft-oriented. In 2005, the architect Rene Hougaard chose to name his furniture company "Dnmark," in order to explicitly link his designs to Danish Modernism of the 1950s and 1960s in the minds of non-Danish customers. In 2006, the firm C. F. Møller published a long brochure about the company, highlighting its work abroad. Especially noted was the opening of an office in London. Despite its location and the fact that only three out of 14 employees were Danish nationals, the office was described as "[representing] a Danish architectural tradition" and as possessing "a Danish soul." These are just three of many examples of Danish architects and architecture firms with global ambitions who are using a national label to promote their work abroad. While not every architect trades on his or her nationality, some do, and do so in ways that are worth investigating. Rather than attempting to argue that a particular architectural object embodies "Danishness," this project examines the ways in which the narrative of Danishness is established around the architect and the object, and thereby examines the persistence of the national within the discourse of architecture.

IV

On November 10, 1978, the Electronic Fund Transfers Act was enacted to regulate the interaction between consumers and a new bank space, the Automated Teller Machine (ATM). This law followed the popularization of the ATM, accomplished by Citibank, just ten months earlier, when it took advantage of New York City's worst blizzard in ten years. Over less than two days, the bank ran forty-three radio commercials that highlighted the convenience of automated, 24-hour banking available at its Citicard Banking Centers (CBCs). While law mandated controls on the information that flowed through this financial space, Citibank, this chapter argues, understood and exploited the ATM from its inception as a mass medium, capable of transmitting not only the bank's image, but new financial habits throughout the city, unrestricted by temporal pressures.

Although it was not the first bank to introduce the ATM, Citibank was the first to undertake this venture at a massive scale. It dotted its home-base city with two hundred such machines in less than eight months as part of a larger initiative, Branch '77, a complete redesign of its retail experience, aimed at brand unification and better service. Concurrently, as the first to take advantage of new building incentives, it erected midtown Manhattan's third tallest building. Designed by Hugh Stubbins and Associates, as its new headquarters, Citicorp Tower joined Citibank's existing high-rise office buildings, which, being located along a sequence of consecutive stations on the E subway line, formed an administrative axis that came to coordinate the bank's new media outlets. While the ATM was Citibank's answer to an ailing retail banking sector, all of its spatial gestures came to challenge the image of a city, which, having just been denied federal assistance, was on the verge of bankruptcy. This chapter argues that the bank found the form for these undertakings in studies it undertook earlier to identify remedies for New York's malaise. Moreover, it asserts that, by navigating the confluence of changes in law and advancements in technology, Cititbank recognized its retail space as a mass medium and engaged in a spatial communicative strategy that enabled it to influence and in turn be influenced by its environment on the metropolitan scale of the city.

V

My research will investigate intersections of architecture, information technology, and communications media in the postwar museum and its methods of popular instruction. These threads, and their convergence, will be analyzed through a close reading of the Metropolitan Museum of Art under Director Thomas P.F. Hoving, whose tenure (1967-77) was marked by visions of a populist museum-going experience equally forged through entertainment and education.

Hoving's reformulation of the museum's curatorial practices and tactics, coupled with his creation of a Master Plan (1966-71) designed by Kevin Roche John Dinkeloo and Associates (KRJDA) to house incoming collections of art and reorganize existing departments, reveal an emerging emphasis on environmental design in positioning works of art as information for the masses. Yet, most of all, KRJDA's undertaking of the Master Plan--an exhaustive cataloging of human history--signals an unprecedented use of organization systems in both curatorial and architectural design alike, arguably making it difficult to distinguish the two.

This thesis will focus on KRJDA's Met Master Plan, the curatorial programs of Hoving's early "blockbuster" exhibitions, and larger cultural, economic, and epistemological phenomena to critically weigh these systems and question whether they cause an elision of culture and information. In unpacking its origins and mechanisms, I will reveal mass culture's implicit links to organization and information patterns to ask if and how those patterns co-opt new possibilities (or limitations) for subjectivity--a concern that persists in the digital age.

My research includes a comparative analysis of contemporaneous museums with similar objectives, such as KRJDA's Oakland Museum (1961-69)--celebrated as the "People's Museum" upon its opening--and in addition to Renzo Piano and Richard Rogers's Centre Beaubourg (1971-77), envisioned as a cultural center amid the Marais, a working class district in urban Paris. Mid-century writings from media theory, aesthetics, urbanism, and cybernetics will lend a historical framework in positioning mass culture and information design as complicit with emerging morphologies of architecture. Contemporary theorists including Beatriz Colomina, Reinhold Martin, Kristin Ross, Michael Warner and Jacques Rancière will provide critical lenses for assessing the Hoving/KRJDA Master Plan and its ongoing relevance, as digital media technologies expand forums of public access and therefore patterns of mass culture.

VI

Geographically situated between the Orient and the Occident, Turkey exists in an in-between space of shared heritages. That is why throughout the Republican period (1923-today), the question of identity has always revolved around dualities such as East-West, religious-secular, national-universal and so on. This thesis will be taking Istanbul as a case study, because the city depended on and benefited from its place as a major crossroads of trans-regional economic and cultural relations. As the "west" and "east" divide came to consolidate itself politically, spatially and ideologically, the city became a terrain where this divide played itself out dramatically.

From a historical perspective, what makes Istanbul somewhat exceptional is its deep history as an interface between different economies, cultures and politics. Long-distance interactions and interconnectedness with its changing form, density, and velocity over time has been an essential part of the city's history and identity. Istanbul not only occupies a distinct geographic location at the interstices of multiple regions--Asia, Near East, and Europe--but also, for much of its history, it functioned as a central node in long-distance trade and cross-cultural exchange, as a cultural center of two world religions, and as a political center of two world empires. These different experiences play themselves out in the contemporary discourses that shape the city today.

The country has been forced to adapt to worldwide geopolitical and economic changes on many occasions. My research will investigate three major economical and cultural turning points, which had major influence on this radical transformation of the architectural culture and urbanscape of Istanbul. Through the analysis of key historical moments and major projects (1950s and the Istanbul Hilton, 1980s and the Corporate Banks, 2000s and Golden Horn renovation projects), my thesis aims to address broader questions. In what ways can architecture be used by political entities as a part of nation building and identity formation? How do worldwide economic and political processes affect this process? How global trends become local processes. And how do local/national actors, themselves, turn out to be forces that initiate and help this process?

V
INFORMATION ARCHITECTURE
DAVID SADIGHIAN
Mass Culture, Organization,
and Interface Design at
the Metropolitan Museum of Art

VI
NATIONAL IDENTITY, POWER
AND ARCHITECTURAL CULTURE
OZLEM CAGLAR TOMBUS
The Case of Istanbul

3RD FLOOR

Faculty

JEFFERY BLANCHARD
KARLA BRITTON
PEGGY DEAMER
BRYAN FUERMANN
JAN GADEYNE
SOPHIA GRUZDYS
STEPHEN HARBY
JOHN JACOBSON
TERRY KIRK
ALEXANDER PURVES

Students

JAMIE BERG
CHENG HUI CHUA
YIJE DANG
PALMYRA GERAKI
JANICE HAHN
GREGORY MELTINOV
CHRISTOPHER PALENCIA
CARLOS FELIX
    RASPALL-GALLI
KAREN RIZVI
ZAK SNIDER

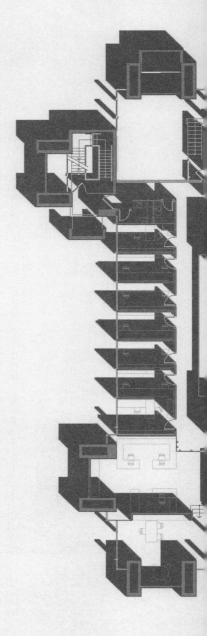

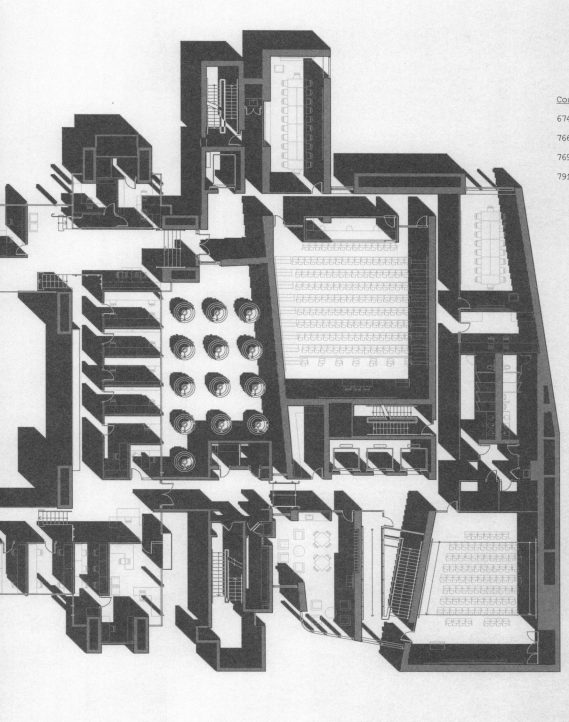

674A

ARCHITECTURAL PRODUCT DESIGN

This studio course attempts to broaden the design experience by concentrating on the design and innovation of three-dimensional architectural objects not usually found within architectural commissions. Students are required to design and fabricate full-size, working prototypes of five small objects such as weather vanes, andirons, step stools, mailboxes, bird houses, etc. Emphasis is on wood and metal, but all materials are considered. Issues of detail, scale, proportion, aesthetics, manufacturing, and commercial viability are explored.

I
UNTITLED
JAMIE BERG

II
UNTITLED
YIJIE DANG

II
UNTITLED
CARLOS FELIX RASPALL-GALLI

I

II

III

JAMIE BERG   YIJIE DANG   CARLOS FELIX RASPALL-GALLI

INTRODUCTION TO BRITISH LANDSCAPE HISTORY

766B

The Yale Center for British Art is the largest and most comprehensive collection of British art outside the United Kingdom. It is an unparalleled resource amongst American universities. Students of the course have the opportunity to examine firsthand British painting, sculpture, drawings, watercolors, rare books, and manuscripts and use these primary sources in tracing the evolution of the idea of nature in Britain as represented in its literature, art and architectural history, and landscape architectural history from 1650 to 1900.

The methodology of the course is interdisciplinary. In the first half of the term students focus primarily on gardens, landscape parks, and garden theory. Literature, painting, and prints supplement the discussion. The second half of the course shifts focus to literature, painting, watercolors, architecture, the decorative arts, as well as mid-nineteenth-century discoveries in the natural sciences. Gardens, parks, garden theory, and debates on horticulture supplement the discussion. The course culminates in a trip to Britain to examine these issues first hand.

Throughout the term the course examines the idea of nature within a wide cultural arena: aesthetics, politics, philosophy, psychology, science, commerce, imperialism, colonialism, and nationalism. Many of these issues have become the focus of landscape studies in the past two decades and the assigned readings reflect these critical perspectives.

DANIEL YODER AT CASTLE HOWARD

ANGEL BEALE & ROSIE WEINBERG
AT CANTERBURY

769B

RELIGION &
MODERN ARCHITECTURE

The design of religious architecture challenges the creative capacities of prominent architects, yet this domain has largely gone unnoticed within the field. In an inter-religious and interdisciplinary context, this seminar offers a fresh examination of the history of modern architecture through a close analysis of a single building type--the religious building (mosques, churches, synagogues, and temples). Drawing on guest speakers, this course opens a discourse between the disciplinary perspectives of philosophy, theology, liturgical studies, and architectural history and theory on the influence religion has come to exert in contemporary civic life, and the concretization of that role in the construction of prominent religious buildings. Questions addressed include: How can the concept of the "sacred" be understood in the twenty-first century, if at all? In what contexts is it intelligible? In a pluralist society, in which the spiritual is often experienced individually, how can architecture express communal identity or tradition? How are concepts of the ineffable realized in material form? Architects discussed included Perret, Plecnik, Lutyens, Wright, Le Corbusier, Mendelsohn, El-Wakil, Tange, Kahn, Ando, Barragan, Moneo, Eisenman, Hadid, and Shim.

I
POSTWAR SENTIMENT IN THE MIKVEH
ISRAEL SYNAGOGUE
GREGORY MELTINOV

II
ELÁDIO DIESTE AND LUIS BARRAGÁN
CHRISTOPHER PALENCIA
Sacred Architecture and Critical Modernism in Latin America

III
THE VOLATILITY OF SACRED SPACE:
AYODHYA & THE BABRI MASJID CONFLICT
KAREN RIZVI
No discussion of religion and sacred space is complete without acknowledging the darker aspect of religious belief. History offers us numerous examples of how religion can spawn fanaticism, territoriality, and hegemonic tendencies. The spaces associated with religion can become highly charged and contested areas--often the site of horrific violence, where the stakes of ownership are not merely to control land or buildings, but to hold the power to revise history and to perpetuate an ideology. This paper explores two of the most contested sacred sites in the world: the first is what Jews call har ha-bayit, the temple Mount in Jerusalem, otherwise know by the Muslims as al-haram al-sharif, or the Noble Sanctuary. The second is the ancient city of Ayodhya in India, the locale of recent and intense Hindu-Muslim conflict. Both sites are instances of a volatile, multi-layered and contested sacred territory where the interconnection of memory, landscape and religion is particularly alive. Using the cultural and religious theories of sacred spaces and memory by theorists such as Mircea Eliade, Walter Capps, and Simon Schama, this paper explores these sacred places as crepuscular territories, changed by, and changing, the volatile world around them, and yet tethered to a vanished, idealized past. These sites are discussed in their social, political, and spatial complexities as sacred territories that express a final link to the things worth saving, and worth dying for.

I

Kahn believed that art, architecture included, was the language of God. He also believed that it was in man's nature to express himself through art, "Art is man's only real language since it strives to communicate in a way that reveals the 'human' and that the will to be (the Existence Will) in man is really the will to express." Thus, what was timeless about art was man desire to express and to speak the language of God. Kahn's work for the Mikveh Israel Synagogue was an artful composition of rooms and a reference. Throughout his career he sought to give meaning to space by developing an architectural vocabulary rooted in common culture. Despite increasingly flexible attitudes in organized religion, Kahn sought to put religion back on its pedestal, making architecture integral to worship. Work on the Mikveh Israel project only stopped when Kahn's commissions grew to include projects of truly monumental proportion. Kahn was commission to design iconic projects for fledging states on a scale of significance matching that of Independence Hall. The Hurva Synagogue in Jerusalem was not realized due to Kahn's death. However, the National Assembly Complex at Dhaka, Bangladesh--an edifice of a postwar religious state--was completed after Kahn's death.

II

Considering the work of Eládio Dieste and Luis Barragán, and in particular the churches at Atlántida, San Pedro, and the Chapel of the Capuchinas, the works reveal a number of ways to approach a discussion of sacred architecture. A strictly formal discussion will focus on the ways these churches attempt to create bridges to the transcendental via the formal and compositional manipulation of material, light, and in the case of Barragán, color. A second layer of analysis, however, reveals two architects grappling with some of the most contentious issues of modern architecture, and indeed, modernity itself. Having been charged to re-invent and re-create by the avant-garde functionalists, Dieste held to an ethical position that modernity and progress were not simply matters of technological innovation. For Dieste, a more ethical approach to architecture, for the Uruguayan situation at least, did not insist on concrete and glass, but rather on an intelligent and critical engagement of materials and technologies already available in Uruguay. This approach, Dieste believed, would yield formally strong solutions, and in the case of the Atlántida and Duraznos churches, become the basis of an architecture of community.

In contrast to Dieste, Barragán reveled in the planar, orthographic basis of aesthetic modernity. Barragán's skepticisms, however, went beyond the aesthetic and questioned the effects of industrial modernity on human life. Though Barragán's architecture is one of supreme compositional abstraction, the turn to color, texture, and thickness in articulating the concrete wall speaks to a longing for the simplicity of a pre-industrial Catholic mysticism. To be sure, the architectures of Barragán and Dieste are quite different from one another. But what they hold in common, and in contrast to the high modernists, is a critical attitude about the articulation of modernism in Latin America. Both architects understood that modernization had been constructed around a formalism of concrete and glass. In contrast, Barragán and Dieste's concerns went beyond form, and insisted on the primacy of the poetic, the emotional, and the human dimensions of space.

III

GREGORY MELTINOV   CHRISTOPHER PALENCIA   KAREN RIZVI

JEFFREY BLANCHARD   BRYAN FUERMANN   JAN GADEYNE   SOPHIA GRUZDYS
STEPHEN HARBY   TERRY KIRK   ALEXANDER PURVES

ROME:
CONTINUITY & CHANGE

This intensive four-week summer workshop took place in Rome and provided a broad overview of that city's major architectural sites, topography, and systems of urban organization. Examples from antiquity to the twentieth century were studied as a sequence of layered accretions. Joined by knowledgeable archeologists and historians of Rome, students were given in-depth lectures and on site guided tours. The seminar examines historical continuity and change as well as the ways in which, and the reasons why, some elements and approaches were maintained over time and others abandoned.

    Drawing was used as a primary tool of discovery during explorations of buildings, landscapes, and gardens, both within and outside the city. The course is guided by the conviction that an essential part of an architect's formation is the first hand experience of a broad range of buildings and places from of all periods and styles. True possession of them comes about not only through the intellect but through the body by inhabiting and measuring them and through the hand by drawing them.

I
UNTITLED
PALMYRA GERAKI

II
UNTITLED
JANICE HAHN

II

I

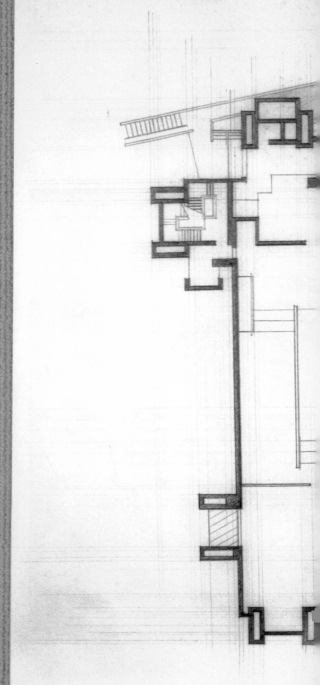

2ND FLOOR

Faculty

KARLA BRITTON
PEGGY DEAMER
ARIANE LOURIE HARRISON
DOLORES HAYDEN
KYUNG SUN MOON
DIETRICH NEUMANN
PALOMA PAJARES
EEVA-LIISA PELKONEN
JOEL SANDERS
CARTER WISEMAN

Students

BRYAN BERKAS
LAUREN CHAPMAN
CHENG HUI CHUA
CORY COLLMAN
SEHER EDROGAN
MARK GAUSEPOHL
PALMYRA GERAKI
JACQUELYN HAWKINS
REUBEN HERZL
MEREDITH MCDANIEL
PATRICK MCGOWAN
SHANE NEUFELD
MIEKO OKAMOTO
ZACH PURSLEY
MATT ROMAN
DAVID SADIGHIAN
ZAK SNIDER
OZLEM CAGLAR TOMBUS
ADAM TOMSKI
ANDREA VITTADINI
LEAH WEINBERG
MATT ZYCH

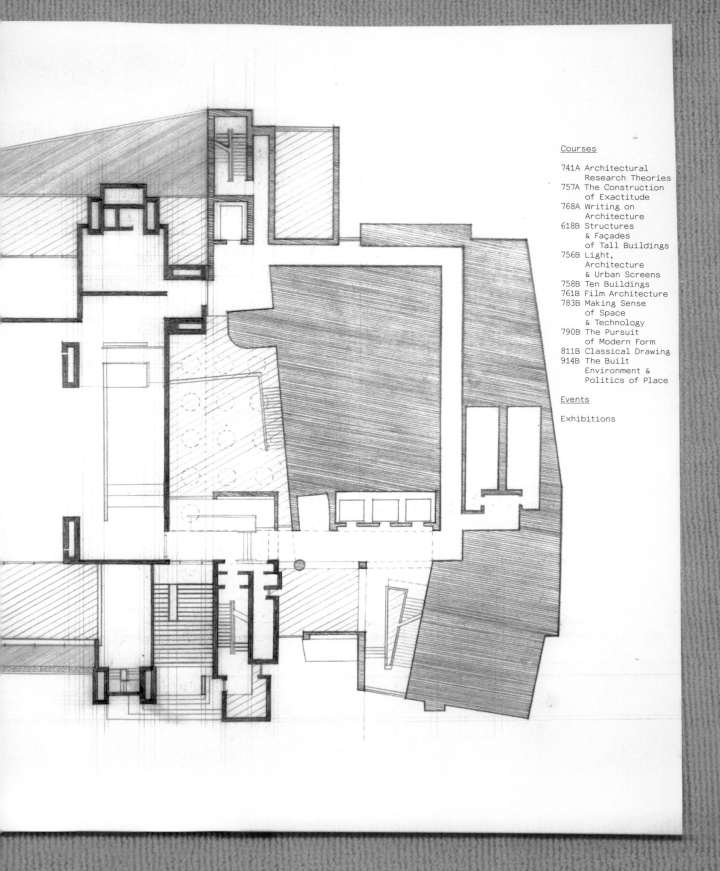

ARCHITECTURAL RESEARCH THEORIES

741A

This course introduces students to methods of architectural writing and research, laying the groundwork for an advanced research project. By investigating various text genres, such as surveys, journalism, manifestos, scholarly essays, critical essays, and narratives, this course studies ways of writing about architecture, urbanism, and the environment. Recent debates concerning the relationship between architectural history and theory and the questions about disciplinary and interdisciplinary boundaries are explored. Students are introduced to hands-on research through a series of library, archival, and GIS workshops that take place outside of class time. Students are expected to present different writing styles and formats through weekly assignments.

I
MIGRANT ELDERS AND THE WELFARE STATE
MIEKO OKAMOTO
A Retirement Village Development in Subic Bay

II
THOMAS HOVING AND THE PLEASURES OF TEXTUAL INDETERMINACY
DAVID SADIGHIAN

I

Off the west coast of Luzon in the Zambales Province, about 120 kilometers from Manila, is the Subic Bay. A port town bustling with McDonalds and jipneys, the memories of protracted military conquests seem forever sealed by the silent asphalt on which Subic's hyper-modern facilities and interstate highways sit today. This site has undergone a dramatic transformation into an arsenal for the Spanish colonialists in the late 19th century, a temporary stronghold for the Japanese invaders during WWII, and the largest U.S. military base abroad during the Cold War. In the early 1990s, the illustrious layers of history have been papered over once again by its conversion into the Subic Bay Freeport Zone.

Freetrade zones are indeed a contemporary phenomenon. Yet, the forbidden fruits that these spaces yield are not necessarily privileged economic viability or cultural imperialism. Today, the clients who turn to pieces of the global market are the welfare states in the first world. Rarely taken up in the discourses on the decline of national sovereignty, borderless production, and rule by Empire is the impending "silver era" on the global scale.

Where and how do we situate the elderly in the age of Empire? What happens to the worker when they reach the so-called "retirement age" and are no longer deemed labor? If the modern welfare system was established by governments to mobilize industrial labor, and if those nation-states no longer command the sovereignty they did before Empire's ascension, then how can we understand the relevance of state involvement in elderly care today?

The development of retirement "villages" in the Philippines and the emerging urban landscape predicate themselves upon an extremely tenuous balance of power between the first-world countries (which ship off expired human labor elsewhere), and the third-world host countries (which could benefit as long as the pension system in client countries remains defunct).

II

A 1967 cartoon in The New Yorker illustrates Thomas Hoving's induction as Director of the Metropolitan Museum of Art as a moment of free-wheeling public jubilee. Fireworks pop in the sky, kites and balloons soar, and the churning masses--some pushing hot dog carts, some hawking cheap goods--swarm beneath a banner ("Welcome Mr. Hoving"!) draped across the museum's Beaux Arts façade. Caricature aside, such forms of spectacle were not unknown to Hoving at the time.

Prior to accepting the directorship of the Met, Hoving was appointed New York City Parks Commissioner under Mayor John Lindsay--a tenure marked by publicity stunts and scandal. Hoving left a successful curatorial career at The Cloisters to accept the Commissioner bid with the aim of animating the city's parks into sources of leisure and pageantry--transforming New York City into "Fun City." Hoving's proposition for reclaiming a public for the city's parks was through forms of recreation, which he coined "happenings."

Arriving at the Met with his populist Parks ideologies intact, how was Hoving to make the Met--an archive of human history; a bastion of civic identity--happen to invite the masses? While the New Yorker cartoon might suggest euphoric utopia, it also contains shades of cynicism: Hoving's park public has here metastasized, and an elite fortress of art and society seems buried--even lost--in the spectacle.

If, per Michael Warner's definition, a public is attained through textual circulation, how does architecture attain persisting social relevance in its physical permanence?

Textual circulation operates on the assumption of mass legibility: the ability to create a public through shared language, through the act of communication. To invite the masses, architecture must offer a textual space for reading as a form of engagement. Yet obviously this presents ethical dilemmas, in that it destabilizes the idea of meaning as sustained and shared truth, opting instead for performance--the Hoving happening. Yet more than temporary social engagement, the ultimate problem pertains to endurance: can the masses attain a lasting built form?

While the New Yorker cartoon suggests that the masses exist in opposition to architecture, Hoving's directorship at the Met sought to transform a moribund institution into a stage of mobility and exchange. To attain the mass address of a public enveloped with media forms and spectacles, the museum had to become a space of textual inundation.

THE CONSTRUCTION OF EXACTITUDE

757A

This seminar critically considers modern classicism not only as a compositional design method and as an evocation of precedents, but also as a language of clarity, reduction, and economy resistant to an unquestioned avant-gardist predilection for the "new." Beginning with the fixed principles that were the legacy of nineteenth-century French and German Neoclassicism (unity, symmetry, proportion), the seminar continues up through the Rationalism and Formalism that followed the Second World War. Issues explored include the concepts of the ruin and monumentality; the Modern Movement's analogies to the classical; and the representation of interwar national and political ideologies. Works studied include those by architects, literary/ artistic figures, and theorists such as Richardson, Garnier, Perret, Le Corbusier, Rossi, Asplund, Lutyens, Terragni, Speer, Mies, SOM, Kahn, Valéry, Gide, de Chirico, Calvino, Rowe, Krier, Eisenman, Stern, Porphyrios, and Colquhoun.

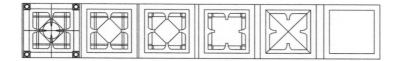

I

I
LOUIS SULLIVAN & THE GEOMETRY OF ORNAMENT
ZACH PURSLEY

For my final project I am proposing a series of models that study Louis Sullivan's development of architectural ornament and how his process represents a logical series of geometric operations. Within all of Sullivan's ornament lies a rational set of operations that can be traced though the design. While most of Sullivan's ornament looks as if it is derived directly from nature I will strive to show the geometric process that led to these works.

The models that I will produce will look similar to the process steps that Sullivan illustrates in the image above. I will produce a series of smaller process models that are about 8"×8" while also producing a final model that is 12"×12". I hope to show that the relationship between order, rationality, and structure in Sullivan's architecture can be clearly seen through his development of ornament.

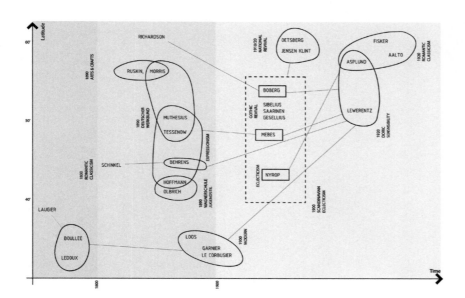

II

II
NORDIC CLASSICISM: ASPLUND, LEWERENTZ & THE WOODLAND CEMETERY
ANDREA VITTADINI

From this viewpoint, Neo Doricism and Functionalism could appear as culturally impoverished versions of Classic and Modern originals, deprived of their cultured contents and reduced to merely constructive or linguistic systems. Nevertheless such reduction of cultural complexity was potentially legitimate or even healthy, since in Europe both had already degenerated into the rhetoric exercises of Beaux Arts Revivalism and International Style: Neo Doricism and Functionalism thus gain value insofar as they manage not to restore the original orthodoxy, but to revitalize through new cultural contributions.

It is thus legitimate for Asplund and Lewerentz to use Classic and then Modern as a pretext to continue exploring themes held dear by Scandinavian culture: local materials, constructive methods, landscape and environmentalism, education and social welfare. Technical and poetic concerns rather than theoretical and ideological denoted a craftsmen sensibility rather than academic intellectualism.

This alternative approach produced unexpectedly successful results since the beginning, when an incredible aesthetic delicacy, compositional wisdom, and sophistication of detail could already avoid an incoherent collision of diverse cultural fragments, blending towards a balanced whole and achieving an effect of pleasant weirdness and calibrated bizarreness.

768A

WRITING ON ARCHITECTURE

The goal of this course is to train students in the principles and techniques of nonfiction writing as it applies to architecture. The course includes readings from the work of prominent architects, critics, and literary figures, as well as varying types and lengths of writings, such as brief reviews of books and exhibitions, opinion pieces, and formal presentations of buildings and projects. The main focus of the course is an extended paper on a building selected from a variety of types and historical periods, such as skyscrapers, private houses, industrial plants, gated communities, malls, institutional buildings, and athletic facilities.

I
REUSED AMERICANA
CORY COLLMAN
Dia: Beacon

II
SCHOLARSHIP VERSUS ELITISM
MATT ZYCH
The Residential College System at Yale

I

In the Hudson Valley, sixty miles north of New York City, lies a museum that has been largely overlooked as a work of architecture. It is neither flashy, nor figural. It is neither conceited, nor conceptual. It houses, however, one of the most important collections of American art in the world, and in spite of its simplicity, the unique dialogue between the museum and the artwork contained within it invokes a powerful reaction. The building is the Dia Art Foundation's home in Beacon, New York.

The effect of Richard Serra's Torqued Ellipses is meant to be destabilizing, but this is a difficult effect to produce if the surrounding walls of the gallery are dynamic as well. This is one of the reasons why Serra has cited his feeling that his work is less successful when displayed in Frank Ghery's Guggenheim Museum in Bilbao. The success of the Torqued Ellipses at Dia: Beacon relies on its context, which both serve as a reflection of its genesis and as a contrast that further defines it. Sandback and Serra have therefore both preferred to show their work in former industrial buildings as opposed to museums with more monumental or sculptural white walls. The reason for this is the specific kind of dialogue that takes place between the work and the space. As Anthony Vidler writes, "reciprocally, the architectural space that acts as site for the sculpture generates an equal and opposite experience, as architectural space for its own sake, without the existence of which the sculpture would have little to tussle with." It is for this reason that the former box factory in Beacon was chosen and why many of the artists in Dia's history have preferred to co-opt cast iron buildings in Chelsea and Soho for use as art galleries. These buildings are not simply neutral spaces, instead they provide an understood and familiar field or spatial framework within which the artwork is set. These settings suggest an American urban industrial landscape, which grounds the work in an abstract yet perceptible cultural context.

II

At the time when Yale University has announced plans to construct two new undergraduate colleges, this analysis revisits the founding of the residential college system. Constructed by the American architect and Yale alumnus James Gamble Rogers between 1917 and 1935, the colleges attempt to define a behavioral code for their students, evoking an image that is not and never was central to Yale's student body.

Unallied to any stylistic orthodoxy for the new campus (contrasted to Harvard's Georgian typology or the High Gothic at Princeton), Rogers assumed considerable liberties in his interpretation of historic precedents. His selection of the Gothic model derived little from the body of reactionary moralism published by Ruskin and his conservative following in Europe during the mid-nineteenth century. Conversely, it appeared that Rogers borrowed from the Gothic for primarily esthetic effect; his buildings employed modern forms and construction methods, as opposed to the traditions of the Gothic canon, but such pragmatism and contemporaneity were cloaked in a diverse shield of historicist décor to reference the aura of their English predecessors. For example, his compositions resist the axis which would have been central to a Gothic plan, but instead offer a picturesque promenade. The resulting amalgam of styles creates something which resists any strict taxonomy; the colleges appear European and disparate from the New England vernacular, and require both the imagination of students and their historical stereotypes to link the new complex to its English brethren.

The social matrix of Yale College at the time illuminates the notable irony in selecting this icon of nostalgia as a model for the college: socially and culturally, the atmosphere of Yale could not have been further away from the piety and sobriety of Gothic monasteries. Rogers and the Presidents of the college conversed regularly as to the atmosphere which was desired for the young men of Yale, and it was the his task to use whatever building vocabulary possible to achieve this; the Gothic was a point of departure for Rogers, not a destination.

In the end, Rogers' architecture is the embodiment of a social doctrine. Exemplified by a lack of allegiance to any ideology--stylistic, theoretical, or historical--his buildings depend on a considerably diverse repertoire of atmospheric ploys to generate architecture of impact. While this analysis has exposed the fallacy of simply classifying Roger's campus as "collegiate Gothic," the resulting effect on its population fashioned a legacy that would identify not only the campus, but Yale itself. Rogers' essentially rational and modern buildings, shrouded in historical detailing, are in fact a pristine metaphor for the architect himself: an intelligent, pragmatic, middle-class man who at times masqueraded his sober practicality behind the cultural and social spirit that he learned as a student at Yale in order to obtain its commissions. Like a folly of a historic subject that never did in fact exist, the elusive, even ironic subjects to which the buildings allude is far more provocative than the specifics of the designs. At Yale, for better or worse, this is what has come to dominate the physical and social trajectory of the school since Rogers' first project nearly a century ago.

CORY COLLMAN

MATT ZYCH

EXHIBITIONS

I
HAWAIIAN MODERN
The Architecutre of Vladimir Ossipoff

II
MODEL CITY
Buildings & Projects by Paul Rudolph
for New Haven and Yale

III
WORLDS AWAY
New Suburban Landscapes

618B

STRUCTURES & FACADES OF TALL BUILDINGS

This seminar investigates the dynamic interrelationship between technology and architecture in tall buildings. Among the various technologies involved, emphasis is placed on structural and façade systems, recognizing the significance of these systems, the separation of which in terms of their function led to modern architecture, and allowed the emergence of tall buildings. This seminar reviews contemporary design practice of tall buildings through a series of lectures and case study analyses. While most representative structural and façade systems for tall buildings are studied, particular emphasis is placed on more recent trends such as diagrid structures and double skin façades. Further, this seminar investigates emerging technologies for tall buildings and explores their architectural potentials. Finally, this course culminates in a tall building design project and presentation.

I
VEILED TOWER
CHENG HUI CHUA & ZAK SNIDER

Sited at the intersection of the Chicago River and Lake Michigan, this 2050 foot-tall super tower is the product of sky-scraper research during the first half of the semester. Vortex shedding led to the concept of a double shell system. The inner diagrid structure varies in angle from 63 degrees at the top to 80 degrees at the base, responding to greater loads. The secondary shell is cantile-vered from the structural core and inner diagrid. These outer shells are primar-ily oriented south to shield against solar heat gain, capture energy through photovoltaic panels, and act as massive chimneys for heat escape. In section, the space between the diagrid and outer shell provide atria establishing a visual connection between floors.

I

154

CHENG HUI CHUA
ZAK SNIDER

LIGHT, ARCHITECTURE & URBAN SCREENS

This seminar explores the history, theory, and practice of architectural illumination and the notion of electric light as a "building material," and considers the current interest in urban screens and media façades. The course follows a historic trajectory from ca. 1900 to the present and introduces students to the most important techniques, protagonists, and debates over the past 100 years. In conjunction with the preparation and current research for an exhibition at the School of Architecture in the fáll of 2010, particular emphasis is placed on the work of Yale's theater and architectural lighting designer Stanley McCandless and his student Richard Kelly, who became the most important lighting designer in twentieth-century modern architecture, profoundly changing the appearance of seminal buildings by Louis Kahn, Ludwig Mies van der Rohe, Richard Neutra, Eero Saarinen, and others.

I
IIT
SEHER EDROGAN

III

Richard Kelly selected a lighting approach in working with Eero Saarinen on Washington Dulles airport (1958-1962) that integrated directly into the expressive form of the airport's design. The lighting scheme of this project shows the results of Kelly's direct involvement throughout the design process. In each situation we see lighting reinforcing the dominant lines of this structure. The success of this lighting design was only possible through early collaboration with the architect. Preliminary detail drawings showing the lighting fixtures cast directly into the concrete evidence the early collaboration between Saarinen and Kelly.

I

Richard Kelly focused his design for this project on the importance of expressing the character and intent of the architecture. He capitalized on the power of accent and contrast, available at night, to amplify the highly expressive qualities existing in one of Saarinen's best works. The soaring expression of the roof and heroic stature of the columns become more salient at night as a direct result of Kelly's highly effective lighting theme.

Dulles airport, serving as a key gateway to the nation, stands as an institution signifying arrival and departure to and from the United States. The importance of expressing that significance at night was not lost on Richard Kelly.

II
HORSE ISLAND
REUBEN HERZL

II

III
MODERN IS THE NIGHT
MARK GAUSEPOHL
The Lighting Design of Richard Kelly for Dulles Airport

758B

TEN BUILDINGS

This seminar provides a close reading of ten buildings and projects that mark a point of inflection in the works of Moretti, Mies, Le Corbusier, Kahn, Stirling, Venturi, Rossi, Koolhaas,
Libeskind, and Gehry. Students are encouraged to probe the rationale for selection of these
seminal works, examining alternative readings and relationships to precedents.

I
THE PROBLEM OF APERTURE
MEREDITH MCDANIEL

A diagrammatic analysis of how Frank
Gehry deals with the problem of
aperture produced multiple strategies
which were then applied to the redesign of a personal studio project.
Taking Gehry's monograph as a textbook,
relevant projects were categorized
by window typology. Persistent themes
emerged as the data was charted over
the course of his career.

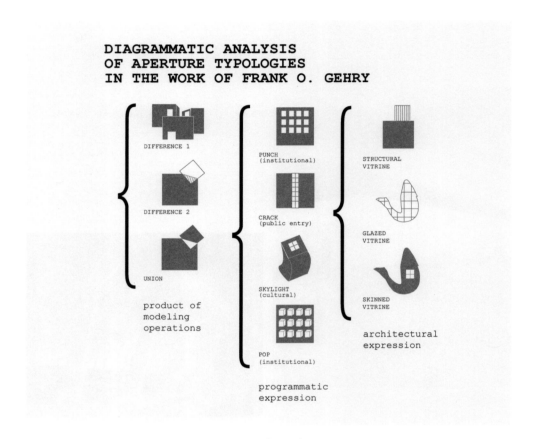

I

II
PROTOTYPE/MORETTI
SHANE NEUFELD

II

FILM ARCHITECTURE

This lecture course analyzes selected chapters in the history of cinematic set design through the twentieth century and presents masterpieces, major movements, protagonists, and crucial theoretical debates. In addition, the course examines the depiction of the city through film and the role of the movies as a reflection, commentary, and experimental laboratory for contemporary architecture. Attendance at the lectures and weekly one-hour discussion sections is required. A fifteen-page research paper or short video project as well as a final examination is required.

I

Arguably one of Hitchcock's best films, Vertigo, is teeming with mid-century psychoanalytic nuances. Voyeurism is a theme that is masterfully captured by the cinematography and spaces in the film. Particularly in the first half of the film, Hitchcock makes certain to frame nearly all shots of Kim Novak's character Madeline (as viewed by James Stewart's character Scottie) with a literal frame in the extreme foreground. The effect is a sense of 'peeping,' allowing the audience to feel as if they, themselves, were spying on the lovely Madeline. One clever shot frames the narrowly-exposed face of Jimmy Stewart right next to a tight mirror reflection of Kim Novak. Other 'reflection' shots appear in the film, which seem to hint at Madeline's (or Judy's?) double life. In addition to instilling a sense of voyeurism, these techniques lend an air of removal to the Madeline character. She is always viewed in a petri dish, as a distant puzzle to be deciphered by Scottie, as well as the audience.

This sense of removal also reinforces Madeline's role as a performer. The 'Madeline' that Scottie keeps watch of actually does not exist at all--she is an apparition fabricated by the deceptive Judy and aggrandized in the mind of Scottie. By framing her character within a frame, Hitchcock puts her on a virtual stage or screen of her own in which she can perform for Scottie.

Along the same lines, Hitchcock uses calculated architectural layering to thicken the sense of mystery in the film. Most interesting is Hitchcock's use of the courtyard typology as a means by which to add depth to the Scottie's pursuit of 'Madeline'. Many of Madeline's mysterious visits culminate in some sort of classical building with a labyrinthine series of spaces that must be passed before arriving at her final destination on the interior. One example of this is when Madeline visits the cemetery at a mission-style church, having to first pass through a courtyard and then through the chapel itself in order to visit the grave of her alter-ego Carlotta Valdes out back. Scottie's resulting pursuits seem to be a metaphor for him finding his way into the depths of her complicated psyche. Deep in her mind, it suggests, the answers might be revealed.

II

David Lynch and Anthony Masters agreed that the foremost task in bringing the universe to life was the depiction and articulation of the four planets. The political divisions, cultures and the biospheres described in the book became a starting point for figuring out the material realities of each world. Masters presented sketches of objects or sets to Lynch without the director's prior input. Those pieces would provide a logic that effected everything else in that world. For example, the Atreides lived on Caladan, a wet, forested planet, with a hierarchical military society. So wood is a dominant material, as are leather and animal skins. The weapons, musical instruments, and even some machinery are adorned with wood details. The men are always in uniform, and the women wear their hair in tight, elegant arrangements. This logic would often supersede the descriptions of things and places in the novel, and Lynch felt free to reinterpret them in the film. No sets are alike, and as Lynch demands it, all are able to support the close scrutiny of the audience. Each set is literally a world apart from the others.

Geidi Prime is the home planet of the film's villain, Baron Harkonnen. It is covered by oceans of oil and has little useable land mass. The entire surface of the planet is blanketed in a single gridded structure, an urban environment that is best described as a malignant factory. This disturbing over saturation of order was made manifest in Archizoom's No-Stop City project. Andrea Branzi provocatively proposed a diabolically systematic infrastructure of continuous gridded interior space as dominant organizing feature of the city. The gargantuan steel framework of Geidi Prime matches this maniacal repetition, but is further aestheticized, holding back a kind of sickening green glow, and undetermined programmatic possibilities. There is an overall lack of differentiation. In Master's own words, the environment was "as appealing as a cross between Victoria Station and the inside of a fire hydrant."

783B

MAKING SENSE OF SPACE & TECHNOLOGY

Challenging our traditional "ocularcentric" understanding of architecture, this seminar explores the overlapping relationship among sight, sound, and touch. Seminar discussions based on required readings treat this subject from a socio-historical perspective, examining how prevailing cultural assumptions about the human body shape and in turn are shaped by the design of the built environment. The seminar considers the impact of technology on the senses. Since the nineteenth century, new inventions--from gramophones to iPods--have transformed the human sensorium, profoundly altering how we perceive and interact with the designed environment. After charting these historical developments, the seminar speculates about the future: How can architects harness new materials and technologies to craft new ways of synthesizing multi-sensory experiences in space? How can we devise new representational strategies that convincingly portray our sensory experience of space?

I
DEPENDENCY
CHENG HUI CHUA

Dependency

Aircraft depend heavily on navigational systems, as well as information given to them from ATC sources.

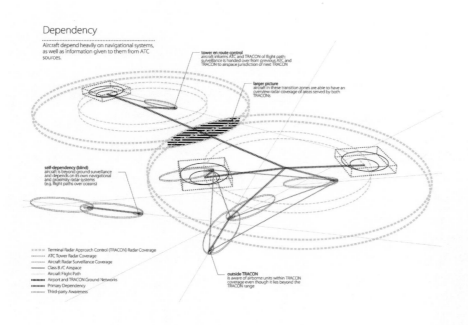

tower en route control
aircraft informs ATC and TRACON of flight path; surveillance is handed over from previous ATC and TRACON to airspace jurisdiction of next TRACON

larger picture
aircraft in these transition zones are able to have an overview radar coverage of areas served by both TRACONs

self-dependency (blind)
aircraft is beyond ground surveillance and depends on its own navigational and proximity radar systems (e.g. flight paths over oceans)

outside TRACON
is aware of airborne units within TRACON coverage even though it lies beyond the TRACON range

```
••••••  Terminal Radar Approach Control (TRACON) Radar Coverage
------  ATC Tower Radar Coverage
------  Aircraft Radar Surveillance Coverage
──────  Class B /C Airspace
──────  Aircraft Flight Path
▬▬▬▬  Airport and TRACON Ground Networks
••••••  Primary Dependency
──────  Third-party Awareness
```

I

II
UNTITLED
PATRICK MCGOWAN & ZAK SNIDER

II

III
AURAL HISTORY
DAVID SADIGHIAN
Acoustic Technology in Exhibit Design

III
It is now common to be guided by a chorus of disembodied voices throughout the course of one's day. These mellifluous streams of polite instruction--indeed, they're often female--ensure that we properly align with a desired spatial or architectural orientation: "Stand clear of the closing door, please"; "Mind the gap"; "Exit approaching, 300 feet". The built environment, it seems, is increasingly hardwired with an overlaid audio track, as though visual cues no longer suffice in codifying information.

Unlike mobile audio players (e.g. the Walkman, even the car stereo) these apparatuses serve a highly localized function; rather than offer an aesthetic distance from place, they reify the body as a material substrate in relation to its surroundings. Yet while this contemporary condition might be open to a Foucauldian reading of a controlled or disciplined subject, this is in fact not my argument. In this paper I will chart a history of portable audio information technology--the museum audio guide--as an instrument in democratizing institutional space.

My research will assert that contrary to the traditional narratives of democratization, which rely on institutional critique, populist rhetoric, and even merchandising, these structural changes to the museum experience were achieved through the Acoustiguide, and thereby originated from within curatorial practice. By injecting the disembodied voice into the pedestrian museum experience, the audio guide precipitates a new subjectivity between viewer, voice, and space, localizing the body while co-opting a sense of enclosure and privatization.

While the Acoustiguide, which debuted in 1957, has its formal and epistemological precedents in the European avant-garde's critique of the bourgeois gallery, the focus of my research will not be to trace this lineage. Instead I will unpack the implementation of portable audio technology as an overlooked chapter in post-War American museology...an unprecedented combination of curatorial design and audio technology, blurring the physical and sensory envelopes of exhibition design and its participatory subject.

Yet despite what I argue were seismic shifts in the consumption of information space (the gallery), this transformation of the museum experience through audio technology was all but imperceptible--it now seems an assumed, if perfunctory, component to how we digest the "importance" of an art object. Occurring decades prior to now-canonical performance pieces by Vito Acconci, Janet Cardiff, and Andrea Fraser-- all of whom using the aural medium as operative criticism--the audio guide was in fact a silent revolution that transformed how we, as embodied subjects, consume information through the mediated sensorium.

CHENG HUI CHUA

PATRICK MCGOWAN
ZAK SNIDER

DAVID SADIGHIAN

THE PURSUIT
OF MODERN FORM

The seminar surveys theories about the genesis and meaning of modern form put forward by architects and theorists during the early part of the twentieth century. The focus is on what it means to be modern and what constitutes a modern form. The seminar considers different design methods and formal theories that aimed to take into account issues central to modernity, such as dynamism, mobility, internationalism, geopolitics, and new types of experience. Students study texts and works by key architects and theorists, such as Alvar Aalto, Hans Arp, Adolf Behne, Le Corbusier, Siegfried Ebeling. Naum Gabo, Jean Marie Guyau, Hugo Häring, El Lissitzky, László Moholy-Nagy, Antonio Sant'Elia, Filipo Thommaso Marinetti, Mies van der Rohe, and Henry de Velde. Key artistic and philosophical ideas, such as elementarism, futurism, functionalism, vitalism, constructivism, and biocentrism are addressed. Students produce a research Web site, which allows comparison and cross-referencing between different theories.

In Pursuit of Modern Form

Constructivism
De Stijl ⁵⁶
Expressionism ³²
Werkbund
Art Nouveau ²²
Futurism ¹²

I

Constructivism might be seen as a very particular paradigm of modernism, both culturally and politically. What is intriguing about Constructivist art and architecture is that it cannot be described or understood completely according to normative modern dialectics: individual/mass, liberal/conservative, craft/industry, nationalistic/global. While the movement vigorously upheld the renewed power of the masses, having found its political roots in Communism, the individual artist remained a central cultural figure. This dichotomy was characterized by a strong belief in the transformative and revolutionary potential of such art, still thought by many to exist within the individual citizen. In fact, what might have led to Constructivism's inevitable decline as an avant-garde artistic movement was the mounting friction between the will of the artists and their obligations to an increasingly domineering political system. By the late 1920s and early 1930s many of the symbolic formal tropes employed by these Russian artists--forms that had once been driven primarily by internal disciplinary experimentation--were appropriated into the language of propaganda and political rhetoric. Similarly, there arose a tension between strong nationalistic motivations and participation in an emerging international scene. This tension was productive for Constructivist artists and architects, as it enabled a broad exchange of ideas that cat-alyzed the already strong formal project in Russian circles. As much a political and social philosophy as it was an artistic movement, Constructivism remains deeply influential precisely because it put into material form the conflicting and contradictory aspects of modern life.

I
IN PURSUIT OF MODERN FORM
JACQUELYN HAWKINS & MATT ROMAN

811B

CLASSICAL DRAWING

This seminar teaches advanced representational skills through the study of classical architectural forms. Both traditional and contemporary graphic techniques are explored. Classical drawing skills are acquired through a series of graphic exercises that also provide an understanding of how parts of classical architecture are made and how they are put together into meaningful wholes. Exercises include rigorous full-color measured drawings of outstanding examples of Western classical architecture. The final exercise has a small design component. Lectures and readings address related topics, such as beauty, order, symmetry, hierarchy, proportion, ornament, and meaning.

I
A PAVILION FOR BRYANT PARK
BRYAN BERKAS

For a corner entrance to New York City's Bryant Park at Forty-Second Street and Sixth Avenue, two classical pavilions are intended to carry the thematic elements of Manhattan's urban architecture in the transitional park setting. The simplified Corinthian order is responsive to the nearby New York Public Library, and the overall form takes cues from landmarks visible in either direction. The constellations on the ceiling invoke Grand Central Terminal to the east, while the subtle dome is a nod to the World Financial Center to the south. The analytique was completed using three-dimensional computer modeling in Rhino and post-production in Photoshop.

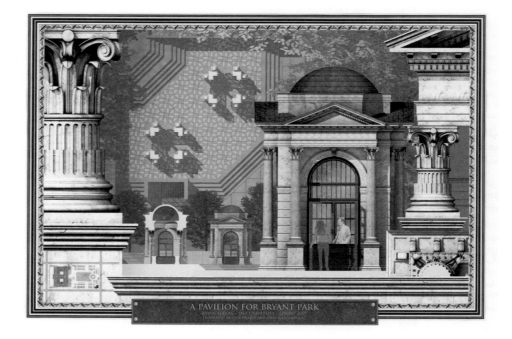

I

THE BUILT ENVIRONMENT & POLITICS OF PLACE

914B

Call it the built environment, the vernacular, everyday architecture, or the cultural land-scape--the material world of built and natural places is intricately bound up with social and political life. This seminar explores research methods involving the built environment. It includes readings from urban and suburban history, geography, anthropology, and architecture as well as readings on narrative and graphic strategies for representing spaces and places. Students are required to present papers.

I

In his Nobel Prize winning autobiographical memoir Istanbul: Memories and the City, Orhan Pamuk wrote about the vast cultural change that had happened in Istanbul during his life. It was the unending battle between the modern and the receding Ottoman past. For Pamuk, the reason for this melancholy was the void of separating a nation from its past without filling in the enormous gap with a new ideal. The proposed but unfulfilled ideal was modern-ization or, as synonymously called in Turkish, 'westernization'. There has been the use of 'westernization' starting form the late Ottoman period, however, the geographical connotations of what 'West' means differed in years. The historical context of the Istanbul Hilton Hotel represents a certain shifting moment in this process. French influence of 19th century was replaced by German presence in the early repub-lic, and by 1950's the locus of inspiration gradually shifted to the United States. As a reflection and result of this process, the Istanbul Hilton Hotel became the icon and initiator of the International Style a la USA and what might be called Americanization as an alternative model for modernization.

The Istanbul Hilton Hotel, overlooking the famed Bosphorus, is one of the most impres-sive and luxurious hotels in Europe.

The Istanbul Hilton Hotel, sitting on a prime hilltop location overlooking the Bosphorus, built both with the financial and architectural collaboration of the USA and Turkey, was pub-lished in various international architectural magazines, and is still the subject of many discussions. The Hilton Hotel, being a sample of Turkey's willingness to westernize and United States' role in internationalization of its culture, was seen as a concrete example of many dichotomies: East/West, National/International, local/global, interior/exterior, modern/ver-nacular. The Istanbul Hilton marked the city with the desired American modern. America was represented through the architecture and the contents of the building, as argued in detail by Annabel Wharton, and became the source for the new modernization process that would be taking place in Turkey within the next decades.

II

The story of Monterey Place in New Haven, Connecticut and its predecessors, Elm Haven, and the original late 19th century "slum", are direct results of the Federal laws which funded and guided their designs and construc-tion. Elm Haven and Monterey Place were de-signed to fulfill the perceived needs of low income families at discreet moments in the twentieth century. By those determining policy, these perceived needs changed over time, and different minimums were tolerated by the Ameri-can consciousness. These needs stretched from the most basic--a house in a "slum" for shel-ter in the early twentieth century, to a yard, driveway, and other trappings of middle class suburban America in the late twentieth century. The beliefs that supported these needs changed as projects and policies failed through the last century. The land that Monterey Place now occupies was once a crowded slum, which was cleared for the intermediary Elm Haven Project. At this point in time, a contentious recipe for housing is being used across the country which in many ways matches the development of Monterey Place. The role of housing the city's poor will be explored through these three stages of development. Will the changes in the list of needs of Monterey Place make it a success or are we merely repeating Elm Haven's mistakes?

I
AMERICAN CULTURE AS ROLE MODEL
OZLEM CAGLAR TOMBUS
Post World War II Turkey and Architec-ture in the case of Istanbul Hilton

II
FROM BLOCK TO BOX
LEAH WEINBERG
The Changing Perceived Needs of Residents of Public Housing

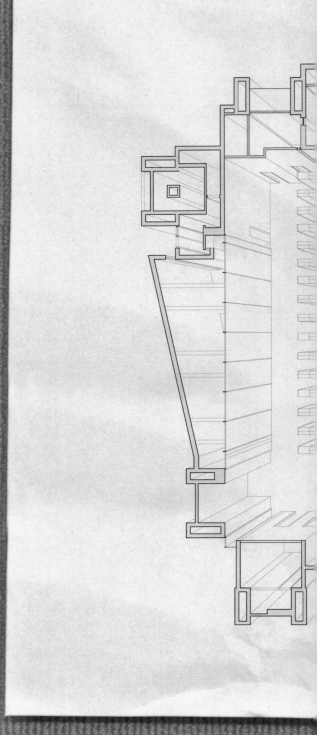

1ST FLOOR

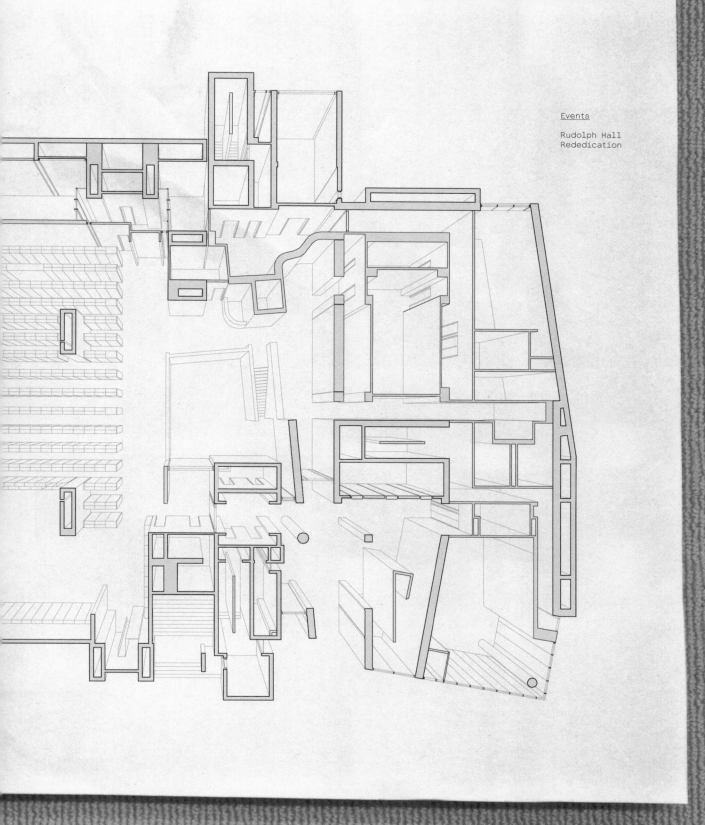

NOVEMBER 7-8, 2008:
RUDOLPH HALL REDEDICATION

ROBERT A.M. STERN

MERCEDES BASS
SID BASS

ANDREW HAMILTON

RÉJEAN LEGAULT

ROBERT A.M. STERN „Good evening to everyone in „ the room, and to the many others in the various „ rooms throughout the building. I'm sorry we „ all cannot be in one room, but churches should „ not be designed for Easter Sunday and this is „ our Easter Sunday; a packed crowd all here to „ celebrate and recognize this amazing occa- „ sion. We have students, faculty, alumni, and „ friends that are too numerous to name, but I am „ thrilled that you are all here for the dedica- „ tion of Paul Rudolph Hall and the celebration „ for the completion of the Jeffrey Loria Center „ for the Study of Art History and the Robert B. „ Haas family library. I am Robert Stern, dean „ of the school of architecture and in a sense „ I am the equivalent of the last living Civil „ War veteran. Forty-five years ago when Paul „ Rudolph Hall was dedicated on November 9th, „ 1963 I was a third-year architecture student „ fortunate enough to be in attendance at the „ ceremony and reception that followed. It was „ a glorious occasion which has very special

„ personal memories for me. Since then much „ has happened to this building, but we can all „ rejoice in its restoration.
I would like to thank a few of the many people „ who worked so hard to make this celebration „ possible. Sadly time does not permit me to ac- „ knowledge all those who helped, but I do wish „ to recognize Jean Sielaff, my administrative „ assistant; Martha Lewis, our associate event „ planner for the office of development who worked „ closely and tirelessly with Richard DeFlumeri, „ our events coordinator in the architecture „ school; and his assistant and colleague Robie- „ Lyn Harnois. Perhaps most of all I want to „ thank John Jacobson, the associate dean of „ the school who bore the brunt of this entire „ operation. Not only the celebration weekend, „ from our school's point of view, but actually „ representing the school, dean, and faculty, in „ the magnificent process of seeing this building „ to completion. I want to acknowledge Charles „ Gwathmey, the architect and alumnus, who cre-

„ ated Loria Hall and the extraordinary renova-
„ tion of the Rudolph Building.
I also want to thank Sid Bass, whose extraordinary
„ gift made this restoration possible. Sid Bass
„ began his engagement with the Art and Archi-
„ tecture building when he was an undergraduate
„ at Yale College. Inspired by Professor Vincent
„ Scully's discussions of Paul Rudolph's work,
„ Mr. Bass made it a point to closely follow the
„ construction of the Art and Architecture which
„ so impressed him that over time he was instru-
„ mental in commissioning a number of important
„ buildings from Paul Rudolph, including his own
„ residence in Fort Worth that ranks amongst the
„ Twentieth Century's greatest modernist houses.
„ As work proceeded on the restoration of the
„ Art and Architecture building, Mr. Bass made
„ it perfectly clear that he did not wish the
„ reborn building to bear his name but to in-
„ stead honor its architect. This gesture speaks
„ volumes about the modesty, consideration, and
„ humanity of Sid Bass.

When I became dean in 1998, I set the restoration
„ as a top priority while during my tenure at
„ Yale. To achieve this, I needed and received the
„ support of Richard Levin, the president of the
„ university, and the support of Sid Bass, who
„ joined with Jeffrey Loria and Robert B. Haas
„ to graciously underwrite the entire project.
„ With the completion of this restoration, Paul
„ Rudolph Hall once again begins to enjoy the
„ critical and public esteem that it deserves.
„ I would also like to thank Turner Construction,
„ especially Arthur Heyde, for accomplishing
„ this renovation in record time. Please join me
„ in thanking all of the people, named and un-
„ ammed, who were instrumental in this project.

ROBERT HAAS

STANLEY TIGERMAN
CHARLES GWATHMEY

HAROLD R
KEVIN RO

CHARLES GWATHMEY

KAREN DAHLBERG
ELIHU RUBIN

STANLEY TIGERMAN

JUDITH HUNT
WALTER HUNT

ALLAN GREENBERG
ALEX TZONIS
STANLEY TIGERMAN

PETER L. GLUCK

NORMAN FOSTER
CARL ABBOT

ALLAN GREENBERG
ALEX TZONIS
STANLEY TIGERMAN
PAUL GOLDBERGER

MARK FOSTER GAGE

RALPH LAUREN
RYOUNG KIM
TAI SOO KIM

EMANUEL PETIT   BARBARA PINE
RYOUNG KIM   MARSHALL RUBEN
TAI SOO KIM   CAROLYN GREENSPAN

RALPH LAUREN

ROBERT A.M. STERN

PAUL GOLDBERGER

BARBARA PINE
DEAN SAKAMOTO

FRED CLARKE
GERALD HINES

BASEMENT

Faculty

KENT BLOOMER
PETER EISENMAN
ARIANE LOURIE HARRISON
PALOMA PAJARES

Guest Jurors

FORTH BAGLEY
KELLER EASTERLING
PETER EISENMAN
LIZA FIOR
MARK FOSTER GAGE
NICK JOHNSON
JOHN KALISKI
GEORGE KNIGHT
IRVING LAVIN
RALPH LERNER
BARBARA LITTENBERG
LESLIE LU
ED MITCHELL
ADRIANNA MONK
BEN PELL
ALBERT POPE
HILARY SAMPLE
DAI SONGZHOU
BILLIE TSIEN
HUIJIN TU
JAMIE VON KLEMPERER
WANG BOWEI
ADAM YARINKSY

Students

ANNE-MARIE ARMSTRONG
BRYAN BERKAS
CARMEL BONFIGLI
NATHAN BRIGHT
JACOB DUGOPOLSKI
FRANCES EDELMAN
NICHOLAS GILLILAND
GARY KU
LIAM LOWRY
J.D. MESSICK
DANIEL MARKIEWICZ
BRIAN SPRING
JIA-JUN YEO

Lecturers

ALEJANDRO ARAVENA
CHARLES ATWOOD
ROBERT CAMPBELL
MATTHEW COOLIDGE
PETER EISENMAN
YVONNE FARRELL
LIZA FIOR
ADRIAN FORTY
KURT FORSTER
TERUNOBU FUJIMORI
WALTER HOOD
TOYO ITO
CARLOS JIMINEZ
GREG LYNN
FRANCISCO MANGADO
SHELLEY MCNAMARA
TIMOTHY ROHAN
JOHN PATKAU
SHIH-FU PENG
WILLIAM SHARPLES
CAMERON SINCLAIR
EEVA-LIISA PELKONEN
ANTHONY VIDLER
LÖIC WACQUANT
NICHOLAS FOX WEBER

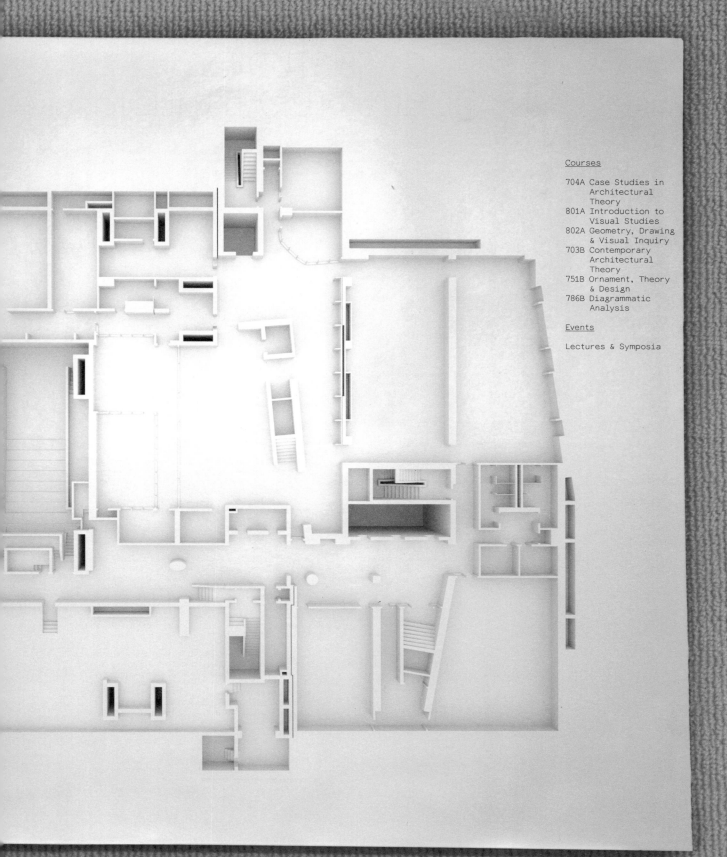

Courses

704A Case Studies in
     Architectural
     Theory
801A Introduction to
     Visual Studies
802A Geometry, Drawing
     & Visual Inquiry
703B Contemporary
     Architectural
     Theory
751B Ornament, Theory
     & Design
786B Diagrammatic
     Analysis

Events

Lectures & Symposia

704A

CASE STUDIES
IN ARCHITECTURAL THEORY

The history of Western architectural theory, 1680-1987, through the close reading of primary texts. Lectures place the readings in the context of architectural history; the texts are discussed in required discussion sections. Topics include the architecture of the Enlightenment, the picturesque, debates regarding style, historicism, and eclecticism, Gothic Revival, questions of ornament, architectural modernism, functionalism, new monumentality, critiques of modernism, and various currents of postmodernism.

I

UNFORTUNATELY, WE ALL ARE NOT SPECIAL
CARMEL BONFIGLI

II

ABSTRACTION TAKEN TO ITS LOGICAL
CONCLUSION
GARY KU
Ludwig Mies van der Rohe & Kazuyo
Sejima (Finding Buildings Too Heavy)
take the architecture out
of Architecture

I

Piranesi circuitously concludes what unacademic common sense dictates: that exceptionality is an exception. In doing so, he defines an avant-garde as being, by definition, populated by a few rather than the many. If everybody crams into the front, there is no front--only an uncomfortable, cramped, linear disorder. Piranesi, it seems, does not subscribe to contemporary self-esteem culture. Strangely, perhaps Robert A.M. Stern best encapsulates Piranesi's notion of an avant-garde when he discusses his own work in a 2007 New York Times article:

> "Many modernist works of our time tend to be self-important objects, and that's a real quarrel that I have," Mr. Stern said. "Buildings can be icons or objects, but they still have to engage with the larger whole." {...} "I'm not considered avant-garde because I'm not avant-garde," he added. "But there is a parallel world out there–of excellence."

What excellence means in the context of contemporary architecture is certainly beyond the scope of this paper, but the seeming irrelevance of excellence is often cited as having origins in an over-emphasis on the primacy of the avant-garde and, therefore, Piranesi's work. However, the paradox (and the contemporary misconception) of Piranesi is that, while he can be understood as an originator of the genius architect or the architect as expressive artist, he does not advocate expression for everyone. While he clearly reviles dogmatic and anachronistic linguistic conventions in architecture, he does not propose that his own work is a model. This omission is significant and telling. Piranesi suggests that, unfortunately, we all are not special.

II

Inexplicably, a group of architects find themselves in an abandoned warehouse. Many are contemporary: Rem Koolhaas, Winy Maas, Joshua Prince-Ramus, Frank Gehry, Zaha Hadid, Kazuyo Sejima. Some are freshly reanimated: Le Corbusier, half-naked and dripping wet; Mies van der Rohe, clutching the cigar he was buried with; Bernard Tschumi, protesting that he's not actually dead yet. Testing the door, they find it locked. Under a bare bulb is a platter of vol-au-vent, a seared monkfish liver within each pastry. The architects slowly munch.

Suddenly, a disembodied voice: build me a table.

Surprised, Koolhaas drops his Penthouse, Prince-Ramus his business card; Maas shoots a furtive glance to Tschumi, chalking dance steps on the floor. Ever unshakeable, Le Corbusier shouts: how will it be used? No response. Nervously, they begin exhaustive studies of common table usage patterns, the rise and fall of international table futures contracts, Stanley Kubrick's innovative use of the table in Barry Lyndon. Eleven months later, the programmatically-driven architects feel justified in beginning.

Gehry, Hadid, Mies, and Sejima are confident that they maybe already know what a table does, and honestly, may be don't care too much. They begin immediately--objects are their forte. Hadid, inspired by the spectacularly smooth excrement of the Caspian Tiger, mimics it in laboriously CNC'd Carrera marble. Gehry, inspired by fish, makes a fish table. (Chanel and Vitra order a thousand copies of each, respectively.)

Mies van der Rohe and Sejima, meanwhile, are taken aback by each other's designs. Yes, their differences are immediately apparent. Mies van der Rohe's table is resolute composition of two independent yet precisely balanced elements, a square plane and a precise cross that together create a table. By contrast, Sejima's table is more a drawing of a table than a physical object, its top an almost two-dimensional circle, its legs drawn with a ruler and a technical pen.

However, beyond the differences are intriguing similarities. They are both pursuing a difficult purity beyond literal ideas of program or form--an abstract "lightness" only tangentially related to an actual reduction of weight. Mies relies on the rhetorical separation of parts while maintaining a functional whole; while Sejima relies on tectonic abstraction to create a graphic architecture visually at tension with the idea of physical tactility. Both invoke techniques of uniformity and repetition to create objects of uncertain scale and mass. Both recognize that "lightness" is ultimately manifest within the mind of the viewer, not the physicality of the architecture.

INTRODUCTION
TO VISUAL STUDIES

801A

What is critical composition? Critical composition is not so much how to draw, but how to draw with an understanding of the object that goes beyond any primary perception; to understand if the building is a critical building, and what makes it so. Criticality, therefore, is a commentary on what existed at some moment in time. The purpose of your drawing each week is to see if you can visualize in drawing what can be thought. Seeing, therefore, becomes a way of thinking and drawing a reading or a text as a product of this way of seeing.

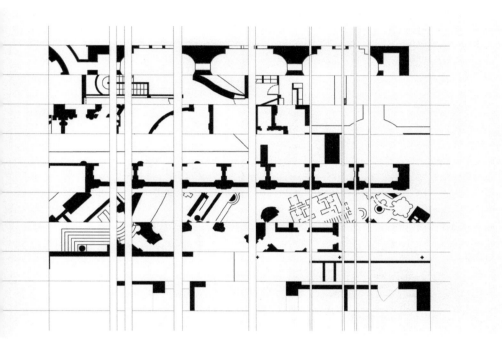

I

I
LATE STYLE IN BEETHOVEN
LIAM LOWRY
This project was an attempt to draw the idea of "Late Style" as presented in Teodor Adorno's article "Late Style in Beethoven": "…the sudden discontinuities that more than anything else characterize the very late style of Beethoven, are those moments of breaking away; the work is silent at the very instant when it is left behind, and turns its emptiness outward. Not until then does the next fragment attach itself, transfixed by the spell of subjectivity breaking loose and conjoined for better or worse with whatever preceded it; for the mystery is between them, and cannot be invoked otherwise than in the figure they create together."

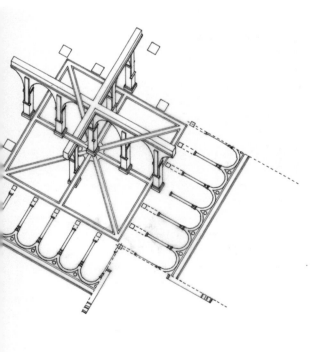

II

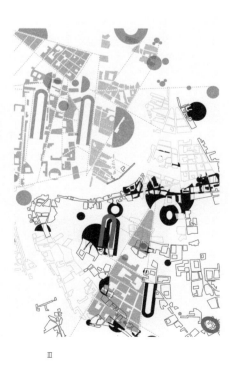

III

II
SANTA MARIA DELLA PACE/URBINO
DANIEL MARKIEWICZ

III
PIRANESI/NOLLI
BRIAN SPRING

LIAM LOWRY   DANIEL MARKIEWICZ   BRIAN SPRING

802A

GEOMETRY, DRAWING & VISUAL INQUIRY

This course introduces students to the fundamentals of drawing architectural subjects by hand. Students complete graphic assignments using traditional techniques, with an emphasis on watercolor on pencil. They acquire an understanding of the basic geometry that regulates architectural compositions through a series of projects that include freehand drawing and rigorous measured drawing of buildings and their details in orthogonal projection, axonometric, and perspective. Assignments are designed to enhance the students' ability to observe, analyze, understand and represent architectural forms.

I
PIERSON COLLEGE
JACOB DUGOLPOSKI

II
BERKELEY COLLEGE
FRANCES EDELMAN

I

II

III
STERLING MEMORIAL LIBRARY
JIA-JUN YEO

III

JACOB DUGOLPOSKI   FRANCES EDELMAN   JIA-JUN YEO

ARIANE LOURIE HARRISON

CONTEMPORARY ARCHITECTURAL THEORY

This course occurs at a time when the role of theory in architectural practice is yet again under scrutiny; the leveling strategies of the globalized marketplace and pervasive media suggest to some that theory is over, proposing we locate an "Intelligence after Theory." Others invert theory's modality asking "critical of what?" or proposing alternative forms of criticality such as the post-indexical.

Bringing together a series of lecturers from across the spectrum of the architectural practice--from well established architects, to emerging firms, to young practitioners, seeking to integrate advanced research into a critical architectural practice--this course focuses on theoretical texts by architects and from outside of the discipline.

I

In 1978, Bernard Tschumi published a small collection of drawings that attempted to transcribe these motivated spaces beyond architectural experience. Two of the sketches, The Dance and The Fight, were not only nascent attempts at implementing movement notation through cinematic translations, but were extrusions of those notations into the pictorial space of the drawing itself. In The Dance, Tschumi begins with the plan of dance steps similar to Andy Warhol's Dance Diagram (1962). Yet in breaking from Warhol's bounded horizontality, Tschumi projects axonometrically downwards into the depths of the page, transforming motion into a three-dimensional volume. The flattened plane of theory emerges activated in a new spatial praxis--a manifestation of Oskar Schlemmer's spatial relationships:

> If one were to imagine a space filled with a soft, pliable substance in which the figures of the sequences of the dancer's movements were to harden as a negative form, then this would demonstrate the direct relationship of the geometry of the plane to the stereometry of space.

An equal operation is discovered in The Chase where movement is turned upwards into distinct volumes of architectural form. No longer restricted to the diagrammatic, Tschumi has given dimension and resemblance to the intangible. These drawings are an inversion of Le Corbusier's architectural promenade--the transcendent moment of modern architecture. In its cinematic movement, the promenade frames architectural experience within the approaches to the object:

> It is appreciated by walking, on foot; it is by walking, by moving, that one sees the order of architecture developing…it's a question of a real architectural promenade, offering constantly changing views, unexpected, sometimes astonishing.

If to be modern is to be about motion, then it is a motion embedded in the interstices. Tschumi, however, suggests the opposite, that movement itself has substance and volume. "Here, the events are formalized in the same way as a room is a formalized space. These events 'regulate' these spaces. The spaces are determined by an événement régulateur." In his reference to Le Corbusier's tracé régulateur, Tschumi shifts the discussion from object-centered principles to one where the dynamic emerges as a mode of organization. It is an inversion of both the Nolli plan and of Rowe's acropolis-forum, where voids can no longer be taken as empty, gaining comfort through the density of their enclosures.

II

In a period of extreme social and political upheaval, two artistic/architectural partnerships, on opposite sides of the Atlantic, were born out of a common desire to re-establish the increasingly neutralized subject through disruptive physical and mental action. In each case, the medium of intervention was spatial, interrogating the themes of grounding, gravity and dynamics. Repulsion and pain were the extreme forms of this new engagement.

It is significant that the term topology has been co-opted in both cases: for the French it was primarily a geometrical and spatial critique; in the later work of ABRW, the word topology is grafted onto biotypology, to form Biotopology in response to more current concerns for disembodiment through biotechnologies.

The critical sources of these desires to incite movement and self-directed change were highly varied: a disciplinary response to urbanism and architecture's position in a changing cultural landscape; a political critique of modern speed, power and alienation; a transhumanist critique desiring to literally re-engage the bodily subject from the inside.

The alter-disciplinarity of each of these bodies of work (A.P. via a theatrical, total-art approach and its own dissolution; A.B.R.F. through their status as "artists") has allowed them to maintain a conceptual and critical autonomy which is rare in current practice. As Virilio's concepts of global uniformity are realized with increasing speed, a generalized awareness of the topology of discomfort can provide a useful tool toward reinvesting the subject.

I
THE SEARCH FOR CONCEPTUAL ARCHITECTURE
NATHAN BRIGHT

II
THE TOPOLOGY OF DISCOMFORT
NICHOLAS GILLILAND
Pain, Space and Utopia

751B

ORNAMENT THEORY & DESIGN

This course reviews the major theories governing ornament in Western architecture, with special emphasis on nineteenth- and twentieth-century arguments. The ultimate focus is on the language of ornament in the framework of building and urban space today.

I
17 SYMMETRY OPERATIONS
BRYAN BERKAS

To display all seventeen symmetry operations in a single composition, a simple geometric motif of a 30-60-90 triangle that fits into a hexagonal grid is implemented in narrow bands so that the edge of any of the 17 patterns can join and combine with the motifs of any of the other 17 patterns to produce a single continuous, incrementally changing pattern.

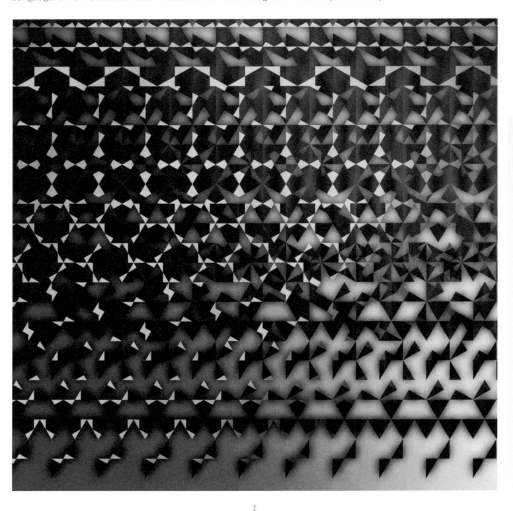

I

II
ORNAMENTATION AND TRANSFORMATION
J.D. MESSICK

This project was an exercise in transforming a flat, regular geometry into a more complex ornamentation through its application to a three-dimensional surface. The process of transformation was based upon projecting the initial geometric pattern onto a three-dimensional object and then shifting the perspective of the projected geometry from above to a side view. By shifting one's perspective of the projected geometry, the pattern takes on a completely new character which is informed entirely by the surface of the three dimensional object it is applied to. The interaction of surface, pattern and geometry yields a new, undetermined geometry that offers a new way to interpret and approach the design of pattern and ornament.

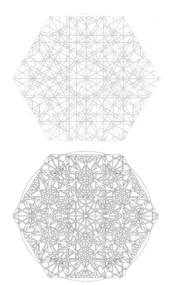

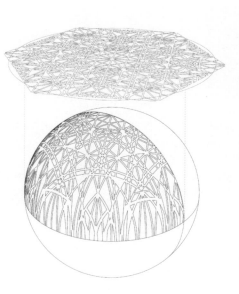

II

BRYAN BERKAS

J.D. MESSICK

DIAGRAMMATIC
ANALYSIS

786B

While formal analysis is sufficient to understand the genesis of historical buildings up until the French Revolution, that approach is no longer sufficient to understand the complexity of contemporary work, which, despite formal moments, introduces new relationships. This seminar is intended to explore analytic methods that provide an understanding of the complexities of current architectural production. The seminar begins with discussions of new material practices and relationships to the production of form. Students are required to make a presentation, whether it be drawings, writing, or animation, of a diagrammatic analysis of a recent building, such as the Seattle Public Library by Koolhaas, his Porto Concert Hall, Herzog and de Meuron's de Young Museum, Zaha Hadid's Rome Market project, or Zaera Polo's Yokohama Harbor Project.

I
LE CORBUSIER
ANNE-MARIE ARMSTRONG

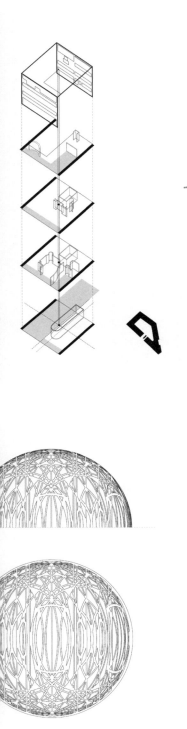

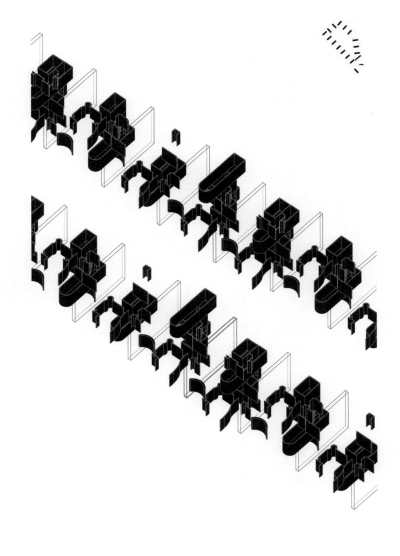

I

FALL LECTURES & SYMPOSIA

CHARLES ATWOOD „The company that owned Holiday
„ Inns purchased Harrah's casinos from the estate
„ of Bill Harrah in 1979. It was a small company,
„ with two casinos based in Reno and Lake Tahoe.
„ No history of mob ties and no presence in Las
„ Vegas. As a young employee of Holiday Inns,
„ that's how I came to the gaming industry. The
„ Strip was the new center of gravity in Las
„ Vegas. And our company was ready to follow
„ the money. But banks didn't lend to casinos.
„ When we bought Harrah's, we needed to borrow
„ the money to close the deal. But banks were
„ concerned about how to protect their lien,
„ what would they do if they had to foreclose?
„ The answer for us was to secure the loan with
„ our hotel assets around the country. Even into
„ the 1980's, the only way to get the money to
„ build a casino was to either, a) already have
„ the money, or b) have other assets to secure
„ a loan. Wall Street would eventually step
„ in with new financing mechanisms, like junk
„ bonds…that's how Steve Wynn financed Mirage.
„ The casino industry could generate the high
„ rates of return necessary to pay off the financ-
„ ing. Even then however, it was easier to secure
„ financing to invest in the Strip, and harder to
„ invest downtown.
In one decade, from 1989 to the turn of the mil-
„ lennium, the Vegas Strip of "Learning from Las
„ Vegas" was essentially erased. The scale of
„ the signs and buildings--so carefully plotted
„ by the 1968 Yale Studio, and so fundamental to
„ the thesis of the book--was not just changed,
„ it was irrelevant next to the scale of the
„ mega-resorts that now dominate. The buildings
„ themselves, even entire resorts, had morphed
„ into symbols in space.
The casino resorts of the Strip are not designed
„ to be impressive in architectural terms; they
„ are designed to be attractions. The guid-
„ ing ethos of the nineties was to get the new
„ buildings up as fast as possible so that the
„ guests would start bringing in the return on
„ investment as fast as possible. Successes
„ were copycatted. Did a new resort with a theme
„ succeed? Then, by all means, try a variation.

ROBERT CAMBELL „First of all, I'm not going to
„ "deliver" a lecture, as Bob said I would. I am
„ not capable of doing that. I see many friends
„ in the audience and I'm sure you'll put up
„ with whatever I do. I'm a critic, you're used

„ to having architects come who can show you
„ their work, or scholars who can bombard you
„ with their ideas. I don't have any works, I
„ don't have any ideas, and what I'm going to
„ do is talk about whatever is biting me at the
„ moment, which is what I usually do. I want to
„ thank Bob Stern for giving me a wonderful tour
„ of this building, or at least it was wonderful
„ once he got over his apoplectic fit of seeing
„ me carry a cappuccino cup across the orange
„ carpet. But he warmed up after a--
ROBERT A.M. STERN „Uncovered cappuccino cup!
{Laughter}
ROBERT CAMPBELL „I think he thought it was a
„ terrorist act. Standing here at Yale, I am
„ reminded of a lecture that I saw by Philip
„ Johnson. I know everyone has to start a lec-
„ ture here with a comment about Philip Johnson.
„ But he came to Boston, and he was a major
„ speaker at a meeting of the Society of Boston
„ Architects, and the evening waxed a little bit
„ late, and he finally got up the lecturn, and he
„ stood there and he looked around and he said,
„ "Any questions?" And I've always thought, will
„ I ever have the nerve to begin a lecture by
„ saying, 'any questions?' My other favorite
„ architecture lecture was by Henry Cobb, the
„ architect of the Hancock Tower in Boston who
„ gave a lecture at Cornell, and as illustration
„ he used only an image of the famous painting
„ The Raft of the Medusa, by Géricault. There is
„ a storm at sea, and the ship has sunk, and the
„ raft is bouncing up and down, and it's total
„ panic: people are climbing on it and falling
„ off it and it's utter chaos, and he left it on
„ the screen for his entire lecture on The Future
„ of Architecture at Cornell.
{Laughter}

MATTHEW COOLIDGE „We work on projects across
„ the United States, and most of our work is
„ about the United States. We are a non-profit
„ educational organization that employs tools
„ of the arts but also tools of the sciences and
„ other disciplines in pursuing the stated mis-
„ sion: to increase and diffuse information about
„ elevations, lands, apportioned, utilized and
„ perceived.
All of this fits in the banner of anthropogeomor-
„ phology, which arguably is everything on the
„ planet. Geomorphology is created or changed
„ by humans. I don't think there is a molecule
„ on the surface of the earth that hasn't been
„ affected by human agents of some kind. The
„ world has been denaturalized, at least in the
„ classical sense of the term.
What we look at is the ground. It's very basic:
„ what is that thing, how did it get there, who
„ owns it, what does it do, how does it connect
„ to other things, how does it fit in the context.
„ We look at American culture by looking at the
„ artifacts we create, both intentionally and
„ unintentionally: the byproducts, the things
„ that happen because of other things that hap-
„ pen. It's like throwing an archaeological grid
„ across the entire nation and looking at what
„ transpired there.
The ground is our medium, but by itself it means
„ nothing, we bring readings to it. You con-

„ struct meaning in your mind, which relates to
„ the basic notion of modern art that Duchamp
„ made clear a long time ago that art is in the
„ viewer and not necessarily in the object on
„ the wall. We look at landscape in a similar
„ way. Our work really lies in the ephemeral
„ area above the ground, the zone between the
„ physical ground and the eye of the beholder.
The other thing we keep in mind with all our
„ programs and projects is to consider that
„ every time you point something out, by defini-
„ tion, you're also un-pointing out everything
„ else, you're turning your back on the things
„ non-observed. The act of observation is also
„ an act of obfuscation. The foundation of the
„ organization is a collection of information.

PETER EISENMAN „ It is my contention that
„ Rudolph's early work with Ralph Twichell, in
„ Florida, from 1947 to 1951, was heavily influ-
„ enced by the work of Giuseppe Terragni. What-
„ ever the influences, these were certainly left
„ behind by 1959-60, when crucial changes appear
„ in both Rudolph's massing and drawing style.
„ First, there are studies of Rudolph's Sarasota
„ High School, of 1958, which seem similar to
„ the early studies for the A&A Buildings. For
„ example, one only has to look at the Milam
„ House of 1960 to see the change. But there
„ are also two Yale-related events that might be
„ said to have precipitated, if not participated
„ in, these changes.
One was the appearance of Jim Stirling at Yale
„ in fall 1959 as a visiting critic. Another is
„ John Fowler (who went on to work with Rudolph
„ in 1961 and is most certainly the author of
„ the incredible drawing for the Yale Married
„ Students Housing of Rudolph's of 1961) and
„ Michael McKinnell, of Boston City Hall fame,
„ who were living with me in New York City in
„ 1959. At that time they taught me the Graphos
„ style rendering, which they certainly would
„ have picked up at the Regent Street Poly in
„ the years prior. In another, perhaps more in-
„ teresting note, McKinnell claims that Gerhard
„ Kallmann, his partner in the Boston City Hall
„ competition was doing one-point perspectives
„ long before Rudolph's famous section of the
„ A&A Building.

WALTER HOOD „ I'd like to talk a little bit tonight
„ about this idea of how I've been trying to push
„ myself to begin to think about my training and
„ experience but also those experiences I've had
„ over the years and how that can begin to shape
„ a practice as well as a pedagogy. I teach at
„ the University of California, Berkeley. I'm a
„ full time professor there. As well as I have
„ a studio in Oakland California where I'm an
„ active practitioner. Everyone's always asking

„ me how do I do it and I have no idea, you just
„ do it. But the practice and the pedagogical
„ framework is based around three basic ideas.
„ One, that of advocacy. Advocacy in the urban
„ environment. Meaning, that I am out there ad-
„ vocating with community residents, politicians
„ alike to make the public realm a better place.
„ And I look at this as research. Research in
„ making projects. So the actual advocacy is not
„ political, it's actually making projects and
„ trying to get projects built. The second part
„ of the practice and pedagogy is this notion
„ of hybrid improvisations. For the last fifteen
„ years, I've tried to be very critical about the
„ field in which I work, Landscape Architecture
„ and particularly, trying to understand those
„ products which we are responsible for whether
„ they are parks, streets plazas, or gardens, or
„ squares. To be very critical about why do we
„ need them, why do we have to have them, and who
„ are they for? And over time it's been my, sort
„ of, I guess, position that maybe the American
„ landscape is much more of an enmeshed public
„ experience that these types--no longer does
„ the figure ground hold true, but in a very
„ heterogeneous society we need more spaces
„ that literally work with one another versus
„ separate one another. And lastly, the everyday,
„ mundane public objects that inhabit most of
„ our public landscapes. And these, everything
„ from garbage cans to lights to benches to
„ trees to trellises; these are things that we
„ don't take the time to make.

CARLOS JIMÉNEZ „ In Houston this expansiveness
„ of the horizon without any geographical limit
„ whatsoever tends to create this illusion of
„ freedom. As if the city, as if the mandate of
„ the city, is to perpetuate this endless horizon
„ in its own metaphoric possibilities. So what
„ you see here is typical of our city, which is
„ this finesse, and this exquisite propagation of
„ infrastructure. Houston perhaps is more known
„ by its infrastructure than by its architecture.
„ Except obviously with examples like the Menil
„ and examples of Eric Johnson's early work and
„ other architects that have been able to work
„ in the city, but primarily the city promotes
„ its desires in this incredible proliferation
„ of these infrastructures that you see so
„ well captured in this image. These rivers of
„ endless traffic that move in and out for two
„ hours, perpetuating this image of the Ameri-
„ can dream, American freedom, when in fact we
„ know that it's quite the opposite. There is
„ a quiet sentence that is quietly not spoken
„ about these people driving in and out of this
„ massive, fort-like city in the country. It is
„ only at night that we come to witness perhaps
„ or to understand the true vastness or improb-
„ ability at times in anyone's imagination of
„ the size of this monster city, a monster city
„ that fascinates as much as it might repulse.
„ And I would say that the fascination can be
„ misunderstood sometimes, in a romantic way,
„ in the sense that, in particular, European
„ architects have celebrated Houston as some
„ kind of new aperture to live in in a world of
„ multiple possibilities, but in fact it's not
„ as such when you live in this place. It has
„ enormous problems, and it has probably, very
„ equal to that vastness, it has a vast solitude.
„ In Houston they are rather radical in the
„ sense that they retain this philosophy, this
„ auspicious sort of vertiginous velocity of the
„ city. And I have found in the last 32 years
„ that it is that slowness, that kind of pause,
„ as I like to call it, that gives me great

„ pleasure, and in fact reinvigorates my faith
„ in architecture as an instrument of optimism,
„ as an instrument of making place.

FRANCISCO MANGADO „We have to recognize the
„ lack of hope and aspiration that are char-
„ acteristic of today's powerful market era.
„ Everything goes, but there are no references.
„ In spite of the fact that we are continuously
„ communicating, we are not entirely present
„ in the moment. Everything, in my opinion, is
„ superficial. There is an absence of loyalty.
„ The devaluated quality of architecture is a
„ reflection of its times, and as a consequence,
„ is a reflection of these times. This has led
„ to a recent phenomenon that I have observed
„ in which architecture is more about seeming
„ than being.
It is in this context that I will share my work
„ with you. It is a humble and personal response
„ to these moments in history, particularly in
„ the Spanish context. Please forgive the con-
„ tradiction that it contains. Being fifty, I am
„ a very young architect. I have been lucky to
„ receive a lot of commissions, many of them,
„ the majority, I will say all of them, have been
„ won by competitions. But I have to recognize
„ this contradiction.
My work is not a global answer to our times, of
„ course, but is my response to the world that
„ I perceive.
Now I will say a few thoughts on what does and
„ does not interest me in architecture today. In
„ some ways this is the notion of the meaning
„ of architecture made with the left hand. I
„ am not very interested in architecture that
„ is concerned only with image, the image that
„ responds only to the demands of the market. I
„ am not very interested, we are not very inter-
„ ested in my office, in architecture that strives
„ to proclaim itself as an isolated object as if
„ it existed in a laboratory. This architecture
„ consists of objects that are important inde-
„ pendently to the society and the reality that
„ has made them possible.
Architecture is a richer and more complex is-
„ sue full of ideas that are much more than
„ mere objects. Within the relationship between
„ architecture and the other disciplines, archi-
„ tecture implies, has always implied, an intel-
„ lectual curiosity. This curiosity, we could
„ say is a prerequisite to making architecture.

SHIH-FU PENG „Transparency is not any kind
„ of research position that we've taken over
„ the years that's focused our work. It's more
„ something that we thought through and decided
„ that, as a word, best describes how we ap-
„ proach what we do, both in terms of how we ap-
„ proach architecture as an object and also the

„ methodology through which we actually produce
„ this so-called 'object.'
One example of the approach: recently, we were
„ doing a project for the extension for the Na-
„ tional Gallery in Ireland, and we were asking
„ the client for a survey. They said, 'we gave
„ you the survey for the site already,' and what
„ I said was that from our point of view, what
„ we're more interested in is a survey which
„ encompasses the area two kilometers outside
„ the site. In many ways, that is how we see our
„ work--that it is highly contingent on these
„ peripheral conditions and it's that transpar-
„ ency between the kind of events that occur and
„ how it actually mediates or breaks down the
„ borders with the actual building itself.
The second example of our methodology is when
„ the RIBA visited Kildare about two years ago.
„ The client showed them everything about the
„ building, the lighting, the services, the
„ concepts between the outdoor rooms and the
„ façades. In the end, the RIBA representative
„ turned around to the client and said, 'So what
„ did the architects do?' And in some ways, that
„ really describes how we feel our approach to
„ design is--that somehow through the degree
„ of close collaboration, the authorship is
„ somehow completely melted into the overall
„ production of the object. The object, in some
„ ways, only emerges from the fact that many
„ different minds from many different disciplines
„ actually produce this so-called 'shape' at the
„ very end.

TIMOTHY ROHAN „Rudolph received his first com-
„ mission for Yale in 1957, when he was still
„ a visiting critic. With the Greeley Memo-
„ rial Laboratory (1957-1959), Rudolph again
„ challenged the International Style when he
„ inflected what could have been a standard,
„ rectilinear box with pre-cast concrete col-
„ umns whose bold, Y-shaped capitals recalled
„ the whiplash-like lines of the Art Nouveau--
„ a style Modernism had long disparaged for its
„ decorative qualities. The columns supported a
„ ceiling of poured-in-place concrete beams and
„ pre-cast panels with deep coffers that together
„ expressed "the nature and direction of the roof
„ stresses," according to Rudolph. The building
„ was a prelude to the expressive architecture
„ Rudolph would create for the university and
„ city over the next two decades.
By the early 1960's, Rudolph and his contem-
„ poraries believed that prefabrication was
„ the enormous scale and affordable housing.
„ Rudolph experimented with a molded concrete
„ block produced by the New Haven company
„ Plasticrete for Crawford Manor (1962-1966),
„ a fourteen-story tower with one hundred and
„ nine apartments for the elderly located on
„ Park Street, in New Haven. Working at a larger
„ scale, Rudolph employed factory-produced
„ mobile homes for Oriental Masonic Gardens
„ (1968-1971), a cooperative housing complex on
„ New Haven's outskirts. Calling it the "twenti-
„ eth-century brick," Rudolph predicted that the
„ prefabricated mobile home would become the
„ basic unit for gigantic mega-structures of the
„ future, such as his visionary but never built
„ Graphic Arts Center (1967) for a site near the
„ World Trade Center, in New York.

SPRING LECTURES & SYMPOSIA

ALEJANDRO ARAVENA „Elemental is today a for-
„ profit company which actually partners with
„ the university and the Chilean oil company,
„ but it started back in 2000, simultaneously
„ at Harvard and Universidad Católica, as an
„ initiative aiming to try to do better social
„ housing within the current conditions of the
„ policy. The cost, time, scale, whatever it
„ was, we wanted to add within the set of rules
„ that was out there, and within that set of
„ rules, try to do better. We knew that we had
„ to build, and we knew that we had to achieve
„ a certain scale from the very beginning. My
„ partner at the beginning, and still today, is
„ Andrés Lacobelli who is a transport engineer,
„ who was doing his Master's in the school of
„ government at Harvard, and with him it was
„ very clear that that was the way we had to
„ start. I'm going to show today this project
„ over here, a few pictures of the first project
„ that we did: studios at Harvard, trying to
„ test what to do with social housing, to try
„ to understand what the problem we were trying
„ to solve was, then build a project, and si-
„ multaneously run an international competition
„ because we wanted to test other conditions
„ for the same problem, throughout Chile, that
„ pretty much offers all the geographical variety
„ that one would encounter trying to escalate
„ the project to other places. And as you see
„ here, there are other branches that began to
„ appear, like transport and infrastructure and
„ public space and I'm going to show a couple of
„ images of those projects as well. The title of
„ the lecture is "Architecture in an Urban Age"
„ and what I'm trying to say with that is that in
„ the end we're architects and we do buildings,
„ we do plans, and try to translate, as Dean
„ Stern said, ideas into facts. The thing is that
„ more than ever, today, being an architect is
„ going to be, and is going to keep on being,
„ and more and more, within an urban context.
„ And that not just as this way of saying "more
„ density," but as a network of opportunities
„ that we haven't seen before in mankind.

LIZA FIOR „ 'Architecture' and 'Art' sits together
„ in the practice name independent of each
„ other, but critically informing those respec-
„ tive disciplines and our way of doings things.
„ And yet, they're very different, because if ar-
„ chitecture has as its premise the duty of care,

„ then knowing as much as you can in advance of
„ the situation, and beginning the engagement
„ with a client with some sense that you're going
„ to describe what they're going to end up with,
„ then in our practice, the duty to care is to
„ process. Sometimes, the means is the project.
„ In different ways, these two disciplines have
„ informed each other. Dean Stern has given one
„ history of the name 'MUF,' but I know from at-
„ tending two previous lectures, that Dean Stern
„ enjoys a nice trajectory, and so I brought, for
„ the first time, the other history of the name
„ of the practice, MUF. This is a drawing of
„ the relation between the garden of my child-
„ hood--the garden with the dots around it--
„ to the Long Garden, a privately-owned garden
„ belonging to the Martins of Northampton, who
„ owned this part of London. The Long Garden
„ was prohibited to girls. The boy children who
„ lived by the garden were allowed to climb over
„ the walls and play cricket there. And so con-
„ sequentially, my entire childhood was played
„ out in balancing tactics, balancing along
„ that wall, climbing in early in the morning,
„ and generally standing on that place between
„ those two sides. And so, what I learned early
„ on in those early morning forays was just as
„ personal as it was political as it was spatial,
„ and perhaps that is why sometimes the name of
„ the practice does seem like a relic from the
„ early days of setting up practice, sometimes
„ it continues to be just as relevant now.

KURT FORSTER „ I am thrilled that you are all
„ here to participate in this boundless celebra-
„ tion, to which I must add a somewhat surpris-
„ ing comment. After hearing my C.V., even in
„ brief, you know I love architecture. But I also
„ love chocolate, and, like Josephine Baker,
„ j'ai deux amours. With the difference that I do
„ not sing about Paris, but about Palladio. That
„ is why I am tempted to compare the exquisite
„ qualities of his work with that other rare
„ substance that was introduced into Western
„ culture in the sixteenth century. Both ar-
„ chitecture and chocolate derive from a base
„ substance that must be artfully refined to
„ reach a high degree of purity and virtually
„ indescribable consistency. That sort of thing
„ that melts on your tongue, and so forth. En-
„ joyment comes as a reward of the laborious
„ process by which brick and mortar is coaxed
„ into a geometrical configuration that we recog-
„ nize as an architectural idea, like the grainy
„ and somewhat strangely bitter bean that needs
„ to be turned into a velvety drink or cast in
„ tablets as the ingots of delectation for the
„ cognoscenti. Dangers lurk of course in culture
„ raised on Hershey bars and chocolate chips,
„ but Marcel Duchamp comes to the rescue of
„ America, as he has so many times before, and
„ in The Big Glass he represents those churning
„ granite wheels that smooth down the hard ca-
„ cao beans into buttery consistency. It is not
„ cacao, as such, but only chocolate that must be
„ considered a cultural achievement. Similarly,
„ neither local tradition, nor disembodied
„ dimensions, nor fame are alone the stuff Pal-
„ ladio is made of. Fragments of Palladian con-

REASSESSING RUDOLPH:
ARCHITECTURE AND REPUTATION
"Matter Immaterial: the paradox
of concrete architecture"
Keynote to symposium, the Paul Rudolph
Lecture presented by ADRIAN FORTY
on Friday, January 23

ANCHOR & ANIMATION
Presented by GRAFTON ARCHITECTS:
YVONNE FARRELL & SHELLEY MCNAMARA
on Thursday, February 12

ARCHITECTURE AND NATURE--WHAT IS
TERUNOBU FUJIMORI'S ARCHITECTURE?
Presented by TERUNOBU FUJIMORI
on Monday, April 20

„cepts may give us a hint, shavings of chocolate „a taste, but the real McCoy lies in an idea „emulsified completely with matter. And that is „precisely where the problem arises. Is there „such a substance and what is it expected to „produce when admixed to others? Is the es- „sence of Palladio to be found on the pages of „his Four Books, or in the brick and mortar of „his buildings? The conundrum originates with „him. For he chose to publish his work, not just „as a medley, but systematically. He structured „the book and his pages as expertly as he laid „out his plans and compartments.

ADRIAN FORTY „All over the world you see large „exposed concrete buildings constructed in the „1950's to the 1960's, many of them unloved. „Even at the moment of their completion, there „was not much affection for them. Nor in many „cases has their reputation improved over time. „Neglect has led to decay, adding to their „infamy and in some cases the result is demoli- „tion. The story is so well known and familiar „to you that it might seem tedious and possibly „inappropriate on this occasion to return to „it. However, you must forgive me for doing so. „I want to because much of the discussion that „has taken place around these large concrete „buildings and their reputations seem to have „been so very limited and disappointing about „what their reputations say about them. I won- „der if we can do any better.
One of the peculiarities of concrete is that „amongst architects it has always been regarded „as a virtuous material. To build well in con- „crete is, in the architecture and engineering „community, a mark of superior achievement. „But against this professional enthusiasm for „concrete--this belief that concrete alone „amongst all building materials has the ca- „pacity to disclose what architecture is truly „about--what are we to do about this discrep- „ancy between professional enthusiasm and „popular disenchantment? Will we be able to „avoid a repetition of the same thing happen- „ing again? By repetition, I don't much mean „the chance of concrete monsters filling up our „cities. Rather, the same misjudgment might be „repeated where architects find that what they „earnestly believe in is met with utter disen- „chantment. For this I think we can be justified „in returning to the history of large concrete „buildings.

TERUNOBU FUJIMORI „When I was an architecture „student forty years ago, the first foreign „architecture book I read was Le Corbusier's „Vers Une Architecture. The second foreign lan- „guage book that I read was in English, and it „was called Modern Architecture. It was quite

„insightful to me, and the author of that book „was Vincent Scully. And forty years ago, when „I read that book, I thought to myself, 'Vincent „Scully must be someone very important, and a „little bit old.' When I knew that I was going „to be coming to New Haven, I thought perhaps „Professor Scully had left New Haven to go to „'Old Haven.' However, I learned that he had „not yet moved out, and so I was very surprised „and quite pleased, because inside my head, he „must me more than a hundred years old now. It „pleased me very much to be able to speak here „in this school of architecture, where Vincent „Scully taught for so many years.
I've shown projects that use natural materials, „like earth, plaster, charcoal, stone, wood, „and these are materials that I like to use, „but there's one problem inherent in them, and „that is when there's precipitation and a lot of „rain, they start to rot. So I looked for another „man-made material that would fit well with the „natural materials that I use. The theme is „how to make architecture and nature as close „together as possible. This is abstract, but „even thinking about a geometrical space, it „can all be tied together with nature. Another „important theme I think about is how to bring „nature into architecture. The first architect „to do that, in modern architecture, was Le „Corbusier. Of his five points, the first was „pilotis, the fifth was a roof garden. Because „I have studied architectural history for so „long, I knew that the architectural histories „in each country are different, that they are „never the same.

GRAFTON ARCHITECTS „'Anchor' and 'animation' „reference two worlds we inhabit as architects: „the real and the imagined. Real anchors for us „are place, material, culture, pattern, experi- „ence, and building. Real animations are the „paths of the sun, the changing seasons, people, „movement, and use. Philosophical anchors are „things that remain true, things that stand the „test of time. Philosophical animation comes „from being open to new ideas, new experiences, „new influences, and conversations that change „the way we look at the world.
This image is an aerial view of Dublin. Weaving „through it is the River Liffey. We have spent „our architectural career weaving and making „within this city. What's interesting for us „is the phenomenon of city. Within our work, „urbanity is something that we really value. „We value the lives of people; we value the „streets and avenues and squares that make up „this amazing conglomerate of living. We're in- „terested in watching people's lives, and what „is interesting in the internationalizing of „the world is that we, as architects, through „material and pattern and grain, set into use „in this city--which is a metaphor for every „city on the earth--and that we are responsible „for describing the architectural phenomenon „of this space.
One thing that happened on the day the (Univer- „sita Luigi Bocconi in Milan) project opened „that was incredibly important for us was that, „once the gates were open, the citizens of „Milan came to visit, and one of the people who „came was a woman in her nineties. We walked „down with her from the first level to the lower „level, and this little lady, who had to be „helped along, said to us in Italian, "The „structure is immense, but it embraces you."
For us, in the end, architecture is a disci- „pline you have to stand in with your body, „and you have to bring your mind and your eyes

„ and all your sensations together. When this
„ elderly woman spoke those words to us, it
„ was important in the sense that architecture
„ had communicated. That, in the end, is what
„ architecture is.

TOYO ITO „ It is my belief that architecture
„ today should be based on fluid and dynamic
„ concepts and ideas rather than firm, fixed and
„ steady ideas. So far architecture has been
„ about cutting-out spaces from the environ-
„ ment, and after this space is cut-out, you
„ would then create some order within it, like
„ in classical architecture. But in the 20th
„ century, a new system, the grid, was developed
„ that sought to make a fluid connection between
„ architecture and the environment. So this new
„ grid system enables us to go anywhere on the
„ globe and produce cities and architecture in
„ a very short period of time, but the result of
„ it is a very even and uniform kind of building.
„ Even today, we have to depend on this grid sys-
„ tem to build large buildings, like high rises;
„ there aren't so many other ways we can depend
„ on. However, this system has made us live in a
„ very defined and isolated system that is very
„ apart from what is happening around us in the
„ environment. Even human beings are forced to
„ live in this standard environment, which is
„ making humans universal and uniform. So, in
„ the last 10 years, I have been experimenting,
„ in my modest sized projects, with how to break
„ this confined system and have a more relative
„ relationship between architecture and the
„ environment.
Is interesting looking at a trees, and what
„ you can learn from it. The tree forms itself,
„ it forms as it grows. As the tree splits into
„ branches, it is a very simple act, but if you
„ repeat it, in the end it becomes a very complex
„ form. The tree's order, as well as its form,
„ is really determined by its neighbors and its
„ environment and its own balancing act; they
„ are open to the outside environment. They also
„ have a fractal system. It is my belief that we
„ will never be able to make architecture that
„ transcends what a tree already has. This sums
„ up what I think of as "generative order".

GREG LYNN „ So plasticity in form, I always be-
„ lieved, was distinct from plastic the material.
„ At least that's what I always kind of told my-
„ self. A couple of churches which we also went to
„ see outside of Turin, again, struck me as being
„ something that could have come off of one of
„ the Yale students' computers upstairs. I mean
„ the sense of modeling a surface, and defining
„ a building envelope as the play of embossed
„ and debossed surfaces in this baroque period
„ is something that is very contemporary to see

„ again. Okay so, when thinking about plastics,
„ I've always started with the cons, instead of
„ the pros. Plastics tend to be associated with
„ featureless yet shapely surfaces; they tend to
„ be monolithic and hollow, used for packaging
„ or wrapping; they're arrested liquids in the
„ sense that they're molded and cast, typically;
„ they're disposable; they're cheap; they're
„ recyclable; they're base; they're a kind of
„ everyday material we throw away; and they're
„ colorful and glossy and low-quality. All of
„ those things are also what is so interesting
„ about plastics. They're voluptuous, they can
„ be sculpted; they're good at producing volume
„ with surface; they're moldable, deformable;
„ they're cheap and recyclable; they're connect-
„ ed with the language of popular culture; and
„ they're glossy and translucent and can carry
„ color. So all of the things that I kept telling
„ myself would make plastics not relevant to
„ architecture, really the only thing that is
„ so problematic is this monolithic quality of
„ plastic objects. So what I've found is that in
„ the last maybe eight, probably if you go back
„ to stereo lithography models, for the last
„ fifteen years, I've been working a lot in plas-
„ tics. And so I thought for this lecture I would
„ pull together first a quick little compendium
„ of some of the plastic components, and what
„ I noticed is, they're starting to scale up,
„ larger and larger and larger for me to the
„ scale of buildings.

JOHN PATKAU „ It's a great pleasure to be here,
„ especially in this wonderful building which
„ was an icon of my student days and is in won-
„ derfully restored condition and it's a great
„ pleasure to be here. In the August 2005 edition
„ of the RIBA journal there is an interview with
„ Shigeru Ban, in which he is asked, Why the
„ switch from Frei Otto to Cecil Balmond? His
„ response was, "I am still working on projects
„ with Otto, we have to take advantage of him
„ and his ideas, but this is my challenge: to
„ move from form-finding, which Frei Otto does so
„ well, to form-making." To me, this statement
„ is both provocative and disconcerting. At the
„ outset of our practice, my partner Patricia
„ and I pursued a very self-conscious process of
„ form-finding. We would often initiate a project
„ by searching for what we would call the "found
„ potential" of a project: those aspects of site,
„ climate, building context, program, or local
„ culture for example that would facilitate the
„ development of an architectural form which was
„ evocative of circumstance. The result of this
„ approach was that individual projects often
„ took on distinctive identities in response
„ to circumstance, and consequently the formal
„ relationship between our projects was loose at
„ best. To us this was an appropriate expression
„ of the diversity within which we live. The dis-
„ tinction between form-making and form-finding
„ is not necessarily precise, however. It might
„ even be said that approaching architectural
„ design as a process of form-making or of
„ form-finding is tied intimately to personal or
„ cultural sensibility. For example, if you take
„ a sporting analogy, if punching is the boxing
„ analog of form-making, then counter-punching
„ is the boxing analog of form-finding. On the
„ other hand, the architectural form-finding that
„ I admire in the work of Shigeru Ban is perhaps
„ more at home in Eastern cultures, like Judo
„ rather than boxing. Or like a Japanese saw
„ that cuts by pulling, rather than a Western saw
„ that cuts by pushing. The Japanese saw acts
„ in tension, and therefore can be much more

GENERATIVE ORDER
Presented by TOYO ITO
on Thursday, January 22

IS CIRCUMSTANCE ENOUGH?
Presented by JOHN PATKAU, EERO
SAARINEN VISITING PROFESSOR
on Thursday, January 8

PLASTIC FORM
Presented by GREG LYNN,
DAVENPORT VISITING PROFESSOR
on Thursday, April 9

ARCHITECTURE, MODERNITY,
AND GEOPOLITICS
Presented by EEVA-LIISA PELKONEN
on Thursday, March 26

WHEN SUSTAINABILITY IS
A MATTER OF LIFE AND DEATH
Eero Saarinen Lecture Presented by
CAMERON SINCLAIR on Monday, April 6

VIRTUAL PROTOTYPING:
LIVE DESIGN AND
THE SEARCH FOR A NEW METRICS
Presented by WILLIAM SHARPLES,
LOUIS I. KAHN VISITING ASSISTANT
Professor on Thursday, April 2

„ slender than the Western saw, the resulting
„ cuts much finer. Nevertheless, I would argue
„ that form-finding is every bit as much a part
„ of Western culture as form-making. To quote Le
„ Corbusier, "Creation is a patient search."

EEVA-LIISA PELKONEN „As you notice from the
„ slide, my subject is the Finnish architect
„ Alvar Aalto. I find it interesting that more
„ than any other architect Aalto has been tied
„ to his home country. This raises an interest-
„ ing methodological question: how does one
„ make sense of architecture's relationship to
„ a particular geographical location? We often
„ take this relationship for granted; we talk,
„ for example, about American modernism and
„ International Style, without giving a second
„ thought what these attributes mean. The idea
„ of genius loci, according to which a timeless
„ spirit of place flows without any friction into
„ architecture, dominates Aalto scholarship.
As the title indicates, I want to revise this
„ reading by placing Aalto within a broader
„ terrain of geopolitics, which exposed him to
„ situations that were often beyond his con-
„ trol. I will show that Aalto's life and career
„ evolved unpredictably in unpredictable times.
„ In addition, I want to press that Aalto's rela-
„ tionship to his home country was complicated
„ and that this relationship changed in time. To
„ be sure, when we think about the 20th century,
„ we must be reminded that all geography was
„ then politically highly charged. The century
„ was marked by Civil Wars, two World Wars, and
„ culminated in the end of the Cold War, which
„ only led to new wave of nationalist and re-
„ ligious hatred. Yet, amidst all the horrors,
„ it was also a century of social, political
„ and artistic experimentation. Geographic at-
„ tributes, such as "international," "pan-Euro-
„ pean," "regional" and "universal" were some of
„ the many alternative political world-orders.
Aalto 's architecture must be understood within
„ the complex web of individual actors, dis-
„ course, geography, society, politics, and
„ power. To the question of how relevant Finnish
„ history is to understanding Aalto's architec-
„ ture I would simply answer that we cannot
„ understand Aalto without Finland, nor can one
„ understand Finland without Aalto.

WILLIAM SHARPLES „Obviously, the last 6 months
„ has had a profound impact on our profession,
„ and as with every negative, there is always a
„ positive. And I think from this standpoint,
„ the optimism that we see and how our office is
„ going to continue to evolve in the coming six-
„ to-twelve-to-eighteen months is pretty repre-
„ sentative of a lot of offices our size in the
„ United states, as well as a lot of opportunity

„ for young designers in the architecture and
„ engineering community. Where I'm focusing
„ this discussion today is the medium in which
„ we process design and manage the construction
„ process; that evironment where in the early
„ days of SHoP it was in the 2 and 3D, we are now
„ moving into the 4, 5, and 6D.
Before we get to that, quickly, for those of
„ you who don't know who we are, we are five
„ Columbia graduates: a set of identical twins
„ and two married couples. And one of the reason
„ we stay together as a five principal firm is
„ that we all have a very diverse background
„ and we attack things from different angles.
„ In addition, over half of our staff comes from
„ disciplines outside architecture, and their
„ fields speak for themselves. The idea that
„ architects remain specialized and focused in
„ how they develop a particular design from one
„ or two media is changing, our idea is that we
„ do many different things, from environmental
„ performance to engineering and construction.
„ This is no different from the Master Architect
„ of the renaissance. Brunelleschi, to us, is
„ the epitome of what we are after: a person who
„ not only conceives the building, but is also
„ in control of the means and methods by which
„ it is actualized.

CAMERON SINCLAIR „Today is an auspicious day.
„ It's exactly ten years today that we began
„ this organization so I kind of changed the
„ presentation a little bit. We started this
„ organization to get architects, designers,
„ engineers, planners involved in humanitarian
„ crises around the world. The thing about this
„ organization is it's not about a responsi-
„ bility of our profession to get involved in
„ these situations. It's actually a unique op-
„ portunity. Many of our designers take a kind
„ of tour of duty. They're usually graduates;
„ they do five years in the profession and then
„ have a mid-twenties nervous breakdown as they
„ realize that the umpteenth hotel doorknob that
„ they designed is not fulfilling their desire
„ to be an architect. So they go out into the
„ field. They take six months, a year and what
„ happens is they come back with a profound
„ understanding of what it means to design in
„ the world. You may be affecting the lives of
„ a family, a village, even a city. But what
„ you really understand and what you really get
„ to do is to really realize the dreams of an
„ architect, and that is to make an impact on
„ this planet that is positive. Also, we're not
„ a pro bono, do-gooder organization. It's not
„ like, "Oh I really care about these people,
„ just send me over there." It's about providing
„ professional design services. It's about giv-
„ ing an area of expertise that many communities
„ do not have. It's done for two reasons. One
„ is because that's what our skill-set is. But
„ secondly it's to improve the way that most of
„ community and most of the world thinks about
„ architecture, that we're not elitists, that we
„ can provide our services for all.

ANTHONY VIDLER „The main thrust of tonight's lecture is on the archive of James Stirling's work; its nature, form and interpretative potential. An archive is not a biography, despite the fact it may contain biographical information, nor is an archive a history or a theory, despite the fact that it may contain material leading to one or the other. Rather, an archive is at once more neutral and potentially more dangerous and exciting than either one of these options.
Over the seventeen years since his untimely death, the built work of Stirling has emerged as controversial, the upkeep of his early buildings have failed up uphold their integrity, and a number of his works have aroused scorn from traditionalists and modernists alike for their transgression of both canons. Reyner Banham writing in 1988, declared "The only approvable attitude towards James Stirling is one of sustained execration and open accusations of incompetetance", while more sympathetic critics have seen his work move through a series of brilliant and eclectic modernist and post-modernist styles; from Corbusian to Brutalist to Constructivist.
Stirling's initial reliance on both modernism and traditional classicism was, in retrospect, not at all contradictory with the main thrust of modernism itself, as delineated in the 1920s and 30s by the likes of Corbu and Breuer. For the modern movement was, on the one hand, committed to a modernism of collage, montage and avant-garde formalism in service of a new social order; on the other hand, modernism sought a timeless relationship with society based on an abstraction of traditional construction which seemed to go hand-in-hand with the inherent principles of classicism, minus the rhetoric of the orders.
However, the archive reveals a very different kind of process from that understood as the conventional "history of a design"; the identification of sources, the tracing of projects and evolutions, and so forth. While one can find things in the archive, Stirling's work resists the easy linear narrative of cause and effect, source and imitation and theory to practice; the sorts of narratives we construct in the absence of further evidence. It is out of the resistance of the archive that the common place notions of a critical narrative that we can begin to extract a working definition of what might be called "Stirling's Theory".

LÖIC WACQUANT „It is an honor and pleasure to deliver this lecture, and to have my work noted and engaged by scholars in architecture. I was raised in a European intellectual tradition with a low disciplinary threshold, so I consider myself not a sociologist but rather a social scientist who happens to be in a sociology department. I consider as part of my general duty to engage issues across disciplinary boundaries, including boundaries between the more scholarly crafts and the more professional crafts. At the same time, this is a bit daunting, and I am not one who is easily intimidated, because it's hard to sense the interests, concerns, and expectations of the audience from a field which is quite remote (from my own).
What I am going to try and do is to bring you external stimulation on an issue which I've spent about a decade working; which is the issue of obtaining forms of urban marginality in advanced societies or what I call urban polarization from below. What I propose to do is to give you an analytic synoptic linkage between my two most recent books; the first one Urban Outcasts that looks at the transformation of the black American ghetto since the wave of riots in the 1960's and answers the question what happened to that particular urban socio-spatial constellation in the American metropolis and what we can learn from the transformation of the black American ghetto in relation to changing European working classes. Volume two, in a sense, is what is the policy innovation that sought to react to the rise of urban marginality and try to contain it. It's called Punishing the Poor: the New Liberal Government of Social Insecurity. In this book I look at the reactionary policy that arises from urban marginality.

NICHOLAS FOX WEBER „Well, we biographers are merciless. We'll hear anything from anyone we can, we'll ask all sorts of questions, and one of the first people I was lucky enough to meet was Le Corbusier's doctor, Jacques Hindermeyer, who was in his early eighties when I met him, living on the Boulevard Saint-Germain, and eager to talk about this great architect whom he had treated as a young man. And he began to talk to me, quite specifically, about Le Corbusier's death. He had only been treating Corbu in the last years of his life (he had also been treating Corbu's wife) and Dr. Hindermeyer described that summer of 1965 when the day before he went for his annual month in Southern France, Corbu said that he was feeling "rats in the plumbing." And "rats in the plumbing" was a reference to a heart problem. Dr. Hindermeyer treated him for it, and made him promise, at age 76, not to swim twice a day anymore. Only to stick to his afternoon swim. And Corbu swore by it. Well Corbu, as many of you know, died drowning, and he drowned at 10 AM. So one thing we knew is that he had certainly disobeyed his doctor. I then spoke with a young architect who had worked with Corbu and as a boy had served his parents––he was sort of a waiter––in the seafood shack next to Corbu's house. And he described to me how three days before Corbu's death, he was talking with Corbu who said, "Robert, would you please take back to Paris a manuscript that I've been working on, I've made some notes on it, it's really a summary of my life, and I'm consigning it to you." And Robert said, "But Corbu, you know I'm going to Venice to work on our hospital project there, and why do you want me to take it back? You go back to Paris always on the first of September." And Corbu simply insisted. And he died on August 29th, 1965.

JAMES STIRLING, ARCHITECT & TEACHER
"James Stirling: Entering the Architve"
Keynote to symposium presented by
ANTHONY VIDLER on Saturday, May 9

LE CORBUSIER: THE SURPRISES
Brendan Gill Lecture Presented by
NICHOLAS FOX WEBER on Thursday,
January 15

SPATIAL ILLITERACIES
"Designing Urban Seclusion
in the 21st Century"
Keynote to symposium, the Roth-Symonds
Lecture presented by LÖIC WACQUANT
on Friday, March 27

SUB-BASEMENT

Faculty

PETER DE BRETTEVILLE
BRENNAN BUCK
JOHN EBERHART
EDWARD PARKER

Students

JASON BOND
CRAIG CHAPPLE
ISAIAH KING
ELIZA HIGGINS
QIWEI LIANG
CALEB LINVILLE
PATRICK LUN
VENESSA MENDOZA
CARLOS FELIX
  RASPALL-GALLI
KATE THATCHER
EMILY ARDEN WELLS

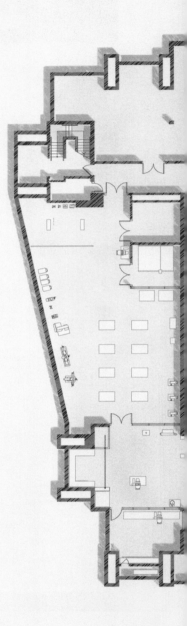

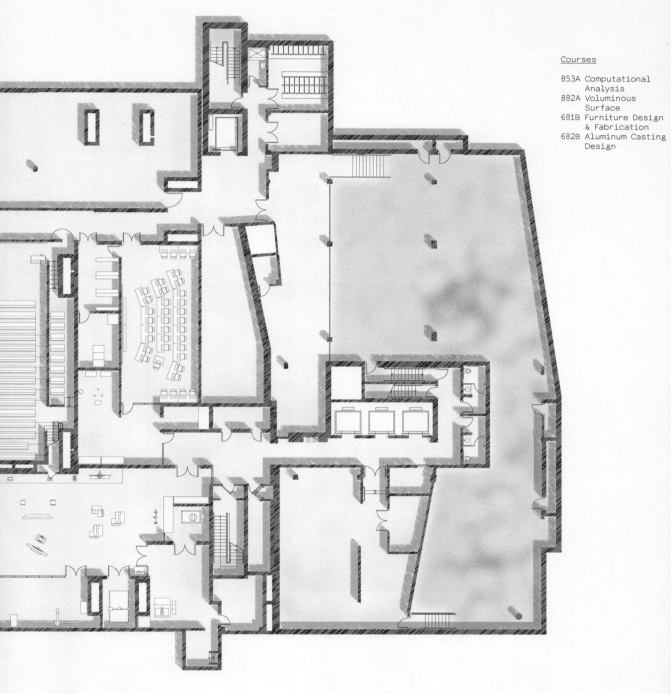

COMPUTATIONAL ANALYSIS

853A

This course investigates and applies emerging computational theories and technologies through the design and fabrication of a full-scale building component and/or assembly. This investigation includes various static, parametric, and scripted modeling paradigms, computational based structural and sustainability analysis, and digital fabrication technologies. Students design, analyze, and fabricate a full-scale constructed piece.

I
FRACTURES: SCHOOL FOR THE PERFORMING ARTS IN BOSTON
CARLOS FELIX RASPALL-GALLI

This design exercise explores the application of multiple digital technologies from the initial phases of the design process to the fabrication of a large scale prototype. Initially, the use of 3D Voronoi subdivision algorithms guided the distribution of the massing and program. As the project evolved into different structural systems, the application of parametric tools allowed the development of more complex organizations, as well as the emergence of unexpected arrangements. Finally, the project tested, in several models and prototypes, the use of a variety of digital fabrication techniques, including CNC plasma cutting and CNC milling.

II
PERFORM
ELIZA HIGGINS

This investigation of the black box theater proposes a pre-fabricated system of adaptable framing and enclosure. Being a performance venue, by nature it must be able to convey and establish the perception of "anyplace," through spatial and technical flexibility. This system uses an adjustable hard interior surface and soft exterior skin allowing for a shift in spatial arrangement inside that is revealed through relief and shadow on the exterior surface. This relationship between inside and outside yields two levels of performance. In this way, the theatre is a place of action for those inside and a theatrical device to the passersby, drawing intrigue without revealing the narrative within.

III
DYNAMIC PANELLING FAÇADE
QIWEI LIANG

Taking the studio work (Boston performing art school) as a case-study, this research about parametric panelling aims to adjust the digital process to the whole design which is still based on classical architectural concepts, like context, function and circulation, etc. This façade system makes a gentle transition from transparent to opaque, representing how open the space behind the façade is, and how acute the changing from public to private takes place. With Grasshopper for Rhino, two separated system is generated. System one is a user-defined panelling system-- every cell in which can self-adjust its size according to the distances from it to the regulating surface. System two is a material system with all the cells the same size and same shape, allowing the panels from system one to be cut in a set of uniform base material.

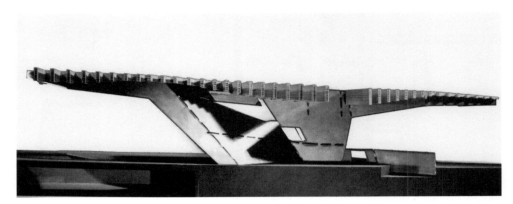

I

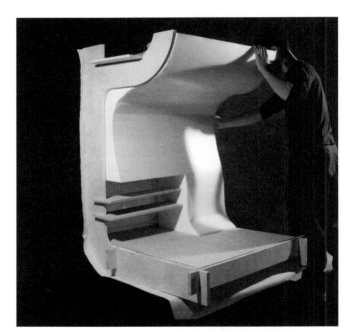

II

III

CARLOS FELIX RASPALL-GALLI   ELIZA HIGGINS   QIWEI LIANG

VOLUMINOUS SURFACE

This seminar examines the architectural preoccupation since Venturi with surface, investigating techniques of articulation and expansion to solve the contemporary limitations of architectural surfaces. Surface is generally posited in opposition to the modernist notion of even and infinite Cartesian space; contemporary architectural surfaces are infinitely thin and constantly various. Surface has also prompted a renewed concern for the interior and an interest in building skins that articulate a distinction between inside and out, are present rather than invisible, and are opaque or translucent rather than transparent. But an architecture of surface presents its own difficulties: digital and geometrical purity, monotonous smoothness, and immaterial thinness. This seminar seeks solutions to the problems of surface by revisiting multiple notions of space and interior volume. Within this context, students take advantage of the inherent complexity of material fabrication, developing full-scale architectural envelope systems that synthesize surface geometry, panelization, structure, and envelope. Each project articulates an agenda about inside and out, geometry and material, and atmosphere and construction.

I
BANANA WALL
JASON BOND & CRAIG CHAPPLE

This surface is bananas. Ventilation, solar control, and graphic façade are all spelled B-A-N-A-N-A-S. A flat steel sheet is imparted with volume and variable opacity through a process of cutting and pulling. Three scales of arc cuts twist under axial force to create aperture or collapse to graphic figure in areas of flatness. One side is a rusty brown fresh from the freezer while the other is a ripe powder coated yellow.

I

II
HONEYCOMB
ISAIAH KING & KATE THATCHER

This prototypical mock-up is concerned with creating a maximum amount of effects from a minimum amount of formal manipulations and materials. Designed as a repeatable module, the striated transparent areas of the surface are created by the offset of a vanishing point between the two sides, allowing for the modulation of both view and light. The surface is constructed from a double-wall, two-sided corrugated cardboard that is laser cut and layered. The layering acts to create multiple effects of perspective, porosity, focus, and blur within each module. The cardboard, coated with aluminum foil on one side, creates different affective responses on either sides of the surface, adding reflectivity that further dematerializes the solidity of the material.

II

JASON BOND
CRAIG CHAPPLE

ISAIAH KING
KATE THATCHER

681B

FURNITURE DESIGN & FABRICATION

The final product of this design class, a finished, working, full-scale piece of furniture, is understood as a part of the set of courses addressing the role that the direct consideration of materials contributes to architectural design. The required materials, sequences, and programs emerge from an effort to relate the work of this class to questions of process and materiality in architecture more generally. So the attitude toward materials and their assembly should be prejudiced toward those that to some extent mimic architecture. The emphasis is on common materials joined and formed by standard procedures to serve unique purposes in unusual contexts and adapted to new programs.

I
YACARÉ: CHAISE LONGUE
CARLOS FELIX RASPALL-GALLI
This chaise longue is conceived as a gradient both in the material properties [hard/soft] and the formal quality [faceted/smooth], which moves from the exterior surface of the chair to the layer in contact with the human body.

I

II
TRANSFORMER CHAIR
EMILY ARDEN WELLS
The intention of the design is one of a multi-use piece of furniture. It functions as a coffee table, a bar stool, and as a lounge seat. The geometry is generated by the conflict of the limits of the different functions: the height of the barstool creates the limit of the width of the lounge seat, and the height of the coffee table limits the width of the barstool seat. It is made out of half-inch square steel tube stock, and filled with 14-Gauge sheet steel for the seats and table surfaces. The seats are padded with neoprene and covered with cow-hide, further emphasizing the difference between the inside and outside of the overall form of the box.

II

CARLOS FELIX RASPALL-GALLI   EMILY ARDEN WELLS

ALUMINUM CASTING DESIGN

682B

This seminar follows the critical path of designing and producing an object (furniture, sculpture, assembly, etc.) by combining aluminum castings and stock materials. Input from a local foundry included.

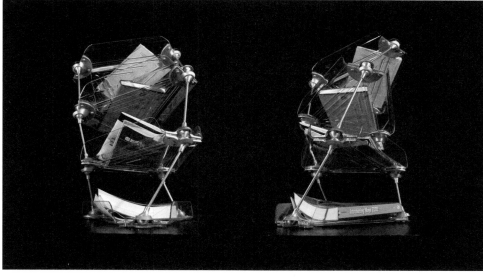

I

I
NEO-MECHANISM
QIWEI LIANG

Neo-mechanism is a digitally gener-ated and calculated structural system expressed in machine language, which tries to recombine language and func-tion. Double-ball joints that can rotate to any direction and support each other allow connections resulting in different shapes by changing the length of the connecting bars.

The sample using the new mechanism is a bookshelf with dynamic structure. Following an architectural logic, the bookshelf has four plates oriented differently, which defines the frequency of the usage. The more frequently read book will be placed higher where it is easiest to reach. It is a dramatic view of "freed books," and the current reading situation of the shelf owner.

II

II
TABLE
CALEB LINVILLE

III

III
TABLE
PATRICK LUN

The goal was to create a table using discreet elements (wood and aluminum) and combine them through form to make a unified table. The concept of the form comes from the inherent relation-ship between surface and edge. The aluminum legs were designed to take advantage of the casting process, while trying to minimize weight, and labor involved for joinery.

YALE URBAN DESIGN WORKSHOP

DIRECTOR
ALAN J. PLATTUS
   PROJECT MANAGER
ANDREI HARWELL
   FACULTY ASSOCIATES
JAMES AXLEY
DIANA BALMORI
ALEX FELSON
KEITH KRUMWIEDE
EDWARD MITCHELL
HILARY SAMPLE
   STUDENT FELLOWS
SEHER ERDOGAN
MWANGI GATHINJI
VANESSA MENDOZA
ROBERTO ROSSI

Founded in 1992, by Alan Plattus, then Associate Dean and Professor at the Yale School of Architecture, the Yale Urban Design Workshop (YUDW) is a community design center based at the School of Architecture.

In all its work, the YUDW is committed to an inclusive, community-based process, grounded in broad citizen participation and a vision of the design process as a tool for community organizing, empowerment, and capacity-building. These projects are staffed mainly by current graduate professional students at the Yale School of Architecture supervised by faculty of the School, but often also include Yale College undergraduates, recent graduates of the School as full-time staff, faculty and students from Yale's other professional schools (including the Law School, the School of Forestry and Environmental Science, the School of Management, the School of Public Health and the School of Art), as well as outside consultants and other local professionals.

As part of collaborative group "Orange," the YUDW was named a finalist and a special jury selection in the 2008 RIBA Make Me A Home, Northshore competition. The competition entry was exhibited earlier this year in Stockton-on-Tees, the CUBE Gallery in Manchester, and at the North East Festival of Architecture in Newcastle.

This year, work of the YUDW was also included in an exhibition in Berlin titled "Community Design, Involvement and Architecture in the US since 1963," organized by the journal, An Architektur.

In May 2008 a YUDW team of faculty and students helped to organize and lead a design charrette in the Jordan River Valley, to develop plans for a 1200 acre Peace Park straddling the border between Israel and Jordan. The project is a cross-border environmental and economic development initiative conceived by Friends of the Earth Middle East, an NGO involved in environmental peace-making in the region. The Yale team worked on site along with Jordanian, Israeli and Palestinian professionals and students, and presented the results of the charrette in both Amman and Jerusalem.

TRIP TO JORDAN RIVER VALLEY

RIBA "MAKE ME A HOME"
COMPETITION ENTRY

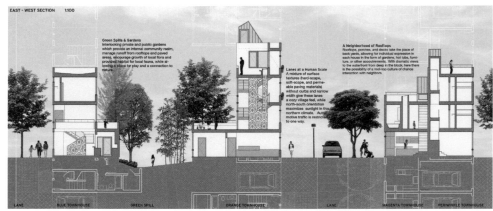

RETROSPECTA 2008-2009
Published by the Yale School of Architecture
Dean Robert A.M. Stern

For more information and copies of this book,
please write, call, or visit us at:
180 York Street
New Haven, CT 06511
(203) 432-2288
www.architecture.yale.edu

Editors
Kyle Stover, MArch., 2011
    Editor-in-Chief
Anne Mason Kemper, MArch., 2011
    Assistant Editor
Andrew Smith-Rasmussen, MArch., 2011
    Assistant Editor
Emmett Zeifman, MArch., 2011
    Assistant Editor

Editorial Assistants
Melissa Bauld, MArch., 2011
Jacob Dugopolski, MArch., 2011
Kathryn Everett, MArch.,2011
Shirley Hsu, MArch., 2011
Alfie Koetter, MArch., 2011
Meredith McDaniel, MArch., 2010
Marianna Mello, MArch., 2009
Kristin Mueller, MArch., 2009
Jonah Rowen, MArch., 2011
Tyler Survant, MArch., 2011
Matthew Zych, MArch., 2011

Graphic Designers
Caspar Lam, MFA, 2010
Ke Cao, MFA, 2010

Design Consultant
Pentagram, New York

YSOA Photographers
John D. Jacobson
Brandt Knapp
Susan Surface

Additional Photography
Lauren Chapman
Jacob Dugopolski
Palmyra Geracki
Alejandro de Mesa
Rafael Ng

Printer
Finlay, Bloomfield, CT

Typeface
Everson Mono
Lever Sans

Paper
FiberMark SuedeTex Black 0.025
Finch Opaque Vellum Text Bright White 89 gsm

We would like to extend
our most sincere gratitude to:
Dean Robert A.M. Stern
Sheila de Bretteville
Michael Bierut, Pentagram, New York
Richard Kaplan, Finlay Printing
John La Russo, Finlay Printing
Gwathmey Siegel & Associates Architects
Richard DeFlumeri
Jean Sielaff
Robie-Lyn Harnois
John D. Jacobson
Nina Rappaport
Monica Robinson
Robert Liston
Rosemary Suggs Watts
Maria Huling
Marilyn Weiss
Donna Wetmore
Jonah Rowen (M. Arch 2011)
Matthew Zych (M. Arch 2011)
And all the faculty, staff, students, friends,
and families who have smoothed our way to a
successful publication.

We would also like to acknowledge the support
of the Rutherford Trowbridge Memorial Publication
Fund and the Paul Rudolph Publication Fund,
established by Claire and Maurits Edersheim,
for their invaluable support.

RUDOLPHALL